THE NEW WORLD ORDER IN ACTION

VOLUME 1

TAKIS FOTOPOULOS

THE NEW WORLD ORDER IN ACTION

VOLUME 1

GLOBALIZATION, THE BREXIT REVOLUTION AND THE 'LEFT'

— Towards a Democratic Community of Sovereign Nations

THE NEW WORLD ORDER
IN ACTION,
Volume 1:
Globalization, the Brexit Revolution and the 'Left' —
Towards a Democratic Community of Sovereign Nations

By Takis Fotopoulos. All rights reserved.

Second edition

Updated with a new chapter on
the US presidential election of November, 2016;
released December 16, 2016 by
ProgressivePress.com,
San Diego, Calif.

List Price: $17.95. Length: 122,000 words on 353 pages
ISBN: 1-61577-247-2, EAN: 978-1-61577-247-6

E-book edition: 978-1-61577-811-9

Cover design by Jose Ernesto de la Torre and Spyros
Methenitis

BISAC Subject Area Codes
POL033000 POLITICAL SCIENCE / Globalization
POL047000 POLITICAL SCIENCE / Imperialism
CUR010000 CURRENT EVENTS / Poverty
CUR004000 CURRENT EVENTS / International
HIS031000 HISTORY / Revolutionary

Contents

PART II
THE NEW WORLD ORDER'S MYTHS

PART III
TOWARDS A DEMOCRATIC COMMUNITY
OF SOVEREIGN NATIONS

Acknowledgements

I would like first to thank the friends and colleagues David Gabbard, Steven Best, Peter McLaren, Arran Gare and Dr Chamsy el-Ojeili for their perceptive comments which encapsulated the essence of the entire New World Order project.

Second, I am grateful to John-Paul Leonard, the courageous Progressive Press publisher. He not only was glad to publish this controversial book, which was effectively banned by the NWO publishers (as expected) as well as by the globalist 'Left' publishers (some of whom even tried to censor it!), but also helped enormously with his patience for such a major project as well as his general useful advice. It's needless to mention the valuable help of my companion Sia and my son Costas who have helped me with their advice and important support throughout the preparation of this book.

Last but not least, I would like to express my gratitude to Dr Peter Rhys-Evans, without whose decisive help this book might have never been finished.

For my grandchildren Nasia and Panos

Preface to the second edition

The two major processes that marked the end of the 20th century and defined the contours of the 21st are the emergence of the New World Order (NWO) of neoliberal globalization, and the collapse of actually existing socialism. Both are processes rather than just events, which are of course interconnected.

Thus, the process leading to the NWO, i.e. the new form of internationalized market economy that has been established in the last forty years or so, represents a structural change, a move to a new form of modernity. This is a move from statist to neoliberal modernity, rather than simply a change in economic policy, or in ideology, as the integrated into the NWO 'Left' (the globalist 'Left') argues. Therefore, today's globalization is indeed a new phenomenon, which is the outcome of the interaction of the social struggle with the grow-or-die dynamics of the self-regulating system of the market economy that was established over two centuries ago and had led to the marketization process.

Similarly, the collapse of actually existing socialism was also the outcome of a historical process going back to the Soviet Revolution of 1917, which, in turn, was part of the revolutionary era that began in the 17th century and probably ended in the 20th. However, although the collapse of actually existing socialism had very serious implications for the Left in general, which I will examine in connection to the rise of the present globalist 'Left', this is not the main aim of this book, which is, in fact, the first volume of a major project on the NWO that will extend to at least three volumes.

The aims of this project are first to demystify the meaning of the NWO of neoliberal globalization, dissociating it from the usual conspiratorial definitions. In this framework I will show how the NWO emerged while exposing the myths its propaganda is based on. My second main aim is to show that the real mechanism, which secured the production and then the reproduction of the NWO, is economic violence, which can be accompanied by military violence.

This volume develops the analytical background within which one can explain seemingly unrelated phenomena, such as the destruction in the Middle East (Iraq, Afghanistan, Libya, and Syria), the coup in

Ukraine and the Greek economic catastrophe. It is shown that the main consequence of the NWO expansion is the phasing out of national sovereignty (through economic and/or military violence) and its replacement by a kind of transnational sovereignty administered by a Transnational Elite. This is the network of the elites mainly based in the G7 countries, which control the world economic and political/ military institutions (WTO, IMF, World Bank, EU, European Central Bank, NATO, UN and so on), as well as the global media that set the agenda of the 'world community'. Furthermore, the mythology used by the elites about sovereignty and the multipolar world are considered, as well as the corresponding mythology of the globalist 'Left', and its consequent political bankruptcy. It is shown that it was the failure of the Left which is the ultimate cause of the rise of neo-nationalist movements in Europe but also in the USA that were quickly embraced by most of the victims of globalization, particularly the working class that used to support the Left.

A major part of this volume deals with what I call the Brexit revolution and the inevitable counter-revolution that was launched by the Transnational and national elites to effectively annul the referendum result. Brexit was very much a popular revolution not only because the entire movement was a movement from below, i.e. from the victims of globalization themselves against the entire (local and international) establishment and the minority which benefits from it. But also because it was, in effect, the first battle in the new class struggle that emerged in the era of globalization. That is, the struggle between the beneficiaries of globalization and the overwhelming majority of its victims. In this sense, Brexit was in fact a class issue reflecting the popular reaction to the class nature of globalization.

The significance of the Brexit revolution became immediately eminent when it was followed, a few months afterwards in the same historical year 2016, by a very similar revolution in thinking in the USA, the metropolis of the NWO. The real issue therefore at the moment, which is examined in this book, is whether this revolution, from Britain and USA yesterday, to Italy today, and France tomorrow, will mature into a huge anti-globalization movement for economic and national sovereignty and self-reliance, as well as a new internationalism.

No wonder that the present volume concludes with the crucial dilemma whether humanity should submit to the present violent world order perpetuating and expanding the privileges of the few at the expense of the vast majority of the world population, or whether instead the class struggle against the NWO, which is already developing at full speed, would manage to create the conditions for the development of a democratic world community of sovereign and self-reliant nations to replace the present NWO of neoliberal globalization. This would imply that the fundamental aim of the social struggle today should be a complete break with the present criminal NWO of neoliberal globalization — which has already destroyed the lives of billions of people all over the world — and the building of a new world democratic community, in which economic and national sovereignty have been restored, so that peoples could then fight for the ideal society, as they see it.

A significant implication of this sort of social struggle would be the development of a new genuine internationalism based on the values of mutual aid and solidarity, as against the present order based on the values of competitiveness and violence, which are destroying both society and the environment. This would also be the precondition for any systemic change that would have to be determined through direct democratic procedures.

In the following volumes, it will be shown how the use of economic and military violence in the Middle East and Europe was successfully used for the full integration into the NWO of Iraq, Libya, Syria, as well as of Greece and Ukraine.

Takis Fotopoulos
London, December 2016

Introduction

Obama's West Point Speech as an introduction to the New World Order (NWO)

Perhaps the best introduction to the themes to be developed in this book was Barack Obama's 2014 speech, at the West Point Military Academy, which he complemented with his Polish freedom day speech a few days later. As the Nobel Peace Prize laureate (who managed to bomb 7 countries in the first 6 years of his presidency)[1] stressed in his speech:

> America does not simply stand for stability or the absence of conflict, no matter what the cost; we stand for the more lasting peace that can only come through opportunity and freedom for people everywhere.[2]

What of course he meant was that a more lasting peace could only be realized through the global expansion of neoliberal globalization, where free markets of capital, goods and labor are the magic wand that distributes opportunities and freedom. And so as to leave no doubt at all, he went on to elaborate the meaning of his words in the following significant passage:

> America's support for democracy and human rights goes beyond idealism; it is a matter of national security. Democracies are our closest friends and are far less likely to go to war. Economies based on free and open markets perform better and become markets for our goods. Respect for human rights is an antidote to instability and the grievances that fuel violence and terror.[3]

So, at the outset, Obama made crystal clear that the cash register ("the markets for our goods") is the ultimate goal of "opportunity and freedom" offered by the expansion of the New World Order (NWO) of neoliberal globalization. That is, the unipolar world run by the Transnational Elite consisting essentially of the G7 countries, within which US is a hegemonic force — but not the 'Emperor'.

---

[1] "O, bomber! Obama bombs 7th country in 6 years", *RT*, 23/9/2014
http://rt.com/usa/190048-usa-bombing-six-country/
[2] Full transcript of President Obama's commencement address at West Point, *Washington Post*, 28/5/2014
[3] ibid.-

Then, he had no qualms about stating with incredible impudence that 'democratic' countries are far less likely to go to war than non-democratic ones. This, despite the fact that it was the 'democratic' countries (on which the Transnational Elites are based), which under US hegemony have launched, since the emergence of the NWO about three decades ago, a series of wars: Yugoslavia, Afghanistan, Iraq and Libya, apart from the wars by proxy in Syria and Ukraine, which had a huge human cost in terms of dead, wounded and displaced people.

At the same time, we have not seen any of the regimes which Obama and the Transnational Elite describe as 'undemocratic' (Russia, China, North Korea, Cuba, Venezuela, etc.) launch similar wars, thousands of miles away from them — not even in their own backyard! By contrast, the Transnational Elite does not hesitate to encircle Russia with protectorates, the latest example being Ukraine which has already been integrated into the EU as an associate member. No wonder that Obama in his state visit to Poland stressed that the Ukrainian people are trying to reach the same freedom and opportunities that Polish people celebrated, which is worth the effort. And, in a crescendo of impertinence, he went so far as to proclaim that the days of empires and spheres of influence are over, stressing that:

> Bigger nations must not be allowed to bully the small, or impose their will at the barrel of a gun or with masked men taking over buildings. And the stroke of a pen can never legitimize the theft of a neighbor's land.[4]

Apparently, the U.S.A and other members of the Transnational Elite are exempt from these rules having, just a couple of years ago, made a successful coup 'from below' in Ukraine to incorporate it into the NWO, using armed masked men who occupied public buildings. These same men have, since then, massacred anyone who resisted the NWO, first in Odessa and Mariupol and then in East Ukraine as a whole. Neither, of course, does the Transnational Elite have any objection to working with armed, self-declared, fascist storm troopers to turn Ukraine into a protectorate. But, at the same time, in other countries, like Greece, which, in the last five years or so, has developed into a protectorate of the Transnational Elite in all but name,

---

[4] David Jackson, "Obama to Poland, Eastern Europe: You are not alone", *USA TODAY*, 4/6/2014 http://www.usatoday.com/story/news/world/2014/06/04/obama-polish-freedom-day-speech-russia-and-ukraine-tiananmen-square/9946925/

the elites had no qualms about imprisoning for many months and without any trial, those whom they identified as fascists, despite the fact that they themselves deny being fascists (albeit some of the leadership of Golden Dawn have obvious sympathies to Nazi collaborators) and have never occupied public buildings or been found possessing any arms beyond shotguns!

Needless to add that what Obama meant by 'democratic countries' was simply the 'parliamentary juntas', which have been established everywhere by the Transnational Elite in the NWO of neoliberal globalization. This is a parody of parliamentary 'democracy' (which is itself a parody of democracy![5]), where local elites of professional politicians have the 'franchise' of the Transnational Elite — i.e. the authorization to sell "opportunity and freedom" in some region, similar to the authorization that subsidiaries of multinationals have to sell goods and services in their region. This license is complemented by the decisive help of the mass media of the 'international community' (i.e. the world media controlled by the same Transnational Elite), and the local mass media controlled by the subordinate elites, to promote any systemic intellectual or actor etc. into a media personality and then into a parliamentarian, a Minister and so on. As I will try to show in this book, national sovereignty is impossible today for every country integrated into the NWO and only transnational sovereignty is possible for those countries exercising significant transnational power. But parliamentary democracy presupposes national sovereignty and therefore no parliamentary democracies in the proper sense of the word exist anymore in the NWO.

However, there was one thing that Obama was right about when he asked, rhetorically, how one could allow the dark tactics of the 20th century to be repeated today. Indeed, after Iraq and Afghanistan, where the Transnational Elite achieved its objective of regime change, so that a regime based on a national liberation movement (Ba'athist Iraq) and a fundamentalist one respectively (Afghanistan) could be toppled — although at a considerable cost in terms of casualties suffered by its own forces — a new tactic dawned on the Transnational Elite strategists for the integration of countries into the NWO in a way that will not involve a heavy (human) cost for the Transnational Elite itself, so that the political repercussions at home could be minimized.

---

[5] Takis Fotopoulos, *Towards An Inclusive Democracy* (London: Cassel, 1997), Ch. 5

Thus, the 'Obama era' includes a combination of some sort of 'democratization' (in the above sense of parliamentary Juntas, as e.g. in Tunisia) and engineered 'insurrections' that eventually take the form of armed rebellions (Libya, Syria, Ukraine), without direct military assistance by the Transnational Elite . The only exception was Libya but, even in that case, its direct military attack did not involve Western 'boots on the ground' but only criminal air attacks.

This new approach has received crucial assistance from the globalist 'Left' (i.e. the Left that does not question globalization and its institutions, i.e. the WTO, IMF, EU and so on), which has supported all these uprisings, as supposedly 'progressive' insurrections. The inevitable result was that there has never been a single large demonstration against the Transnational Elite and the massacres it has organized in all these countries with the clear aim to integrate them into the NWO! This has already led to dramatic changes. In fact, if Russia finally capitulates to the Transnational Elite, as the 'globalist' faction within the Russian elite attempts to achieve at the moment with the decisive help of the Transnational Elite, the global autocracy of the latter will be absolute and only the peoples' mass resistance could then abolish it. Alternatively, if Russia does not capitulate to the Transnational Elite after all, a generalized military conflict could well follow, as indicated by the fact that the US Pentagon has recently announced that it is more than quadrupling its spending in Europe "to reassure allies and deter so called Russian aggression."[6] At the same time, the view is promoted (and celebrated!) by some in US establishment circles that "moving past the last fifteen years, the United States military is once again focusing on great power conflict."[7]

---

[6] "Pentagon wants $582bn in 2017 budget, quadrupling of spending in Europe", RT, 2/2/2016 https://www.rt.com/usa/331009-pentagon-budget-war-big/
[7] Dave Majumdar, "America reveals 'Great power' plans against Russia and China", *The National Interest,* 3/2/2016 http://nationalinterest.org

PART I

THE NEW WORLD ORDER OF NEOLIBERAL GLOBALIZATION AND THE TRANSNATIONAL ELITE

Chapter 1.

The rise of the New World Order

In this part of the book I will examine the causes and the consequences of the rise of the New World Order (NWO) of neoliberal globalization, as well as of the emergence of a Transnational Elite that informally runs it. I will also try to show the seismic changes that the rise of the NWO had at the political level — apart from those at the economic level. At the political level, the rise of the NWO meant the effective demise of the Left, which was mostly incorporated into it, while the victims of globalization are abandoning it almost en masse, moving towards neo-nationalist movements that express the demand for economic, political and cultural sovereignty, i.e. for national sovereignty.

The ascent of the New World Order of neoliberal globalization

A basic characteristic of the present globalization era is the multiple confusion about the meaning and significance of the New World Order (NWO) and the role played today by the main power centers within it. In the context of this confusion, which is often deliberate, one may hear various myths about the present World Order that we shall examine in Part II.

The popular conception of the NWO is in terms of some sort of conspiracy theory, according to which secretive power elites — usually defined in ideological, if not religious or ethnic terms and sometimes in geopolitical, or crude economic terms — rule the world. In all these cases, the NWO is not interpreted in terms of systemic structures and the historical changes in them but, always, in terms of conspiracies by some elites. However, it is simply a myth that the NWO is the result of conspiracy. Instead, we should see it as the product of historical changes, spanning over two hundred years now, to the prevailing system of the capitalist market economy and the associated long-term changes in political structures.

This does not of course mean that there are no conspiracies in history. Far from it — take, for example, the Transnational Elite's conspiracy on the supposed weapons of mass destruction in order to dismantle the Iraqi Ba'athist regime. Yet, whether a conspiracy will succeed or not always depends on the outcome of the social struggle and it is only when the appropriate subjective and objective conditions have been created that such conspiracies can lead to historical changes, as the outcome, always, of this struggle.

In a nutshell, we may distinguish between three main phases in the development of the system of the capitalist market economy, roughly, a new phase for each of the three centuries since the rise of this system:[8]

a) The *liberal phase* in the 19th century that led to an attempt for globalization at the beginning of the 20th century. This, however, failed as the universal opening and liberalization of markets — the necessary condition for globalization – was impossible in the colonial era.[9]

b) The *statist phase* in the last century, which effectively began in Nazi Germany in the pre Second World War period[10] but was universalized in the West only in the aftermath of the war, in the form of social democracy and the welfare state.

c) The present *neoliberal phase*, which was associated with the advent and massive expansion, since the 1980s, of

---

[8] See for a detailed analysis of this periodization, Takis Fotopoulos, *Towards An Inclusive Democracy* (London: Cassel, 1997), Part I

[9] See for evidence to substantiate the fact that trade openness (a major index of globalization) contrary to what the globalist "Left" asserts, was at historically record levels at the beginning of the new millennium, which were not comparable to trade openness at the beginning of last century, Takis Fotopoulos, *The Multidimensional crisis and Inclusive Democracy*, (English translation of the book with the same title published in Greek, Gordios, 2005) http://www.inclusivedemocracy.org/journal/pdf%20files/Multidimensional%20Crisis%20Book.pdf p.71-72

[10] Michael Bleaney, *The Rise and Fall of Keynesian Economics* (London: Macmillan, 1985), p. 66

Transnational Corporations (TNCs). This crucial socio-economic development marked the emergence of globalization. And given it coincided (not by accident!) with another epoch-making development – the collapse of 'actually existing socialism' i.e. of the USSR and the soviet bloc – we may well talk about the emergence of a New World Order, which is defined in terms of these two major systemic developments, i.e., the rise of TNCs and the collapse of 'actually existing socialism'.

Thus, as I attempted to show elsewhere, [11] the new form of internationalized market economy, that has been established in the last forty years or so, represents a structural change. That is, a move to a new form of modernity, i.e., a move from statist to neoliberal modernity, rather than simply a change in economic policy, or in ideology, as the globalist 'Left' argues. In this sense, today's globalization is indeed a new phenomenon which, in fact, is the outcome of the interaction of the social struggle with the dynamics of the self-regulating system of the market economy that was established over two centuries ago and led to the marketization process, as described by Polanyi. [12] That is, the process of minimizing social controls on the markets and particularly those aiming at the protection of society (e.g. labor and the environment) from the markets, given that such controls were coming inevitably into conflict with economic "efficiency" and profitability.

Indicative is the way in which the process is described by Lawrence Summons, a Harvard professor, who had to concede the crucial role played by the elites when he tried to explain the present revolt against globalization:

> Driven by domestic economic progress, by technologies such as containerized shipping and the Internet that promote integration, and by legislative changes within and between nations, the world has grown smaller and more closely... The core of the revolt against global integration, though, is not ignorance. It is a sense, not wholly unwarranted, that it is a project carried out by elites for elites with little consideration for the interests of ordinary people — who see the

---

[11] Takis Fotopoulos, "Globalization, the reformist Left and the Anti-Globalization "Movement"," *Democracy & Nature*, Vol. 7, No. 2 (July 2001).
[12] Karl Polanyi, *The Great Transformation* (Beacon Press, 1944) Ch. 5

globalization agenda as being set by big companies playing off one country against another.[13]

In fact, the emergence and rapid expansion of Transnational Corporations (TNCs), which is a new phenomenon in the history of the capitalist market economy, initially led to an informal opening and liberalization of markets that was later institutionalized by Thatcherism and Reaganomics. It was this development that, together with the change in the subjective conditions i.e. the decay of the labor and socialist movements — signaled the collapse of social democracy and the rise of neoliberal globalization. In turn, the decay of the labor movement was the inevitable outcome, on the one hand, of de-industrialization in the West (which was a result of the globalization process itself and the subsequent depletion of the proletariat) and, on the other hand, the collapse of the soviet bloc.

Today, the evidence about globalization as a new phenomenon, which in the last two decades has taken the dimensions of hyper-globalization, is overwhelming. A significant recent study[14] on globalization, among others, confirms the above trends. The main feature of this hyper-globalization has been the rise of Transnational Corporations (TNCs) that, by 2009, numbered more than 80,000, accounting for about two-thirds of world trade. However, hyper-globalization is beneficial only to small sections of the world population, whereas the vast majority of people are victims. This was the inevitable outcome of the opening and liberalization of markets that has led to a huge concentration of power in the hands of TNCs, as scientific studies, such as a 2011 study by the *New Scientist,* have established.[15] This study, using a database listing 37 million companies and investors worldwide, identified 43,060 TNCs and the share ownerships linking them. It revealed that, of these TNCs, just 1,318 core companies, through interlocking ownerships, own 80% of global revenues. Furthermore, they found that just 147 companies (i.e. less than 1 per cent of the network) form a 'super entity', controlling 40 per cent of the wealth of the entire network!

---

[13] Lawrence Summers, "Global trade should be remade from the bottom up", *Financial Times,* 10/4/2016
[14] Arvind Subramanian and Martin Kessler, "The Hyper globalization of Trade and Its Future", Global Citizen Foundation, *WORKING PAPER 3,* JUNE 2013
[15] Andy Coghlan and Debora MacKenzie, "Revealed – the capitalist network that runs the world", *New Scientist* Magazine, issue 2835 (24/10/2011)

In other words, the rise of the Transnational Corporations, (or multinationals) was the main contributing factor to the emergence of the NWO of neoliberal globalization. Here is a brief description of what it is all about:

> Companies are rightly responding as quickly as possible to those new demands and, as a result, we are witnessing a level of international outsourcing that we could never have imagined. "Made in" labels mean little nowadays: companies based in the west often have their production plants elsewhere and use components sourced from third countries; and are financed by investors in yet other countries. If that were not complex enough, when countries impose trade barriers and erect controls, companies simply move overnight. Regulators and governments often do not stand a chance.[16]

Within this framework even modern 'slave trade' has developed, as described by the same author who is a partner at Dechert LLP specializing in international trade (and wife of Nick Clegg, the Liberal Democrat leader who was deputy Prime Minister of Cameron between 2010 and 2015). Thus, although the author has no problem with countries being able to produce cheaper products on the basis of their competitive advantage — including lower labor costs, as this is, as she stressed, "what free trade is all about" — she objects to the "abuse of human rights," while admitting that government action to control this new kind of "slavery" is ineffective:

> The UK government has taken the initiative in this area with the modern slavery bill. But such a bill does not attach any consequences for companies that are aware that there is modern slavery in their supply chain. Without tougher consequences, the chances of this changing things on the ground will be virtually zero.[17]

Yet, as a good globalist she celebrates the fact that "no matter how much protectionists wing, free trade has now won."[18] Needless to add that what she means by "protectionists" is all those fighting at this very moment against globalization all over the world — a phenomenon

---

[16] Miriam González, "Free trade has won: adapt or die is the only option left to us ", *The Observer*, 17/4/2016
[17] ibid.
[18] ibid.

which, those who do not understand its real significance, compare to the free trade expansion of the 19th century and the ideological and political battles between 'free traders' and 'protectionists'! [19]

The consequences of globalization and the propaganda of the Transnational Elite

The globalization process has already led to an unprecedented concentration of income and wealth, which several studies have confirmed.

As regards to the concentration of income, according to Nobel laureate in economics Joseph Stiglitz:

> Large segments of the population in advanced countries have not been doing well: in the US, the bottom 90% has endured income stagnation for a third of a century. Median income for full-time male workers is actually *lower* in real (inflation-adjusted) terms than it was 42 years ago. At the bottom, real wages are comparable to their level 60 years ago.[20]

Also, as regards the concentration of wealth, according to a Credit Suisse report, the richest 1 percent on the planet owned 48.2 percent of the world's wealth in 2014, (up from 46 percent the year before), whereas the bottom half of the global population owned less than 1 percent of the total wealth![21] Furthermore, more recent data suggests there has been an acceleration in the concentration of wealth. Thus, according to a very recent OXFAM report, the net worth of the 62 richest people is equal to the combined wealth of half the world (3.5 billion poorest people). Furthermore, as the same study showed, this trend has accelerated sharply, in the last five years or so, as the wealth of a circle of billionaires consisting of 388 people has risen by 44 per cent, (or half a trillion dollars) since 2010, while the wealth of the poorest fell by 41 per cent (more than a trillion)! [22]

---

[19] see for instance Larry Elliott, "How free trade became the hot topic vexing voters and politicians in Europe and the US" , *The Guardian*, 28/3/2016

[20] Joseph E. Stiglitz, "Globalization and its New Discontents",*Project Syndicate*, 5/8/2016 https://www.project-syndicate.org/commentary/globalization-new-discontents-by-joseph-e--stiglitz-2016-08

[21] "Richest 1% own 50% of world wealth- Credit Suisse report", RT, 16/10/2014 http://rt.com/business/195816-richest-1-percent-credit-suisse/

[22] Sam Joiner, "Richest 62 in world worth the same as poorest 3.5 billion", *The Times*, 18/1/2016

The social consequences of the huge inequality created by globalization, even in the USA, the country that played a leading role in promoting the opening and liberalization of markets throughout the post-war period, are well known. Thus, a very recent study published in the *Journal of the American Medical Association* implicitly showed that the more a country is integrated into the NWO the greater the negative impact on health and life expectancy. The result is that, as average life expectancy in developing nations continues to rise, lifespans in parts of America are getting shorter. This has reached the point where the poorest American men, at the age of 40, have a life expectancy comparable to the average 40-year-old man in Pakistan and Sudan! Rightly, therefore, Dr Deaton, a professor of economics at Stanford University, noted that the "infamous 1 per cent is not only richer" they have "ten to 15 more years to enjoy their richly funded lives," with their life expectancy being better than the average for any nation on earth.[23]

Even the *Financial Times,* the systemic financial organ of the Transnational Elite, recently had to admit the catastrophic consequences of globalization. As one of its main commentators pointed out: "We are close to the point where globalization and membership of the Eurozone in particular have damaged not only certain groups in society but entire nations," describing in some detail the economic shocks that 'inevitably' result from globalization.[24] The economic shocks concerned are: the stagnation of real average incomes for two decades but also the global financial crisis — a consequence of globalization — and its permanent impact on long-term economic growth. The overall effect, according to the same report (written just before Brexit!) was:

> In large parts of Europe, the combination of globalization and technical advance destroyed the old working class and is now challenging the skilled jobs of the lower middle class. So voters' insurrection is neither shocking nor irrational. Why should French voters cheer labor market reforms if it could result in the loss of their jobs, with no hope of a new one?... In 2014, almost 90 per cent of Germans were in favor of free

---

[23] Will Pavia , "Poor Americans have same life expectancy as Sudanese", *The Times,* 13/4/2016

[24] Wolfgang Münchau, "The revenge of globalization's losers", *Financial Times,* 23/4/2016

trade, according to a YouGov poll. That has fallen to 56 per cent. The number of people who reject TTIP outright has risen from 25 per cent to 33 per cent over the same period of time.[25]

No wonder that, following in particular the victory of Brexit and the fact that one of the two presidential candidates in the forthcoming US elections has adopted many of the demands of the victims of globalization, the Transnational elites have been terrified by this rapid rise of the anti-globalization movement. Particularly so as it is not anymore just the neo-nationalist movements in East Europe (such as those in Hungary and Poland) which challenge globalization. Following Brexit, the Eurosceptic Alternative for Germany party (AFD) came second, ahead of Chancellor Angela Merkel's CDU, in regional elections held in September, while similar parties and movements in Italy, France, Austria and the Netherlands have also seen a rise in their popularity.

This could explain the recent concerted attack against the rising new anti-globalization movement by some of the prominent members of the Transnational elite, such as the head of the IMF, the president of the European Central Bank and the president of the European Council.[26] All of them suddenly discovered the gross inequality in the distribution of income and wealth as a result of globalization and blamed the political elites for not taking enough measures on boosting support for low income workers and reducing inequality. Yet, they are fully aware of the fact that any such measures are impossible, in an environment of open and liberalized markets. Such measures, if they are designed to be effective (as present circumstances demand), they are bound to affect negatively competitiveness — the foundation of globalization itself. Not surprisingly, the arch-gatekeeper of globalization, the EU Commission President, immediately came out to 'restore order' and declare that the recipe for combating growing discontent in Europe was "more union" including a military headquarters "to co-ordinate efforts towards creating a common military force", rightly prompting Le Pen, the leader of the French FN,

---

[25] ibid.
[26] Claire Jones & Alec Barker, "Do more to help globalization's losers, say champions of liberalism", *Financial Times*, 13/9/2016

to ask "What is the EU protecting us from — are you protecting us against prosperity?"[27]

It is therefore clear that these two strategies (i.e. the 'good cop' strategy of improving the image of globalization and the 'bad cop' strategy of force to impose 'law and order') are going to define the response of the Transnational Elite in the future to the emerging revolt of the victims of globalization. Yet, the disquiet of globalists cannot anymore be hidden, as it happened in their latest big family reunion in New York.[28]

Globalization as a conspiracy

Clearly, globalization was not the result of some conspiracy by 'bad' economists and politicians, who were exploiting any kind of crisis in order to introduce neoliberal measures through "shock therapies" etc., as some best-seller conspiracy theorists (promoted by the Transnational Elite media!) suggest.[29] Instead, this was just the inevitable outcome of the collapse of the social-democratic model, which, being based on national markets, inevitably, became incompatible with the growing internationalization of the market economy. In other words, governments had to follow neoliberal policies in the new framework, in order to make their economies competitive and capable of continuing the expansion of the consumer society.

However, when in the last ten years or so, the full consequences of globalization, and the control over it exercised by an elite based mainly in the G7 countries started becoming common knowledge, a new propaganda campaign was launched by the Transnational Elite with the following manifold aims:

a) To diminish the significance of the vast expansion of TNCs and globalization itself, with some even speaking about the coming death of globalization based on the fact that for the past four years or so, international trade flows have increased more

---

[27] David Charter, Juncker calls for more union to beat 'galloping populism', *The Times*, 14/9/2016
[28] Anand Giridharadas, "Besieged Globalists Ponder What Went Wrong", *New York Times*, 26/9/2016
[29] See e.g. Naomi Klein, *The Shock Doctrine*, (Penguin, 2007)

slowly than global GDP.[30] However as the deputy governor of
the Bank of England recently stressed, "globalization is not
reversing, but it is simply changing"…while, following the
financial crisis of 2007-8, "banking flows are de-globalizing,
market-based flows — such as foreign direct investment and
portfolio flows — underwent a recovery post-crisis."[31]

b) To propagate the myth of a multi-polar world being created,
due to the rise of the BRICS countries (Brazil, Russia, India,
China and South Africa). Even the elites within these countries,
strangely enough, adopted this myth (see Ch.4) so that they
could pretend to be independent of the NWO and the
Transnational Elite. In fact, this is only partially true as far as
Russia is concerned and much less so with respect to China, the
dispute over the Pacific islands notwithstanding (Ch. 5)!

c) To attack the rapidly rising global movement against the NWO
of neoliberal globalization. The concrete aims behind this
attack by the ideological organs of the Transnational Elite in
the media, universities, think tanks, NGOs and the like, were
either to slander as 'fascist' any popular anti-globalization
movements and/or to defame as conspiratorial, any talk about a
NWO controlled by a Transnational Elite.

Thus, any popular neo-nationalist movements against globalization,
like Le Pen's FN in France or UKIP in Britain, were characterized by
the usual gatekeepers of "EU values" (such as Martin Schulz, the
President of the European Parliament) as racist or even fascist. At the
same time, they were looking the other way with regard to the actions
of the real fascists in Ukraine, whom the elites used as their main
organ for a 'coup from below,' instigated there in order to achieve the
country's integration into the NWO.[32]

The EU propaganda machine also marginalizes or even defames as
a conspiracy theorist every writer who does not toe the Transnational
Elite's line on globalization, while it directly or indirectly promotes
liberal or even Marxist authors and publications who "ignore"

---

[30] Heather Stewart, "The borders are closing, the banks are in retreat. Is globalisation
dead?", *The Observer*, 24/5/2015
[31] Minouche Shafik, "Globalisation is changing, not going into reverse", *Financial
Times*, 14/4/2016
[32] See Takis Fotopoulos, *Ukraine, The attack on Russia and the Eurasian Union*,
(vol. 2 of the NWO in Action project)

globalization and the Transnational Elite. In other words, this propaganda promotes all those authors who prefer to talk about today's reality in terms of completely outdated theories of the past two centuries, developed well before the emergence of globalization, such as the theory of Imperialism. Clearly, this kind of Paleolithic Marxist Left — with the exception of some enlightened Marxists who attempted, in a genuine Marxist fashion, to use the classical Marxist tools to develop new theories for today's reality[33] — is politically dead and theoretically bankrupt.

Neil Clark aptly described the systematic effort by the media organs of the Transnational Elite to misrepresent as a 'conspiracy theory' any effective critique of present reality:

> The labeling of people as 'conspiracy theorists' by gatekeepers in the West has nothing to do with how much evidence there is to support a claim or the quality of that evidence, but is a political call, based on who the conspiracy theory concerns and who is making it. Establishment gatekeepers are not objective judges, but are heavily biased and label any idea they don't like as a 'conspiracy theory'. Labeling someone a 'conspiracy theorist' is their standard way of declaring that person to be 'off-limits', i.e. he/she is an unreliable source and a 'crank'. It's a way that dissent and debate is stifled in what appear to be free, democratic societies - and how people who challenge the dominant establishment narrative are deliberately marginalized.[34]

Thus, a common slander against the very conception of the Transnational Elite is that it implies the presence of a well-organized international elite, which decides for the planet's future in a way that implies that "History is written on the basis of the commands of this elite which represents the 'New World Order.'"[35] This is an obvious and (far from sophisticated) distortion of my views since, as I have consistently stressed, History is always a creation. Such a view of

---

[33] See e.g. Leslie Sklair, *The Transnational Capitalist Class* (Oxford: Blackwell, 2001).
[34] Neil Clark, 'Conspiracy theories? No one does it better than West's elite', RT, 13/11/2013 http://rt.com/op-edge/conspiracy-theory-west-poisoning-648/
[35] See e.g. a collective work on "The conspiratorial discourse in the Greek political system", University of Thessaloniki, 2010

History rules out both conspiracy theories, as well as any 'objective' laws determining historical outcomes.[36]

Neoliberal globalization vs. neoliberal ideology

The post-war internationalization of the market economy, which led to the present globalization, was actively encouraged by the advanced capitalist countries, in view in particular of the expansion of 'actually existing socialism' and of the national liberation movements in the Third World. However, as I showed elsewhere, [37] the internationalization was basically the outcome of 'objective' factors related to the dynamics of the market economy and in particular the expansion of transnational corporations' (TNCs) activity and the parallel growth of the Euro-dollar market.

The Euro-dollar market provided a regulation-free environment where US dollars (and later other strong currencies such as the yen, mark etc.) could be borrowed and lent free of any US regulatory and tax requirements. The growth of this new market, which simply reflected the growing needs of TNCs, was instrumental in the later lifting of exchange and capital controls. This was because the exchange controls of nation-states, particularly those in Britain where the Euro-dollar market originated, [38] were put under severe strain, throughout the 1970s. This informal, at the beginning, opening and liberalization of markets to cover the needs of TNCs was then institutionalized, initially by conservative politicians (Thatcher and Reagan) to be followed later by governments of every persuasion: from Christian democrats and conservatives to social democrats, liberals and any combination between them.

In fact, the vast expansion of TNCs, a new phenomenon in the history of the capitalist market economy — which characterizes (together with the collapse of the Soviet bloc) the New World Order – would have been impossible without open and liberalized markets for commodities and capital. However, this was not the result of some conspiracy by 'bad' economists and politicians exploiting some kind of crisis, as some best-seller conspiracy theorists of the 'Left,' suggest, particularly promoted by *The Guardian*, the flagship of the globalist

---

[36] Takis Fotopoulos, *Towards an Inclusive Democracy*, (London: Cassel,1997), ch 8
[37] ibid. ch 1
[38] For a description of the gradual lifting of capital controls in Britain under market pressure, *see* Will Hutton, *The State We're In*, (Vintage, 1996)

'Left'. Instead, this was just the inevitable effect that followed the collapse of the social-democratic model, which was based on national markets and, as such, was not compatible anymore with the growing internationalization of the market economy.

It is also well known that, as even *Le Monde Diplomatique* recently pointed out:

> since the end of the second world war, the US empire has been the engine of trade liberalization, and the consistency of views has been absolute among successive presidents, Democrat or Republican, from John F Kennedy to Ronald Reagan, George W Bush to Barack Obama.[39]

In fact, it was only Donald Trump who, despite his – possibly critical — inconsistencies and contradictions, moved against this trend, supporting an informal anti-globalization movement that is rising among the victims of globalization (i.e. blue collar workers, small farmers and others), inevitably, uniting the entire US establishment and the Transnational Elite against him.[40] It was funny however to see, not only the entire political establishment (from Obama to George W. Bush and Bernie Sanders, the 'socialist' candidate), the whole economic establishment, as well as the entire press corps, (let alone the CIA![41]) but also the US globalist 'Left' siding with Clinton. Thus, from the *Nation* to Michael Albert's *Znet* up to the self-declared "anarchist" Noam Chomsky and many others, all declared their ('reluctant') support for the criminal candidate of the Transnational Elite. A candidate, no less, (in)famous for her memorable exclamation: "we came, we saw, he died." A remark she made after hearing of the brutal lynching of, Muammar Gaddafi, the Nasserite leader of the Libyan national liberation movement, at the hands of the 'revolutionaries,' funded by the Transnational Elite and supported by

---

[39] Serge Halimi, "Why fire-fighters are against free trade", *Le Monde Diplomatique,* April 2016
[40] see e.g. Philip Stephens, "US politics is closing the door on free trade", *Financial Times*, 7/4/2016; see also Jon Rappoport, "TPP, TTIP: Eliminating Nations, Turning over the World Economy To Mega-corporations", *Global Research*, 2/5/2016 http://www.globalresearch.ca/tpp-ttip-eliminating-nations-turning-over-the-world-economy-to-mega-corporations-obamas-secret-trade-deals-vs-trump-and-bernie/5522947
[41] Patrick Martin, "Why the CIA is for Hillary Clinton", *Global Research*, 6/8/2016 http://www.globalresearch.ca/why-the-cia-is-for-hillary-clinton/5539997

the State Department, which she headed at the time. Even Slavoj Žižek, one of the protagonists of the globalist 'Left,' seemed worried about the image of the 'Left,' presenting a total consensus in favor of Clinton — something that even the worst kind of one party systems have never achieved:

> Everybody is in there, from Wall Street to Bernie Sanders supporters, to what remains of the Occupy movement, from big business to trade unions, from army veterans to LGBT+, from ecologists horrified by Trump's denial of global warming and feminists delighted by the prospect of the first woman-president, to the 'decent' Republican establishment figures terrified by Trump's inconsistencies and irresponsible 'demagogic' proposals.[42]

For this politically and theoretically bankrupt American 'Left', the fact that the working class (for which supposedly they fight) fully supports Trump is irrelevant, or, alternatively, these 'libertarians', think workers are stupid enough so that they have to be 'educated' by these enlightened people about whom to vote for! This, despite the fact that Trump had drawn mass support and won elections and public opinion not just because he is a 'populist demagogue' (as they claim) but because, as even a prominent member of the globalist 'Left' admitted,[43] he rejected the free trade agreements which allowed TNCs to exploit labor all over the world. Furthermore, domestically, he questioned the uncontrolled importation of cheap immigrant labor, called for large-scale public investment, opposed the new cold war with Russia and China, and rejected US support for NATO's military build-up in Europe and intervention in Syria, North Africa and Afghanistan. In fact, even Julian Assange, another prominent member of the globalist 'Left', had to criticize her devious attack on Trump about supposedly having links with Russia and Vladimir Putin, whom she called the "grand godfather of this global brand of extreme nationalism." As Assange told Fox News:

---

[42] Slavoj Žižek, "The Hillary Clinton Consensus Is Damaging Democracy", *Newsweek*, 12/8/2016 http://europe.newsweek.com/slavoj-zizek-hillary-clinton-donald-trump-us-presidential-election-bernie-489993?rm=eu
[43] See James Petras, "Obama versus Trump, Putin and Erdogan: Can Coups Defeat Elected Governments?", Global Research,10/8/2016 http://www.globalresearch.ca/obama-versus-trump-putin-and-erdogan-can-coups-defeat-elected-governments/5540500

She has palled up with the neo-cons responsible for the Iraq war and she has grabbed onto a kind of neo-McCarthy hysteria about Russia and is using this to demonize the Trump campaign.[44]

In fact, this criminal professional politician tried at a stroke something much worse: to smear the worldwide popular struggle against globalization by the millions of its victims. Needless to say, none of her supporters in the globalist Left had anything to say about this — another nail in the coffin of this kind of 'Left'.

Of crucial significance to the globalization process was the creation of the World Trade Organization in 1995 that replaced GATT, the General Agreement on Tariffs and Trade, which commenced in 1948. This development marked the success of "free traders" all around the world. However, following the collapse of the Doha round to further expand free trade, the WTO was effectively sidelined in the last few years by multilateral agreements such as the Transatlantic Trade and Investment Partnership (TTIP) and the companion agreement covering the Pacific area the Transpacific Partnership (TPP). Both agreements were initiated to promote further freedom in the movement of goods and services, as we shall see next, in the process of creating a system of global governance.

In other words, governments in the new framework had to follow neoliberal policies to make their economies competitive and capable of continued growth involving further expansion of the consumer society. It was this requirement that was behind the austerity policies consistently adopted by UK, US and the EU elites and not some sort of ideological dogma or shortsightedness, as the globalist 'Left' maintain.

Lionel Barber, the *Financial Times* editor, gave a brief description of the institutional changes intrinsic to what he calls Globalization 1.0 (to distinguish it from what he calls Globalization 2.0, which emerged after the 2007-8 financial crisis). As it is significant in describing the Transnational Elites' thinking on the matter, I will reproduce this description almost in full:

For 500 years the west was on the rise, culminating between the late 1970s and 2007, in Globalization 1.0... The end of the

---

[44] "Assange slams Clinton for 'Russian hysteria' & US media for politicized election coverage", RT, 26/8/2016 https://www.rt.com/usa/357306-wikileaks-clinton-russia-agents/

cold war further accelerated institutional change: the creation
of the EU in 1993, and launch of the single currency in 1999;
the 1994 Uruguay Round agreement on global trade
liberalization and the establishment of the World Trade
Organization; the opening of a market economy in communist
China followed by entry into the WTO in 2001; and far-
reaching changes in national and international laws driven by
the deregulatory spirit of the Thatcher-Reagan era. The fall of
the Berlin Wall and the collapse of the Soviet Union brought
about an even bigger shift. The 'client states' of the world's
two superpowers — the US and the Soviet Union — were no
longer hemmed in by the geopolitical constraints of the cold
war and were now free to pursue their own development. As
the 'winner' of the cold war, many states chose to follow the
advice of the 'western' model prescribed by the US-influenced
global institutions: The World Bank, International Monetary
Fund and WTO-led trade liberalization — the so-called
Washington consensus. At the end of the cold war, around 1bn
people counted themselves in market economies. With the rise
of emerging markets and the transition in India and China that
number rose to between 3bn and 4bn people — a truly seismic
shift. The progressive abandonment of controls on capital,
goods, services and labor — epitomized in this period by the
creation of Europe's single market and the birth of the euro —
reached its apogee in the summer of 2007.[45]

As it should be clear from the above analysis, neoliberalism was
not just an invention, a dogma, or a 'political project' adopted by some
bad economists and politicians, whose advice was adopted by greedy
capitalists, as the intellectually bankrupt globalist 'Left,' suggests. It
was, instead, the inevitable outcome of a capitalist globalization based
on TNCs, which could only be neoliberal. This is because the opening
and liberalization of markets — a pre-requisite for the efficient
functioning of TNCs — was aimed at creating a level playing field for
the TNCs, not only with respect to the economic framework within
which they had to operate, but also with respect to the social
framework. For instance, capitalist globalization implies not only the
homogenization of legislation with respect to the hiring and firing

[45] Lionel Barber, "Globalization 2.0 — an optimistic outlook", *Financial Times*, 14/1/2016

workers ('flexible' labor relations). It also implies the homogenization of social services to the least common denominator, i.e. to the least expensive 'welfare system', so that TNCs could get the best possible conditions for profit maximization (in terms of very low taxation etc.), in any country fully integrated into the NWO.

However, one has to draw a clear distinction between the ideology of neoliberalism, and neoliberalism itself, in the same way that one should draw a clear distinction between capitalist or socialist ideology and capitalism or socialism respectively. The neoliberal ideology is simply the system of ideas and ideals used to justify, ('objectively', as every systemic ideology is supposed to do) the need for the opening and liberalization of markets, on which neoliberal globalization was founded. In other words, it was the structural change signaled by the emergence and massive expansion of Transnational Corporations — a result, in turn, of the grow-or-die dynamic of the system of the capitalist market economy – which led initially to an informal opening of markets (e.g. the Eurodollar market and similar markets) that later on was institutionalized.

Yet, the globalist 'Left', (including many in the antisystemic Left, even Marxists) do not draw this crucial distinction and, instead, usually confuse — sometimes deliberately — the systemic phenomenon of neoliberal globalization, which belongs to the economic base, with the ideologies of neoliberalism and globalization that belong, in Marxist terms, to the superstructure. This way, they derive an ahistorical 'theory' about 'bad' capitalists/politicians conspiring to impose 'neoliberalism', as a means of expanding profits, capital accumulation, smashing the labor movement etc. at the expense of workers. No wonder that even Eric Hobsbawm, the doyen of Marxist historians, was predicting — not very perceptively! — the imminent end of neoliberalism at the very beginning of the new millennium.[46] Today modern Marxists, (more modestly!), declare that although neoliberalism is not dead yet, it is certainly "dying" and all we have to do is to replace the neoliberal institutions. As Boris Kagarlitsky put it:

> The time has therefore come to turn the page and to reorient development strategies toward production, toward more educated, better-paid labor, toward reindustrialization, and

---

[46] Perry Anderson, *New Left Review,* No. 1, (new period) (Jan/Feb 2000), p. 10.

toward social programs and a new welfare state. But to do this we have to tear down the economic and political institutions of neoliberalism, just as neoliberalism earlier destroyed the social-democratic and communist institutions of the one-time *Sozialstaat* (social state). Can this be achieved without revolutions? Perhaps in some cases, but only in the context of revolutions elsewhere, in something like the way that Scandinavian social democracy benefited from the Russian Revolution of 1917. [47]

Others, like Noam Chomsky, talk about the 'bad' capitalism of today compared to the 'good' old capitalism, arguing that the problem is the corporatization of the market economy, which, supposedly, represents "an attack on markets and democracy." [48] However, as I showed elsewhere, [49] the problem was not the corporatization of the market economy, as this development was unavoidable anyway within the grow-or-die dynamic which characterizes the market economy system. The problem was that, as this dynamic was not reversed by the social struggle, it was bound to lead to the corporatization of the market economy. In other words, the problem in a capitalist market economy is not its corporatization — as if some other kind of capitalist market economy was feasible and desirable by the elites — but the capitalist market economy itself. Otherwise, one may easily end up blaming the elites for violating the rules of the game, rather than blaming the rotten game itself.

A more 'sophisticated' kind of 'antisystemic' Left effectively dismisses neoliberalism as "a political project carried out by the corporate capitalist class, as they felt intensely threatened both politically and economically towards the end of the 1960s into the 1970s." [50] According to this pseudo-antisystemic approach, the aim of

---

[47] Boris Kagarlitsky, "Economic policies after the death of neoliberalism", (Russian) *Institute for Global Research*, 8/4/2015
http://english.igso.ru/articles.php?article_id=45
[48] Noam Chomsky, 'Domestic Constituencies', *Z Magazine*, May 1998; see, also, his 'Power in the Global Arena', *New Left Review*, no. 230, July-August 1998, pp 3-27
[49] Takis Fotopoulos, "Mass media, culture and democracy" *Democracy & Nature*, vol.5, no.1 (March 1999) pp. 33-64
http://www.democracynature.org/vol5/fotopoulos_media.htm
[50] David Harvey, "Neoliberalism is a Political Project" , *Jacobin,* 23/7/2016
https://www.jacobinmag.com/2016/07/david-harvey-neoliberalism-capitalism-labor-crisis-resistance/

this project was, effectively, to smash labor, i.e. the project was a counter revolutionary one aiming, as Harvey put it, "to nip in the bud what, at that time, were revolutionary movements in much of the developing world — Mozambique, Angola, China etc. — but also a rising tide of communist influences in countries like Italy and France and, to a lesser degree, the threat of a revival of that in Spain."[51]

This approach not only is theoretically wrong and historically unfounded, as it ignores the basic fact that capitalism has gone through various phases, from the liberal phase of the 19th century to the statist phase of the 20th to the neoliberal phase of today,[52] but it is also disorienting. This is because the starting premise of neoliberalism, as a kind of conspiracy by the capitalist elites to smash labor, inevitably results in misleading conclusions. Such as Harvey's conclusion that "it's possible that you can make a better capitalism than that which currently exists" (although he adds "by not much"!) as well as his sort of 'alternative' conclusion "I would rather be talking about anti-capitalism than anti-neoliberalism." [53] However, if neoliberal globalization is not just the product of some sort of conspiracy but, instead, the present stage in capitalism's evolution — which, if it eventually covers the entire world in the form of global governance, will be its final one — there is no 'improvement' at all possible. Apart, of course, from the pseudo-improvements the Transnational Elite itself may decide in order to make slavery tolerable!

On the ideological front, liberal economists (as opposed to 'statist' Keynesian ones, who were dominant in the immediate post war period, during the statist phase I mentioned above) created a mix of liberal economic theory with monetarism and supply-side economics (what was usually called by its critics '*neoliberal economics*'), which involved policies aiming at the abolition of any effective social control of the economy. That is, it involved the shrinking of the public sector, through mass privatizations, the effective dismantlement of the welfare state and the squeezing of government spending, as well as the deregulation of the markets for commodities, labor and capital. The aim of shrinking the public sector was to enhance, instead, the role of the private sector, so that the scope of action of the TNCs, which

---

[51] ibid.

[52] see for an analysis of these historical phases of capitalism Takis Fotopoulos, *Towards an Inclusive Democracy* (Cassell 1997) ch. 1

[53] David Harvey, "Neoliberalism is a Political Project", op.cit.

control it in the globalization era, could be expanded accordingly. In a very recent confirmation of these trends, it was announced that in Britain, for instance, the number of public sector workers has tumbled to the lowest level since the Office for National Statistics began compiling records and that the massive reduction in public sector work has been more than offset by the private sector, where employment has risen to the highest level in history.[54]

Yet, the globalist 'Left' (Chomsky et al.) created another myth to dispute the obvious decline of the role of the public sector in the globalization era, effectively, disorienting the victims of globalization. Thus, inadvertently identifying the scope of the public sector with government spending they concluded that the public sector has not in fact shrunk because government spending as a proportion of GDP has not declined between the Keynesian and the neoliberal eras. This is strictly speaking true,[55] although the former period was characterized by conditions of almost full employment while the latter by conditions of disguised mass unemployment and growth in poverty. This fact is crucial in understanding this apparent paradox and could easily be explained if one examines the changes in the structure of government spending between the two periods. Then, one could see that the main reason why government spending, in the narrow sense of current government spending, has not fallen as a proportion of GDP between the two periods is that the decline of it, following the mass decrease in the size of civil service that we saw above, was more than matched by the rise in spending on defense and security. That is, the extra spending needed to cover the expenses on the wars of the Transnational Elite and the consequent anti-terrorist campaign. On the other hand, government spending, in the broader sense of overall state expenditure, has not fallen as a proportion of GDP between the two periods because any induced by neoliberal governments decline of it was matched by the steep (automatic) rise in social government

---

[54] Philip Aldrick, Public sector employment drops to record low, *The Times,* 14/9/2016

[55] According to World Bank data, current government expenditure (which excludes public investment, government social spending on subsidies, benefits, etc.) as a percentage of GDP for high income countries had remained stable between the Keynesian and neoliberal eras. Thus, government expenditure as a proportion of GDP was 17.0 in 1965 and 1988 during the Keynesian era (*World Development Report 1990*, Table 9) and it stayed about the same in the neoliberal era, i.e. 17.0 in 1995 and 18.0 in 2008 (*World Development Indicators 2010*, Table 4.8).

spending to cover the extra demands created by the growth of unemployment and poverty.[56] Yet, the globalist 'Left' had no qualms about using a distorted view of the statistics involved in order to dismiss the analysis about neoliberal globalization!

The new neoliberal ideology was, of course, also adopted by the mass media controlled by the TNCs and other press magnates. They promoted neoliberalism as the dominant *social paradigm* of the new era – where a social paradigm is defined as "the system of beliefs, ideas and the corresponding values which are dominant in a particular society at a particular moment of its history."[57]

Yet, the globalist 'Left', in its desperate effort to present neoliberalism as just a bad ideology, (or, alternatively, as an erroneous policy that was then adopted and promoted by 'baddies' in economics and politics), had no qualms even about distorting the history of economic thought. Thus, George Monbiot, a prominent British member of the globalist 'Left' (in its 'Green' variation, one of the worst variations, as Cohn-Bandit's Greens have amply shown) — christened as neoliberals two prominent members of the old liberal school, Ludwig von Mises and Friedrich Hayek, who, supposedly, "came to define the [neoliberal] ideology."[58] He then went on to call Friedman a neoliberal, simply because he wrote an article in 1951 on pre-war neoliberalism,[59] at a moment in his career when he was still in his first academic years at his university of Chicago post and had not yet even developed his comprehensive critique of Keynesianism. Yet, the neoliberalism he referred to was simply an inter-war development of the old liberal school, as Friedman himself stressed, which had little to do with modern neoliberal economics:

> Neo-liberalism would accept the nineteenth century liberal emphasis on the fundamental importance of the individual, but

---

[56] Spending on social security and welfare, which is now the dominant element of central government expenditure, has increased in high income countries from 55% of total government spending in 1985, (WB, World Development Report 1998/99, Table 17) to 62% in 2008 (WB, World Development Indicators, 2010, Table 4.11)

[57] Takis Fotopoulos, "Mass media, Culture and Democracy", DEMOCRACY & NATURE, vol.5, no.1 (March 1999), pp. 33-64
http://www.democracynature.org/vol5/fotopoulos_media.htm

[58] George Monbiot, "Neoliberalism – the ideology at the root of all our problems", *The Guardian*, 15/4/2016

[59] Milton Friedman, "Neo-Liberalism and its Prospects", *Farmand*, 17/2/1951

it would substitute for the nineteenth century goal of laissez-
faire as a means to this end, the goal of the competitive order…
The citizens would be protected against the state by the
existence of a free private market; and against one another by
the preservation of competition.[60]

In other words, this pre-war neoliberalism was essentially an
attempt to improve the liberal economics' attack on 'collectivism', at a
time when the latter was not only ideologically hegemonic but also
politically rising. However, this first generation of neoliberalism had,
inevitably, very little to do with neoliberal globalization in general and
neoliberal economics in particular. Inevitably, because pre-war
liberalism and neoliberalism referred of course to the pre-globalization
era, i.e. the era of nation-states, within which Keynesianism could only
thrive. At that time the issue was how to improve, through the state
mechanism, the social control over markets in order to protect society
and the environment from them. On the other hand, the issue today is
whether social controls are possible at all in the globalization era of
open and liberalized markets, which make the implementation of
neoliberal economics a one-way street — unless one is prepared to
break with the NWO of neoliberal globalization.

The emergence of a new kind of 'growth economy' in the NWO

Few doubt today that major structural changes are taking place
within the NWO of neoliberal globalization. These changes are
expressed both as a direct effect of globalization, (i.e. the huge and
growing concentration of income and wealth, following the vast
expansion of trade and investment through the activities of TNCs) and
as an indirect effect of the opening and liberalization of markets. Thus,
in the globalization era, a new type of "growth economy" is emerging
involving also a new kind of dual consumer society, as we shall see
next. This new kind of growth economy involves two contradictory
effects on growth implied by the opening and liberalization of markets
brought about by globalization.

There is first a positive effect on growth, as a result of the
expansion of exports and investment brought about by the opening and
liberalization of markets and their implications on aggregate demand
through the multiplier effects created by the extra spending of the

---

[60] ibid.

social groups that are the beneficiaries of globalization. But, there is also a negative effect on growth as a result of an enforced kind of 'de-growth' brought about by the suppression of aggregate demand, following the opening and liberalization of markets (particularly of the labor market), which suppress real wages and incomes (and therefore the demand) of the victims of globalization.

In other words, the huge and growing concentration of income and wealth brought about by globalization is the effect, first, of the expansion of incomes, due to the rise of profits, but also wages and salaries of those who found a job within the globalization process, (because of the expansion of, mainly foreign, investment) and, second, of the suppression of incomes, due to the suppression of wages and salaries of the victims of globalization (full-timers becoming part-timers or unemployed etc). It is therefore the net result of these two contradictory effects of the growth process that determines the overall growth pattern of a country. In case the positive effect outweighs the negative effect, as for instance in the present 'miracles of globalization' (China, India, etc.), then the overall effect is positive, but where the opposite happens, as in most countries of the world, the overall effect is either negative, or, at most, a low-growth kind of economy. The fact that China's growth rate is slowing down lately is therefore due to the fact that the negative effect of globalization on growth becomes increasingly more significant than the positive effect — a process leading eventually to a low growth economy.

In more detail, the institutional framework that has been established today all over the world, (i.e. in all countries integrated into the NWO), consists of a model in which economic growth – sometimes for its own sake — is the fundamental economic aim. In this framework, the continuation of growth depends on a process of further internationalizing the economy, a fact that implies a self-perpetuating vicious circle. This process can be briefly described as follows:

- The destruction of economic self-reliance, as a result of globalization and the consequent opening of markets which necessitates a growing dependence on imports;
- As imports expand, this creates in turn further pressure to expand exports in order to finance them;
- However, greater exports presuppose more competitiveness and therefore corresponding improvements in productivity that,

in the end, can only come about through more investments in technology, research and development (or, alternatively, through austerity policies, as shall see below);

- Therefore, it is the Transnational Corporations (TNCs) that control world trade and investment in a globalized economy, as they alone possess the productive and technological base that allows the constant improvement in productivity, which is required by the cutthroat international competition.

Given therefore, as mentioned above, a few hundred TNCs control the bulk of global revenues, it is hardly surprising that, by the beginning of the new millennium, the fifth of the world's population living in the world's richest countries — from where the TNCs mostly originated (mainly the G7 countries) — enjoyed 86% of world GDP and 82% of world exports.[61]

The victors in this process are, necessarily, the most competitive economic actors, who possess the production and technological structure that allow for the continual increase in productivity required by the tough international competition. However, high competitiveness can be based on either high productivity, due mostly to a strong production and technological base (e.g. Germany) or, alternatively, on very low production cost due to very low wages (e.g. India) and/or low taxes on TNCs (Ireland etc.).

So, in the NWO, it is no longer nation-states that rule the world, fighting among themselves for the division of world markets, but rather the transnational corporations. It is these huge oligopolies that are always the victors, irrespective of where they base their activities. Therefore, the fact that today China or India look like economic superpowers (or rising superpowers) is not, in fact, an economic miracle but rather an economic mirage. If any of these countries stopped offering the 'comparative advantages' they presently do, particularly in terms of cheap production cost they offer to the TNCs, then the economic miracle would end overnight — i.e. as soon as the TNCs move to one of the other countries begging them to invest in their own area.

---

[61] UN, *Human Development Report 1999* (NY: Oxford University Press, 1999), p. 3
More recent national data are mostly unreliable, given the growing practice of TNCs in the last twenty years or so, to use various practices (including accounting practices), which have become easier in the framework of open markets, to minimize taxes and therefore maximize profits (see e.g. Amazon, Apple etc.)

In other words, the myth that competition within the NWO is 'good for the people' assumes that people are just consumers looking for the cheapest possible price for what they buy. However, consumers also have to be producers (of goods and/or services), so that they can buy, i.e. they should have the necessary disposable income for their purchases. In fact, as we shall see next, the NWO of neoliberal globalization did not lead to a further expansion of the mass consumer society, which was created in the West during the immediate post-war period (the statist phase of capitalism). Instead, the institutionalization of neoliberal globalization under Thatcherism and Reaganomics, at the end of the 1970s, (i.e. the opening and liberalization of markets that globalization necessitated), has led to a dualist consumer society within a new type of growth economy. This was the result, mainly, of the continuous suppression of real wages and incomes brought about by the globalization process and in particular the opening and liberalization of labor markets. So, globalization is too good for a small minority of the world's population and too bad for the vast majority of it and, as we saw above, it has led to a huge concentration of economic and therefore of political and all other forms of power in a few hands.

The mechanism through which the real incomes of the victims of globalization have declined works through the lifting of any significant *social* controls on markets imposed in the past to protect society and environment from markets. The effective lifting of social controls aiming at the protection of society from the markets means that transnational corporations are today free to move capital and commodities all over the world, while having to face regulatory controls only. Furthermore, the 'liberalization' of labor markets, which is part of the same process, implies effectively the lifting of social controls to protect labor, for the sake of attracting foreign capital, (i.e. the transnational corporations), and making the economy more 'competitive'. 'Flexible' labor is the norm in this process, i.e. a vast expansion of part-time or occasional labor, zero hours contracts etc. - all of which have the effect of artificially reducing the level of unemployment at the expense of real incomes, i.e. incomes which are essentially frozen in real terms.[62]

---

[62] See e.g. Ed Conway, "The UK is paying the price of its jobs miracle," *The Times* 14/10/2014

Furthermore, liberalization of labor markets meant also the opening of borders that facilitated the movement of labor, particularly among the EU countries, through the Lisbon and Schengen Treaties. The result of this was the present migration crisis in the EU that threatens its very foundations. The EU elites are of course in favor of labor market liberalization, so that real wages are suppressed in the EU area but the precondition for such a policy to be effective is that they would be in control of the labor flows. It is exactly the violation of this precondition that has created the present crisis.

Today's controls on markets are of the kind I called in the past *regulatory controls*,[63] which have usually been introduced by the Transnational Elite controlling the market economy in order to 'regulate' the market. In other words, the aim of regulatory controls is to create a stable framework for the smooth functioning of the market economy without affecting its essential self-regulating nature. Such controls have always been necessary for the production and reproduction of the system of the market economy but whereas in the past the aim of such regulation was the control of the domestic market economy, today's regulatory controls aim at the transnational market and are imposed through transnational institutions controlled by the Transnational Elite, such as the World Trade Organization, or the EU bureaucracy as far as the European market is concerned.

It is the same opening and liberalization of markets which tends to universalize the rudimentary US 'welfare services' system, as well as the associated low corporate taxation system and the consequent shrinking of the public sector through privatizations etc. A new lowest common denominator is created to which any country wishing to have growth and employment has to conform. Why? Because growth and employment in an economy integrated into the NWO of neoliberal globalization, (which is characterized by open and liberalized markets for capital, labor and commodities), crucially depends on competitiveness. It is relatively high competitiveness, which will attract more Transnational Corporations and therefore more investment and that, in turn, will lead to more growth and employment. This is in contrast to the era of nation-states, when growth and employment crucially depended on the national market, as markets were not open at the time. Clearly in that case, it mattered a lot

---

[63] Takis Fotopoulos, Towards An Inclusive Democracy, (London: Cassel, 1997) Ch. 1

whether governments were pursuing policies of balanced budgets (a milder version of what we call today 'austerity policies') or whether instead they were adopting expansionary policies to boost aggregate (domestic) demand, even if this implied deficit budgets, particularly in periods of recession — as Keynesian economics, which was dominant at the time, prescribed.

Some view the presently emerging low growth economy in the West as a kind of temporary phenomenon, usually related to the 2008 financial crisis. This is what Paleolithic Marxist approaches usually suggest, unless, they argue — based on national statistical data that is mostly irrelevant in the globalization era — that capitalism suffers from an over-accumulation of capital and lack of investment! However, it is well known that TNCs, in the framework of open markets which facilitate such practices, tend to artificially 'distribute' their activities, among the various countries where they operate, with the aim to minimize their taxes and maximize their profits accordingly. Luxembourg (from which Jean-Claude Juncker the present president of the EU Commission originated!) has specialized in such practices to hide the real profits of TNCs (e.g. Amazon). This forced the EU Commission, in the light of the 'Panama Papers', to unveil a set of draft rules that would compel companies with global revenues of more than €750m per year to provide a public country-by-country breakdown of key financial information. The argument was that this move would hit complex corporate arrangements intended to avoid tax.[64] However, given this is the fourth EU attempt within the last couple of years or so to "to roll out country-by-country reporting for companies," one may have very serious doubts that this process will ever get real momentum. This is especially so in view of the recent corruption scandals, which, apart from tax evasion, make a mockery of national statistical data. In fact, it was recently revealed that Germany, the effective leading power within the EU, is against the plan, with the German Finance Minister Wolfgang Schäuble explicitly stating at a Eurogroup meeting "sometimes there is a contradiction between transparency and efficiency."[65] It seems therefore that this will be the

---

[64] See Jim Brunsden, " Brussels plans to force multinationals to open up on profits", *Financial Times*, 13/4/2016
[65] Jim Brunsden, "German finance minister objects to tax transparency proposals", *Financial Times*, 24/4/2016

end of the 'rebellion' against the TNC's — if such a rebellion ever happened and it was not just a EU propaganda trick!

Furthermore, the financial crisis, which functioned as the catalyst for the present economic and social catastrophe of peoples in the periphery of the EU (Greece, Portugal, Spain, Ireland), was, in fact, as I tried to show at the time, merely a symptom of neoliberal globalization.[66] In this sense, the emergence of a low growth economy is a systemic phenomenon rather than a temporary one.

Others attempt to explain the same phenomenon in terms of the supposedly radical changes brought about by the 'financialization' of the economy, which is claimed to represent "a new historical period in the development of capitalism" in which globalization is simply "a notable feature of the historical period of financialization!"[67] Clearly, such a completely disorienting approach is based on a highly distorted view of the current reality that ignores the dominant phenomenon of our time: the mass expansion of transnational corporations and the consequent neoliberal globalization, as the economic dimension of the NWO.[68] No wonder that, in this completely a-historical approach, there is neither a NWO nor a Transnational Elite that administers it. Consequently, the frequent wars of this elite in the last two decades are simply blamed on intra-imperialist conflicts, although one may wonder how exactly the entire Transnational Elite managed to be so remarkably and unprecedentedly united in all these wars — apart from some tactical divisions between them, as for instance with the invasion of Iraq.

Still others try to explain the present low growth economy of the West on the basis of ecological factors, particularly related to the Limits of Growth approach. These approaches mainly rely on the

---

[66] See Takis Fotopoulos, "The myths about the economic crisis, the reformist Left and economic democracy", *The International Journal of INCLUSIVE DEMOCRACY, Vol. 4, No. 4 (October 2008)*
http://www.inclusivedemocracy.org/journal/vol4/vol4_no4_takis_economic_crisis.htm
[67] Jennifer Tighe, "Costas Lapavitsas Discusses the Financialization of Capitalism", *Verso,* 28/1/2014 http://www.versobooks.com/blogs/1509-costas-lapavitsas-discusses-the-financialization-of-capitalism ; see, also, C. Lapavitsas, "Globalization or Financialization" (in Greek*), Iskra,* 24/8/2014)
[68] Takis Fotopoulos, "Globalization, the reformist Left and the Anti-Globalization 'Movement'", *DEMOCRACY & NATURE vol.7,* no.2, (July 2001)
http://www.democracynature.org/vol7/takis_globalisation.htm

premise that growth for growth's sake is unsustainable, as it pushes the limits of the biosphere. On the basis of this premise, they draw the conclusion that it is the growing scarcity of resources (particularly of energy resources), which indirectly caused the financial crisis and historically has led to a long-term capitalist crisis. Yet, as I tried to show elsewhere,[69] neither the history of capitalist development since the Industrial Revolution, nor present developments with respect to the almost historically low price (in real terms) of oil — despite the political machinations involved we shall consider in vol. 2 — are consistent with the scarcity of energy approach.

The new dual consumer society

The main characteristic of the 'new growth economy' is that, unlike the old type of growth economy founded on a mass consumer society, the new growth economy relies on growth for the few and de-growth for the rest. This implies a new dual consumer society that consists of:

- The 'normal' consumer society, which, however, nowadays covers only the needs of the privileged social strata that benefit from globalization in both the "North" and the "South", i.e. a small minority of the world population;

- The emerging today new "subsistence consumer society" covering the needs (mostly basic needs) of the rest of the population, which is condemned to permanent unemployment or low wages/salaries/ pensions, zero hours contracts, part time or occasional employment etc.

In this dual consumer society, the 'normal' consumer society is sustained mainly by the beneficiaries of globalization, i.e. the privileged social strata that benefit from globalization and push forward for further economic growth based on mass consumption. On the other hand, today's emerging new 'subsistence consumer society' is sustained by the victims of globalization, in the framework of an effective de-growth process. De-growth in this context does not mean

---

[69] See Takis Fotopoulos, "Disaster theories and the crisis: the peak oil case", *The International Journal of inclusive Democracy*, Vol. 7, No. 2/3 (Summer/Autumn 2011)
http://www.inclusivedemocracy.org/journal/vol7/vol7_no2_3_takis_disaster_theorie s_peak_oil_crisis.html

negative growth but simply low growth, enough to reproduce the labor force.

The net effect of these two trends, as I stressed above, determines whether overall growth will be fast or whether, instead, it will be slow, or even negative. The former case is the one of the BRICS 'miracles', where the rapid expansion of the consumption of the rising middle classes far outweighs the low growth of the majority of the population. However, in the last few years, these 'miracle cases' showed their limitations, with very low or even negative growth rates in some of them being noticed (see Ch. 5). On the other hand, the latter case is the one of the peripheral EU countries, e.g. the Mediterranean countries and also the ex-soviet bloc countries etc. Needless to add that a dual consumer society, (which is based on the division in each country that is integrated into the NWO between beneficiaries and victims of globalization respectively), is already present in the G7 countries themselves, leading to the rise of anti-NWO movements. Such movements are the anti-EU movements in Europe[70] (on top of France and UK, a similar flourishing of neo-nationalist movements is noticed in countries such as Poland, Austria and others) or even in the USA where Donald Trump's support in effect draws on various anti-globalization trends emerging in the country.

It should be noted that this kind of de-growth is a distorted kind of de-growth and not the kind promoted by the supporters of a movement under the same name,[71] as the elements of sharing, co-operation, etc., stressed by them, are missing. However, the net ecological effect may be significant, as the new growth economy could significantly reduce the pressure on energy sources. Furthermore — crucially for the system — this could be achieved without the need to abolish the growth economy itself, as radical ecologists have always demanded based on projections for the scarcity of resources founded on the old kind of growth economy, i.e. on projections that are clearly irrelevant

---

[70] Editorial, "The People's Revolt", *The Times,* 11/10/2014
[71] See the de-growth debate, *The International Journal of INCLUSIVE DEMOCRACY,* vol 3 no 1 (January 2007)
http://www.inclusivedemocracy.org/journal/vol3/vol3_no1_Takis_degrowth.htm
and the de-growth debate revisited, ibid. vol 6 no 4 (Fall 2010)
http://www.inclusivedemocracy.org/journal/vol6/vol6_no4_takis_degrowth_simpler_way_id.htm

to today's reality. Needless to add that this "success" is paid for by the lower strata, which are the main victims of globalization.

Therefore, the de-growth debate is not only irrelevant to the present reality but also disorienting, especially as far as the victims of globalization are concerned, since, indirectly, it justifies the various austerity policies imposed by the NWO of neoliberal globalization. However, although the ideologues of neoliberal globalization do not dare of course to justify austerity policies on the basis of ecological rationality, the present enforced de-growth does create a perverse effect. Thus, many people, particularly in the middle classes, could find attractive this new kind of growth economy, on account of the above ecological "alibi". This, in turn, could well function as an additional reason to induce them to vote for the parties constituting the local parliamentary juntas imposed by the NWO. Particularly so, if we take into account the fact that, today, it is mainly those belonging to the middle class who, being among the beneficiaries of globalization themselves, and having already sorted out their own survival problems, can afford to worry about ecological issues.

But, leaving aside the potential beneficial ecological effect that could result from the emergence of the new type of growth economy described here, its overall socio-economic effect is the suppression of real wages and aggregate demand. It also involves the creation of conditions of fake full employment — like those prevailing in Britain at present — with flourishing zero hours contracts,[72] part time and occasional work and so on. In other words, the net socio-economic effect of the new growth economy is the perpetuation of the present huge concentration of income, wealth and power in a few hands, without the parallel dismantling of the image of a consumer society. This image is particularly important for the reproduction of the system as a whole, given that consumerism is the only reason for which most people in the world still tolerate the present criminal system. No wonder that economic migrants from Asia and Africa (many masquerading as refugees) demonstrate in Greece with the slogan "open the borders", choosing in the process even their best destination, Germany, presumably because higher wages there could

---

[72] In March 2016 the Office for National Statistics in UK said the number of workers on zero hours contracts had increased by more than 100,000 over the previous 12 months to exceed 800,000 for the first time, Phillip Inman, Use of zero-hours contracts goes beyond short-term flexibility, says thinktank, *The Guardian*, 8/9/2016

meet their consumerist aspirations! This is in consistency with recent studies that show that, happiness is in direct proportion to per capita gross domestic product. As an analyst put it: "To change your life you need a boat (to emigrate), not a party!"[73]

In fact, all the above hypotheses are justified by statistical evidence, like the 2014 International Labor Organization (ILO) report, according to which, for a large number of developed countries, "including Greece, Ireland, Italy, Japan, Spain and the United Kingdom – average real wages in 2013 were below their 2007 level", while "overall, in the group of developed economies, real wage growth lagged behind labor productivity growth over the period 1999 to 2013".[74] This implies a continuous redistribution of income all these years against the lower income groups living out of wages and salaries, and in favor of the higher income groups living out of profits and dividends respectively.

This huge redistribution of income (and consequently wealth as well) is the basic cause of the new type of growth economy and of the dual consumer society described, as well as the main effect of the establishment of the NWO of neoliberal globalization.

Is neoliberal globalization or 'the austerity delusion' the real enemy?

In this framework, as we shall see also in more detail in Ch.6, it is not the austerity policies imposed by some 'baddies' in the political and economic elites that are the cause of the present low-growth economy, given their unwillingness to adopt expansionary Keynesian policies to boost incomes and demand. However, austerity policies are simply the symptom of globalization in the sense that, if investment on research and development to improve competitiveness is not available, the alternative 'cheap' way to achieve the same result is through the suppression of domestic wages and prices, by means of some sort of austerity policies. Yet, the globalist 'Left' simply blames austerity policies for the present low or negative growth, as they do not wish to question is any way the ultimate cause of such policies: globalization itself!

But, whereas in the 1990s and 2000s, the globalist 'Left' included at least in its vocabulary the word 'neoliberal' — deliberately

---

[73] Ivan Krastev, "Fear and loathing of a world without borders", *Financial Times,* 6/4/2016
[74] International Labor Organization, *The Global Wage Report 2014/15,* 5/12/2014

confusing of course the systemic phenomenon (neoliberal globalization) with the ideology justifying it — in this decade it, often avoids even using the word, in a clear attempt to turn people's minds away from their real enemy. That is, from the systemic phenomenon of neoliberal globalization and the implied opening and liberalization of markets, which is the ultimate cause of the dismantling of the welfare state and of Keynesian economics itself.

In fact, today, not only naïve economists belonging to the globalist 'Left' support Keynesian policies — presumably still living in a nation-state time capsule with its Keynesian policies and all its ideological paraphernalia — but even Nobel laureates in economics, who cannot of course be accused for naivety but rather for deliberate disorientation. This is the case for instance with Paul Krugman who, in a 2015 article in the *Guardian*,[75] the flagship of the globalist 'Left', systematically attempted to bypass the crucial issues of our era — particularly globalization and its neoliberal ideology — and concentrated, instead, on the austerity 'delusion' or 'obsession' (as he called it) of policy makers, particularly in UK. This way, he not only conveniently 'forgot' that these are also the policies of the EU, as well as of the US administrations since Reagan, but he also ignored the fact that these are the policies of the Transnational Elite. That is the policies which are imposed, one way or another, on every country integrated into the NWO.

Thus, in a 6,000 word article, the words 'neoliberal' and 'globalization', let alone 'competitiveness', are not mentioned even once. So, Krugman 'forgetting' that we live in a globalized world in which competitiveness is crucial even for growth and employment, talks about why Keynesian policies are best for each nation-state! At least, however, this apologist for globalization (who justifiably was awarded by the Transnational Elite — through the Nobel prize committee which does a very good job in promoting, directly or indirectly the apostles of globalization — the highest accolade for any systemic economist) had the frankness to admit that big business, unlike economists like himself and politicians, love austerity policies. But then he went on to disorient, yet again, about their reasons for doing so:

---

[75] Paul Krugman, "The austerity delusion", *Guardian*, 29/4/2015

I've already suggested one answer: scare talk about debt and deficits is often used as a cover for a very different agenda, namely an attempt to reduce the overall size of government and especially spending on social insurance. This has been transparently obvious in the United States, where many supposed deficit-reduction plans just happen to include sharp cuts in tax rates on corporations and the wealthy even as they take away healthcare and nutritional aid for the poor.[76]

In fact, however, the cuts in public spending and the shrinking of the public sector in general, (through privatizations etc.) and of the welfare state in particular, are caused by the cuts in corporation and capital taxes, which are induced by governments keen to stimulate productive investment and improvements in competitiveness. On the other hand, capitalists prefer to invest, instead, in such paradises as India or China. Yet, the consequent lack of domestic investment in the countries of origin of TNCs is taken by calamity 'Marxists' as proof of a crisis of over-accumulation and lack of investment!

However, although 'austerity policies' constitute the inevitable consequence of neoliberal globalization, Krugman does not want to talk about globalization and competitiveness – these are the 'dirty' words businessmen and politicians have to say. On the other hand, Krugman's mandate, as a Nobel laureate in economics, is to disorient people from their real enemy, the NWO of neoliberal globalization, and turn them instead against non-systemic factors, which do not challenge the system itself but just the 'baddies' in the political elite who implement the austerity policies!

The political consequence of such disorienting views is that, when the globalist 'Left' that adopts such misleading ideas comes to power, instead of attempting to break with the NWO itself, it simply turns against the austerity policies[77] implemented by the political personnel running the NWO. This is, for instance, the case of Greece, where the victory of the globalist Left (SYRIZA), instead of leading to an exit from the EU and the implementation of self-reliance policies, has led to the present fiasco. That is, where a "Left" government is implementing the strictest austerity policies possible, which are also accompanied by the selling out of social wealth, with the obvious aim

---

[76] Ibid.
[77] See on the Left's myths with respect to austerity policies Ch. 6

to secure a bit more time in power from the EU elites. On top of this, the same Greek 'Left' government does not have any qualms about celebrating the criminal policies they implement and presenting their total submission to the Troika as a kind of victory! In so doing, they confirm the worst suspicions of the Greek people that their 'Left' government is just a bunch of con artists interested only in power for power's sake!

Chapter 2.

The role of the Transnational Elite

The meaning of the Transnational Elite in the NWO

The creation of an internationalized market economy necessitated some sort of international economic and political 'regulation'. When the market economy was mainly national, the role of enforcing the market rules was assigned to the 'nation-state' (which included the old national empires, like the British colonial empire that, in effect, had its own internal market for trade and capital investment) and the political and economic elites controlling it. However, a transnational economy needs transnational political and economic elites to control it. Therefore, although the state monopoly of violence still remains in the present internationalized market economy, it is now supplemented by a transnational form of violence enforced not just by one state — even if this could (wrongly) be seen as the last 'empire' in the classical sense of the word (USA) — but by the main military powers in the G7 i.e. France, UK, US (the 'FUKUS' powers which acted collectively and very effectively in destroying Libya). But, even though economic power is concentrated today among a few hundred TNCs, which originated, mainly, in the G7 countries, (i.e. FUKUS plus Germany, Japan, Canada and Italy), the USA, due to its unambiguous military supremacy, has a de facto leading position — although it is not the Emperor. In other words, the NWO is an 'Empire', in the sense of a unipolar world, but without an Emperor – unless we consider as 'emperor' the entire Transnational Elite.

In this framework, we may define the Transnational Elite as the elite that draws its power (economic, political or generally social power) by operating at the transnational level — a fact which implies that it does not express, solely or even primarily, the interests of a particular state. It consists of a network of interconnected elites controlling each major field of social life (economic, political, ideological and so on). Therefore, the following elites constitute the major components of the transnational elite:

➤ *The transnational economic elites* in charge of economic globalization, which control the main TNCs and consist of corporate directors, executive managers, major shareholders of the main TNCs, as well as the directorates of the main international economic organizations (IMF, World Bank, OECD and so on). It is the transnational economic elites which determine, usually indirectly and informally, the economic policies of the countries integrated into the NWO of neoliberal globalization (see e.g. the role of the European Round Table of Industrialists, which consists of the main TNCs effectively running the EU by influencing its economic program, such as the content of the Maastricht Treaty);[78]

➤ *The transnational political elites* in charge of political globalization, which control the distinctly politico-military dimension of the NWO and consist of transnational bureaucrats and professional politicians functioning either within major international organizations (EU, NATO etc.) or in the state machines of the major market economies, (principally the G7 countries). It is the transnational political elites, which discuss, informally at present (e.g. in the context of the annual meetings of the Bilderberg Group or at Davos), the geopolitical strategies, as well as the economic policies, of the countries integrated into the NWO of neoliberal globalization. The political complement of a capitalist market economy integrated into the NWO is a parliamentary 'democracy', which in the NWO takes the form of a 'parliamentary junta'. This is a hybrid between representative democracy and a political junta,

---

[78] See the official site of the European Round Table of Industrialists http://www.ert.eu; see, also, the film by Friedrich Moser & Matthieu Lietaert, *The BrusSels Business: Who Runs the European Union?* (2012). Finally, see George Monbiot, "Still bent on world conquest", The Guardian 16/12/1999.

in the sense of a committee that leads or governs on the basis of a prearranged program that may have very little relationship to its electoral program. A parliamentary junta consists of a political party or parties, elected to government through some sort of electoral and parliamentary process. This is a process that has very little to do with the electoral process involved in the parliamentary democracies of the past, when mass political parties with clearly distinct electoral programs were competing for the vote of an electorate that participated in the process en masse. Today's national political elites are seriously constrained by rules designed by forces outside the national parliaments. It is estimated, for instance, that at least 65% of domestic legislation of EU member states has its origin in Brussels.[79] Furthermore, the competing elites for government are well aware of the fact that their programs are simple variations of the same theme, i.e. the neoliberal globalization program. That is, a program which is being implemented by governments of every persuasion in Europe, the USA, Australia etc., and that it is imposed through the NWO institutions, such as the WTO, the IMF and World Bank, the EU, NAFTA etc.

➤ *The transnational propaganda elites* in charge of promoting the ideology of the New World Order of neoliberal globalization, through their control of transnational mass media (e.g. CNN, BBC and the like). They include also the elites involved in implementing this ideology when dealing, for instance, with the protection of human rights, (e.g. the leading cadres of international NGOs such as Human Rights Watch, Amnesty International, etc.). All these organizations are financed, directly or indirectly, by the transnational economic elites (George Soros plays a leading role here) or the transnational political elites (e.g. the US State Department). In fact, Transnational media and NGOs, together with the so-called 'social media' of the Internet (blogs, Facebook, twitter etc.) play a crucial role in the manufacturing of 'news', legitimizing the selected 'insurgents' (in Libya, Syria, Ukraine)

---

[79] "Definitive study reveals EU rules account for 65% of UK law", Business for Britain, 2/3/2015 http://businessforbritain.org/2015/03/02/definitive-study-reveals-eu-rules-account-for-65-of-uk-law/

who are then promoted into rebels, as well as in supporting the propaganda about the supposed progressive role of criminal organizations like NATO. It is now known, for instance, that DARPA — the Pentagon-run, Defense Advanced Research Projects Agency — has, in one way or another, funded several studies recently that set out to explore the use of social networking sites, (as well as the Social Media in Strategic Communications, or SMISC, program), toward the general goal of pure manipulation of social data information, so that the Transnational Elite's line is filtered through them. As its goal is described: *"Through the program, DARPA seeks to develop tools to support the efforts of human operators to counter misinformation or deception campaigns with truthful information."*[80]

➤ *The transnational academic elites,* namely the prominent systemic academics in various transnational organizations (foundations, institutes, think tanks and the likes), which are in charge of creating/improving the ideology of the NWO and globalization, 'scientifically' justifying the need for globalization (see e.g. the role of these elites with respect to Brexit, Ch. 8), as well as disorienting people on the real causes of the present multi-dimensional crisis. Within this process, the Transnational Elite takes care to put prominent members of its own in charge of the most prestige universities. Thus, whereas in the past, university directors of prestige universities, like the London School of Economics (LSE), were drawn from the academy, nowadays, it is prominent technocratic members of the Transnational Elite occupying such places, giving an indirect signal to the academics involved of what is the 'correct' line of research and teaching. No wonder that the newly appointed Director of the LSE is an ex Director of IMF and deputy governor of the Bank of England (which carried out a fierce attack against Brexit).[81] Furthermore, the media that are controlled by the Transnational Elite can even determine who is a prominent academic today: either directly (i.e. through

---

[80] Pentagon spent millions studying how to influence social media in Darpa-funded research, RT, 8/7/2014 http://rt.com/usa/171356-darpa-social-media-study/
[81] Philip Aldrick, "Shafik closes Bank account before going back to school", *The Times,* 12/9/2016

2. The role of the Transnational Elite   61

the mass media owned or controlled by it), or indirectly (i.e. through the social media funded by it). Pierre Bourdieu has shown the way in which the media, particularly television, control not just the information flow, but also the production of culture, by controlling the access to them by academics, who in turn — as a result of being recognized as public figures — gain recognition in their own fields.[82] One example of how media (both the mainstream and the social media) are so effectively used today to disorient peoples is to see how they can produce media 'stars' who promote, directly or indirectly, the ideology of globalization, from a supposedly 'progressive' viewpoint. If one wants to understand better the massive propaganda campaign by the ideological and cultural organs of the Transnational Elite to promote its own globalization 'stars', she/he would only have to look at the list of the 'greatest thinkers on Earth' for 2015 chosen by social media users — social media being one of the main instruments of cultural globalization which was used extensively by the Transnational Elite in the "Arab Spring".[83] As these 'stars' are presented by *Prospect* Magazine, they range from the 'serious' ones (Thomas Piketty, Paul Krugman et al) up to the less serious ones — to put it mildly — (Naomi Klein, Russell Brand and Yanis Varoufakis!).[84] Needless to add that the common characteristic of all those at the top of the list is their publicity due to their massive promotion by the Transnational Elite's media, including the social media that often simply reproduce the propaganda of the mainstream media for a different 'audience'! It is through this all-encompassing combination of mainstream and social media that the ideological and cultural globalization has become hegemonic in the NWO.

➤ *The transnational cultural elites* in the film and music industries. The former is mainly controlled by the Transnational and Zionist elites that control the dominant Hollywood industry and plays a crucial role in propagating the

---

[82] P. Bourdieu, *On Television and Journalism*, (London: Pluto Press, 1996), pp. 46-7 & 54

[83] See Takis Fotopoulos, *Subjugating the Middle East* (vol. 3 of The New World Order in Action)

[84] Valentine Low, "The world's fourth greatest thinker? Er, Russell Brand", *The Times*, 26/3/2015

values of globalization and the 'normal' way of living — which, 'by coincidence', happens also to be the one consistent with globalization values. The music industry — particularly the pop industry — is also controlled by TNCs. It is through the combined efforts of the transnational propaganda elites, the academic elites and the cultural elites that the ideology and culture of globalization is promoted. That is, the ideology of civil liberties, instead of collective self-determination; the promotion of the free movement of capital, labor and commodities, instead of national sovereignty and patriotism; the effective flattening of cultural differences in the name of a supposed multiculturalism; the erasing of the history of each particular people in the name of a pseudo-brotherhood in a consumerist global village and so on. A typical example of cultural homogenization through the globalization process is the annual Eurovision contest song. When it began, 60 years ago, only seven European countries took part and for the first two or three decades only European countries did so, with songs in the language of each country, expressing the various European cultures. However, in the last thirty years or so, not accidentally coinciding with the flourishing of globalization, English has gradually replaced all other song languages, individual cultures have disappeared, countries outside Europe but friendly to the Transnational Elite (e.g. Israel and Australia) had become contesters, while the entire show has become big business for the record industry and the TNCs which control it. In other words, this supposedly multicultural show has become a commercial one-culture show, which has created a huge market with millions of potential customers all over the world, ready to buy the latest homogenized cultural product of this huge promotion industry. On top of this, far from being an a-political song contest, as Eurovision rules prescribe, it is highly politicized, as long as the entries support the Transnational Elite's line. In the 2014 contest, for instance, Hungary was forced to censor one of the captions in the song's video which contained the words: '2014 Gaza two-thirds of the victims were civilians, including more than 500 children'. On the other hand in the 2016 contest, Ukraine's highly political song against Russia (its theme was, formally, an attack on Stalin's deportation of pro-Nazi Tatars from Crimea) was selected against all the odds as the winner, in a clear rebuke of Russia's action to re-unite Crimea with Russia in 2014. Clearly Soros and his 'color revolutions machine' had a hand in this, as Neil Clark, a liberal analyst, hinted: "I'm sure George Soros, uncrowned King of Ukraine, approves heartily."[85] This year's change in the voting system regulations, as well as the introduction of a process whereby the jury vote and the public vote are calculated separately, actually made it easier for such an act to take place behind-the-scenes. Needless to add that the Russian entry won the public vote but was far behind in the jury vote (which ensured that the Ukrainian entry came first) and therefore Russia came third overall. Obviously, the EU machine and the Soroses of this world, who have every motive to engage in some crude Russia-bashing, saw a much bigger chance to achieve their aim this year since all they needed was to influence the few jury members, rather than the public at large – given that the final result is derived from a 50/50 combination of the two kinds of votes!

In a nutshell, the Transnational Elite consists of a network of interconnected transnational elites, which are mainly based in the G7 countries and control all major fields of social life (economic, political, ideological, cultural and so on). The Transnational Elite today plays the role that the national governments used to play in the pre-globalization era, when they had the function of expressing the general interest of the national elites, to which the specific interests of these elites had to submit. Similarly, in the present globalization era, the Transnational Elite expresses the general interest of the elites controlling all forms of transnational power (economic, political, ideological, cultural etch.) to which the specific transnational interests have to submit, for the sake of the general interest of the New World Order. One may therefore argue that the Transnational Elite is simply a new kind of informal (for now) global governance, as celebrated by Simon Peres, the ex-President of Israel, in his 2013 talk in front of the European Parliament.[86]

The Transnational Elite is an ***elite***, because its members possess a

---

[85] Neil Clark, "Ukraine's 'Song for Europe' violates the spirit of Eurovision", RT, 15/5/2016, https://www.rt.com/op-edge/333580-ukraines-song-europe-jamala/
[86] See "Full text of Peres speech to European Parliament in Strasbourg" *Haaretz,* 13/03/2013.

dominant position within society, as a result of their economic, political or broader social power. Also, it is a ***transnational*** elite, because its members, unlike the national elites, see that the best way to secure their privileged position in society is not by ensuring the reproduction of any real or imagined nation-state but, instead, by securing the integration of every country in the world into the NWO of neoliberal globalization. In other words, this elite draws its power (economic, political or generally social power) by operating at the transnational level — a fact which implies that it does not express, solely or even primarily, the interests of any particular state, even if this has a hegemonic position with regard to the control of the crucial transnational military power, as is the case with the USA today.

However, as the political elite in the USA has to secure political approval by its electorate even as regards its transnational actions (mainly but not only the military ones), the leading power position of USA within the Transnational Elite may create sometimes problems in the running of the NWO, which are usually expressed in the political struggle for the US presidency — as is the case with the candidacy of Donald Trump at the moment. Trump, in his effort to win the presidency, has explicitly appealed to the victims of globalization in the US calling for the protection of the domestic labor force from international competition, the national control of borders, the containment of NATO power etc. — i.e. policies in direct conflict with the Transnational Elite's policies. If therefore by any chance Clinton, the transnational elite's candidate, is not elected as US President in November and if Trump does not betray his voters as soon as he is elected (two big "ifs"), one could expect drastic changes in the world order.

The de-centered nature of the Transnational Elite

Clearly therefore transnational power is dispersed, as a result mainly of the fact that the transnational economic power — which in a capitalist market economy system is the dominant form of transnational power — is spread among hundreds of transnational corporations (TNCs). [87] This is why it is meaningless, if not deliberately disorienting, to talk of economic power in terms of what part of the global output a country produces, when it is TNCs which

---

[87] Andy Coghlan and Debora MacKenzie, "Revealed – the capitalist network that runs the world", *New Scientist* Magazine, issue 2835 (24/10/2011)

take the important economic decisions (what, how and for whom to produce) and not the host countries, which usually exercise very little, if any, control over them, as happens even with most of the BRICS countries!

Therefore, the Transnational Elite sees its interests in terms of transnational 'spaces' (markets, political and military institutions, media, etc.) rather than 'national' ones, although the emergence of transnational forms of political and economic power does not imply the complete abolition of national forms. States are still needed for the local institutionalization and enforcement of transnational strategies and policies, which any country integrated into the NWO of neoliberal globalization, has to implement.

In other words, the Transnational Elite is a decentered apparatus of rule not in the sense of decentralization but in the sense of the lack of any territorial center of power. This means that the Transnational Elite members are not necessarily based on a superpower like the USA. Yet, they do not hesitate of course to utilize the power of a particular state to achieve its aims — even more so when this state happens to be today's leading military power. In this sense, the archaic Marxist approach that still sees USA as an 'empire', albeit a declining one, is obsolete, as it is based on the outdated notion of the concentration of political and economic power at the state level. The transnational elite is not defined geographically and consists of members having a dominant position within the 'world community', as a result of their transnational economic, political or broader social power, rather than as a result of holding power in any single nation state.

From this viewpoint, it is indicative that even when enlightened Marxist analysts (i.e. those who, unlike obsolete Marxists, have understood the significance of globalization as a new systemic phenomenon) still use the term 'empire' — presumably to secure a Marxist audience — they usually give it a meaning that closely corresponds to the meaning of the transnational elite, as defined above. Thus, Hard & Negri [88] see the 'Empire' as "a *decentered* and *deterritorialising* apparatus of rule," (although the NGOs and the UN are not included!) [89]

---

[88] Michael Hardt and Antonio Negri's *Empire* (Harvard University Press, 2000)
[89] See for a critique of *Empire*, Takis Fotopoulos & A. Gezerlis, "Hardt and Negri's *Empire*: a new Communist Manifesto or a reformist welcome to neoliberal

Also, in a more recent study, Anthony Mustacich, (who uses the term 'trilateral imperialism' to refer to US, EU and Japan), stresses that "the neo-liberal empire of today is not the empire of one imperialist nation, but the empire of transnational corporations, based in the Triad, and enforced through U.S. and NATO military force."[90]In fact, the Transnational Elite 'rule' is not just imposed through US and NATO military force, as Mustacich argues. This is only partially true, as it refers to the transnational military power alone, in which the dominant force is indeed the US. However, the transnational economic power, which is much more dispersed than military power, is enforced through various informal networks such as The European Round Table of Industrialists (which consists of the main TNCs effectively running the EU), as well as the various international economic institutions controlled by the elites that are based in the G7 countries, i.e. the EU, WTO, IMF, World Bank etc.

Correspondingly, transnational political power is enforced though the UN Security Council (UNSC), where, however, there is the 'anomaly' (as far as the Transnational Elite is concerned) of the veto power of some countries that are not among its members (Russia and China) but, for historical reasons, are members of the UNSC. No wonder the Transnational Elite has to resort increasingly to ad hoc 'alliances of the willing' to achieve its aims. It is not surprising also that many members of the Transnational Elite talk today about reforming the UNSC, with the exclusion of any countries not controlled by it, and their replacement by obedient BRICS countries such as India and the like.

Similarly, transnational ideological power is enforced through the international mass media controlled by the Transnational Elite, as well as through the local media controlled by the client elites that reproduce the same line (see e.g. the monolithic line adopted on Russia and Ukraine), and various think tanks such as the Brookings Institution, Levy Economics Institute, *Demos* and the likes.

globalization?" in *The Communist Manifesto*, by K.Marx, ed. by Frederic L. Bender (Norton, 2013)
[90] Anthony Mustacich, "Imperialism, The Cold War, and the Contradictions of Decolonization", *Global Research*, 12/5/2013
http://www.globalresearch.ca/imperialism-the-cold-war-and-the-contradictions-of-decolonization/5334692

Finally, transnational cultural power is enforced through the cultural institutions the Transnational Elite controls, (Hollywood and other major cultural institutions controlled by the TNCs), the distribution networks (of film, music etc.) controlled by it and so on.

The pre-globalization World Order run by Nation-States vs. the NWO of neoliberal globalization

The twofold aims of the Transnational Elite since the rise of the NWO have been:

a) First, to expand globalization into countries which have not yet lost all national and economic sovereignty within the globalization process, mainly Russia and also the countries still controlled by governments that came to power either through national liberation movements (Syria and Iran — following the successful destruction of Iraq and Libya by the Transnational Elite and their conversion into failed states for the time being; see vol. 3) or, alternatively, through socialist movements, which are now in decline (China, Cuba, Venezuela). In fact, the Transnational Elite has been highly successful in integrating many of these countries into the NWO through military violence (Iraq and Libya and possibly Syria too if the Transnational Elite succeeds in its plan to dismember it) and/or economic violence combined with 'infiltration', as e.g. with respect to the EU peripheral countries (Greece Portugal, Spain etc.), as well as Venezuela and possibly Cuba in the near future. Furthermore, it does not seem unlikely at the moment that the Transnational Elite may integrate eventually countries like Venezuela and Iran and possibly even Russia itself, unless the informal patriotic front in the latter manages to overcome the globalists who have infiltrated the Russian elite (particularly the economic elite, the media and so on).

b) Second, to deepen the globalization process into areas not yet covered by the World Trade Organization rounds and secure in particular the movement of capital, whose complete freedom to move, up to now, has been secured mainly through the EU and NAFTA, or bilateral and multilateral agreements. The same aim of deepening globalization is pursued at present by transnational treaties, such as the Trans-Pacific Partnership (TPP) among 12 Pacific Rim countries, the agreement for which was signed in February 2016 and the companion agreement on a Transatlantic Trade and Investment Partnership (TTIP) between EU and USA, the negotiations for which have been effectively suspended until the end of the US presidential election, so that the chances of success of the Transnational Elite candidate, Hillary Clinton, are not jeopardized (see Ch.4).

Clearly, in pursuing these general aims it is inevitable that political differences could arise between members of the Transnational Elite, exactly as they did between members of national ruling elites. Yet, such differences are always tactical, never strategic, i.e. they never refer to the very strategic aims of these elites to reproduce and expand their transnational political and economic power. The national government was also supposed to play exactly the same role, i.e. to accommodate the tactical differences between its members, so that the strategic aims would not be jeopardized. Therefore, the silly arguments, put forward for instance by the liberal globalists within the Russian elite in favor of exploiting the differences between members of the Transnational Elite (e.g. their divisions with respect to the invasion of Iraq) simply ignore the fact that these were tactical divisions, never strategic. In fact, all Transnational Elite members agree on the primary aim to reproduce and further expand the NWO of neoliberal globalization. In this context, Russia is an enemy for all parts of the Transnational Elite, although there are obvious tactical divisions between them on how best to integrate Russia into the NWO: through economic warfare, or, as some would argue, through a combination of economic and military violence.

However, there is a basic qualitative difference between the pre-globalization World Order which was run by nation-states, some of them major imperial powers in almost constant conflict between them (British Empire, French colonial empire, Imperial Germany, Russian empire, the Ottoman Empire) and the New World Order that emerged in the era of globalization, which is run — albeit informally for the time being — by the Transnational Elite. Thus, the non-antagonistic nature of the tactical differences between members of the Transnational Elite implies that they have very little resemblance, if any, to the intra-imperialist differences mentioned in Marxist literature.

An indicative example is the case when the leading country in the Transnational Elite, the US, fined a French multinational (BNP Paribas) $9bn for helping countries like Cuba and Iran to avoid sanctions. This forced even Michel Sapin, the French finance minister, to call for a "rebalancing" of the currencies used for global payments (at the moment the US dollar is the main world reserve currency accounting for over 60% of global transactions) stressing that the BNP Paribas case should "make us realize the necessity of using a variety of currencies."[91] The implication was obvious: EU countries should also use Euros as a reserve currency. This was, clearly, a torpedo to the hegemony of US dollar as the main (if not sole) reserve currency, which is an arrangement that allows US to adopt policies that non-reserve countries cannot follow. Yet, within hours of the above statement, members of the transnational economic elite (mainly bankers) 'restored order', as the following extract from the same *Financial Times* report made clear:

> Despite efforts to diversify, many central banks say that they still see no real alternative to the safety and liquidity of the US Treasury market, and hold more than 60 per cent of their reserves in dollars. A senior French official cast doubt on the government's ability to stimulate the further use of the euro in international trade: "In the end it is hard to know what they can really do. The market really decides these things."[92]

However, the 'market' is obviously distorted in this case because the main reserve currency is the US dollar and, as long as it is generally acceptable as such, no other currency can de-throne it and therefore deprive US of the associated benefits. One major such benefit has been the US power to finance its own wars, (from the Vietnam war up to the Iraq invasion) by simply printing more dollars — something that no other member of the Transnational Elite could do. This had caused a serious conflict in the past, when the French President De Gaulle forcefully raised the issue. However, back then, the world order was still run by nation-states, and therefore the US was still de facto the emperor. But even today, it seems that, as a result perhaps of some kind of tacit agreement between the Transnational Elite members, they all accept the dollar as the main reserve currency (although the Euro in particular could well challenge the dollar, had the European members of the Transnational Elite decided to do so), presumably as a kind of compensation for the huge military expenses

---

[91] Michael Stothard, "France hits out at dollar dominance in international transactions", *Financial Times,* 6/7/2014
[92] ibid.

that the US has to incur to maintain the Transnational Elite's military hegemony.

Yet, some politicians and obsolete Marxists attempt, even, today to dismiss an analysis like the above on globalization and the Transnational Elite, either with reference to a supposed "Europe vs. America" conflict, or alternatively by referring to the existence of 'many' capitalisms. Thus for some, what we face today is a conflict between the 'goodies' and the 'baddies', where the former are represented in geopolitical terms by 'Europe' and the latter by 'America', while others talk about a conflict between two main power centers, a political-military one (USA) and an economic one (Germany). Finally, for others still, what we face is 'many capitalisms', which are increasingly un-coordinated in the globalization era — a fact that raises, albeit implicitly, the issue of the need for a global governance. Clearly, therefore, the above confusions and corresponding myths play an important role in understanding today's reality and in deciding what to do about it.

I will examine here briefly the views of Russian globalists, whereas I will consider in more detail the views of the Western Left in Ch.6. At the outset, Gorbachev had no qualms about stating, (when celebrating — next to Merkel — the unification of Germany) the following: "*Europe can have a very positive impact on the situation. After all, it must become the locomotive in the creation of the new world.*"[93] In other words, for Gorbachev (one of the protagonists of the integration of Russia into the NWO), as well as for the globalist part of the Russian elite in general, there is nothing wrong with the EU and there is, in fact, no reason for a new world pole expressing the need for a new democratic world order based on sovereign nations, like the one envisaged by the Eurasian Union, i.e. the union of Eurasian states established in 2014 consisting of Russia, and other former Soviet republics as an economic and political union of sovereign states, at about the same level of development. Presumably, Gorbachev envisions Russia (with or without the other members of the Eurasian Union) could well live together in the same unipolar world defined by the NWO and run by the Transnational Elite, as long as Russia is recognized as an equal member of the Transnational Elite.

---

[93] Gorbachev- It's up to Europe to prevent new Cold War between US and Russia, RT, 1/12/2014 http://rt.com/news/210463-gorbachev-us-russia-europe/

Similarly, far from reality are various views proposed usually by the European globalist 'Left' and reproduced also by the Russian globalist faction within the Russian elite. Such views, usually based on the myth that there is an independent European economy, conclude that the USA strangles Europe under the cover of the Ukrainian crisis.[94] This, forgetting the actual stand of Germany on the crisis, which was essentially an opportunistic stand aiming to persuade Putin to incorporate the Eurasian Union into the NWO, if not to the EU itself. It is clear however that if the German elite becomes persuaded that this is impossible, they will have no qualms about siding fully with their supposed enemies, the US elites, in their aim to crush Russia and the Eurasian Union, on the economic front (in fact, they have already showed signs of such an attitude with their stand on sanctions against Russia).[95]

However, perhaps the most representative description of the Russian 'globalists' case was given by Sergey Karaganov, (Dean at the National Research University – Higher School of Economics in Moscow) in the *Financial Times* and the dialogue which followed with Martin Wolf, the associate editor of the same paper. In it, Karaganov, after describing Gorbaschev's exhortation in the late 1980s for "A common European house" (or as George HW Bush called it, in full agreement with Gorbachev, "a Europe whole and free"), he went on to characterize globalization as the West's "crowning accomplishment", which now "they are destroying with economic sanctions."[96] No wonder Martin Wolf, in replying to this apologetic description of the present conflict by a Russian globalist, had only to refer to the supposed superiority of the West in order to put him in his place. As he stressed, in a way very much similar to that of the master admonishing his ignorant pupil:

The west "proclaimed itself victor in the cold war", according to Mr. Karaganov. Maybe the origin of the tragedy can be

---

[94] See e.g. the views expressed by Vladimir Bruter and Aleksey Drynochkin interviewed by *Pravda.ru* in "USA strangles Europe under the cover of Ukrainian crisis", *Pravda.ru*. 25/12/2014 http://english.pravda.ru/world/europe/25-12-2014/129387-usa_europe-0/

[95] See vol. 2 of the *NWO in Action: UKRAINE: THE ATTACK ON RUSSIA AND THE EURASIAN UNION*

[96] Sergey Karaganov, "Western delusions triggered conflict and Russians will not yield", *Financial Times*, 14/9/2014

found in this remark. The west did not just proclaim itself victor; it *was* the victor. A defensive alliance defeated the Soviet Union because it offered a better way of life. That is why so many wanted to escape the Soviet prison, including many once-optimistic Russians.[97]

As Martin Wolf explained, Russians wanted, (like the other East Europeans who already joined the 'free world') to join "the world of civilized modernity." Wolf then went on to explain the meaning of "civilized modernity."

It means intellectual and economic freedom. It means the right to engage freely in public life. It means governments subject to the rule of law and accountable to their people.[98]

So, Wolf, in effect, unashamedly declared, one of the most barbaric societies in human history, America, and its imitators all over the world, as a country of many 'freedoms' i.e. intellectual, economic, political, legal etc. On this, even the self-declared "anarchist" Noam Chomsky would also agree, as he did when in an interview described USA as "an unusually free country!"[99] Wolf only neglected to mention that all these 'freedoms' depend on one fundamental precondition: namely, enough wealth and income to adequately influence the appropriate political, economic, judicial and media processes! But in that case the appropriate term to describe the US political system is 'plutocracy' rather than 'democracy'.

---

[97] Martin Wolf, "Russia is our most dangerous neighbor", *Financial Times*, 16/9/2014
[98] ibid.
[99] See Noam Chomsky's interview in the Athens daily *Eleftherotypia* (the second-biggest newspaper in Greece, before it was closed down, effectively by the Troika, during the present EU-induced catastrophic crisis, see vol.2 of the NWO in Action) 31/7/1995

Chapter 3.

The phasing out of national sovereignty in the NWO and the rise of neo-nationalism

Transnational vs. national sovereignty

Few believe today that, in the era of globalization, national sovereignty, in the classical sense of the word, is still the norm. Some, like Umberto Pascali, simply stress the power of banking interests:

> This is the big secret that now cannot be covered anymore. The governments of the US and the European countries are NOT independent entities; they are not sovereign. They do not have the will or even the ability to act on behalf of their people. They are controlled by powerful banking interests.[100]

However, although it is true that powerful economic interests — and not just banking interests — do control all the governments of countries integrated into the NWO and that there is a close interconnection between economic, political, media and cultural elites and the corresponding aspects of the Transnational Elite, the issue of sovereignty still arises in the globalization era, albeit not in the sense of the traditional national sovereignty. This is made clear if we take into account the fact that the power centers (economic, political, military, academic, media, cultural) that make up the Transnational

---

[100] Umberto Pascali, "The Ukraine Crisis and Vladimir Putin: A New Financial System Free from Wall Street and the City of London?" *Global Research*, 22/3/2014 http://www.globalresearch.ca/the-ukraine-crisis-and-vladimir-putin-a-new-financial-system-free-from-wall-street-and-the-city-of-london/5374785

Elite, or at least strongly influence it (e.g. strong trade unions), are mostly geographically concentrated in the G7 countries (the US/Canada, the major EU countries and Japan).

So, we may assume that today we have a system of double sovereignty. There is, first, the national sovereignty, which is all but disappearing today. This is the kind of sovereignty that was established as a result of the creation of nation-states, mainly in the 19th and the 20th centuries. In fact, the basic characteristic of a nation-state was national sovereignty, i.e. the state's authority to exclusively control its own national economy, particularly its currency, as well as the political and military institutions within the state. Controlling the national economy implied of course not just the implementation of economic policies but, even more important, the enforcement of social controls to protect society from the market.

However, both the control over economic policies as well as the power to impose social controls on markets, was drastically eroded in the globalization era. This is why, as I stressed about twenty years ago, nation-states have been in a process of withering away during the entire era of globalization:

> The role of the nation state (in the neoliberal internationalized economy) does not involve anymore the enforcement of social controls to protect society from the market. The state's role today is exclusively related to securing the reproduction of the market economy through its monopoly of violence and to creating the stable framework for the efficient functioning of the markets.[101]

It is, therefore, a truism that if a government does not control its economic policy it does not have any economic sovereignty and therefore any national sovereignty. But, this is exactly what happened in the globalization era, where a new kind of sovereignty, a transnational sovereignty developed. This is the kind of sovereignty resulting from the significant degree of transnational power (economic, political, cultural and media power) the elites in the advanced capitalist countries, from where most of the transnational corporations have originated, have concentrated in their hands.

---

[101] Takis Fotopoulos, *Towards an Inclusive Democracy*, (London/NY: Cassell/Continuum, 1997), pp. 50-51

Forms of transnational institutions and of transnational sovereignty

The elites based in these countries, *the Transnational Elites,* although they do not have a formal governing body (yet!), in fact, control all forms of power in the world. They do so by controlling the various transnational institutions, namely:

- The transnational economic institutions, such as the World Trade Organization (WTO), the IMF, the World Bank, the European Central Bank;
- The transnational political/military institutions, such as the UN, and NATO;
- The major transnational world media, which are mainly located in US, Germany, UK and France;
- The transnational world culture, i.e. the major universities and research centers, think tanks, as well as the film and music industries located also in the G7 countries.

This is clearly a transnational kind of power, which is consistent with transnational, not national, sovereignty, in the sense that it relies on controlling political, economic and other forms of power at the transnational, rather than the national, level.

Therefore, sovereignty in the globalization era does not mean national sovereignty any more, as in the era of nation-states, but, instead, a transnational sovereignty. Consequently, sovereignty within the NWO has to be re-defined to indicate the fact that its basis — as far as every country fully integrated into it is concerned — is no longer the national economy and the nation-state (which is withering away within it) and the associated national power centers (economic, political, media, cultural), but, rather, the internationalized market economy and the globalized power centers I mentioned above. The elites controlling these power centers share various degrees of transnational sovereignty depending on the transnational economic, political/military, media, cultural power concentrated in their hands. Correspondingly, the countries in which most members of these elites are found (the G7 countries) share a significant degree of transnational sovereignty.

Thus, the countries belonging to the Transnational Elite can be shown to concentrate in their hands all forms of transnational power and therefore the bulk of transnational sovereignty. That is:

- Transnational economic sovereignty, in the sense that all major Transnational Corporations (TNCs), which control the world markets for commodities and capital can be shown to be based (not just in the legal sense but mainly in the financial sense) in these countries, whereas all major international economic organizations (WTO, IMF, WB etc.) are also controlled by the elites of the same countries;
- Transnational political/military sovereignty, in the sense that all major international political-military organizations (UN, NATO, etc.) can also be shown to be controlled by the Transnational Elite countries;
- Transnational media power in the sense that all international media controlling world public opinion (what euphemistically is called the 'world community') are also based in the same countries; and, finally,
- Transnational cultural power, in the sense that all major institutions of the 'culture industry' controlling world culture are overwhelmingly held by the Transnational Elite — although of course in the NWO this has little, if anything, to do with the general cultural level and much more to do with controlling the major production and distribution networks of culture (see e.g. the world dominance of Hollywood's sub-culture!)

One way to see how transnational sovereignty is transcending national sovereignty today is to examine more closely the EU composition in relation to the distribution of power. We may distinguish between two main sets of countries within the EU.

There are first, the advanced capitalist countries, which are also members of G7 (Germany, France, Italy and Britain), which have a significant degree of what I call *transnational sovereignty*, in the sense that a significant number of the transnational corporations controlling the world economy today have originated in these countries. Not surprisingly, European transnational corporations possess also a very significant degree of political power. It has been shown, for instance, that the European Round Table of Industrialists, which is an informal meeting of the main transnational corporations in Europe, had drafted all the main constitutional treaties that the EU now implements: i.e. the

Maastricht treaty, the Lisbon treaty and the treaties based on them.[102] As the kind of constitution these treaties imposed was, in fact, the essence of neoliberal globalization, one may conclude that all the neoliberal measures that are implemented today by the EU are the policies suggested by the transnational corporations.

Then, there is a second set of countries within the EU, what we may call the peripheral countries, which do not have any significant degree of transnational power (economic/political/ideological and so on), i.e. Greece, Portugal, Ireland as well as the 'new' East European members. The peripheral countries do not in fact control their economic policy, which is controlled instead by the European Central Bank and the Eurogroup. Although each member has formally one vote in these decision-taking bodies, clearly, it is the countries with some degree of transnational power that dominate their decisions, given their economic and associated political power.

In between these two main sets of countries, there is a third set of countries exercising some degree of transnational sovereignty but not enough to be members of the Transnational Elite in the G7 (e.g. the Scandinavian countries, the Benelux countries and Austria). These countries usually align with the first group of countries, as their level of economic development and their economic interests are closer to the first group of countries rather than to the second. Furthermore, the electorates in these countries have many more similarities between them than with the electorates in the peripheral countries. This is why the conservative-liberal group is also the dominant one in the Euro-parliament, as we will see below. However, the fact that within the EU there are no countries with significant national sovereignty (apart from some degree of national sovereignty still enjoyed by EU members which are not also Eurozone members) is only an indication of what will eventually happen to every country being integrated into the NWO. Yet, as we shall see in connection to the BRICS countries, although their transnational sovereignty is marginal, if not nil, still, some of them, and particularly Russia, do maintain a significant degree of national sovereignty and could potentially constitute the foundation on which a new Democratic Community of Sovereign Nations would be built (Ch.11).

---

[102] George Monbiot, "Still bent on world conquest", *The Guardian* 16/12/1999.

It is therefore crystal clear that the only way for a country today to have any sort of national power, or national sovereignty, is to break with the NWO of neoliberal globalization and its institutions (WTO, IMF, World Bank and so on). Of course, this is inconceivable for the biggest country in the BRICS group, China, which very recently declared that it would only withdraw from the WTO if it is not awarded full "market economy status". [103] India, will not even contemplate withdrawing from the NWO and therefore the only BRICS country that could potentially take such a step is Russia. This is why I think that the Eurasian Union could potentially be a step in this direction, provided, however, that certain important conditions, which we will examine in Chapter 11, are met.

To sum it up, when a country is fully integrated into the NWO of neoliberal globalization and at the same time it does not exert any significant control over the major power centers, its transnational and, also its economic sovereignty, is nil. This, in turn, means that, in the present globalization era, the only kind of sovereignty that such a country could have is national sovereignty, provided that it can achieve the necessary degree of economic self-reliance. On the other hand, the more a country is integrated into the NWO, the lower the degree of self-reliance possible and, correspondingly, the degree of economic and national sovereignty attainable. Only therefore the break with the NWO could allow the degree of self-reliance necessary for national sovereignty. This is why a new Democratic Community of Sovereign Nations is a vital and imperative need today in the process of building a new society and a new world based on the values of solidarity, mutual assistance and democracy in the real sense of the word (political, economic, social and ecological). [104]

The phasing out of national sovereignty and the 'fascism' of the Transnational Elite

It is clear now that the aim of the Transnational Elite that administers the NWO is to convert nation-states — within the process of the phasing out of their economic and national sovereignty — into, at best, some sort of 'local authorities' within a system of global governance, or, at worst, informal protectorates (e.g. Greece). In this

---

[103] Lucy Hornby and Shawn Donnan, "China fights for market economy status", *Financial Times,* 9/5/2016
[104] Takis Fotopoulos, *Towards an Inclusive Democracy*, chs. 5-6 op. cit.

context, the Transnational Elite launched a series of major wars against peripheral countries, which resisted their integration into the NWO. As it can be shown, all these wars of the Transnational Elite were aimed at the forceful integration of the respective countries into the NWO: from the NATO war against Yugoslavia[105] and the war in the Gulf that was followed by the invasion of Iraq[106] and the war against Afghanistan,[107] to the war against Libya and the proxy war on Syria. [108] In other words, all these wars, which marked the era of neoliberal globalization, were implicitly or explicitly due to the social struggle that followed the phasing out of national and economic sovereignty within the New World Order.

In all these wars, as well as in the Transnational Elite-engineered new conflict in Ukraine,[109] there were no qualms about allying with various local butchers, which specialize in the use of purely fascist methods to overthrow national liberation regimes: from the jihad butchers in Libya and Syria (who later took the name ISIS, Al Nusra etc.) to the self-declared fascists of the Right Sector in Ukraine. The result of all these, essentially fascist wars, was hundreds of thousands of dead people and millions of people whose lives have been destroyed and uprooted, many of them in their desperate effort to avoid the catastrophe of their own countries, as is being shown today with the conversion of the Mediterranean into a 'vast cemetery' of refugees from these areas[110] and the corresponding conversion of Greece into a huge concentration camp for refugees with its borders blocked by its

---

[105] See Takis Fotopoulos, "New World Order and NATO's war against Yugoslavia", *New Political Science*,vol. 24, no.1, (March 2002), pp. 73-104; see also, 'The First War of the Internationalised Market Economy', *Democracy & Nature*, vol. 5, no. 2, (July 1999) <http://www.democracynature.org/vol5/fotopoulos_balkans_2.htm>
[106] Takis Fotopoulos, "Iraq: the new criminal 'war' of the transnational elite", *Democracy & Nature* ,vol.9, no.2, (July 2003) pp. 167-209; <http://www.democracynature.org/vol9/takis_war2.htm>
[107] See Takis Fotopoulos, "The global "war" of the transnational elite", *Democracy & Nature* (Volume 8 Number 2, July 2002), pp. 210-240 <http://www.democracynature.org/vol8/takis_globalwar.htm>
[108] Takis Fotopoulos, *Subjugating the Middle East* (Vol. 3 of the NWO in Action)
[109] Takis Fotopoulos, *Ukraine: the attack on Russia and the Eurasian Union (vol. 2* of the NWO in Action)
[110] Gianluca Mezzofiore, "EU migrant policy turns Mediterranean into 'vast cemetery' says UN rights chief" *International Business Times*, (20/4/2015) http://www.ibtimes.co.uk/eu-migrant-policy-turns-mediterranean-into-vast-cemetery-says-un-rights-chief-1497418

'partners' in the EU.[111] These wars were fascist not in terms of the ideology used to justify them, which is of course the ideology of globalization, but in terms of both the deceitful methods used to secure their fake 'legitimacy' and, even more so, in terms of the massive war crimes and crimes against humanity committed by the Transnational Elite and its organs in overthrowing the targeted regimes.

Rightly, therefore, John Pilger, the veteran anti-war journalist, called the 'fascism' of the Transnational Elite 'a modern kind of fascism', which the elites try to hide at all cost, inciting instead the people to fight the old historical fascism and anti-Semitism, in an obvious attempt to disorient the victims of globalization, within the context of the old 'divide and rule' tactics:

> Fascism is preserved as history, as flickering footage of goose-stepping Blackshirts, their criminality terrible and clear. Yet in the same liberal societies, whose war-making elites urge us never to forget, the accelerating danger of a modern kind of fascism is suppressed; for it is their fascism.[112]

A very significant contributing factor to the creation of the present Orwellian '1984' kind of society has been the emergence of an integrated into the NWO globalist 'Left', which effectively tolerated (if not approved) all the Transnational Elite's wars and engineered insurrections. Particularly so, as this kind of 'Left' encompasses today almost the entire traditional Left: from the reformist 'Left' of the SYRIZA and Podemos kind, to most of the antisystemic Marxist and Green Left. The former aims at a 'better' globalization under the disorienting slogan of Porto Alegre: "Another World is possible", while the latter still supports the messianic expectation of a world socialist revolution that will overthrow capitalism together with the NWO, or, correspondingly, dreams of the emergence of a Green society through the rise of intelligent and networked eco-villages, or the change of "imaginaries."

A clear indication of the globalist 'Left's' integration into the NWO was its stand on the Transnational Elite's wars and engineered insurrections, which was, at best, one of keeping 'equal distances'

---

[111] Editorial, "Europe turns its back on Greece over refugees", *Financial Times*, 28/2/2016
[112] John Pilger, "Why the rise of fascism is again the issue", RT, 26/2/2015 http://rt.com/op-edge/235807-fascism-mideast-ukraine-neo-nazi/

between the competing 'imperialisms', and, at worst, a stand of open support for the supposed "revolutionaries" in Syria, Libya etc. — as Trotskyites and 'libertarians' of various sorts did. Not surprisingly, this stand of the 'Left' was significant in helping the Transnational Elite to destroy the last remnants of national liberation regimes in the Middle East, and of sovereign nations in Europe (e.g. Yugoslavia). Yet, national and economic sovereignty is the necessary condition (though not the sufficient condition) for any kind of systemic change, which is still supposed to be the main aim of the Left!

In this context, today's social struggle is not anymore just a struggle for social liberation, as it used to be in the past but, also, a struggle for national liberation. This does not of course mean the return to an era of nation-states fighting each other for economic reasons (the division of markets) or geopolitical reasons (allocation of spheres of influence). In other words, this struggle has nothing to do with "a reordering of world affairs based on 'spheres of influence'[113] — as the ideologues of neoliberal globalization and promoters of the plan for world governance argue, in an obvious attempt to denigrate the struggle of peoples for sovereignty and self-determination. Instead, this struggle could lead to the creation of a new democratic world order, like the one I will describe in Part III.

However, some could counter-argue here that the risk may well arise in such a scenario that, when a nation breaks from the NWO, new forces may emerge that could use the recovered national-economic sovereignty in order to implement racist or xenophobic policies. Yet, one wonders whether such arguments can still be supported today, particularly by such self-processed democratic beacons of the globalization era like the US and Israel. That is two power centres which have clearly shown their true racist faces: the former, when on top of the intrinsic economic violence against the Afro-Americans, it now shows that the built-in physical violence against them has never stopped, (although usually covert at present), while the latter is now in the process of legislating the second rate status of the indigenous population, the Palestinians.[114]

---

[113] Gideon Rachman, "China, Russia and the Sinatra doctrine", *Financial Times,* 24/11/2014

[114] Thus, as *Le Monde Diplomatique* recently commented on the matter: "Netanyahu is hoping to push through a constitutional bill that redefines Israel as the nation-state of the Jewish people, and provides for legislation to be inspired by the principles of

In other words, globalization can certainly not be a real alternative to national societies based on racism or xenophobia. As we shall see in the last part of this book, only a democratic community of sovereign nations could hope to eliminate such misanthropic tendencies.

However, as the terms 'fascist', 'neo-fascist' and 'nationalist' are used today in common parlance indistinctly, I think it is necessary at this point to draw some clear distinctions between these terms and their origin.

The rise of neo-nationalism in the NWO

As it is well known, nationalism and the concept of nation itself were unknown in antiquity as well as in the Middle Ages. In fact, as I tried to show in the past, the emergence of the modern nation-state in the 17th-18th centuries played an important role in the development of the system of the market economy and vice versa:

> The nation-state, which was just emerging at the end of the Middle Ages, played a crucial role: first, by creating the conditions for the 'nationalization' of the market (mercantilist phase) and, second, by freeing the market from effective social control. The emergence therefore of the nation-state, which preceded the marketization of the economy, had the effect not only of destroying the political independence of the town or village community but, also, of undermining their economic self-reliance. At the ideological level, the formation of national states was accompanied by the rise of nationalism: in other words, a new ideology, which attempted to create an identification between the individual and the abstract entity of the state, in place of the former identification of it with the community. Still, the fact that the state usually played a crucial role in the marketization process, and that, during the nineteenth century in particular, many of the newly formed nation-states were involved in a systematic effort to establish and protect a domestic market economy, does not imply a strict causal relationship. In other words, it would be wrong to

---

Judaism. The law would define the regime as democratic, but only Jews would have collective rights; Muslims and Christians — 20% of the population — would only enjoy individual rights provided by law," Charles Enderlin, "Israel loses its grip on democracy", *Le Monde Diplomatique,* March 2016

attribute a cause and effect relationship to the rise of the nation-state and the rise of the national economy.[115]

However, whereas the 'nationalization' of the market was necessary for the development of the 'market system' out of the markets of the past, once capital was internationalized and therefore the market system itself was internationalized, the nation state became an impediment to further 'progress' of the market system. This is how the NWO emerged, which involved a radical restructuring not only of the economy, with the rise of TNCs, but also of polity, with the present phasing out of nation-states and national sovereignty.

Inevitably, the phasing out of the nation-state and national sovereignty led to the flourishing of neo-nationalism, as a movement for self-determination. Yet, this development became inevitable only because the alternative form of social organization, confederalism, which was alive even up to the time of the Paris Commune, had in the meantime disappeared. As Murray Bookchin rightly pointed out:

> Confederalism remained a viable alternative to the nation-state well into the latter half of the last century. As late as 1871, the Paris Commune called upon all the communes of France to form a confederal dual power in opposition to the newly created Third Republic. Eventually the nation-state won out in this complex conflict, and statism, in fact, was firmly linked to nationalism. The two were virtually indistinguishable from each other by the beginning of this century.[116]

In other words, the peoples' need for self-determination, in the NWO, had no other outlet but the nation-state. Particularly so, as up to a few years ago the world was dominated by nation–states, within which communities with a common culture, language, customs etc. could express themselves. Therefore, the nation-state became again a means of self-determination, as it used to be in the 20th century for peoples under colonial rule struggling for their national liberation. The national culture is of course in clear contradiction with a globalist

---

[115] Takis Fotopoulos, "The Nation-State and the Market", *DEMOCRACY & NATURE: The International Journal of INCLUSIVE DEMOCRACY*, Vol.2, No.2 (1994) http://www.democracynature.org/vol2/fotopoulos_nation.htm
[116] Murray Bookchin, "Nationalism and the "National Question", *DEMOCRACY & NATURE: The International Journal of INCLUSIVE DEMOCRACY*, Vol. 2, No. 2, (1994) http://www.democracynature.org/vol2/bookchin_nationalism.htm

culture like the one imposed now 'from above' by the Transnational and national elites. This globalist culture is based on the globalization ideology of multiculturalism, identity politics, the protection of individual human rights (as opposed to collective self-determination) etc. In fact, the globalization ideology is an extension of the classical liberal ideology to the NWO. Not accidentally, globalist ideologists characterize the present flourishing of what I called neo-nationalism, as the rise of 'illiberalism.'[117]

This neo-nationalist movement had already created strong roots all over the EU, from its older Western part (France, UK, Austria) up to the newly added Eastern part (Hungary, Poland). Even in the USA itself, Donald Trump, who has called on Americans to resist "the false song of globalism", expresses to a significant extent neo-nationalist trends and yet may be tomorrow the next President of the 'Free World'. Of course, given the huge political and economic power that the elites have amassed against these neo-nationalist movements, it is possible that none of them will ever take over, and even if they do, they may well be forced to fizzle out, as is happening today with the Brexit revolution. Yet, this will not of course stop social dissent against the phasing out of national sovereignty, which is an aspect of today's class struggle between the victims of globalization and its beneficiaries.

On the basis of the above discussion we may therefore distinguish the following differences between old (or classical) nationalism and present neo-nationalism:

a) Nationalism developed in the era of nation-states as a movement for uniting communities with a common history, culture and usually language under the common roof of nation-states. Such states were emerging even as late as in the 20th century when various national liberation movements managed to get their independence from the last colonial empires. On the other hand, neo-nationalism has developed in the era of globalization i.e. the last 30 years or so, when various movements emerged aiming to protect the sovereignty of their nations (national sovereignty), which was under extinction because of the integration of their states into the NWO;

---

[117] Tony Barber, "Illiberalism takes root in Europe's fertile centre", *Financial Times,* 13/5/2016

b) Nationalism's emphasis was on the nation-state (or the aspiration for one), whereas neo-nationalism's emphasis is not so much on the nation-state as such, but rather on sovereignty, which has been phased out in the globalization process at the economic but also at the political and cultural levels,;

c) Unlike old nationalism, neo-nationalism raises also demands that in the past were an essential part of the Left agenda, such as the demand for greater equality (within the nation-state and between nation-states), the demand to restore social services, the demand to minimize the power of the elites, even anti-war demands.

Naturally, given the political origin of many neo-nationalist parties and their supporters, it is not difficult for elements of the old nationalist ideology to penetrate them, (e.g. various Islamophobic and anti-immigration trends), which then provide the excuse to the elites and the media to dismiss these movements in toto as 'far right', anti-immigrant, racist etc. However, it can easily be shown that the refugee problem itself is also part and parcel of globalization and of the '4 freedoms' (capital, labor, goods and services) that its ideology preaches. In other words, the anti-immigrant nature of several neo-nationalist movements arises out of the economic consequences of globalization rather than out of any racist or anti-immigrant beliefs of their supporters.

Therefore, neo-nationalism is basically a movement that arose out of the effects of globalization, particularly the liberalization of labor markets, so that labor could become more competitive. The present 'job miracle', for instance, in Britain, (which is characterized as "the job creation capital of the western economies"), hides the fact that, as an analyst pointed out, "unemployment is low, largely because British workers have been willing to stomach the biggest real-terms pay cut since the Victorian era."[118] It is not therefore surprising that even the conservative London *Times* had to admit that this was due to globalization — a fact that the globalist left ignores!

> The surge in support for UKIP is not simply a protest vote. The party has a constituency among those left behind by globalization... the globalization of the economy has produced

---

[118] Ed Conway, "The UK is paying the price of its jobs miracle", *The Times*, 14/10/2014

losers as well as winners. As a rule the winners are among the better off and the losers among the least affluent.[119]

But, it is mainly Le Pen's National Front party, more than any other neo-nationalist party in the West, which realized that globalization and membership in the NWO's institutions are incompatible with national sovereignty. As Le Pen stressed, (in a way that the 'Left' has abandoned long ago!):

> Globalization is a barbarity, it is the country which should limit its abuses and regulate it [globalization]... Today the world is in the hands of multinational corporations and large international finance"... Immigration "weighs down on wages," while the minimum wage is now becoming the maximum wage.[120]

In fact, the French National Front is the most important neo-nationalist party in Europe and may well be in power following the next Presidential elections in 2017, unless of course a united front of all globalist parties, supported by the entire Transnational Elite and particularly the Euro-elites and the mass media controlled by them, prevents it from doing so. This is how Florian Philippot the FN's vice-president and chief strategist aptly put its case in a FT interview:

> The people who always voted for the left, who believed in the left and who thought that it represented an improvement in salaries and pensions, social and economic progress, industrial policies... these people have realized that they were misled.[121]

As the same FT report points out, to some observers of French politics, the FN's economic policies, which include exiting the euro and throwing up trade barriers to protect industry, read like something copied from a 1930s political manifesto, while Christian Saint-Étienne, an economist for *Le Figaro* newspaper, recently described this vision as "Peronist Marxism".[122] In fact, in a more recent FT interview, Marine Le Pen, the FN president, went a step further in the same

---

[119] Editorial, "The People's Revolt", *The Times*, 11/10/2014
[120] "Globalization is barbarous, multinationals rule world" – Marine Le Pen, RT, 10/1/2015 http://rt.com/news/212435-france-pen-globalization-barbarity/
[121] Adam Thomson, "France's far-right National Front seeks voters from the left", *Financial Times,* 4/1/2015
[122] ibid.

direction and she called, apart from exiting from the Euro — a development she expects and hopes to lead to the collapse of the Euro, if not of the EU itself — for the nationalization of banks. At the same time she championed public services and presented herself as the protector of workers and farmers in the face of "wild and anarchic globalization…which has brought more pain than happiness."[123] For comparison, it never even occurred to SYRIZA (and Varoufakis who now pretends to be a radical!) to use such slogans before the elections (let alone after them!) Needless to add that her foreign policy is also very different from that of the French establishment, as she wants a radical overhaul of French foreign policy in which relations with the regime of Syrian president Bashar al-Assad would be restored and those with the likes of Qatar and the Gulf states, which she alleges support terrorism, reviewed. At the same time, Le Pen sees the US as a purveyor of dangerous policies and Russia as a more suitable friend.

Furthermore, as it was also stressed in the same FT report, "the FN is not the only supposedly rightwing European populist party seeking to draw support from disaffected voters on the left. Nigel Farage, the leader of the UK Independence party has adopted a similar approach and has been discussing plans "to ring-fence the National Health Service budget and lower taxes for low earners, among a host of measures geared to economically vulnerable voters who would typically support Labor." [124] Similar trends are noticed in other European countries like Finland, where the anti-NATO and pro-independence parties effectively won the last elections,[125] as well as in Hungary, where neo-nationalist forces are continuously rising.[126] In fact, Orban's government in Hungary has done a lot in protecting its country's sovereignty, being as a result, in constant conflict with the Euro-elites, up to the point that one of the EU's gatekeepers, Luxembourg, has even called for the exclusion of Hungary from the

---

[123] Anne-Sylvaine Chassany and Roula Khalaf, "Marine Le Pen lays out radical vision to govern France", *Financial Times*, 5/3/2015
[124] Adam Thomson, "France's far-right National Front seeks voters from the left", *Financial Times,* 4/1/2015
[125] "Anti-NATO parties grab top spots in Finland general election", RT, 19/4/2015 http://rt.com/news/251065-finland-election-centre-party/
[126] Hungary's far-right Jobbik party wins key seat, BBC News 13/4/2015 http://www.bbc.co.uk/news/world-europe-32281713

EU![127] Finally, the rise of a neo-nationalist party in Poland enraged Martin Schulz, the loudmouthed gatekeeper of the Transnational Elite in the European Parliament, who accused the new government as attempting a *"dangerous 'Putinization' of European politics."*[128]

However, what Eurocrats like Martin Schulz 'forgot' is that since Poland joined the EU in 2004, at least two million Poles have emigrated, many of them to the UK. The victory of the Law and Justice Party (Prawo i Sprawiedliwosc, PiS) in October 2015 was due not just to a backlash by traditional Polish voters to the bulldozing of their values by the ideology of globalization but also to the fact, as Cédric Gouverneur pointed out, that:

> the nationalist, pro-religion, protectionist, xenophobic PiS has attracted these disappointed people with an ambitious welfare programme: a family allowance of 500 zloty ($130) a month per child, funded through a tax on banks and big business; a minimum wage; and a return to a retirement age of 60 for women and 65 for men (the party had planned to raise it to 67 for both). [129]

In fact, PiS used to be a conservative pro-EU party when they were in power between 2005 and 2007, following faithfully the neoliberal program, but since then they have become increasingly Eurosceptic. As a result, in the last elections they won the parliamentary elections in both the lower house (Sejm) and the Senate, with 37.6% of the vote, against 24.1% for the neoliberals and 8.8% for the populist Kukiz, while the 'progressive' camp failed to clear the threshold (5% for parties, 8% for coalitions) and have no parliamentary representation at all!

It is therefore obvious that the globalization process has already had not only devastating economic and social consequences on the majority of the world population, but has also resulted in tremendous changes at the political and the cultural levels, in the past three decades or so. Furthermore, it has led to a series of major wars by the

---

[127] "Exclude Hungary from EU, says Luxembourg's Asselborn," *BBC News, 13/9/2016* http://www.bbc.co.uk/news/world-europe-37347352
[128] Martin Summers, "Poland, Hungary used by US as wedge between EU and Russia", RT, '13/1/2016
https://www.rt.com/op-edge/328758-eu-poland-hungary-putin/
[129] Cédric Gouverneur, "Poland's populist revenge", *Le Monde Diplomatique,* March 2016

Transnational Elite in its attempt to integrate any country resisting integration into the New World Order (NWO) defined by neoliberal globalization (Yugoslavia, Iraq, Afghanistan, Libya and Syria).

There is little doubt anymore that it was the intellectual failure of the Left to grasp the real significance of a new systemic phenomenon, (i.e. the rise of the Transnational Corporation that has led to the emergence of the globalization era) and its consequent political bankruptcy, which were the ultimate causes of the rise of a neo-nationalist movement in Europe. This movement is embraced by most of the victims of globalization all over Europe, particularly the working class that used to support the Left, whilst the latter has effectively embraced not just economic globalization but also political, ideological and cultural globalization and has therefore been fully integrated into the New World Order. In fact, today, following the successful emasculation of the antisystemic movement against globalization, thanks mainly to the activities of the globalist 'Left', as well as of the World Social Forum and the various Foundations funding it, the neo-nationalist movement has become the only political force left to fight against globalization in general and the EU in particular.

Almost inevitably, in view of the campaigns of the Transnational Elite against Muslim countries (Iraq, Afghanistan, Libya, Syria), worrying Islamophobic trends have developed within several of these neo-nationalist movements, some of them turning their old anti-Semitism to Islamophobia, supported on this by Zionists themselves![130] Even Marine Le Pen did not avoid the temptation to lie about Islamophobia and anti-Semitism, stressing that there is no Islamophobia in France, although she accepted a rise in anti-Semitism. Yet, she is well aware of the fact that Islamophobia was growing in France well before Charlie Hebdo, [131] with racial attacks against

---

[130] Adam Sage, "French Jews turn to Le Pen after Muslim attacks," *The Times* (24/2/2015).
[131] See e.g. Clemence Douchez-Lortet. "Growing Islamophobia in France: towards a revival of the extreme right?", *St. Andrews Review*, 16/10/2014 http://foreignaffairsreview.co.uk/2014/10/growing-islamophobia-france/ Although the article clearly attempts to blame the National Front for all Islamophobia in France, (presumably because the author belongs to the globalist Left), still, it is undeniable that the party plays electoral games on this crucial issue, attempting to exploit the anti-immigration feelings of French workers by turning them against immigrants rather than by attacking the real enemy, i.e. globalization

Islamic immigrants, (most of whom live under squalid conditions in virtual ghettos) being very frequent. At the same time, it is well known that the Jewish community is mostly well off and shares a very disproportionate part of political and economic power in the country to its actual size, as it happens of course also — and to an even larger extent — in the UK and USA.

This is one more reason why Popular Fronts for National and Social Liberation have to be built in every country of the world to fight not only Eurofascism and the NWO — which is of course the main enemy — but also any racist trends developing within these new anti-globalization movements and neo-nationalist parties. This would also prevent the elites from using the historically well-tested 'divide and rule' practice to divide the victims of globalization.

Neo-nationalism vs. Eurofascism

The rise of neo-nationalism in the globalization era, as a movement for national sovereignty, has nothing to do with the rise of what we may call 'Euro-fascism', mainly in the ex-soviet block countries of East Europe (Ukraine, the Baltic countries etc.) The unifying element of 'Euro-fascists' is that they implicitly or explicitly accept the NWO of neoliberal globalization, if not in their official ideology, at least in their practice. This is the case, for instance, of Ukrainian Euro-fascists who were massacring people in Maidan and in Odessa under the EU flag (sometimes next to swastikas!) and were fully backed and funded by the Transnational Elite, both by the EU parts as well as its US parts (Victoria Nuland, the US assistant Secretary of State for European and Eurasian Affairs was seen distributing biscuits to the Maidan Eurofascists!)

Therefore, in the globalization era, we have to make a clear distinction between Euro-fascists and neo-nationalists. Eurofascists, although they usually use as their point of reference National Socialism, they do not really question their countries' membership of the EU and sometimes they are even funded by the Transnational and European elites! In fact, their only relation to historical fascism (in a general sense, covering also National Socialism) concerns their practices, but not their real ideology. On the other hand, neo-nationalists are patriots and nationalists, who are 'recruited' from every part of the political range, from left to Right, including sometimes people with sympathies to historical fascism and Nazism, as for instance is the case with the Golden Dawn party in Greece.

As we saw in the last section, the unifying element of neo-nationalists is their struggle for national sovereignty, which they (rightly), see as disappearing in the era of globalization. Even when their main immediate motive is the fight against immigration, indirectly their fight is against globalization, as they realize that it is the opening of all markets, including the labor markets, particularly within economic unions like the EU, which is the direct cause of their own unemployment or low-wage employment. Yet, this is not a racist movement but a purely economic movement, although the Transnational Elite and the Zionist elites, with the help of the globalist 'Left', try hard to convert it into an Islamophobic movement — as the *Charlie Hebdo* case[132] and today's war against burkas and burkinis clearly show — so that they could use it in any way they see fit for the support of the NWO.

In Greece, for instance, at the very moment when people should be in the streets fighting united against the Transnational Elite and the EU elites, which have brought them to an unprecedented economic and social catastrophe, the same elites, with the help of the local elites, the media and the bankrupt globalist 'Left', keep calling the people to the streets — in a clear distraction strategy — to fight 'fascism' and 'racism' that supposedly threaten Greece rather than to fight for national liberation as a precondition of social liberation. At the same time, one of the main protagonists of the present catastrophe in Greece, the ex pop 'Tsar of the economy' Varoufakis, used the same fascist bogeyman to persuade the Transnational Elite to allow some relaxation of its austerity policies in Greece![133]

But, what is the relationship of both neo-nationalists and Euro-fascists to historical fascism and Nazism? As I tried to show elsewhere,[134] fascism, as well as National Socialism, presuppose a nation-state, therefore this kind of phenomenon is impossible to develop in any country fully integrated into the NWO, which, by definition, cannot have any significant degree of national sovereignty.

---

[132] see *Subjugate the Middle East*, (vol.3 of *The NWO in Action*)
[133] By Mark Lowen, "Why did Greece's Varoufakis bring up Nazis in Berlin?", *BBC News*, 6/2/2015 http://www.bbc.co.uk/news/world-europe-31170591
[134] Takis Fotopoulos, *Ukraine: the attack on Russia and the Eurasian Union* (vol.2 of *The NWO in Action*)

As I tried to show in this book, the only kind of sovereignty available in the NWO of neoliberal globalization is transnational sovereignty, which, in fact, is exclusively shared by members of the Transnational Elite. In other words, fascism and Nazism were historical phenomena of the era of nation-state before the ascent of the NWO of neoliberal globalization, when states still had a significant degree of national and economic sovereignty.

However, in the globalization era, it is exactly this sovereignty that is being phased out for any country fully integrated into the NWO. Therefore, the only kind of 'fascism' still possible today is the one directly or indirectly supported by the Transnational Elite (e.g. the 'Euro-fascism' I mentioned), which is in fact a kind of pseudo-fascism — although in terms of the bestial practices it uses, it may be even more genuine than the 'real thing' of the inter-war period. This is, for instance, the case of the Ukrainian Euro-fascists who are the closest thing to historical Nazism available today, not only in terms of their practices but also in terms of their history. However, as there is overwhelming evidence of the full support they have enjoyed by the Transnational Elite and (paradoxically?) even by the Zionist elite,[135] they should more accurately be called Euro-fascists.

It is therefore clear that the neo-nationalist parties, which are all under attack by the Transnational Elite, constitute cases of movements that simply filled the huge gap left by the globalist 'Left'. That is, the kind of Left which, instead of placing itself in the front line of all those peoples fighting globalization and the phasing out of their economic and national sovereignty,[136] indirectly, promoted globalization itself, using arguments based on an anachronistic internationalism, developed a hundred years ago or so. As a result, the neo-nationalist parties are embraced today by most of the victims of globalization all over Europe, particularly the working class which used to support the Left,[137] whilst the latter has effectively embraced all aspects of globalization (economic, political, ideological and cultural) and has

---

[135] "Communists seek Jewish denouncement of oligarch over E. Ukraine raid sponsorship", RT, 7/11/2014
https://www.rt.com/politics/203111-russian-communists-kolomoyskiy-denounce/
[136] See e.g. "Globalization is barbarous, multinationals rule world – Marine Le Pen", RT, 8/12/2014 http://rt.com/news/212435-france-pen-globalization-barbarity/
[137] Francis Elliott et al. 'Working class prefers Ukip to Labour", *The Times*, 25/11/2014

3. Phasing out national sovereignty, rise of neo-nationalism

been fully integrated into the NWO — a defining moment in its present intellectual and political bankruptcy.

The process of bankruptcy of the Left has been further enhanced by the fact that, faced with a political collapse in the May 2014 elections for a Euro-parliament, it has allied with the elites in condemning the neo-nationalist parties as fascist and neo-Nazis, while in extreme cases they even consented to the use of blatantly fascist methods in order to suppress some of them, as it was, for instance, the case of the Golden Dawn party in Greece. Although this party is an aberration from the main neo-nationalist parties, yet, no arms in its possession have ever been found and the charge that the party itself was involved in the killing of a left wing activist has yet to be proven in court.

So, although it is true that the Golden Dawn party's rhetoric seems to be supporting Nazi collaborators in Greece, and the military junta of 1967, and there is some evidence of it taking part in attacks against immigrants in the past, this in no way justifies the use of purely illegal methods by the state against a formally legal party. Such methods included the imprisonment without any trial of the entire leadership of the party for almost a year and a half, the blocking of its access to the mass media and even the effective prevention of its leader to take part in the advisory meetings of party leaders called occasionally by the Greek President. In fact, the imprisoned Golden Down MPs were not even allowed to exercise their parliamentary duties, in blatant violation of the constitution[138] and when the SYRIZA Speaker of the Greek Parliament sought to rectify this blatant illegality, she was disowned even by her own party, members of which went as far as to say — in a purely fascist way — that the GD votes in parliament should not be taken into account, despite the fact that the party has never been declared illegal! Even the communists, paradoxically enough, approved this blatantly fascist practice in the context of their 'anti-fascist' struggle![139] Therefore, all parts of the

---

[138] Of course, there are always "academics" and solicitors specializing in Constitution law, who will provide a handy interpretation of the law which legalizes any action of the elites, for the sake of the social and economic status they enjoy.
[139] Needless to add that when I criticized such blatant fascist methods (always carried out in the name of an 'antifascist' struggle) I was personally attacked, as a rule by anonymous bloggers, as 'laundering' Greek fascism. One such particularly suspicious case has been the persistent attack (for almost four years now) by somebody under the pseudonym Omadcon who had no problem finding several

Left, from communists to reformists, in silent acquiescence, consented to this blatantly fascist practice, for the sake of fighting fascism! In fact, some of the 'Left' leaders did not hesitate even to christen as 'fascists' almost a tenth of the population who voted for GD. This is of course a deep offense against a people, who had one of the strongest anti-fascist resistance records in Europe during the German occupation, while the fascist movement itself in Greece, historically, has never had any significant appeal to the Greek people — even during the Metaxas dictatorship of 1936-1940 when the regime attempted to promote such trends!

---

fellow travellers in his defamation campaign against me among members of the globalist 'Left', including some 'libertarian' ones, who made their name by translating the works of significant libertarian writers like Castoriadis!

PART II

THE NEW WORLD ORDER'S MYTHS

Chapter 4.

The myth of national sovereignty

In this second part of the book I will examine some of the main myths developed by the propaganda machine of the NWO and particularly the myth that national sovereignty is still possible today, as well as the myth of the multi-polar world that supposedly develops at the moment, particularly with respect to the BRICS countries. Finally, some of the myths promoted in particular by the globalist 'Left' to cover its integration into the NWO will be considered. It is not of course surprising that the Transnational Elite has developed an entire new mythology about the NWO. What is surprising — to say the least — is that this mythology has also been adopted, directly or indirectly, by most of what used to be called the Left.

No doubt, the Transnational Elite had every reason to deepen the confusion about the real significance of globalization, in particular with reference to its effect on national sovereignty, the presumed multi-polar nature of the NWO, the supposedly universal economic benefits of globalization and so on. At the same time, it is not strange at all that the reformist 'Left', takes globalization and its institutions for granted, given that its aim has always been to improve the existing system rather than to overthrow it. What however is, prima facie, paradoxical is the fact that most of the antisystemic Left, also, ignores the systemic changes brought about by globalization — mainly on dogmatic grounds having to do with its failure to renew its outdated theoretical tools of analysis, which were developed more than a century before the emergence of globalization.

To put it simply, the antisystemic Left, particularly of Marxist origin, cannot grasp the fact that both liberal capitalism as well as state capitalism of the past are very different from the capitalism characterizing neoliberal globalization. The fact that the state sees its economic and therefore national sovereignty dramatically declining in the globalization era is completely ignored or underestimated by Marxist analysts. The inevitable consequence has been the present political bankruptcy of most of the Left, which is reflected in the fact that, today, it is the neo-nationalist Right which has replaced the Left in its role of representing the victims of the system in its globalized form, while the Left mainly represents those in the middle class or the petty bourgeoisie who benefit from globalization, or hope to benefit from it. This includes the Marxist Left as well, particularly the European academics, who, apart from their class position, have vested interests (e.g. funding of their research and trips around the world for conferences etc.) in supporting the EU, directly or indirectly.

At the same time, several pseudo-radical movements (indignados, occupation movements, anonymous etc.), substitute for the Left. These are movements which the system can easily integrate or neutralize — if it did not encourage the emergence of some of them in the first place. No wonder it was out of these pseudo-radical movements that the two main 'Leftist' parties in Europe today emerged, particularly PODEMOS in Spain and SYRIZA in Greece. The latter has a longer history than the former, as its main body came from a marginal party of the reformist (Eurocommunist) Greek Left that was formed in the early 1990s, in the aftermath of the collapse of 'actually existing socialism' and the split with orthodox communists (KKE). Once this party came to power in January 2015 (with the tolerance, if not active help, of the Transnational Elite)[140] it has played a decisive role in the present catastrophe of the Greek people, in full co-operation with the foreign and local elites.

The conditions for sovereignty and self-determination

One common myth promoted by the ideologues of the NWO and globalists is that national sovereignty is still possible today. However, as we saw in the first part, the NWO has led to the phasing out of national sovereignty through the opening and liberalizing of markets,

---

[140] See *Ukraine: the attack on Russia and the Eurasian Union* (vol.2 of *The NWO in Action*)

which, in turn, was necessary for the expansion of transnational corporations.

A renowned member of the Transnational Elite, for instance, the financier George Soros, played a leading role in the campaign for open borders, i.e. the free movement not only of labor but also of capital and commodities between countries. It is well known that Soros, through his Open Societies Foundations, as well the NGOs and think tanks he sponsors, has managed to be behind almost every color revolution in Eastern Europe and beyond. Soros' role in undermining national sovereignty was shown in a revealing recent exchange between the neo-nationalist Hungarian leader Victor Orban and him. Thus, when Orban criticized Soros with respect to his role in the migration crisis in Europe, stating, "philanthropists like Soros must assume part of the blame for the current crisis," (i.e. the migration crisis into the EU) the following interesting exchange between them took place:

> *"This invasion is driven, on the one hand, by people smugglers, and on the other hand by those activists who support everything that weakens the nation state,"* Orban told reporters. *"This Western mindset and this activist network is perhaps best represented by George Soros."* Soros responded by issuing an email statement to *Bloomberg Business*, claiming his international organization works to *"uphold European values"*, while Mr. Orban's efforts to fortify the Hungarian border, thereby halting a massive wave of illegal migrants, *"undermine those values... His plan treats the protection of national borders as the objective and the refugees as an obstacle,"* Soros added. *"Our plan treats the protection of refugees as the objective and national borders as the obstacle."*[141]

It is worth remembering at this point that it was exactly the same 'European values' that were invoked by the EU-elites to undermine the economic and therefore national sovereignty of every European country. The Greek people, for instance, have been condemned by the EU elites, first, to be impoverished,[142] and then forced to play the role of a huge storage space for thousands of refugees from the wars of the Transnational Elite in the Middle East. These refugees, in turn, were

---

[141] Paul Craig Roberts, "Soros's 'European values' mean losing your national identity", RT, 4/11/2015 https://www.rt.com/op-edge/320747-soros-european-values-orban/
[142] See vol.2 of *The NWO in Action*, op.cit.

unleashed by the Turkish elite, which followed in effect an open borders policy towards them, with the obvious connivance of the Transnational Elite and the NGOs, funded by it, playing a significant role in this process (see Chs. 7&8). All this for the 'protection of European values' (of course!) and for the sake of humanism and 'philanthropy', despite the fact that it was the same Transnational Elite, which, for the sake of the 'protection of human rights' and the same European values etc., created the millions of refugees in the first instance, through the destruction of Iraq, Afghanistan, Libya and now Syria!

There is therefore no doubt that the Transnational Elite has been engaged, since the emergence of the NWO, in a systematic campaign to destroy national sovereignty in order to secure the free movement of capital, labor and commodities. The means used for this aim ranged from military ones to economic ones. The former included the campaigns in the Middle East to destroy any regime based on a national liberation movement, e.g. the Ba'athist regimes in Iraq and Syria. The latter consisted mainly in economic pressures to integrate peoples into the NWO (through joining its transnational institutions like the World Trade Organization or the European Union), as well as in the activities of well paid by the Transnational Elite NGOs to help the movement of hundreds of thousands of emigrants, under the label of 'refugees', from Asia and Northern Africa into Greece and Italy and from there to Europe.

But, what are the conditions for sovereignty in general, as a pre-condition for self-determination? Here we may distinguish between the necessary and sufficient conditions for sovereignty:

The fundamental *necessary condition* for real self-determination and sovereignty, so that the dependence on the NWO of neoliberal globalization and the Transnational Elite administering it could be eliminated, *is economic sovereignty*. This is the necessary condition so that it is each country's people alone that determines--through the method of allocation of resources that itself decides and without any foreign interference on the entire process — the sort of economic policies (monetary/fiscal policies) and social controls needed to meet basic needs. On the other hand, there is no need to stress that the opening and liberalization of markets, inevitably, leads to the dismantling of economic sovereignty.

The main *sufficient condition* for real self-determination is economic self-reliance, i.e. reliance primarily on a country's own resources, human and natural.

Economic sovereignty and self-reliance

But why is economic self-reliance so important for sovereignty and self-determination? There are two main reasons:

- First, because economic self-reliance is the only way in which a country could become invulnerable to economic warfare (e.g. through economic sanctions) by the Transnational Elite, as this is the main form of warfare used by the Transnational Elite in the globalization era. This is for instance the case of Russia, against which economic warfare is used in lieu of war itself;
- Second, because self-reliance is the only way in which a country's people could determine its production pattern in accordance with the consumption pattern preferred, so that the people will not be dependent on foreign capital (investment and finance capital), as well as on trade, in order to cover even their *basic needs*.

In other words, not only is self-reliance the best defense against economic warfare but it is also the best way to create a self-determined economy and society and avoid full subordination to the NWO, as is the case of Greece today. It is therefore clear that self-reliance plays a crucial role in the peoples' struggle for self-determination, given that economic and therefore national sovereignty is impossible without self-reliance.

Needless to add that economic self-reliance does not just mean import substitution, i.e. the replacement of foreign products by domestic ones. Economic self-reliance means fundamental economic, political and cultural changes that could only be achieved within a democratic community of sovereign nations, which will have to function as an alternative pole to the present unipolar world run by the Transnational Elite.

Likewise, self-reliance does not mean isolation, as globalists attempt to defame it. Instead, it could well imply the creation of a new democratic world order of sovereign nations, which will determine collectively and democratically the division of labor between them. This new division of labor could be based on the principles of mutual aid and solidarity in meeting their citizens' needs, rather than on the principles of competitiveness drawn from an individualistic culture, as is the dominant culture in the present World Order.

It should therefore be clear that self-reliance here is meant in terms of autonomy, rather than in terms of self-sufficiency, which, under today's conditions, is neither feasible nor desirable. A useful definition of self-reliance is the one given by the 1974 Cocoyoc Declaration of non-aligned countries as "reliance primarily on one's own resources, human and natural, and the capacity of autonomous goal-setting and decision-making."[143] Thus, although self-reliance implies maximal utilization of local resources and sources of energy, it should not be confused with autarchy and should always be seen as a sufficient condition for autonomy, in the sense here of political and economic sovereignty. Needless to add that self-reliance in this sense is impossible within the World Trade Organization framework and the limited degree of import substitution allowed by its rules, whereas it could potentially be feasible within an economic and political union like the Eurasian Union, as we shall see in Ch.11.

A real struggle for economic self-reliance could begin through the radical restructuring of the productive base, with the aim of meeting, at least, the basic needs of all citizens, rather than meeting market demands — as prescribed by the Transnational Elite and the Transnational Corporations (TNCs) that control world markets. Furthermore, in a framework of self-reliance, citizens could enjoy the benefits of Social Health, and Education, as well as Social Insurance (through new public organizations that they themselves would control directly) and will also be able to recover the public assets and social goods, which are currently being sold out to TNCs and loan sharks.

It should also be stressed that self-reliance should not be seen only in the narrow context of a single country, even a big one such as Russia, but, also, in the context of the alternative pole of sovereign nations as mentioned above. This implies that another necessary condition for the implementation of such a program is the radical change of geopolitical conditions, so that the 'Libyan' or 'Ukrainian' examples are not repeated in the countries moving away from the NWO. This presupposes the creation of an international front of all countries presently resisting the NWO: from Venezuela, Bolivia and

---

[143] Quoted in Paul Ekins, *Trade for Mutual Self-Reliance* (London: TOES publication), 1989, p. 13.

Cuba up to the countries in the EU periphery — which have been condemned to either mass unemployment or pseudo-full employment and poverty — and the peoples in the Middle East (particularly Syria and Iran), as well as the peoples in the broader Eurasian area, among which post-coup Turkey could potentially play a key role, provided it cuts its links with the NWO and joins the Eurasian Union.

Of particular importance is of course the participation of Russia itself in this front, whose people at present, from communists up to neo-nationalists, and from radical social democrats up to orthodox Christians, are united against the NWO. There is no doubt that Russia, by definition, could play a leading role in a new democratic world order of sovereign nations, creating a new global pole against the criminal pole of the NWO, provided of course that Russia and the Eurasian Union as a whole break their relations with the NWO.

Clearly, therefore, apart from the maximization of the degree of national self-reliance (i.e. the self-reliance achieved by each nation participating in such an economic union), there should also be a collective self-reliance at the level of an economic union formed by the countries resisting the NWO. The size of such a union and the variety of the countries involved (in terms of economic resources, geophysical conditions and so on), will determine the degree at which the union of sovereign nations will be a self-sufficient alternative pole, which would be invulnerable to any kind of economic war against it by the NWO.

With regards to economic growth per se, although growth (or, better, development) may still be necessary in order to meet the needs of the population, there is no reason why a rational society will 'grow for growth's sake'. This is because such a growth process will not only have obvious adverse ecological effects, but also catastrophic social, cultural as well as political effects, given that real democratic processes are clearly impossible in today's centralized societies, which are the outcome of this sort of growth economies. Growth for growth's sake is an irrational process imposed by those controlling production, i.e. the TNCs, which do not have any qualms about creating artificial needs, provided they make more profits and expand further.

Therefore, as long as the fundamental economic decisions about what, how and for whom to produce are not social decisions taken collectively and directly by *citizens* as citizens but, instead, are decisions taken by individual *consumers* through the market, then the resulting allocation of resources will inevitably lead to the present huge and growing inequalities in the world distribution of income and wealth. This, in spite of the myths of orthodox economics, which is based on an imaginary perfectly competitive world that assumes away the crucial distributional aspects![144]

Furthermore, in a globalized market economy there is no possibility that any state, or even a federation of states, or an economic union like the EU, would be able to impose significant social controls on markets to ameliorate this growing inequality, as it used to be the case in the statist period. Despite the myths to the contrary of globalists such as Piketty, Krugman, Stiglitz and the likes, any such interference would by definition make the corresponding state or union, which is integrated into the NWO, less competitive. In other words, in a globalized market economy only *global* social controls could be effective and it is only the Transnational Elite that has the power (but not the will, for obvious reasons) to impose global controls of this kind. Instead, as we shall see next, the Transnational Elite is interested in doing exactly the opposite: loosening even further the still existing social controls and opening the way to privatize any social service still available, following the onslaught of the NWO and the mass neoliberal legislation adopted in the last 30 years or so.

The Transatlantic and Trans-Pacific Partnerships and the myth of sovereignty

In October 2014, and again in April 2016, major demonstrations took place all over the world and particularly in Europe against the NWO of neoliberal globalization and the Transnational Elite. The reason was the latest Transnational Elite plan for a transatlantic trade deal called "Transatlantic Trade and Investment Partnership (TTIP)."[145] Negotiations for this new agreement, which have taken place between representatives of the political and economic elites of USA and EU are, in fact, well advanced behind the scenes and one could assume that as soon as the US Presidential elections are out of the way, with the expected victory of the Transnational Elite candidate (Clinton) and the similar victories of the Transnational Elite candidates

---

[144] See for a critique of orthodox economics on the market allocation of resources, Takis Fotopoulos, *Towards An Inclusive Democracy*, op.cit. pp. 248-250

[145] See e.g. Andrew Walker, "Concerns rise over US-EU trade talks", *BBC News*, 11/10/2014, http://www.bbc.co.uk/news/business-29572475#story_continues_1

in the French and German elections in 2017, the TTIP agreement will be concluded and signed. A similar agreement called The Trans-Pacific Partnership (TTP), which is characterized as "one of the most ambitious free trade agreements ever signed,"[146] has already been agreed between 12 countries across the Pacific Rim, (the US, Japan, Malaysia, Vietnam, Singapore, Brunei, Australia, New Zealand, Canada, Mexico, Chile and Peru), which together account for about 40% of the global economy.

However, the Trans-Pacific Partnership and the corresponding trans-Atlantic one TTP represent, as was recently stressed, a major step towards global governance and therefore a final nail in the coffin of national sovereignty:

> Several major international agreements are under negotiation which would greatly empower multinational corporations and the World Economic Forum is promoting a new model of global governance that creates a hybrid government-corporate structure. Humankind is proceeding on a path to global corporate rule where transnational corporations would not just influence public policy, they would write the policies and vote on them. The power of nation-states and people to determine their futures would be weakened in a system of corporate rule.[147]

But what exactly do these agreements involve? An apt summary of what TTIP is all about was given by Sam Gerrans:

> Under TTIP, public services, education and health services will be open for tender. EU food and cosmetics standards will be brought in line with the much lower standards in operation in the US. What banking protections exist after the last collapse will likely be removed. The walls in data privacy will become porous between the two blocs. And since the US is party to NAFTA, it will mean that EU workers will be in competition

---

[146] "Ambitious TPP trade deal signed" &" TPP: What is it and why does it matter?", BBC News, 3/2/2016 http://www.bbc.co.uk/news/business-32498715
[147] Kevin Zeese &Margaret Flowers, "Stop The Fast Track To A Future Of Global Corporate Rule. The Dangers Underlying the TPP and TTIP "Trade Agreements", *Global Research*, 12/3/2015 http://www.globalresearch.ca/stop-the-fast-track-to-a-future-of-global-corporate-rule-the-dangers-underlying-the-tpp-and-ttip-trade-agreements/5436121

with Mexico... Put nicely, then, TTIP is a drive to the lowest common denominator between the laws which currently exist in the EU and the US combined with the creation of an unaccountable executive branch committed only to the interests of corporations.[148]

More recent research on the basis of 248 pages of classified negotiation papers that were leaked[149] revealed that the TTIP deal between the EU and the US could affect public health, people's rights, internet privacy and the environment badly. Furthermore, they confirmed something we already suspected, i.e. the strong pressure exerted by the US elites on the EU elites to approve the deal. Thus, according to a report published in *Sueddeutsche Zeitung*,[150] based on an analysis of the leaked documents, Washington is blocking European car exports into the US to force the EU to buy more environmentally risky US farm produce. In other words, the environmental protections, on which the EU prides itself, will be thrown overboard for the sake of the profit of TNCs, as soon as the deal goes ahead.

One striking characteristic of these negotiations is that both Russia and China are deliberately excluded from them, for the reasons we shall examine in the next chapter. That is, the negotiations take place exclusively among members of the Transnational Elite, and those fully integrated into the NWO as associate or subordinate members of it. As I will try to show in later chapters, this is because Russia is not fully integrated into the NWO, despite its recent joining the World Trade Organization. That is, the international organization which was set up at the beginning of the globalization era with the explicit aim to fully integrate into the New Order of neoliberal globalization as many countries of the world as possible, provided they would agree to fully open and liberalize their markets for commodities, so that TNCs do not have any tariff or other barriers restricting their activities.

---

[148] Sam Gerrans, "TTIP: Fake freedom moves closer to open slavery", RT, 20/3/2016 https://www.rt.com/op-edge/336362-fake-freedom-moves-ttip/
[149] TTIP risks to health & environment, 'US pressure on EU' revealed in secret docs leaked by Greenpeace, RT, 2/5/2016 https://www.rt.com/news/341591-greenpeace-leak-ttip-deal/
[150] Michael Bauchmüller und Silvia Liebrich, "USA wollen Einfluss auf europäische Gesetze nehmen", Sueddeutsche Zeitung, 2/5/2016 http://www.sueddeutsche.de/wirtschaft/ttip-papiere-usa-wollen-einfluss-auf-europaeische-gesetze-nehmen-1.2975013

However, despite the fact that the World Trade Organization has been highly successful in opening and liberalizing goods markets, it was not so successful in opening services markets, given that many countries still try to protect basic needs services like Health, Education, Transportation and Communications, which are all characterized as social services and are not therefore left free to become easy prey for the TNCs and their profit making activities. This is unlike the US case, where meeting these basic needs depends on market forces, (i.e. on how thick the citizen's wallet is) rather than on collective social decisions taken democratically. On top of this, the World Trade Organization was not particularly successful in opening and liberalizing some production sectors in the "South" (e.g. the agriculture sector), which are still the main production sectors (at least in terms of providing employment) for many of those countries. As an expert on the field stressed:

> To put it mildly, the World Trade Organization has not proven terribly popular. In fact, the organization has mainly been used as a vehicle to force open vulnerable economies and make the rich richer and the poor poorer around the world. Thus, unsurprisingly, talks on further liberalization measures within the World Trade Organizations' global framework have stalled.... Hence, the confusingly abbreviated TTIP and TTP, which are being negotiated by more exclusive sets of countries whose leaders happen to (mainly) agree that it would be a good idea to go much further down the trade liberalization rabbit hole than even the hugely unpopular World Trade Organization has. One of the most concerning ways they want to do this is by seeking to institutionalize what is known as investor-state dispute settlement (ISDS) within the agreements' framework.[151]

And indeed, as the last sentence in the above extract stresses, the new agreements (TTIP and TTP) propose various clauses that will create universal mechanisms to settle disputes between TNCs and states. Thus, unlike individual deals on developing specific natural resources, the TTIP and TTP cover a wide range of what are considered to be TNCs investments in the states. Therefore, as the

---

[151] Roslyn Fuller, Pyrrhic victory for whistleblowers on Transatlantic Trade Agreement, RT, 2/4/2014 http://rt.com/op-edge/transatlantic-trade-agreement-817/

same expert points out "incorporating these clauses would mean that if
a country later makes a law that contravenes the terms of the TTIP or
TTP, (for example, in the interests of protecting public health), a
company that suffers damages (for example, because it has been
making a product that contravenes the new rule) can sue the state for
compliance with the treaty, bypassing the normal court system. In
other words, foreign companies are placed above the law of the host
State through these agreements."[152] Thus, TNCs with a stake in the
UK health service, for instance, could sue the government if it decided
to pursue a program of nationalization. No wonder that Gail Cartmail
(the Assistant General Secretary of Unite, a major British Trade
Union) urged congress delegates in the 2014 TUC conference to
oppose the TTIP and rally support amongst people in the UK to
demand Prime Minister David Cameron keep Britain's health services
out of the TTIP agreement. As it was reported at the time:

> It is clear this government thought they could do this deal in
> secret – a deal that would mean the irreversible sell-off of our
> NHS to America," Cartmail said. "Wall Street financiers like
> Blackrock and Invesco are already heavily invested in the NHS
> – over 70 percent of new contracts are now in private hands.
> Over £11 billion of our money in the hands of casino
> capitalists," she added.[153]

It is not therefore surprising that some of the campaigners against
TTIP worry that once this agreement is converted into EU law and
finds its way to domestic parliaments, it could then open the way to
privatize any social services still available, following the onslaught of
the NWO and the mass neoliberal legislation adopted in the last 30
years or so by both conservative, Christian Democratic and social
democratic parties in power. Environmentalists are also concerned that
the dispute settlement procedure could well be used by TNCs to block
moves to protect the environment.

Finally, it should be noted that the conduct of the negotiations is
also contentious. Campaigners say they are secretive and undemocratic,
as should be expected given they are, in fact, (despite formalities)
carried out between unelected US and EU bureaucrats, who owe their
posts to the transnational political and economic elites, and

---

[152] ibid.
[153] No TTIP: Mass protests slam US-EU trade deal as 'corporate power grab', RT,
11/10/2014 http://rt.com/news/195144-europe-protests-stop-ttip/

representatives of TNCs. If we add to all this the fact that, as it is estimated, up to 65% of each EU country's legislation originates in the EU Commission, we may get a good idea of the sort of sovereignty enjoyed by the EU peoples!

The Scottish referendum, Brexit and the myth of independence within the EU

On the morning the results of the Scottish referendum were announced in October 2014, there was a general climate of euphoria, if not celebration, in all centers of the Transnational Elite: from the City of London and Wall Street to Washington and Brussels. What they were celebrating was that, following an unprecedented and successful general attack by the Transnational Elite, they could declare 'mission accomplished': the victims of neoliberal globalization were utterly defeated! In this attack, not only did the British elite played a leading role, as expected, but also the Scottish economic elite, (of which 90% of the entrepreneurs declared themselves against independence),[154] the US elite,[155] and even Zionist theoreticians of Global Governance.[156] Needless to add that the elites controlling the transnational media – with the BBC (aptly called by Scottish nationalists the "British Brainwashing Corporation") excelled in biased reporting.[157] In this sense, the Scottish referendum was for the elites a dress rehearsal for the much more important Brexit referendum that followed in 2016. It was on the basis of their success in 2014 that the British elites allowed a referendum on Brexit to take place, given the growing pressure "from below". Of course, following the results of Brexit referendum they deeply regretted that fatal decision (see Ch. 8).

However, to begin with, one has to notice that, unlike Brexit, there was never a full mobilization in Scotland of the victims of globalization and its consequent de-industrialization.[158] That is, a

---

[154] Sarah Gordon and Patrick Jenkins, "CBI says most Scottish business against independence", *Financial Times*, 11/9/2014
[155] Robin Harding, Richard McGregor and Geoff Dyer, "US alarmed by prospect of Scottish 'Yes' in independence vote", *Financial Times*, 15/9/2014
[156] Gideon Rachman, "This is a very bad time to break up Britain", *Financial Times*, 15/9/2014
[157] 'Clear split: Scottish support "YES" campaign, UK media "NO" movement', *RT*, 16/9/2014 http://rt.com/op-edge/188176-scotland-referendum-media-bbc-uk/
[158] Christine Jeavans, "Scottish independence referendum in maps", *BBC News*, 19/9/2014 http://www.bbc.co.uk/news/uk-scotland-scotland-politics-29255449

mobilization of the unemployed, the involuntary part-timers, or casual
employees on barely survival salaries, and so on. In other words, of all
those who have abstained from the electoral game all these years, as
they found themselves with no political representation in Westminster,
following the effective institutionalization of neoliberal policies
imposed by the transnational corporations, through the Thatcherites
first, and then the Blairites, Brown & co. Yet, the main victims of
globalization could have potentially formed a joint informal front with
at least part of the middle classes, which had already begun to be
squeezed by the neoliberal policies and were also supporting the
demand for self-determination — as it happened in the case of Brexit.
Naturally, a significant part of the middle classes would never have
joined such a front, in full knowledge that an independence movement
would have to adopt radical policies in government in order to create a
self-reliant economy, which could put them in a much higher risk than
the 'sans culottes'. Yet, a full mobilization of the victims of
globalization, who surely constitute the majority of the Scottish
population, could have overcome this obstacle. But, instead of a full
mobilization of the victims of globalization, there was a full
mobilization only of those who benefit from globalization and the
Transnational Elite's aggressive policies. How can we explain this
paradox, which in effect is a superficial one?

At the outset, it should be made clear that regional independence
is not always beneficial to the people. It is, in principle, a positive step
towards self-determination, only if independence involves not just
political self-reliance, as is self-evident, but also, and, most
importantly in the globalization era, economic self-reliance, which is a
prerequisite for national and economic sovereignty. If, therefore, an
independence movement — sometimes motivated or encouraged by
the Transnational Elite itself — simply ends up with the breaking up of
a powerful and potentially sovereign nation state, allowing for easier
integration into the NWO of the easily controlled statelets resulting
from this development, then, this form of independence is not just
negative, but also destructive (see e.g. Yugoslavia, as well as Iraq,
Libya, and probably Syria[159] soon).

Of course, the case of Scotland does not belong to this category,
given Britain's prominent political/military role within the

---

[159] Takis Fotopoulos, *Subjugating the Middle East,* (Vol. 3 of the *NWO in Action*)

Transnational Elite, which is why the American elite rushed to support its British partner against the looming independence of Scotland. Yet, this was a typical example of double standards, as it was the US elite itself, which presided over the NATO slaughter of Serbs, so that Kosovo could later declare its independence. In that case, regional independence was obviously a 'good thing' for these elites. In fact, it was exactly Kosovo's 'independence' that completed the dismantling of the most self-reliant and powerful state in the Balkans, Yugoslavia,[160] and opened the way for the full integration of the new statelets created by the dissolution of Yugoslavia into the NWO, through their joining the EU, and possibly later NATO. In this sense, it is ironic indeed that the Serbs, who were leading the struggle for a united Yugoslavia, once they were bombed by the Transnational Elite and were defeated into submission, became so degraded politically that they are now begging to join the EU, supporting in the latest general elections the pro-EU parties.[161] No wonder, Serbian Prime Minister Aleksandar Vucic hailed Joe Biden, the US Vice-President who recently visited Belgrade, as a friend of his country, despite the fact that Biden was one of the most vocal supporters of the NATO butchery of Serbia back in 1999![162] All this, at the very moment a full anti-EU tsunami is blowing across Europe.

In fact, the Transnational Elite was particularly alarmed at the anti-war tendencies of the Scots, who were against the wars of the Transnational Elite (in which, of course, Britain had taken a lead), as well as against both NATO and nuclear proliferation. Alex Salmond himself, the leader of the Scottish Nationalist Party at the time of the Scot referendum, was a former anti-NATO activist, and did not hesitate to state that Putin has restored 'a substantial part of Russian pride',[163] receiving the wrath of the Transnational Elite and the British

---

[160] See Takis Fotopoulos, "New World Order and NATO's war against Yugoslavia", *New Political Science*, vol. 24, no.1, (March 2002), pp. 73-104

[161] Andrew Byrne, "Serb voters back pro-EU parties as early results cement Vucic win", *Financial Times,* 25/4/2016

[162] "Serbian PM calls top advocate of Yugoslavia NATO bombing Biden a 'friend of country'", RT, 16/8/2016 https://www.rt.com/news/356197-biden-serbia-us-friend/

[163] Alan Roden & Will Stewart, "Now Kremlin expresses delight at Salmond's praise for Putin as Ukrainian families speak of their 'disgust and betrayal'", *Daily Mail*, 30/4/2014 http://www.dailymail.co.uk/news/article-2616722/Now-Kremlin-expresses-delight-Salmonds-praise-Putin-Ukrainian-families-speak-disgust-betrayal.html#email

elite in exchange. He then later added salt to the wound when he stated that the bombing of Syria cannot be allowed, without a resolution of the UN Security Council.

But, despite the clearly more progressive trends of Scots in general compared with Englishmen, not only on foreign affairs but also on welfare state issues as well, such as education and health (in England, the former is a thing of the past as far as higher education is concerned and the latter is decaying), the crucial question that arises in connection to similar independence movements within the EU, like the Catalans in Spain, is the following: Is the political independence and the economic self-reliance of a country, that is fully integrated into the NWO, feasible? Particularly so when the Scottish Nationalist Party, unlike other neo-nationalist movements in Europe (e.g. in France) does not dispute either the EU or not even the Euro and is not raising the demand for the country to have its own national currency? In fact, the Scottish nationalist party — together with other autonomist parties in the UK, such as the nationalist movements in Wales and Northern Ireland — sided against Brexit (see Ch. 8) and today plays a purely reactionary role in systematically attempting to stop the Brexit process!

It is therefore clear that the Scottish nationalist elite, unlike the lower classes that supported the 'Yes' vote, never wanted to come into conflict with the EU and the Transnational Elite in general. That's why Salmond himself promised tax havens to transnational corporations in order to attract more of them in Scotland.[164] It was not therefore surprising that when he was asked how he would ensure a peaceful and comprehensive welfare state — as he promised — within the NWO of neoliberal globalization, despite the fact that others before him had tried and dismally failed to do so (e.g. Mitterrand and Hollande in France), he had to resort to nonsensical and disorienting arguments (like those of SYRIZA in Greece), that he would be a better negotiator! This, despite the fact, of which Salmond was surely aware, that even the Norwegians, who also have rich energy resources, saw a

---

[164] Seumas Milne, Salmond's Scotland won't be an escape from Tory Britain, *The Guardian*, 11/9/2014

massive retreat from social democracy in their country, even though, formally, they are not EU members![165]

On the other hand, in England, not only the working class but also part of the middle class, which is also squeezed at present as a result of globalization (as everywhere else), has joined the anti-EU forces. Of course, Brexit is only a necessary condition (not a sufficient one) for any political and economic independence. In fact, the reason why Nigel Farage's (UKIP) social policies did not significantly differ from those of Cameron was exactly because he, like Salmond, represented much more the nationalist part of the bourgeoisie rather than the victims of globalization. In terms therefore of the terminology we adopted in the last chapter, we may classify Scottish nationalism as an old kind of nationalism, whereas the Brexit movement expressed mainly a neo-nationalist movement, despite the existence also of some old nationalist elements within it.

In conclusion, true independence and self-reliance, i.e. national and economic sovereignty, is impossible within the NWO in general and the EU in particular. Therefore, had the 'Yes' vote won in Scotland, this would not have been a victory against the NWO, unless it was only the first step in the process of Scotland ceasing to be a protectorate in effect, not only of the British elite but also of the EU and the Transnational Elite in general. However, the fact that the Scottish (as well as the Irish) nationalists turned against the English neo-nationalists who wanted a break with the EU[166] shows that the nationalist movements in Scotland and Ireland are very much dominated by the globalist local elites and, as such, have no chance of leading their peoples to real sovereignty and independence. Furthermore, the fact that the Scottish nationalists declared also their intention to stop the English people from leaving the EU, asking for a separate referendum in Scotland to secure their stay in the EU, shows that this kind of nationalist movements are dominated at the moment by narrow-minded nationalist elites. In other words, their elites are nationalist in the old sense of the word, having no clue about globalization and living instead in a time capsule, sometime at the

[165] Andreas Bieler, "Norway: What Future for Social Democracy?", *Global Research*, 11/10/2013 http://www.globalresearch.ca/norway-what-future-for-social-democracy/5353922
[166] Christopher Hope, "Scottish and Welsh nationalists pledge to stop the English leaving EU", *The Telegraph*, 8/2/2015

beginning of the 20th century!

Clearly, therefore, the victims of globalization in Scotland and Northern Ireland pursue narrow nationalist demands, unlike those in Wales, who, ignoring their nationalist elites, voted in favor of Brexit. The same is true about other similar autonomist movements in France, Italy, Belgium, Spain etc. However, such movements could, in fact, secure a real national and economic sovereignty in case they will opt for a Democratic Community of Sovereign Nations, instead of the present NOW — as proposed in the last part of the book. Given that such a Community does not have to consist only of nation-states, all those peoples, who are really fighting for their economic and national sovereignty, could indeed find real self-determination within it. Thus, if a nation-state consists of several nations (as is the case of UK, Spain etc.) it could be replaced in such a democratic community of sovereign nations by a confederation of the nations involved. This way, political and economic sovereignty, as well as economic self-reliance, for each nation separately, could be achieved.

In fact, such an institutional arrangement does not even require the need to create many powerless statelets, as long of course as the peoples with different national identities prefer to live within the same confederal state. In other words, within the context of a democratic community of sovereign nations, we may see the resurrection of confederalism and the replacement of many nation-states with confederations, without the emergence, in the aftermath of such a historic event, of dozens of new statelets — so much desired by the Transnational Elite in its pursuit of "divide and rule" policies.

Chapter 5.

The myth of the multipolar world and the BRICS

Are the BRICS countries sovereign?

The paradoxical myth that we already live in a multipolar world (or, in a milder version, that a multipolar world is emerging) has grown strongly in the last few years. The paradox lies in the fact that this myth is promoted not only by the Transnational Elite, but also by the elites of the countries constituting the supposedly alternative pole, i.e. the elites of the BRICS countries (Brazil, Russia, India, China and South Africa) themselves! But, as I will try to show in this chapter, the BRICS countries not only do not form part of a multi-polar world, but, in reality, most of them are far from sovereign states in any sense of the word.

The Transnational Elite has, of course, every reason to conceal the growing concentration of transnational economic, political, military, and cultural power in its hands, within the process of creating an informal, at present, system of global governance. On the other hand, the BRICS countries, with the exception of Russia and China, (which however are also integrated into the NWO — albeit not fully), are characterized by very little, if any, national sovereignty, and a corresponding degree of transnational sovereignty. One may therefore assume that, far from the BRICS countries constituting part of a multi-polar world — as the Transnational Elite propaganda machine asserts in order to hide its real transnational monopoly of power — in fact, they are very much part of the present unipolar NWO and this is why the Transnational Elite can still implement means of economic warfare, such as sanctions, even on Russia, creating havoc in its economy. And if even Russia does not share any comparable degree of transnational sovereignty to that of the Transnational Elite members, this is true par excellence for countries like China and India, whose control over the transnational political power is marginal, let alone their control over transnational military, media and cultural power, which is almost nil.

In fact, even the BRICS' control of transnational economic sovereignty is marginal, despite the fact that Russia, for the reasons I will examine later, [167] is much less integrated into the NWO of neoliberal globalization than any of the other BRICS countries. Thus, despite the fact that the five BRICS countries account for nearly three billion people (42% of world population), their combined nominal GDP represents only 20% of global GDP [168] and their total capital investment was estimated to be between a minimum 11% of global capital investment [169] and a maximum 20%, [170] indicating that the degree of transnational economic sovereignty of these countries is marginal, if not negligible, in proportion to their huge populations. So, the fact that the purchasing power of aggregate Chinese GDP has now surpassed US levels (as a result of the fact that the US population is only 23% of the Chinese) by no means implies that China is the world's greatest economic power. In other words, economic power is still concentrated in the West (i.e. mainly the G7 countries) from where all major TNCs originate, and where their power and, frequently, their research and development centers, are based.

Also, if we attempt to project the expected transnational power of the Transnational Elite compared to that of China, even if we add Russia in the equation on China's side, it is obvious that the BRICS bloc will never control, in any foreseeable future, a degree of transnational power comparable to that of the Transnational Elite. This implies that if Russia and China really wish to be independent states enjoying national and economic sovereignty, they have to break from the present World Order that is controlled by the Transnational Elite,

---

[167] *Ukraine, The attack on Russia and the Eurasian Union*, (vol. 2 of *The NWO in Action*)
[168] *World Development Indicators 2014*, Table 1
[169] "BRICS establish $100bn bank and currency reserves to cut out Western dominance", RT, 15/7/2014 http://rt.com/business/173008-brics-bank-currency-pool
[170] Adrian Salbuchi, 'Building a BRICS wall', RT, 15/7/2014 http://rt.com/op-edge/172624-brics-putin-arab-spring

as they should never hope of becoming equal members of the Transnational Elite within it.

In fact, both China and India consist of hundreds of millions of starving people and a few hundred billionaires, as well as a proportionately very small, but utterly greedy, middle class. India, for instance is a country where Mercedes saw a 47% surge in sales recently and where its super-rich have long raised eyebrows around the world with their spectacular spending,[171] whereas at the same time nearly half of India's 1.2 billion people have no toilets at home[172] and nearly 2 million children under the age of five die every year from preventable illness as common as diarrhea, and of those who survive, half are stunted owing to a lack of nutrients.[173] Yet, the Indian elite recently decided that the country could afford to have its own space program and even launched the first satellites![174]

The myth of the Chinese superpower

As far as China in particular is concerned, if there is anything on which China begins to resemble the USA it is only in the number of its billionaires! Thus, 10 years ago China had no billionaires whereas now it has more billionaires than any other country except the US.[175] This is not of course at all surprising, if one takes into account the fact that, even according to official statistics on inequality (which may not be particularly reliable given the 'communist' leadership's high sensitivity on the matter), China shows a high and growing inequality,[176] as a result of the neoliberal policies it had to apply within the NWO to which it is fully integrated. Unofficial statistics, meanwhile, by the Southwestern University of Finance and Economics

[171] Jason Burke, "As India's super-rich list explodes, the shopping has only just begun", *The Guardian*, 25/7/2014
[172]"India unveils cheap new village toilets", *BBC News*, 1/9/2014
http://www.bbc.co.uk/news/world-asia-india-29008713
[173] John Pilger, "In India's land of extremes, resistance is on the rise", *The Guardian*, 3/1/2014
[174] Josh Hrala, "India just launched 20 satellites in 26 minutes and made history", *Science Alert*, 22/6/2016 http://www.sciencealert.com/india-just-broke-a-record-by-launching-20-satellites-in-one-mission
[175] "China Billionaires: Sharp Rise In Richest", *Sky News* 11/9/2013
http://news.sky.com/story/1140129/china-billionaires-sharp-rise-in-richest
[176] China reveals income gap statistics after 12 year of silence, RT, 18/1/2013
http://rt.com/business/chin. -income-gap-reveals-288/

and the Institute of Financial Research, put China at the top of an 'inequality' list of 16 countries on the World Bank website.[177]

Needless to add that the emergence of new significant middle classes in China, India and other BRICS countries implies not only the creation of a huge market for the products of TNCs, but also, the spreading of the values and ideas of globalization. Indicative is the fact that the US and UK universities and schools are presently full of students from these new middle classes from countries like China,[178] forming the future elites of globalization to govern the desperate masses in their own countries, according to the dictates of the Transnational Elite, following their brain washing in western universities and schools.

The myth, in particular, of the emerging new economic superpower in China is based on crude statistical indicators, such as GDP and the concentration of industrial and trade power within that country. But such indicators ignore the huge size of its population, and the fact that it is basically the TNCs which created the alleged economic miracle, including the post-Mao industrial and trade power. Thus, taking into account relative population sizes, the per capita GNP of China and India is still 11% and 3.5% respectively of that of the USA,[179] despite the fact that the celebrated growth rates achieved by both countries in the last decade were over six times higher in China and more than four times higher in India, than in the USA.[180] In other words, the so-called economic 'miracles' of globalization (China, India etc.) are, in fact, the myths of globalization, as their rapid growth and industrialization, in the last 35 years or so, simply mirrors the de-growth and de-industrialization of the West. It was from the West that many TNCs moved to China and India to maximize their profits, exploiting the huge comparative advantage of these countries in terms of cheap production cost (mainly cheap — and usually skilled — labor), as well as in terms of markets free of significant social controls, low taxes, and other facilities offered to investors, particularly in the

---

[177] Data based on Gini coefficients. ibid.
[178] James Pickford and Helen Warrell, "Wealthy Chinese want British education for their children", *Financial Times*, 22/1/2014; see, also, Helen Warrell, "Chinese parents scramble to send children to top British schools", *Financial Times*, 21/3/2014
[179] World Bank, *World Development Indicators 2014*, Table 1
[180] ibid. Table 4

'special economic zones' of slave labor emerging lately in countries like China. Similarly, the allegation recently repeated by Obama of the drastic reduction of world poverty as a result of globalization can also be shown to be a statistical myth. The supposed "elimination" of poverty is almost exclusively due to the fact that the Chinese "communist" leadership removed from the list of the poor more than 400 million Chinese in the period 1981-2001, simply because they became proud earners of US$ 1 dollar a day, thus decreasing with one stroke of the pen the percentage of absolutely poor in China by two-thirds.[181]

Furthermore, the foreign dependence of China has not been reduced by the much-advertised outflow of some Chinese capital abroad lately. Thus, in his annual government work report, Premier Li Keqiang noted that inward foreign direct investment ($120bn) exceeded China's own outward investment ($103bn) in 2014.[182] This belied earlier expectations of a supposed 'historic shift', according to which China was becoming a net exporter of capital.[183] In the event, this was the effect of a boom in the export of capital (to buy mainly real estate abroad) and of a relative fall in the rapidly growing foreign investment flow. The latter simply marked a slowing down in the boom in foreign investment that began in 2001 when China was fully integrated into the NWO, through joining the WTO and offering huge comparative advantages to TNCs in the form of abundant cheap labor, tax concessions etc.

Therefore, China, despite (or rather because) of the rapid marketization of the economy following Mao's death, is still an economy dependent on exports and investment rather than on domestic consumption, as is the case with advanced market economies.[184] This is why Zhang Gaoli, the vice-premier and a member of the politburo, stressed at the 2015 China Development Forum (an annual meeting of

[181] World Bank, *World development indicators* 2005, Table 2.5a. See Takis Fotopoulos, The "elimination of poverty", The International Journal of INCLUSIVE DEMOCRACY, vol.4, no.1, (January 2008) http://www.inclusivedemocracy.org/journal/vol4/vol4_no1_takis_poverty.htm
[182] Tom Mitchell, "For all the sound and fury, China depends on foreign forces", *Financial Times*, 8/3/2015
[183] Jamil Anderlini, "China's outbound investment set to eclipse inbound for first time", *Financial Times*, 22/10/2014
[184] Shawn Donnan, "What the Fed says about China behind closed doors", *Financial Times*, 9/3/2015

top Chinese officials, international business people and policy intellectuals), that the old growth model "featuring high input, high energy consumption and over-dependence on external demand is no longer sustainable."[185]

As for the supposedly huge trade power of China, although this is prima facie true, many, if not most, of its high technology exports and imports are due to the activities of foreign TNCs. This means that the moment the country decides to impose drastic social controls on markets to reduce their 'freedom' to move capital and commodities in and out of their country, (e.g. in order to protect local labor or the environment from the wild exploitation of TNCs), the Chinese 'miracle' could end overnight. And, in fact, there are plenty of causes of social unrest founded on the way this economic miracle was created, i.e. the sheer exploitation of cheap labor and the corresponding wild exploitation of the environment, which has already been leading to something approaching an ecological catastrophe,[186] and which can be mainly attributed to the incompatibility of sustainable development with neoliberal globalization.[187] No wonder both working class labor activism[188] and middle class environmental activism[189] have been thriving lately in China.

I do not refer of course to the recent Hong Kong (HK) 'umbrella revolution', where the middle class 'Facebook youth' demonstrated for 'democracy' and 'freedom'. This 'revolution' was irrelevant to the above activism that was based on genuine demands by the victims of globalization. No need to add that the HK demands were the same demands raised in every color 'revolution' engineered by the Transnational Elite in general and Soros in particular — from Syria

---

[185] Martin Wolf, "China will struggle to keep its momentum", *Financial Times*, 7/4/2015

[186] Joseph Kahn & Jim Yardley, «As China Roars, Pollution Reaches Deadly Extremes, *New York Times* (26/8/2007)
http://www.nytimes.com/2007/08/26/world/asia/26china.html

[187] See for a theoretical explanation of the eco-catastrophic growth in China, Takis Fotopoulos, "Is sustainable development compatible with present globalisation? The Chinese Case", *The International Journal of INCLUSIVE DEMOCRACY*, Vol. 4, No. 4 (October 2008)
http://www.inclusivedemocracy.org/journal/vol4/vol4_no4_takis_chinese_case.htm#_edn16

[188] See e.g. on the Walmart dispute, Tom Mitchell and Demetri Sevastopulo, "China labour activism: crossing the line", *Financial Times*, 7/5/2014

[189] See e.g. Kathrin Hille, "China: Citizens united", *Financial Times*, 29/7/2013;

and the other Arab 'spring' countries up to Ukraine! No wonder that the well-known neocon Zionist war criminal Paul Wolfowitz, considered one of the ideological fathers of the slaughtering of Iraq, (carried out by the war criminals Tony Blair and George W. Bush), was seen in HK with media tycoon Jimmy Lai Chee-ying, in June 2014, while according to the HK populist newspaper *EastWeek*, the National Endowment for Democracy (NED) and its two subsidiaries had been offering training and funding to organizations in Hong Kong.[190] It should not be surprising if we later learn that the protagonists of the umbrella revolution were trained and funded by the same good NGOs, which have been involved in almost all color revolutions of the NWO!

Furthermore, regarding the famous huge financial power of China, this is another bubble of globalization. Although it is true that China's holdings of foreign exchange reserves are gigantic amounting to $4tn in March 2014,[191] yet, its elite cannot even think of using them against the Transnational Elite as, at the moment it attempts to dump these assets, it will be China that will suffer an economic catastrophe, whereas the US can easily find other buyers, as long as the US dollar continues to be generally acceptable as a reserve currency. This fact, as the same study by Wolf & Pilling stressed, "gives America exceptional influence over the shape of global finance and details of global regulation," for many years to come.[192]

Also, one can draw similar conclusions with regards to the other dimensions of transnational economic power, e.g. China's technological power. As Wolf & Pilling pointed out in their study, a clear indication that China remains well behind is that "economy wide average productivity remains a fifth of US levels."[193] Even more important is the absence of world-leading Chinese technology companies, with the principal exception of Huawei, whereas the US by comparison, hosts a significant number of world-leading companies.

---

[190] Kahon Chan,"Office opposes foreign interference in HK", *CHINA DAILY*, 20/6/2014 http://www.chinadailyasia.com/hknews/2014-06/20/content_15142785.html
[191] Martin Wolf and David Pilling, "China: On top of the world", *Financial Times*, 2/5/2014
[192] ibid.
[193] ibid

Yet, the globalist 'Left' reproduces the disorienting propaganda of Chinese 'communists' that "China is advancing to global economic superiority by borrowing and innovating the most advanced methods of production."[194] However, apart from the fact that there are growing signs about a Chinese bubble ready to burst,[195] it is clear that, for this kind of 'Left', there is no need for any country to break with the NWO of neoliberal globalization and help in the creation of a new Democratic Community of sovereign nations, as a first step towards social liberation. Therefore, no need either for Russia and China to break from the NWO and create an economy, which belongs mainly to the victims of globalization — rather than, as at present, to the minorities who are the beneficiaries of it. All the Left has to do, instead, according to globalist 'Left', is to adopt "China's model of growth and stability" and wait for the 'intra-capitalist rivalries' — with the help of 'Left' governments of the kind Brazil and Argentina saw recently (before they were overthrown by the Transnational Elite) — to lead to the overthrow of capitalism, sometime in the next millennium!

Finally, China's global military and political power is consistent with its real global economic power. In other words, China is a major regional power and is seen as such by the Transnational Elite, which has indeed been encircling China, but only because of its need to protect its own regional interests in any conflict between China and its regional allies and, particularly, Japan. In other words, the Transnational Elite's (mainly the US elite's) attempts at encirclement are more about containing regional squabbles than about any serious concern arising from a supposed Chinese threat to the hegemony of the Transnational Elite. Naturally, the Transnational Elite is fully aware of the fact that China by itself cannot even potentially challenge the Transnational Elite's global military and political power, particularly so when its military power is not even comparable to that of Russia.

However, although China by itself does not pose any serious threat to the NWO, in case China and Russia were to join together to question the Transnational Elite's hegemony, then, this could be the

---

[194] Prof. James Petras, "China's Pivot to World Markets, Washington's Pivot to World Wars", *Global Research,* 20/8/2016 http://www.globalresearch.ca/chinas-pivot-to-world-markets-washingtons-pivot-to-world-wars/5541802
[195] see e.g. the article of Ed Conway, economics editor of Sky News, "China's economy is a slow-motion car crash", *The Times,* 30/9/2016

first step in the creation of an alternative pole to the NWO, as we shall see in Ch.11. In fact, such a situation seems developing at the moment both at the military[196] and the economic[197] fronts — although neither China, not even Russia are challenging yet globalization as such, which is a precondition for the creation of an alternative pole to the NWO. Yet, the fact that this scenario cannot be ruled out at the moment is enough reason for the Transnational Elite to exclude both countries from the negotiations about global governance taking place at the moment within the framework of TPP and TTIP.

The BRICS cannot be an alternative pole to the NWO

Clearly, as long as the BRICS countries, as a result of their very low degree of economic self-reliance, depend on the activities of TNCs for the bulk of their growth (financial capital and investment capital, trade) and the development of their technology, they can never be equal members of the Transnational Elite, let alone members of a rival pole. At present, the BRICS countries not only don't form part of a multi-polar world, but in reality are far from sovereign states in any sense of the word. In other words, if their real goal was indeed the creation of an alternative pole of sovereign nation-states, they should have planned at the outset to break their direct dependence on the globalized capitalist market economy, cutting their ties with global institutions controlled by the Transnational Elite (WTO, IMF, WB etc.), and moving towards an economic union of self-reliant nation-states, so that they could regain their sovereignty.

But, as the BRICS economies, far from pursuing such goals, emphasize instead the importance of further opening and liberalizing their markets, according to WTO rules — as the Chinese and Russian elites did, for instance, in the 2014 St Petersburg International Economic Forum [198] and repeated the same pledge this year — inevitably, they can only play a supplementary role to the NWO and its institutions. Furthermore, given that, without economic sovereignty

---

[196] The recent signs of a growing military rapprochement between China and Russia could potentially challenge US military hegemony, see e.g. Roman Kosarev, 'Russia & China military posturing against unfriendly Western countries' RT, 13/9/2016, https://www.rt.com/op-edge/359193-russia-china-military-drills/

[197] Dmitry Babich, "Unwise Obama policy pushes China and Russia closer together", RT, 24/6/2016, https://www.rt.com/op-edge/348210-china-putin-visit-russia-xi/

[198] St Petersburg International Economic Forum, 23/5/2014 http://eng.kremlin.ru/news/7230

political sovereignty is impossible, their national sovereignty will always be subservient to the will of the Transnational Elite.

A very recent confirmation of the above considerations was the agreement just signed between China and the Transnational Elite's protectorate in Ukraine to restart production of the world's largest aircraft.[199] The motive behind the agreement was purely commercial but given that Russia is in a near-war situation with Ukraine, surely this was not an act of an ally in building an alternative pole to the NWO!

Theoretically, the only possible exception among BRICS countries could be Brazil, whose economy is more oriented towards the domestic market than any other BRICS country, including Russia, consequently inviting the corresponding reprimand from the World Bank.[200] However, the fact that Brazil does adopt all the policies for opening and liberalizing markets imposed by the institutions of the NWO (WTO, IMF etc.) indicates that this peculiar — for an integrated country — characteristic is more the result of a slow process of integration into the NWO rather than of any deliberate policy for self-reliance and breaking from it! Furthermore, the very recent replacement of the present regime by an overtly neoliberal one, following the 'palace coup' against its globalist 'Left' President Dilma Rousseff, makes the full integration of Brazil into the NWO an almost certainty.

Again, it is only Russia that lately has adopted deliberate self-reliance policies, albeit as a reaction to the sanctions imposed on the country by the Transnational Elite.[201] This means that any future rapprochement between Russia and the Transnational Elite could well lead to the end of such policies, as happens in Iran at the moment, following its own rapprochement with the West, with the radicals turning only against American TNCs but not against those coming from the EU![202] However, such a rapprochement with Russia is

---

[199] Giant AN-225 plane deal: What China & Ukraine get out of it?, RT, 2/9/2016
https://www.rt.com/op-edge/358071-ukraine-china-plane-ussr/
[200] Otaviano Canuto et al. "The cost of Brazil's closed economy", *Financial Times,* 14/1/2015
[201]"Russia's Putin calls for Russians to be self-reliant", *BBC News,* 4/12/2014
http://www.bbc.co.uk/news/world-europe-30322198
[202] Mario Anzuoni, "Iran bans US consumer goods", 6/11/2015
https://www.rt.com/business/321054-iran-us-consumer-goods-ban/

impossible unless the latter is recognized by the Transnational Elite as an equal — and not a subordinate — member of it. Particularly so when at the moment the gap between the two sides is, in fact, growing and the deterioration could become critical in case the neocon candidate, Hillary Clinton, is elected as the next US President. In my view, Russia will eventually have no other option, in order to maintain its sovereignty, but to break with the NWO and proceed instead to the creation of a real alternative pole around the Eurasian Union that potentially could include China, Iran and even Turkey itself!

The above conclusion that BRICS countries, in effect, play a supplementary role to the NWO and its institutions, is confirmed anyway by the fact that, despite the Transnational Elite's pretense to parity with the BRICS countries, Russia's ostracism from the closed club of Transnational Elite's members is taken for granted. Thus, none of the BRICS countries has been invited to the closed club of G7, which plans all strategic world decisions at the economic and political levels — apart of course from Russia which, however, was promptly thrown out as soon as it expressed its objection to becoming a subordinate member, as the other members effectively demanded. The consequence of this 'non-cooperation' by Russia was that the Transnational Elite's plans to intensify Russia's encirclement were put into action. Furthermore, no BRICS member has been invited to the closed club preparing world governance for the future, through such treaties as the Transatlantic Trade and Investment Partnership (TTIP) or its Asian cousin (TPP). The former includes all the Transnational Elite members (EU and USA), while the latter includes almost half of the Transnational Elite members (USA, Japan and Canada) and two associate members of it (Australia, New Zealand), as well as some protectorates of the Transnational Elite (Chile, Mexico, Malaysia, Peru, Brunei, Singapore and Vietnam). Russia and China have explicitly been excluded from both of them, for the reasons I mentioned above.

All this means, also, that the new international institutions created by the 2014 BRICS summit will inevitably act as *complementary* rather than as *alternative* institutions to the NWO controlled by the Transnational Elite. It is indicative that even the new Chinese-led Asian Infrastructure Investment Bank, (AIIB) did not develop as a substitute, let alone as an alternative to the World Bank, given that, apart from thirty Asian countries which have signed up as founding members of the AIIB, several G7 countries namely, Britain, Germany,

France and Italy have also joined it.[203] In other words, this new Bank, far from functioning as an alternative world institution, is very much a new NWO institution, simply competing for customers with the US-led World Bank, or, similarly, the EU-led European Investment Bank! It should be noted that even the BRICs Development Bank, (now called the New Development Bank, NDB) set up by Brazil, Russia, India, China and South Africa, has not shown any signs so far that it aspires to function as a real alternative to the above NWO Banks. Far from it, as shown by the fact that the Chinese Premier Li Keqiang himself called the opening of the NDB a "helpful supplement to the global financial system," as well as an important step forward in cooperation among BRICS countries.[204] It should be noted that the NDB is headquartered in China, which plays a de facto leading role with respect to the new Development Bank.

An alternative economic and political union would consist instead of sovereign nations operating on the basis of new principles based on complementarity and mutual help within the framework of collective self-sufficiency. This framework would allow for the fundamental right of societies to impose social controls upon markets for the sake of protecting labor and the environment (i.e. societies themselves) from markets. In fact, it is this potential of the Eurasian Union to play a really alternative role to the present NWO that could also explain, at least partly, why Russia under Putin has been targeted by the entire Transnational Elite. This, notwithstanding the supposed political differences between the US and the European part of the Transnational elite on Russia. In fact, however, such differences are just tactical differences, as all members of the Transnational elite agree on the strategic aim that Russia has to be fully integrated into the NWO, as a subordinate member of the Transnational Elite (e.g. in the convenient G7+1 scheme). In other words, their differences refer only to the best tactics to achieve this aim — through economic violence (EU), or through military violence accompanying economic violence (US). But never the strategic aim itself.

---

[203] Heather Stewart, "China builds rival to US financial power", *The Guardian*, 11/4/2015
[204] "NDB president says to work with AIIB", China.org.Cn, 24/7/2015, http://www.china.org.cn/business/2015-07/24/content_36136846.htm

In view of the above, the Transnational Elite's attack on Ukraine was clearly an attack against, not just Russia, but principally the Eurasian Union as a whole.[205]

Towards the end of the BRICS 'miracle'?

A combination of economic and political developments with economic implications, have led lately to serious doubts, even among globalist newspapers, about the BRICS. Some of these events, particularly those regarding the present economic problems of Russia and Brazil, were clearly induced by the Transnational Elite. Thus, Russia's present recession was obviously instigated by the economic war (involving the oil weapon as well economic sanctions) launched by the Transnational Elite on Russia for having the temerity to resist the Transnational Elite coup in Ukraine.[206] Similarly, Brazil's impeachment of the Leftist President Dilma Rousseff seems to have been instigated by the US "to try and get a Brazilian government in power that is more like the governments prior to the Workers' Party, that is, more subordinate to their interests."[207] No wonder the first act of the new Administration was to announce a multibillion dollar privatization plan![208]

These developments have led the media flagship of 'Left' globalization to write the BRICS's obituary: "the fashionable view, popular among western governments and businesses [is], that the BRICS bubble has burst. Members of the exclusive BRICS club of leading developing countries are failing to justify predictions that, separately and together, they will dominate the 21st century world, or so the argument goes."[209] Similarly, an earlier *Observer* editorial stressed that:

> Brazil, which saw its credit rating downgraded to junk last week, is only the latest BRICS economy to crumble in the face of a strong dollar, a global trade slowdown and the prospect of

---

[205] See *The NWO in Action* vol 2 (Ukraine: The Attack on Russia and the Eurasian Union)

[206] ibid.

[207] see interview with Mark Weisbrot, co-director of the Centre for Economic and Policy Research, RT, 14/5/2016, https://www.rt.com/op-edge/343046-brazil-wikileaks-president-temer/

[208] "Brazil starts privatization plan to revive economy", RT, 14/9/2016 https://www.rt.com/business/359285-brasil-privatization-plan-economy/

[209] Simon Tisdall. "Has the Brics idea come tumbling down?", *The Guardian*, 28/3/2016

higher US interest rates. Russia is already in recession; many economists believe China is heading towards a 'hard landing'; and South Africa, which managed to append itself to the emerging-markets club in 2010, is on the brink of recession.[210]

It seems therefore that the only 'miracle' still surviving among the BRICS countries (but only a matter of time before it proves to be another mirage!) is India. That is, a country that owes much of its 'success' to the fact that its high growth rates are a direct result of the survival-wages paradise it offers to TNCs, as a result of the horrible working conditions and mass unemployment/underemployment prevailing in the country. This fact does not of course bother the *Financial Times*, which recently described India as "the country (which) has shifted from socialism with restricted entry to capitalism without exit."[211] Yet, even if some had any illusions on whether the profit-maximizing elite of India would ever consider to question its new masters, they should have been dissolved by now. Particularly so when it was very recently announced that the "US Senate approved the bill about strategic partnership between the United States and India in the field of security. The agreement makes India a NATO ally similarly to the agreement with Israel!"[212] No wonder China now admits that "BRICS faces the risk of retrogressive, rather than progressive, cooperation because of new, intricate circumstances."[213]

Therefore, irrespective of whether the economic problems of the BRICS countries are induced by the Transnational Elite or not, the question is how a country can today restore or maintain its national sovereignty in the present unipolar world environment, which is controlled by the NWO and the Transnational Elite that runs it. This book's conclusion is that only the creation of an economic and political union of sovereign Nations, at about the same level of development, which would be prepared to break with the NWO, could

---

[210] The Observer, "As the Brics collapse and the south staggers, the dollar is suddenly looking almighty again", *Observer*, 13/9/2015; see, also, Jayati Ghosh, "Has growth in the developing world hit a Bric wall? *Guardian*, 24/8/2015
[211] Martin Wolf, "India is now the world's fastest-growing large economy", *Financial Times*, 1/5/2016
[212] Lyuba Lulko, "Russia unexpectedly loses India and Vietnam", *Pravda.ru*, 24/5/2016 http://www.pravdareport.com/world/asia/24-05-2016/134523-india_vietnam_russia-0/
[213] Pepe Escobar, "What is BRICS member India really up to?", RT, 15/9/2016 https://www.rt.com/op-e dge/359428-brics-member-india-escobar/

lead to the creation of a real multi-polar world. Then, a broader economic and political union of peoples worldwide resisting today's unipolar NWO would be in a position to create the conditions to transcend the present downward homogenization (of working and environmental conditions) and lay, instead, the foundations for a different, truly self-managed world society, as we shall see in the last part of this volume.

Chapter 6.

The rise of the globalist 'Left' in the NWO and its myths

Is the traditional Left-Right division meaningful today?

As I hope it is evident from the analysis so far, the rise of the globalization era had very important implications not only at the economic level but also at the political and the cultural levels. In this and the next two chapters, I will concentrate on the effects of globalization on the Left and the traditional political division between Left and Right. It will be shown that the emergence of globalization was associated with the rise of a new kind of Left, what I call the globalist 'Left', which in effect is a hybrid of what used to be called the antisystemic Left with the reformist one. In fact, the emergence of the globalist Left has so effectively blurred the traditional Left-Right division, with supposedly 'Right' political movements and parties adopting policies which traditionally were landmarks of the Left and vice versa, that one may question whether this division is meaningful anymore.

A crucial issue which has clearly shown the blurring of the Left-Right division is the Left's stand on the EU. As I will try to show, the British Left — and the EU Left in general — has now become much more pro-EU than ever before. This, despite the fact that the EU in the last quarter of a century or so excelled at political/military violence abroad (see e.g. its role on the NATO attacks against Yugoslavia and Libya) and economic violence at home (e.g. Greece). It is therefore clear that it is not the EU that has moved towards the Left, but, instead, it is the Left, which has moved towards the EU, as a result of its full integration into the NWO of neoliberal globalization.

However, as this is a general phenomenon, referring not just to the European Left but to the world Left in general, which as a rule has been integrated into the NWO, one could argue that unless we redefine the Left, as this book attempts to do, the traditional Left has no reason for existence and the historical Left-Right division is today redundant.

Antisystemic vs. reformist Left and the globalist 'Left'

The traditional divide within the Left has always been the division between the anti-systemic and the reformist Left. The former (mainly of Marxist origin), has been characterized by a strategy and tactics based on the aim of overthrowing the capitalist system and therefore the World Order as a whole, whereas the latter's strategy and tactics were based on the aim of reforming, or improving, the existing system, even though their past rhetoric sometimes made also reference to the ultimate aim of the replacement of the capitalist system and its World Order — an aim that today's reformist Left has completely 'forgotten'.

However, this traditional (as well as fundamental) division within the Left was blurred in the globalization era with the emergence of what we may call the globalist 'Left', which, although it mainly belongs to the reformist Left, paradoxically, also includes most of the old anti-systemic Left. This is the Left, which, explicitly or implicitly, takes globalization and its institutions — such as the EU, the WTO, the IMF and the World Bank — for granted. In fact, this kind of 'Left' rarely — if ever — mentions globalization and prefers to talk about its symptoms, such as austerity, which it attributes to bad policies! However, as traditionally the Left's main aim was to question the status quo, one can hardly call a party or political organization, which takes for granted the entire status quo, as Left. Particularly so if what is taken for granted is not just the capitalist system, (as the reformist Left has always done), but also the NWO institutions, which even neo-nationalist parties today question. Yet, as the rationale of the anti-systemic Left that belongs to the globalist Left is very different from the rationale of the reformist part of the globalist Left, I will examine the two cases separately.

Thus, those of Marxists, anarchists and other anti-systemic theorists, who effectively take globalization for granted, do so not because they do not believe anymore in the need to overthrow capitalism itself — as those belonging to the reformist part of the globalist 'Left' do (e.g. SYRIZA, Podemos, socialdemocratic parties e.tc.) — but, instead, because they believe that the NWO of neoliberal globalization will be overthrown anyway together with capitalism, or, alternatively, because they implicitly believe that globalization is a necessary stage in the historical process leading to a communist society. Therefore, as a result of their theoretical failure to understand the real significance of globalization — they do not question globalization as such, adopting instead a sort of pseudo-maximalist stand that rejects any transitional strategies in achieving this ultimate aim.

In effect, such anti-systemic writers fail to grasp the fact that globalization is, in fact, a form of occupation, in which economic, political, ideological and cultural means are used, so that the economic and political power of the Transnational Elites and the associated local elites is imposed on the populations. This means that social liberation is impossible unless peoples, first, liberate themselves from this form of occupation. This was also the case in similar periods of military occupation (e.g. during the Second World War), or of colonial occupation before it, when peoples, first, united to liberate themselves from the military or colonial yoke and then to sort out the 'social issue', i.e. the form society should take (state socialist, an Inclusive Democracy and so on). Similarly, today, peoples should first recover their right of self-determination as a people (i.e. their national and economic sovereignty which today has been phased out as we saw in the precious chapters) and then fight for the form of society they wish to have. Unfortunately, globalist anti-systemic writers and activists do not grasp these distinctions, and live in various time capsules ('1917', '1936' and so on) waiting for the revolution, which, in fact, will never come, unless people regain their sovereignty first. At the same time, the victims of globalization all over the world, who cannot afford to theorize endlessly, like their supposed natural leaders in the 'Left', abandon it in droves and join neo-nationalist movements.

Needless to add that I do not refer here to the many varieties of 'post-Marxists', 'post anarchists' and the likes — who, in fact, do not belong to the anti-systemic Left at all — and those in the service of the Soroses of this world, who pretend to be Marxists, anarchists and libertarians of various kinds in order to infiltrate (especially in the internet) anti-systemic movements. I refer instead to orthodox communists or anti-imperialists, for whom globalization is just the latest phase of capitalism (i.e. its monopoly phase) with its industrial cartels or giant monopolies, as described by Lenin's theory of *imperialism*,[214] or, alternatively, in Sweezy & Baran's *Monopoly Capital*.[215] However, the common characteristic of these two major works is that they both have been written before the emergence of neoliberal globalization (i.e. before the late 1970s or so) and therefore are based on the assumptions of nation-states and national capital — instead of the present NWO run by the Transnational Elite, while the economic and national sovereignty of states is being phased out. In other words, this sort of globalist 'Left' is not in a position to analyze the economic processes that were set in motion in the last four decades or so, when he Transnational Elite, which began flourishing in the context of the internationalization of the market economy process, embarked in a double effort:

a) To shrink the public sector's economic role everywhere for the benefit of a vastly expanding private sector — a process that inevitably meant a significant expansion of open unemployment, as well as a huge rise of various forms of disguised unemployment: from part-time and occasional work to zero hours contracts;

b) To open and deregulate markets in order to further enhance the globalization process but also to reduce open unemployment, which was politically unacceptable, and convert it into massive low-paid employment .

Even worse are those in the globalist 'Left' who attempt to 'modernize' the classical Marxist theory by extending it to cover the mass expansion of financial capital and 'financialization'.[216] As it is well known, the new institutional framework of globalization, (i.e. the open and liberalized markets), created the preconditions for a mass expansion of financial capital in the North, following its de-industrialization — a fact which played a crucial role for the outbreak of the financial crisis of 2007-8.[217]

---

[214] Lenin, *Imperialism, the Highest Stage of Capitalism* (1917)

[215] Paul Sweezy & Paul Baran, *Monopoly Capital* (Monthly Review Press, 1966)

[216] See e.g. Costas Lapavitsas, "The era of financialization", *Dollars & Sense*, 15/4/2014 http://www.dollarsandsense.org/archives/2014/0414lapavitsas.html

[217] Takis Fotopoulos, "The myths about the economic crisis, the reformist Left and economic democracy", *The International Journal of INCLUSIVE DEMOCRACY*,

However, the analysis of the crisis in terms of financialization does not trace the financial crisis to its main cause, i.e. the opening and deregulation of capital markets as a result of globalization. Instead, they either ignore globalization, or simply try to fit it into the Procrustean bed of the old Marxist theory, as developed by Lenin and others, before its advent. As a result, the financialization analyses of the crisis were dismal failures compared to the major Marxist works. This was inevitable when it is taken into account that these new 'Marxist' works were written after the advent of globalization. This clearly shows the theoretical bankruptcy of the modern Marxist Left — apart from a few enlightened exceptions, like Leslie Sklair we shall see below — which, instead of attempting to analyze (as Marx and Lenin would surely have done), the new reality of transnational capitalism, and the phasing out of the nation-state, they just ignore it!

On the other end, the reformist 'Left' had its own reasons to ignore globalization and invent various theories, (even conspiracy theories sometimes!) so that they could justify their aim of 'changing the system from within', an aim which is at present deceitful. This is because, following the historic failure of social democracy to achieve permanent social change, most of its social 'conquests' have by now been reversed or converted into the new mix of 'social-liberalism', which is a clear contradiction in terms. No wonder that most cadres in the reformist 'Left' today (e.g. SYRIZA, Podemos etc.) consist mostly of ex-activists involved in the globalist Left movements and now turned into professional politicians, who are using reformism as a kind of ideology, as a means to come into power — effectively, (if not deliberately as in the case of SYRIZA) — by deceiving the victims of globalization to the effect that drastic social changes is possible even within the framework of the NWO!

From the antisystemic movement against globalization to the World Social Forum

However, it should not be forgotten that the anti-globalization movement has not always been a reformist movement. Instead, the strong anti-globalization movement that developed in the late 1990s,

on both sides of the Atlantic, was largely an anti-systemic movement
that was crushed by the combination of state violence (Seattle, Genoa
etc.) and the systematic effort of the globalist Left to undermine it.
This was particularly the case of the reformist part of it, which
developed at the time, with indirect support of the mass media
controlled by the Transnational Elite.

The role of globalist 'Left' was crucial in eventually managing to
convert the anti-globalization movement, from an anti-systemic
movement into a reformist one.[218] The 2001 World Social Forum
(WSF) in Porto Alegre played an important role in this process.
According to the new approach adopted by the anti-globalization
movement, as expressed by the WSF, the globalist institutions
themselves were not to be blamed but, instead, their malfunctioning.
Therefore, all that was needed was a reform of the institutions.
Needless to add that the reformist antiglobalization movement that
emerged at the time, which effectively buried the antisystemic trends
within the antiglobalization movement, was promoted by the reformist
activist organization ATTAC and *Le Monde Diplomatique*, various
NGOs , trade unionists and parliamentarians, and of course the
globalist 'Left' that emerged at the time, with Noam Chomsky (who
has now embraced Varoufakis' Diem 25 for the reform of the EU,
from within),[219] playing a leading role. In fact, Chomsky stressed in
Porto Alegre the following — 'prophetically', as it happened, in view
of what followed a few years afterwards with the wars launched by the
Transnational Elite on Iraq, Afghanistan, Libya and Syria for the
"protection of human rights":

> The World Social Forum offers opportunities of unparalleled
> importance to bring together popular forces from many and
> varied constituencies from the richer and poor countries alike,
> to develop constructive alternatives that will defend the
> overwhelming majority of the world's population from the
> attack on fundamental human rights, and to move on to break

[218] See for an analysis of the forces behind the antisystemic and the reformist sides of
the early anti-globalization movement Takis Fotopoulos, "Globalisation, the
reformist Left and the Anti-Globalisation 'Movement' ", *DEMOCRACY & NATURE:
The International Journal of INCLUSIVE DEMOCRACY*, vol.7, no.2 (July 2001)
http://www.democracynature.org/vol7/takis_globalisation.htm
[219] See YANIS VAROUFAKIS | NOAM CHOMSKY, NYPL, 26/4/2016
https://www.youtube.com/watch?v=szIGZVrSAyc

down illegitimate power concentrations and extend the domains of justice and freedom.[220]

The reformist nature of the WSF was aptly summed up by Eric Toussaint, president of the Committee for the cancellation of Third World debt and participant of the WSF in Porto Alegre, who raised the obviously disorienting question: "is it necessary to "abolish" the World Bank, the IMF and the WTO or can they be reformed? Should we fight in the countries of the periphery for the suspension of the payment of the debt or rely on negotiations without recourse to this measure?"[221]

No wonder that the inevitable result of the combined efforts of all those forces in the reformist 'Left' was the demise of the entire anti-systemic movement against globalization, to the great delight of Transnational Corporations, which were obviously behind this huge campaign, through their NGOs and various foundations funding it — the CIA-related Ford Foundation being the most prominent among them).[222] It is also very interesting to note that exactly the same forces and people (with the addition of a new generation of 'leftists' of the Varoufakis kind) also dominate the systemic propaganda today (under a 'Left' cover always) to condemn as 'fascists' or 'racists' the supporters of the neo-nationalist movements, who took the next obvious step — which the reformist 'Left' tried at all cost to avoid — and demand the abolition of globalist institutions like the EU.

The main difference between the globalist Left and the anti-systemic movement against globalization, which was not explicit at the time but became evident later on, concerned the very object of social struggle. Thus, for the anti-systemic movement against globalization, the cause of the growing concentration of economic power in a few hands is globalization itself, that has led to the present unprecedented inequality, which on the basis of the trends prevailing a year ago, was

---

[220] Text especially written for the Forum launching in Porto Alegre and reproduced on the newspaper *Folha de S.Paulo* (10/09/2000)].
[221] Eric Toussaint, *Another world is possible* (WSF: Porto Alegre, 23/02/2001)
[222] Prof. Michel Chossudovsky," Rockefeller, Ford Foundations Behind World Social Forum (WSF). The Corporate Funding of Social Activism *Global Research*, 11/8/2016 http://www.globalresearch.ca/rockefeller-ford-foundations-behind-world-social-forum-wsf-the-corporate-funding-of-social-activism/5540552

projected to lead to the present stage where 1% of the population owns more wealth than the other 99%.[223]

Furthermore, globalization, as we saw above, in a capitalist market economy can only be neoliberal. That means that neoliberalism, contrary to the mythology of the globalist 'Left', is neither a 'doctrine,' nor the 'bad' policy of some baddies controlling transnational institutions like the EU — as SYRIZA, Podemos, Chomsky, Varoufakis et al. assert in something increasingly looking as a systematic effort to disorient working people about the real aims of the struggle. No wonder that several leading cadres of SYRIZA, including his leader Tsipras, have actually participated in the globalist Left, in the form of the World Social Forum, which was the main organ used at the time to undermine the anti-systemic movement against globalization! For the globalist 'Left' today, as we shall see next, the cause of the present impoverishment of the victims of globalization is not globalization itself but, instead, austerity policies — which are of course only a symptom of globalization, not its cause.

Needless to add that the globalist 'Left' is dominant today within the Left as a whole — a fact, which, in my opinion, is a crucial factor in explaining Left's political demise, as it clearly does not express anymore the needs and aspirations of the working people, who used to be its main supporters. No wonder therefore that some (supposedly Keynesian and 'progressive') economists, such as Thomas Piketty and, even worse, Yanis Varoufakis have become economics 'stars', as a result of their heavy promotion by the mass media of the Transnational Elite. The main characteristic both these stars' share is their utter globalism, i.e. their full support for the NWO of neoliberal globalization.

Thus, Piketty has been massively promoted by the Transnational Elite media, like the *Financial Times,* as a kind of "new Marx" fighting against inequality. In fact, he is an ardent supporter of globalization and therefore a prominent member of the globalist Left, explicitly stating that "if we don't find a way to convince people that everybody can gain from globalization the risk is that a growing faction of the population will turn away from it, against

---

[223] Larry Elliott, "Half global wealth held by the 1%," *The Guardian* (19/01/2015).

globalization."[224] Then, in another interview,[225] which he gave to the leader of Podemos, he went further and revealed himself as a genuine member of the globalist 'Left' aiming, like SYRIZA and Podemos which he strongly praised, to reform EU from within, through its 'democratization'. Needless to add that he never mentioned the role of TNCs and of globalization itself with respect to the growing inequality and concentration of power — a strong indication that he is a laureate in waiting for the Nobel prize in economics (following his mass promotion by the mass media of the Transnational Elite), so that he can join the other 'progressive' (systemic) economists, such as Paul Krugman, Joseph Stiglitz and the likes!

Yet, at least, Piketty, as far as I know, did not have the effrontery to call himself a 'Marxist,' unlike, Yanis Varoufakis, the new 'pop star' of economics and ex Tsar of the Greek economy, who was in charge of the crucial negotiations with the Transnational Elite and calls himself a "libertarian Marxist." He was replaced since the summer 2015, following the total sell-out of SYRIZA to the elites, by another 'caviar Leftist' and self-declared Marxist, Euclid Tsakalotos, with an even more servile attitude — if this is possible! — towards the EU, who has presided over the most catastrophic policies ever imposed on Greece by the Transnational Elite. In fact, Varoufakis' theory and practice has nothing to do with either Marxist or left libertarian theory and practice, as one can easily conclude from his self-presentation, massively promoted by *The Guardian* (the well-known flagship of the globalist Left which supported all the wars of the Transnational Elite in the globalization era). In effect, he is a "liberal pseudo-Keynesian" (i.e. the theoretical version of social-liberalism, similar to the one promoted by Tony Blair and the likes, which is of course utterly incompatible with Keynes' work!) and a fervent globalist, as statements like the following show:

> What good will it do today to call for a dismantling of the Eurozone, of the European Union itself, when European

---

[224] See Martin Wolf, "'Capital in the Twenty-First Century', by Thomas Piketty," *Financial Times* (19/4/2014); see, also, Thomas Piketty, *Capital in the Twenty-First Century* (Harvard University Press, 2014).

[225] "Reforming Europe: Thomas Piketty meets Pablo Iglesias", *Open Democracy*, 20/2/2015
https://www.opendemocracy.net/can-europe-make-it/thomas-piketty-pablo-iglesias/reforming-europe-thomas-piketty-meets-pablo-iglesia

capitalism is doing its utmost to undermine the Eurozone, the European Union, indeed itself?[226]

The disorienting nature of this conclusion is obvious: no need to fight against the EU and the NWO as they are going to dismantle themselves anyway, through their own actions or inactions! In the meantime, as I will try to show below, he had no qualms about participating in a government that was breaking even SYRIZA's mild pre-election commitments to fight the Greek economic catastrophe! Yet, all this did not prevent *Counterpunch*, a leading organ of the globalist Left, from publishing an article under the eloquent title, "Ironman Vardoulakis's Revolutionary Plan for Europe," clearly showing the utter bankruptcy of this sort of 'Left,' which did not have any qualms about concluding that Varoufakis' plan is "Revolution from within. Just don't tell anyone in Berlin"![227] Similar was the line adopted on the matter by the numerous publications of the globalist 'Left' all over the world (Znet etc.),[228] culminating in his election by the social media as the second greatest thinker on Earth, as we saw above.

The outdated (globalist) anti-systemic Left

The anti-systemic Left, particularly the old Marxist Left, sticking to theoretical tools developed a century ago, failed to grasp the meaning of globalization itself and the tremendous significance of the rise of a new phenomenon, namely, the transnational corporation. It was only a few enlightened Marxists such as Leslie Sklair,[229] who attempted to interpret the rise of the new phenomenon of TNCs in terms of a renewed Marxist theory. But Sklair was largely ignored by the hard core of the Marxist Left, which preferred instead to stick to the Old Testament. This way, it could also justify, albeit indirectly, its own complete lack of activity against globalization, (i.e. against the NWO) itself — as, cleverly, the neo-nationalist Right in Europe have done,

---

[226] "How I became Marxist," *The Guardian* (18/2/2015).
[227] Mike Whitney" Ironman Varoufakis'Revolutionary Plan for Europe" Counterpunch, 19/2/2015 http://www.counterpunch.org/2015/02/19/ironman-varoufakiss-revolutionary-plan-for-europe/
[228] See e.g. Tom Walker, "No, Syriza has not surrendered," Red Pepper/Znet (24/2/2015); Serge Halimi "A modest and crazy dream," *Le Monde Diplomatique* (Febr. 2015); "The Greek deal is fair and democratic," *Observer* editorial (22/2/2015) etc.
[229] Leslie Sklair, *The Transnational Capitalist Class* (Oxford: Blackwell, 2001).

uniting the victims of globalization, irrespective of class and political affiliations. The anti-systemic Left, instead, simply sees neoliberal globalization as just the monopolistic stage of capitalism, confusing the Transnational Corporations (TNCs) of the globalization era with the cartels and monopolies of the era of nation-states and waiting for the socialist workers' revolution, sometime in the next millennium!

It is not therefore surprising that the same Left never understood the economic reasons motivating the Transnational Elite and in particular its aim to fully integrate the peripheral countries into the New World Order defined by neoliberal globalization, on top of their perennial need to control the energy-rich countries of the Middle East. It is clear that today's anti-systemic Left in general does not have a clue of these seismic global processes — a basic reason for its political bankruptcy, following the corresponding theoretical one.

The following two cases which are supported by members of the anti-systemic globalist Left, i.e. the case of intra-imperialist conflicts and the case of a variety of capitalisms are illustrative of the confusion reigning in this kind of Left.

a. The case of intra-imperialist conflicts

In the first case, the present geopolitical situation is described in terms of two regional imperialisms, or two power centers, a military one, i.e. USA, and an economic one, a Germany-controlled EU, which somehow collaborate to rule the world by dividing between themselves the global markets and incorporating the new capitalist regimes into their own regional organizations (EU and NATO). Thus, for James Petras:

> While President Bush and Clinton were heralding a 'new world order', based on unipolar military supremacy, Germany advanced its new imperial order by exercising its political and economic levers. Each of the two power centers, Germany and the US, shared the common quest of rapidly incorporating the new capitalist regimes into their regional organizations – the European Union (EU) and NATO – and extending their reach globally.[230]

---

[230] James Petras, 'The Rise of German Imperialism and the Phony "Russian Threat"', *Global Research*, 7/12/2014 http://www.globalresearch.ca/the-rise-of-german-imperialism-and-the-phony-russian-threat/5418498

However, the fact that the NWO is defined in this analysis in purely geopolitical terms — as if we still live in the pre-globalization era of nation states and the imperialisms based on them — inevitably leads to ignoring the role of US and German TNCs in forming the backbone of the respective collaboration of USA and Germany respectively, within the Transnational Elite. But, it is clear that although there may be some tactical divisions between USA and Germany on several issues, including the issue of how best to integrate Russia into the NWO, there is full agreement between them on the strategic aim of reproducing and expanding the present order all over the world, by integrating any countries resisting the crucial elements of neoliberal globalization, i.e. the opening and liberalization of markets for capital and commodities (and to some extent for labor as well). This full agreement between all parts of the Transnational economic elite is shown by the consensus among TNCs (irrespective of whether their economic basis is in the US or the EU) to push the TTIP, TPP and CETA (EU-Canada) agreements through, despite the objections raised by elements of the French, Belgian[231] and even German political elites. The objections of the latter are, of course, due to the fact that they, unlike the economic elites, have to face their electorates.

No wonder that this sort of antisystemic analysis, (which in fact has very little to do with a real Marxist analysis), by ignoring globalization, ends up with completely disorienting conclusions about the actual role played by the globalist 'Left' in Greece and Spain.

Yet, the fact that US and EU are on the same side of the fence was made even more clear very recently by the new EU foreign policy chief, who, as an Italian, belongs to what the 'unforgettable' Donald Rumsfeld had called 'the old Europe'. That is, the Europe which, (unlike the ultra-conservative newcomers to the EU, the East Europeans), had doubts about the Iraq invasion and, at present, about the Transnational Elite's stand on Putin's Russia. Thus, as Federica Mogherini, High Representative of the European Union for Foreign Affairs and Security Policy pointed out in a very recent interview with the Italian daily *La Repubblica:*

> It is not true that there is a soft Europe stance, which opposes the US hard-line position. On the contrary, the latest data

---

[231] Arthur Beesley, "Belgium sinks EU-Canada trade deal after Wallonia veto", *Financial Times,* 24/10/2016

shows that trade between Russia and Europe is declining, while trade between Russia and the US is increasing.[232]

And then she went on to stress that Washington's views on Russia match those of Europe, adding that "everyone wants to get out of the logic of confrontation."[233]

However, in a new version of this thesis, Petras recently returned to the same story of a conflict of national capitalisms, or as he called them, of 'intense intra-capitalist rivalries' within the context of "the struggle for world markets among regional capitalist blocs- Anglo-American, European and Sino-Asian", which define the nature of global instability".[234] Thus, at the very moment the entire Transnational Elite is ready to co-operate, to fight the neo-nationalist movements for national and economic sovereignty and, at the same time impose a regime change in Syria, risking a possibly open conflict with Russia (where the patriotic movement is also thriving), Petras had drawn the following conclusion that may constitute a monument to the theoretical and political demise of globalist 'antisystemic Left':

> In the current phase of global capitalism, the most striking socio-economic dynamics are located in the deepening intra-capitalist conflicts between regions, nations and among segments of the capitalist class. The ideologues of capitalist globalization and regional integration are finally exposed as false prophets. Attempts by the US to impose a new world order that subordinates Europe and Asia have failed; the US now faces internal dissension, notably in US Presidential candidate Donald Trump's 'American First' campaign, pressing for 'national solutions'. The European capitalist elite is now only willing to collaborate with Washington where US-Europe trade agreements can be mutually beneficial – they openly reject being reduced to 'reaping crumbs.' National capitalism has emerged as the new reality on both sides of the Atlantic and across the globe in Asia, as China emerges as the

---

[232] "West wants to end confrontation with Russia over Ukraine – EU foreign policy chief", *RT*, 29/12/2014 http://rt.com/news/218271-eu-confrontation-ukraine-russia/
[233] ibid.
[234] Prof. James Petras, "Inter-Capitalist Rivalries and Political Rebellion against the US Multinational Corporate Elite", *Global Research*, 8/9/2016 http://www.globalresearch.ca/inter-capitalist-rivalries-and-political-rebellion-against-the-us-multinational-corporate-elite/5544729

dominant economic force in the region. China's quest to secure global markets and investment sites has set in motion rival nationalist alignments, which threaten US regional power.

Rebellions by capitalist political elites are the 'new norm' everywhere. Multi-national rivalries over tax evasion and its consequences are leading to 'tit-for-tat' reprisals, which can rupture historical ties.[235]

In fact, this is the world described by Lenin,[236] exactly a century ago, i.e. a world of cartels and monopolies backed by their states fighting for the division of markets! No word about the phasing out of national and consequently economic sovereignty of even the greatest economic powers, the G7 countries, from where most of the TNCs ruling the world originated. No word also about the Brexit revolution, as this analysis is clearly at a loss to analyse its real significance. Finally, this analysis has no clue of the present conflict between the elites and the popular movements against globalization within all countries integrated into the NWO and the consequent attempt by the elites to supposedly meet these demands with pseudo-actions to fight corruption, or fight Apple etc. That is, actions which are of course completely irrelevant to the overall move of the NWO towards more integration and a system of global governance. No wonder that this analysis even dismisses the significance of the mass movement of the victims of globalization in the USA, who are supporting Trump, characterizing it as just a protest campaign pressing for 'national solutions'!

b. The case of a variety of capitalisms

In the second case, which, mostly, is a variation of the intra-capitalist rivalries we have just considered, the problem is the existence of a variety of capitalisms in the globalization era. Thus, for Žižek (although it is a bit of a joke for one to classify this intellectual — highly promoted by the Transnational Elite media — as 'anti-systemic'!):

> The 'American century' is over, and we have entered a period in which multiple centers of global capitalism have been

---

[235] ibid.
[236] Vladimir Lenin, *Imperialism, the Highest Stage of Capitalism*, (1917)

forming. In the US, Europe, China and maybe Latin America, too, capitalist systems have developed with specific twists: the US stands for neoliberal capitalism, Europe for what remains of the welfare state, China for authoritarian capitalism, Latin America for populist capitalism. After the attempt by the US to impose itself as the sole superpower – the universal policeman – failed, there is now the need to establish the rules of interaction between these local centers as regards their conflicting interests.[237]

On the basis of this description, based more on aphorisms rather than any kind of analysis, Žižek concluded that the "principal contradiction" of the New World Order is the impossibility of creating a global political order that would correspond to the global capitalist economy. Yet, Simon Peres, the Zionist ex president of Israel, has already given an answer on how a kind of global governance can be created out of this seemingly disorder. Thus, Peres celebrated as follows globalization in front of a highly enthusiastic audience of the entire European Parliament:

Globalization put an end to racism. It empowers the individual. Global companies do not impose their will upon people. On the contrary, they respect the will of their clients. They can provide scientific know-how for growth. They can assist young people to acquire high education. To create jobs befitting their skills.[238]

Then, Peres went on to describe how the future world based on globalization should be. On this, he simply followed Gideon Rachman, the Zionist chief foreign affairs commentator of the *Financial Times*, who in a well-known 2008 article entitled "And now for a world government" [239] provided the ideological background for global governance, (which many commentators have cited as proof of an elitist plot for its establishment). Thus, for Peres, the new global world

---

[237] Slavoj Žižek, "Who can control the post-superpower capitalist world order?", *The Guardian*,6/5/2014
[238] "Full text of Peres speech to European Parliament in Strasbourg", *Haaretz*, 13/03/2013
[239] Gideon Rachman, "And now for a world government", *Financial Times*, 8/12/2008

would be the same New World Order as at present, plus an informal global governance:

> Our global world has no global government. It has become almost ungovernable. We have to look for an alternative. I believe the future ways of governing shall rely on three pillars: National governments will continue to be in charge of the husbandry of the national state. Global companies will invest in research and development. And the individual will enjoy the capacity to govern themselves by knowing the way their brain functions. Science today is more telling than politics. It is universal and borderless. Armies cannot conquer wisdom. Police cannot arrest science. (...) Facing the lack of global governance, we can foster close cooperation between governments and global companies. Facing the dangers that threaten the values for which we stand, we shall fight terror wherever it is, relentlessly.[240]

So, in almost identical words with the ones used later by Žižek, (who simply added a supposedly Marxist slant to Peres' argument), Peres has shown the way out of this contradiction (in terms, of course), of the present NWO! Yet, as we shall see in the last part of this volume, there is, in fact, a real alternative to this, in terms of a complete break with the present NWO and the building of a new democratic order in which economic and national sovereignty have been restored, so that peoples could then fight for the ideal society, as they see it.

The deceitful (globalist) reformist Left: SYRIZA and Podemos

However, if the anti-systemic Left, despite its outdated theoretical tools, at least, questions the capitalist system and sometimes its main economic institutions (EU, WTO etc.), the reformist Left does not even dare to question such institutions, let alone the system itself! All they usually do is to question the austerity policies, in an effort to differentiate themselves from the old social democratic parties, which are now fully integrated into the NWO in the form of social liberal parties. Yet, it can be shown that any exit from the present economic and social catastrophe in countries like Greece is impossible, unless

---

[240] ibid.

they break with the New World Order of neoliberal globalization, as expressed in Europe by the EU and the Eurozone.

The reformist Left in Greece and Spain, (which are the only countries in which the reformist Left is still politically alive), as represented by SYRIZA and Podemos respectively, is entirely inappropriate to lead the victims of globalization (the vast majority of the population in these countries) onto a path to regain the minimal economic and national sovereignty needed. This is because these parties do not even question the EU, leaving the neo-nationalist anti-EU Right to attract its traditional supporters in the working class. In fact, SYRIZA is a late offspring of Eurocommunism, which has been long dead in the rest of Europe, whereas Podemos has emerged in the aftermath of the Indignados 'movement', which has also long disappeared everywhere without a trace. Yet, whereas the main slogan of the Indignados in Spain in 2011, who used to gather in Madrid's square Puerta del Sol was 'United, the people do not need parties,' today, as Renaud Lambert points out, "the square is no longer occupied. The desire for change remains, but unexpectedly has formed around a new political party, Podemos (We Can)!"[241] However, as it was aptly put by Nuria Alabao, a Barcelona activist, "Podemos has arisen as a way of channeling social energy and the process of large-scale experimentation [of recent years]."[242] Similarly, several members of the Greek Indignados movement, who were invited repeatedly in Athens' Syntagma square to talk about democracy and the crisis (in fact, to promote the pro-EU line!), were candidates of SYRIZA in the 2015 parliamentary elections that followed. Some of them were elected to parliament, with a few even becoming members of the present Greek government, which completed the sell-out of Greece, much more efficiently and thoroughly than their social democratic and Right predecessors!

Thus, even if the parties of the reformist Left in Mediterranean Europe take over, as has already happened in Greece, this in no way would justify the new mythology, which is promoted, directly or indirectly, by the media of the Transnational Elite, that we are on the verge of a historical change in Europe and beyond. In fact, both these

---

[241] Renaud Lambert, "Now can Podemos win in Spain?", *Le Monde Diplomatique*, February 2015
[242] ibid. quoted from Nuria Alabao, "Podemos y los movimientos", *Periódico Diagonal,* 7 November 2014.

two parties, given their commitment to the EU and the Euro, simply exploit, for electoral reasons, the desperation of the victims of the New World Order of neoliberal globalization in these two countries. Clearly, there is no possibility whatsoever that they will take any of the radical steps required to really alleviate the appalling economic condition of the majority of the population in either country — particularly in Greece — within the constraints imposed by the EU, and the constitutional treaties that institutionalized neoliberal globalization at the European level.

So, the rise to power of these parties far from being, as Tsipras, the leader of the Greek SYRIZA party stressed, "a 'historic opportunity' for a left alternative to the current capitalist 'European model" — to the delight of the world globalist "Left"[243] — in all probability, it has already led to the end of the Left in Greece. This is simply the result of its (inevitable) utter failure even to alleviate the effects of the catastrophic crisis imposed on Greece by the Transnational Elite and its local associates. Instead, the SYRIZA government led to the biggest political sell out in the post-war history of the country when, in July 2015, the government of the 'Left' con-artists had no qualms about reversing the result of a referendum, where over 60% of the people effectively voted against any further 'memoranda', and, instead, within days of this resounding slap to the elites, agreed with the Euro-elites on the worst ever memorandum! This latest memorandum involved, among measures to liberalize the labor market, further measures to squeeze pensions, as well as the mass selling-out of the Greek social wealth, including the selling out to foreign 'investors' of ports, airports, transport, communications, electricity, water etc. Although this is deceitfully done in stages, the first stage involving the transfer of ownership from the Greek state to a fund controlled by the Transnational Elite, nobody has any doubt that this criminal act sets the stage for future privatization to repay part of the debt to the banking vultures that constitute the 'lenders'. This is, in fact, the biggest crime of SYRIZA against the Greek people, given that it is almost irreversible, bar a revolutionary change. No wonder that even the worst Right wing governments never dared to commit such a crime en masse. Obviously, the transnational elite found in the 'Left' its biggest ally that could easily pass any criminal legislation, which,

---

[243] See e.g. Leo Panitch, "Europe's left has seen how capitalism can bite back»", *The Guardian*, 13/1/2014.

under a non-Left government, would have caused tremendous social unrest, as history has shown repeatedly in the past.

It is therefore clear that the Mediterranean Left will simply follow belatedly the fate of the Left in the 'North' (Northern Europe, North America etc.) which is already dead and buried, mainly as a result of the fact that it has been integrated into the NWO of neoliberal globalization, at least since the late '90s, as we saw above. No wonder, today, it is the neo-nationalist (and often Islamophobic) Right in the North that has raised the flag of anti-globalization, while, at the same time, the Eurasian Union attracts the patriotic movements in the ex-Soviet countries that are fighting for economic and national sovereignty, which is being phased out in the NWO. [244]

We may therefore conclude that only if Left parties adopt radical policies of economic and national sovereignty, breaking with the EU and the Eurozone (in Europe) and with the institutions of the NWO in general (in the rest of the world), i.e. with WTO, IMF, World Bank etc., can they really implement any appropriate policies to fight austerity and inequality. In other words, the inevitable alternative to sovereignty and self-reliance is the present austerity policies, which are imposed by the European North all over the EU. Within the NWO, these policies are necessary, as we saw in previous parts, in order to sort out the competiveness problem that European multinationals face with respect to their competitors in the Far East and the USA. Particularly so as relatively depressed real wages and/or miserable working conditions are the main foundations of the higher competitiveness in these countries. Therefore, only through a program of self-reliance could a country retrieve the necessary degree of economic and therefore national sovereignty, so that it is the people themselves who will determine the economic process, (i.e. which economic and social needs are to be met and how), instead of leaving these life-and-death issues to 'market forces' and the consequent Social Darwinism.

This would mean that the need for the creation, 'from below', of a Popular Front for Social and National Liberation (instead of relying on the professional politicians of the "Left" or of the Right) is today more urgent than ever before, for countries like Greece or Spain. The

---

[244] See UKRAINE: THE ATTACK ON RUSSIA AND THE EURASIAN UNION, *From the economic violence in Greece to the Ukrainian coup* (vol. 2 of the *NWO in Action*)

government of such a Popular Front would have to formulate a program for the radical changes needing to be achieved in the short term, aiming at restoring full social control on all markets, the unilateral cancellation of the debt and all related legislation imposed by the Troika, following an immediate exit from the EU/Eurozone. Although the socialization of the banking system and of the privatized industries, particularly those covering basic needs (energy, water, transport, communication, etc.) will be necessary even at this early stage, the main medium-term aim will have to be economic self-reliance, so that the basic needs of all citizens are met through the rebuilding of the economic structure, according to social needs rather than according to market demand.

Needless to add that such a break with the NWO would be immensely facilitated if Greece were to join the Eurasian Union, provided of course that the latter also breaks completely from the NWO and becomes a political and economic union of sovereign nations, as it was originally designed. This is particularly the case with Greece, given that Russia has already promised new relations with it, provided of course that it leaves the EU. Thus, as the Russian Minister of Agriculture Nikolai Fyodorov told a news conference in Berlin, almost immediately after SYRIZA took over, "if Greece has to leave the European Union, we will build our own relations with it."[245] Next, Russian Finance Minister Anton Siluanov stated that Moscow wouldn't rule out a bailout to Greece.[246] No need to add that all these indirect Russian attempts to persuade SYRIZA to leave the EU, so that it would then be able to implement its own program, were ignored by Tsipras, Varoufakis, Tsakalotos and similar 'Marxists', as well as the rest of the political gang who took over in January 2015. The inevitable consequence was the present catastrophe in Greece, which would leave the Greek 'Left' and the test of the world 'Left' stigmatized for committing or supporting this huge crime, respectively.

To my mind, the break with the NWO is the only way in which both Greece and Spain (and later on, any other countries in the EU periphery such as Portugal and Cyprus), could achieve their economic and national sovereignty, which is the necessary condition for self-

---

[245] Alexandros Vlachos, "Russia may lift food import ban from Greece if it quits EU - Russian agriculture minister", TACC/EPA (Tass), 16/1/2015
[246] "Russia might bailout Greece – finance minister", RT, 30/1/2015
http://rt.com/business/227751-russia-greece-financial-aid/

reliance. In other words, this is the only way in which their economies could be restructured in a way that will meet the socially determined needs of their own peoples, rather than the needs of a world market controlled by the TNCs.

Not surprisingly, this kind of Left was promoted (before its election to government) even by one of the main organs of Transnational Elite, the *Financial Times*, as the 'radical' Left.[247] Of course, there is nothing radical about this party (or Podemos for that matter), which not only never questioned the EU itself but also never dared even to commit themselves unequivocally to an exit from the Eurozone. Needless to mention that an exit from the Eurozone, which is not accompanied by an exit from the EU, is almost as catastrophic as the present situation, given that the capital, labor and commodities markets will continue to remain open and liberalized, on the basis of the EU and WTO regulations, while the country will still forfeit its sovereignty — a fact that pushed the British victims of globalization to vote for Brexit

It is therefore clear that this kind of Left plays an obviously disorienting role when it just attacks the austerity policies, which, however, are simply the inevitable side effect of integration into the NWO and the consequent adoption of neoliberal globalization. It should not be forgotten anyway that significant social democrats before them, representing important core countries like France and Germany, had also tried to reverse neoliberal policies and either were forced to do a quick about turn (Francois Mitterrand, Francois Hollande) or were even thrown out of the government (Oscar Lafontaine). Nor is there any validity to the argument of Podemos and SYRIZA that this time the Euro-elites will have to reverse neoliberal policies, given that they face the risk of real anti-EU parties coming into power. Clearly, the elites are well aware of the fact that, even if this happens, no government in power has any other choice but to implement the present neoliberal policies, unless of course it breaks with the NWO. However the elites know that, at this moment, no neo-nationalist party will dare taking such drastic action, although of course nothing can be ruled out for the future.

---

[247] Wolfgang Münchau, "Radical left is right about Europe's debt", *Financial Times,* 23/11/2014

The usual devious argument globalist 'Left' parties such as SYRIZA use to justify their blatant U-turns is that this is part of some genius strategy, so that a new 'good' Europe of the peoples could develop at the end 'from within', which would abolish austerity policies — no mention of course of neoliberal globalization, or even of neoliberalism! This is why they never raised the issue of exiting from the EU and creating instead a real Europe of the peoples, in place of the EU of capital, as at present. So, they fight, instead, against the austerity policies imposed by those 'baddies,' despite the fact that such policies are of course the inevitable policies that would have to be implemented by any government which has its markets opened and deregulated, as a result of their integration into the New World Order of neoliberal globalization. As a result, any such integrated country (and its governments) would have to base their growth strategies on foreign investment and on improving competitiveness, with the vain hope that foreign imports would not crowd out domestic production, while at the same time exports would keep expanding.

Yet, although such policies may indeed lead to some kind of growth, which would almost certainly be associated with huge inequalities and poverty for most (as it can be shown both in theory and in practice), they surely cannot lead to a restructuring of production so that the economy could become competitive. What these con-artists hide from their supporters is what open markets mean. In other words, they hide the fact that the products of domestic workers, particularly in EU peripheral countries such as Greece and Portugal, would have to compete with the products of foreign workers abroad working under almost slavery conditions (e.g. India, Pakistan, China and so on) or with the products of foreign workers living in highly advanced countries, in terms of research and development, (e.g. Germany), associated with much higher levels of productivity and competitiveness. Therefore, in an economic union consisting of countries at unequal levels of development, the peripheral countries have no chance to compete with the advanced countries at the center. However, it is at the center where the elites controlling the economic policies of the entire union are based.

It is therefore a disorienting myth that a union like the Eurozone could ever be democratic, as Varoufakis shamelessly declared when he claimed that he was the co-author of the policies imposed on Greece, following his negotiations with the organs of the EU and the IMF! In fact, a democratic union presupposes members of equal economic power, i.e. sovereign nations, and Greece has neither any economic nor national sovereignty within the Eurozone, having to submit to the neo-colonial rules imposed by it. On top of this, only a liberal cretin (or a crook) could assert that a democratic relationship could ever exist between the lender and the borrower, or, alternatively, between those controlling the European Central Bank's purse and the rest, as even systemic writers, like the conservative Dominic Lawson, fully understood:

> As about a quarter of ECB funds are backed by German taxpayers, Schäuble's opinions count much more than those of Varoufakis. (…) So it is hardly surprising that Varoufakis has been humiliated. The terms agreed late on Friday involve acceptance that the bailout package continues to be set and monitored by the International Monetary Fund, the ECB and EU finance ministers; and that if this troika is not satisfied with Greek commitment to economic reform, the money will be frozen — exactly what SYRIZA swore it would never accept.[248]

The main reason therefore why SYRIZA has already dismally failed and a similar fate awaits Podemos, if it ever comes to power has to do with the fundamentally contradictory nature of these parties and their programs. The fundamental contradiction arises from the fact that these parties promise to challenge the austerity policies, imposed by the Transnational Elite in association with the local elites, without questioning in the slightest their countries' participation in the EU and, of course, the Eurozone — which is the ultimate cause of their economic malaise. However, the austerity policies are not some sort of 'bad' policies implemented by some misguided 'baddies' who believe in austerity. Despite the disorienting argument to the opposite by Paul Krugman, the Nobel laureate in economics, such policies are, instead, the necessary policies implied by the full integration of any country into the NWO of neoliberal globalization.

Thus, neoliberal globalization, as we saw in Part I, is not just an ideology, as argued by globalist pseudo-Marxists' who, in fact, function as the ideologues of it and are consequently promoted

---

[248] Dominic Lawson, "Four weeks of Greek hubris, then repulsive humble moussaka," *Sunday Times* (22/2/2015).

appropriately by the mass media of the 'progressive' part of the Transnational Elite (*Guardian* e.tc.). In fact, the globalization of the capitalist market economy is founded on the mass expansion of Transnational Corporations (TNCs) and, as such, can only be neoliberal. In this sense, neoliberalism represents not just a policy change, or a sinister dogma, as most of the Left asserts today, but a structural change marking the shift to a new form of modernity that was necessary for the efficient functioning of TNCs. In this latest form of modernity, international competitiveness is the utmost criterion of success (and therefore of survival) for any business or country and, vice versa, low competiveness is the utmost curse for any of them.

However, the causes of the competiveness problem in peripheral countries of the South are very different from the causes in the advanced countries in the North. Thus, low competitiveness in peripheral countries is a long-term structural problem, which cannot be sorted out without the building of a new productive base that presupposes a process of self-reliant development. On the other hand, low competitiveness in advanced countries, which have already built a competitive economy with high productivity, is a matter of changes in relative prices, which can be sorted out by squeezing wages and incomes (through austerity policies), so that their commodities become as competitive as those made in China and India — to which many TNCs have moved their production (Apple, Nokia etc.). All this implies that even if the SYRIZA government in Greece decided on a Grexit from the Euro (but staying in the EU), the reintroduction and significant devaluation of the drachma would bring only some temporary positive results — unless such policies are accompanied by a parallel radical restructuring of the productive structure. But such a restructuring cannot of course be left to the decisions of profit-maximizing investors and the TNCs. Instead, it has to be based on social decisions — a process which is impossible for any country integrated into the NWO, where such crucial decisions are left to the market forces and those controlling them 'from behind'.

Therefore, left approaches to the contrary are not only wrong, but also completely disorienting, as they ignore the fact that the current devastating crisis in peripheral EU countries is due to structural factors. Such factors have everything to do with the uneven capitalist development process, which is further exacerbated in the era of neoliberal globalization and the consequent policies implemented by the EU. Conversely, they have very little to do with the broader financial crisis and 'financialization,' austerity policies, or the debt itself and the ways to deal with it.[249] In other words, austerity policies are a consequence and not the cause of the present devastating crisis. The solution, therefore, to the 'problem' is not just the redistribution of income at the expense of profits and in favor of wages, as globalist supporters of a pseudo-'Marxist' kind of analysis assume.[250] Inequality is anyway nothing new but an inherent characteristic of the capitalist system. Unsurprisingly, despite growing world inequality during the era of neoliberal globalization, the system has enjoyed a sustained period of expansion, with world GDP rising at an average 2.9% in the 1990s and 3.2% in the period up to the beginning of the latest financial crisis (2000-08).[251] Furthermore, the only case that a systematic redistribution of income against the rich took place in a capitalist system was when the tax burden was shifted to the rich during the social democratic period (approx. 1945-1975). However, this kind of redistribution is simply not feasible anymore in the NWO of Neoliberal Globalization, as TNCs can easily move to tax havens like Ireland, India, etc. leaving massive unemployment and poverty behind.

The reasons why neoliberal EU cannot change "from within"

Any attempt, therefore, to change the neoliberal orientation of the EU 'from within,' as globalist 'Left' academics and political parties suggest, is doomed to failure for both economic and political reasons.

The economic reasons have to do with the crucial fact that austerity policies are not just imposed by some 'baddies', (i.e. neoliberal politicians and economists) but by the logic and the dynamics of an internationalized capitalist market economy in which any significant social controls on markets will undermine

---

[249] Takis Fotopoulos, "The myths about the economic crisis, the reformist Left and economic democracy", *The International Journal of INCLUSIVE DEMOCRACY*, Vol. 4, No. 4, (October 2008), http://www.inclusivedemocracy.org/journal/vol4/vol4_no4_takis_economic_crisis.htm

[250] See e.g. the recent book by two members of the SYRIZA leadership, Euclid Tsakalotos (who replaced Varoufakis as the effective "Tsar" of the economy in charge of the crucial negotiations with the Euro-elites and the faithful implementation of the orders coming from the Eurogroup) and Christos Laskos, *Crucible of Resistance: Greece, the Eurozone and the World Economic Crisis*, (Pluto Press, Sept. 2013).

[251] World Bank, *World Development Indicators 2010*, Table 4.1.

competitiveness — the yardstick of success in attracting capital. In such a framework, countries have to compete with each other to attract capital investment through open and liberalized markets that secure the eventual homogenization of real wages and working conditions. It is not therefore surprising that no social democratic or Left government in Europe has managed to discard neoliberal policies within the NWO. In other words, austerity policies and the various 'reforms' (aiming at making labor more 'flexible', simply aim at making countries more competitive, so that foreign mainly investment (by TNCs and others) can be attracted. But, there is no way any country integrated into the NWO could become more competitive through Keynesian policies, as these policies have been designed for a different environment and with a different aim. The intended environment was a nation-state implying a certain degree of economic and national sovereignty, while the aim of such policies was to create a successful growth economy in which growth was led by domestic demand, mainly by consumption and government spending. On the other hand, austerity policies have been designed for countries integrated into the NWO with the aim to enhance an export-led growth. The means to achieve this aim was making production internationally more competitive, either because of the high levels of investment, technology and productivity built-into their production process, and/or because of the low levels of prices and wages.

Within this framework, we may distinguish three types of countries as regards their ability to survive competition in the NWO:

a) the countries in the North which are endowed with highly advanced production structures and technologies and corresponding financial structures;
b) the countries in the South which can base their competitiveness on an extremely 'flexible' labor force such as the Indian subcontinent with the well-known slave labor conditions;
c) the countries in between, e.g. the peripheral European countries, which are bound to suffer when integrated in the NWO and lose their sovereignty, unless they have abundant natural resources (oil, gas etc.) to attract foreign and domestic investment.

So, as long as a country is a member of the EU — even if it is not bound by a specific program imposing austerity policies because of its huge debt etc. — would still be bound by the catastrophic neoliberal rules imposed by the various EU Treaties. That is, the EU treaties that followed the Treaty of Maastricht, which institutionalized the opening and liberalization of the markets for commodities, capital and labor, and which, indirectly, imply also privatizations and the phasing out of the welfare state. This, on top of the severe restrictions imposed on fiscal policy through the stringent rules imposed on budget deficits and debt ratios to GDP (e.g. through the Stability and Growth Pact), which, indirectly, impose austerity.

But if an EU country is also a member of the Eurozone, then, it cannot control even its own currency — the minimum requirement for economic sovereignty — which is controlled instead directly by the Transnational Elite, i.e. its European members and particularly the German elite, through the European Central Bank (ECB). Furthermore, in the case of countries under debt 'programs', such as Greece, low budget deficits are not enough and a huge surplus of up to 4,5% of the GDP may be imposed so that lenders are better serviced, in effect, through drastic cuts in social services (health, education etc.)! That would mean in practice further austerity, particularly in countries where the tax base is not strong enough, or efficient enough, to sustain an adequate level of welfare services. Clearly, this is the bourgeois housekeeping kind of mentality, which, even if it makes sense at the individual level, surely is senseless at the social level. Furthermore, poor countries (the majority of countries in the world) should certainly not have their public schools or hospitals dependent on the 'market' for the provision of such services. In such a system (effectively, a copy of the most inhumane system of covering social needs in the world, i.e. the US system of 'freedom of choice') , only those who can afford it, have even elementary social needs adequately met. This is the most brutal form of a capitalist market economy which, in the NWO of neoliberal globalization, is dominant and deprives a market economy even of its ability to use surpluses created in the good years of a business cycle to cover deficits of bad years — as the social democratic practice used to be in the period before globalization, when nation-states and Keynesian policies were still the norm.

As regards the political reasons for which any attempt to change the neoliberal orientation of the EU 'from within' is impossible, these reasons have to do with the fact that the EU's political structure is dominated by a solid pro-integration bloc that consists of two interlocking alliances:

a) A 'political alliance', which is an alliance of conservative and social-liberal parties (the ex social democratic parties) mainly located in the European North (Germany, France, UK Benelux and Scandinavian countries), where the middle classes that have benefited from globalization are politically dominant. As shown by the research of *VoteWatch Europe,* in the first six months of the new legislature, from July to December 2014, the center-right European People's Party (EPP) and center-left Socialists and Democrats (S&D) voted together in four out of every five votes. Usually, they were joined also by the centrist liberals (ALDE). The common element of all these parties is that they are all convinced supporters of closer European integration, and command an almost two-thirds majority in the parliament, with 478 out of the 751 seats.[252] This is therefore a solid pro-EU and pro-Transnational Elite majority, which can never to be broken by the likes of SYRIZA and Podemos that have simply been assigned to play the role of the approved 'opposition' to this bloc, by the Transnational Elite. As even a FT analyst pointed out, the political differences between Left and Right within the parties in this solid bloc don't play any role whatsoever: "it would not be far off the mark to say that votes in the EU assembly have tended to put not right against left, or left against right, as in a classical parliamentary system, but rather the bulk of the European political establishment against its sworn enemies and critics."[253] Furthermore, a pro-establishment consensus prevailed at Brussels and Strasbourg, even before Europe's anti-establishment parties started making electoral gains, since, "even before the May 2014 elections, the EPP and S&D groups were voting together 73 per cent of the time – only 7 per cent less than now."[254]

b) A 'geopolitical alliance' that was formed mainly by the ex-soviet bloc countries of East Europe, whose dominant parties are fanatical anti-Russian and pro-Western, or more accurately, pro-American. In fact, the unforgettable war criminal and former US secretary of Defense, Donald Rumsfeld, rightly

---

[252] Tony Barber, "EU parliament's biggest parties vote together", *Financial Times,* 11/3/2015
[253] ibid.
[254] ibid.

predicted long ago the role that the new EU members from Eastern Europe were going to play within EU, as client states of the Transnational Elite running the NWO. At that time, France and Germany were still run by the old kind of conservatives and social democrats respectively and, as Rumsfeld pointed out, they were a 'problem' within the Transnational Elite in opposing the Iraq invasion. [255] This 'problem' has of course been sorted out by now, with the complete conversion of both countries into full supporters of all criminal wars of the Transnational Elite, and with France in particular, having been converted, since the Sarkozy era, into one of its most aggressive members. This is true even today, despite the fact that in the meantime another unforgettable war criminal, Sarkozy, was succeeded by the 'socialist' Hollande, who has (rather unsuccessfully) attempted to cover his social-liberal economic policies under the French flag and the national motto originated in the French Revolution *Liberté, fraternité, égalité* (although the latter — i.e. equality — is, as a rule, forgotten today by the French elites — unless they talk about sexual relations!).

It is therefore clear that the pro-EU and pro-Transnational Elite solid bloc which dominates the political and economic agenda of the EU will continue to do so for any foreseeable future, despite the pipe dreams of SYRIZA and Podemos (assuming it is just pipe dreams) to create a new progressive Europe 'from within.' In other words, despite all their rhetoric, neither Podemos nor SYRIZA will ever be able to implement strict social controls on markets, which is exactly the necessary precondition for Spain and Greece to achieve economic and national sovereignty. At most, what these parties can achieve, even if they are in a parliamentary position to fully implement their program, is a kind of growth like the present one in Britain, where open mass unemployment has simply been replaced with disguised unemployment and frozen wages, as well as rising poverty and malnourishment. [256]

---

[255] "Outrage at 'old Europe' remarks*", BBC NEWS*, 23/1/2003
http://news.bbc.co.uk/1/hi/world/europe/2687403.stm
[256] see "Millions of impoverished Britons malnourished – report", RT, 28/12/2014
http://rt.com/uk/218231-millions-poorest-britons-malnourished/

However, as the SYRIZA 'experiment' has already shown, such parties cannot even implement the reformist policies they pledge. The Transnational Elite and the EU elites, together with the local elites, have every means possible at their disposal to impose their own will on them in case they deviate significantly from the prescribed policies. In fact, they will have no qualms even about resorting, if necessary, to a cut of liquidity through various direct or indirect mechanisms available to them, as they did with Cyprus in 2013 and then again with Greece in 2015. Particularly so, as both Podemos and SYRIZA cannot even appeal to their own voters in the event that a real conflict situation develops, as most of them are 'inevitably' EU supporters! Inevitably, that is, because these parties have never attempted to build a popular movement conscious of the radical measures needed and the corresponding difficulties they would have to overcome, (at least, in the initial stage), so that they could break with the EU and implement their own anti-austerity policies and beyond.

Instead, both SYRIZA and Podemos did everything they could to disorient the Greek and Spanish peoples respectively and persuade them that they could implement their anti-austerity policies, even within the EU! Under such circumstances, even if the leadership of such parties was ready to clash with the EU elites (which is a very big 'if' when one knows the usual social status aspirations of such professional politicians of the 'Left'), it would have been too easy for the elites simply to break these parties and/or their parliamentary majorities and impose their will, as they had all the power at their disposal (economic, political, media and so on) to achieve such a task. Therefore, in spite of the myths that these elites (and the media controlled by them) promoted to terrorize the Greek and Spanish peoples about the supposed catastrophe that would result from an exit from the EU and the Eurozone, there has never been the slightest risk of any uncontrolled by the élites development. In fact even well known organs of the Transnational Elite, such as the Brookings Institute,[257] had already admitted it in advance. Worth noting is that the deceitful

and "Low-paid Britons now number five million, think tank concludes", cf. *BBC News* 26/10/2014
[257] see e.g. Douglas J. Elliott, "Will the Greek Election Ultimately Break the Euro?" Brookings Institute, http://www.brookings.edu/research/opinions/2015/01/15-greek-election-break-the-euro-Elliott; Phillip Inman Anne Penketh, "Fears of Greek exit help send euro to nine-year low against the dollar", The *Guardian* 6/1/2015

'Marxist' economists in the SYRIZA leadership (Varoufakis, Tsakalotos, Stathakis, Lianos at al.) have excelled in this dirty campaign to terrorize the Greek people on the horrible consequences of a Grexit, side-by-side with the systemic economists!

In this sense, the parties of the globalist 'Left' like SYRIZA and Podemos, simply play the game of the Transnational Elite and its European component, the EU, as they will never turn against the EU itself. In fact, the EU elites never had any doubts about this, notwithstanding the empty threats issued by SYRIZA during the negotiations with them.

It is exactly for this reason that, as we saw above, the role of anti-establishment parties is not played anymore by the Left, but by neo-nationalist parties, like that of Le Pen's in France, which however can never hope to break the above solid pro-EU bloc at the European level. At most, they can hope to take over power in a particular country, such as France, and try to implement their sovereignty policies. One could therefore speculate that one basic reason the EU establishment is keen now to create its own EU army[258] is not so much to 'fight Russia', as it declares, nor to confirm Europe's independence from the US (as the globalist 'Left,' in a disorienting way, suggests) but simply to crush any neo-nationalist movements attempting to take over power in any particular EU country. This is of course far from surprising given that the only real threat the Transnational Elite in general and the EU in particular face at the moment can only come about from the neonationalist movements, following the sell out of globalist 'Left'.

Having said this, in case Russia does go ahead with the creation of a Eurasian Union of sovereign nations, as a real alternative pole to the present unipolar world of the NWO, then, the declared EU aim for the creation of an 'anti-Russia" EU army to fight Russia may become a self-fulfilling prophesy!

The Left's myths about Internet democracy and freedom of speech in the globalization era

In this part I will examine the claims of 'Anonymous' and others in the globalist 'Left' about the equality and freedom of speech

---

[258] David Charter, "Juncker calls for more union to beat 'galloping populism,'"*The Times*, 14/9/2016; see, also, "European Commission chief urges 'joint EU army,' Germany backs decision", RT, 8/3/2015 http://rt.com/news/238797-eu-joint-army-threat/

supposedly secured by the internet in the NWO of neoliberal globalization, as well as about its mythical relation to direct democracy. The conclusion drawn is that, although some unquestionable benefits are offered by social media, certain wild claims are also made about it, which have very little to do with reality. Furthermore, given the side effects of anonymity, widely used in the Internet for smear campaigns either against other users, or specifically against writers who do not hide behind anonymity in expressing their views, the inevitable conclusion is that there is an imperative need for the introduction of social controls for the self-protection of society. In other words, in the same way that society needs protection from "free markets" in the form of social controls, society also needs protection from the 'free internet', so that it does not end up like 'free markets', i.e. as an effective means to enhance the power of the elites in controlling populations in the NWO.

The issue of the relationship between freedom of speech and the Internet became front-page news in the second half of 2014 because of the following two events.

The first event was, the minor demonstrations around the world — except for some bigger demonstrations in Anglo-Saxon countries — organized by 'Anonymous' with the well-known Guy Fawkes mask. However, the new element in the Anonymous movement was not their (clearly reformist) demands, which had nothing to do with a revolutionary project and strategy. Despite the revolutionary rhetoric and slogans, their demands were merely demands for improvements to the system, i.e. less corruption in the public and private sector, more transparency, etc. - positions which one may easily find in reports of the World Bank and the IMF! The new element, therefore, brought about by Anonymous refers to the means they used to get their message across, i.e. the Internet. Yet, in London, where perhaps their biggest protest march among world cities took place, their members were boasting that "the internet has the power to bring down regimes…It belongs to everyone… we all have a voice now – 7 billion of us... We're all equal." [259] In fact, there are even some 'anarchists' who declare that "the Internet is a form of virtual direct democracy that empowers the subordinate groups to react against the dominant

---

[259] 'Anonymous to RT: 'Internet has power to bring down regimes', *RT*, 5/11/2014 http://rt.com/news/202639-anonymous-power-down-regimes/ ;; see also 'Global Million Mask March as it happened', *RT*, 6/11/2014 http://on.rt.com/mgbjuk

ones."[260] All this, when authoritative anarchist studies have clearly shown in the past the highly dangerous role of the Internet in relation to real democracy.[261]

The second event was the recent hot debate over the issue of anonymous smearing in countries that still want to keep at least the image of a well-functioning representative 'democracy'. In Britain, in particular, where the public's anger over the hordes of anonymous internet mud-slingers, (who slander, insult and use personal data and distorted photos against their victims) had reached its peak and the smear was either directed generally against other users, or specifically against writers who did not hide behind anonymity in expressing their views.[262]The result of this general condemnation was that the elites (which are far from hostile towards the web when it suits them!) were forced to take measures for the protection of the victims of smear, and quadrupled the previous six-month sentence. As it was stressed by the proponents of the new legislation, "no-one would permit such venom in person, so there should be no place for it on social media."[263] This forced even a clearly sympathetic to social media BBC journalist to comment, "For anyone who believed the Internet and social media would foster a new era of free expression and open debate, this is a depressing time." [264]

As far as the "Anonymous" rhetoric about the power of the internet to bring down governments is concerned, it can easily be shown it has very little to do with reality. I am not aware of any regime supported by the Transnational Elite which was overthrown thanks to the internet, even when hundreds of thousands of "Indignados" and "Occupiers" — who had been mobilized mainly through the internet (e.g. Spain, Greece, USA, Britain, etc.) — took part in relevant demonstrations and other acts of civil disobedience. In reality, the only regimes that were brought down under conditions in which the Internet

---

[260] "TROLLING", *Eleftherotypia,* 12/10/2014

[261] Matt Hern and Stu Chaulk, "Roadgrading Community Culture: Why the Internet is so dangerous to real democracy", *DEMOCRACY & NATURE,* vol.6, no.1, (March 2000) pp.111-120. See, also, Takis Fotopoulos' reply in the same issue, pp. 121-123

[262] See e.g.; Jonathan Brown," Laurence Easeman, the activist in Brand row: 'I was smeared' ", *The Independent,* 24/10/2014; see, also, Suzanne Moore, "Trolling is too high a price for freedom" , *The Guardian,* 7/10/2014

[263] "Internet trolls face up to two years in jail under new laws", *BBC News,* 19/10/2014

[264] ibid.

had really played a major role were the ones prescribed by the same Transnational Elite to be brought down through color "revolutions" (Arab 'Spring', [265] Eastern Europe, [266] etc.)!

Also, the allegations about the relation of the Internet to real democracy and equality are even more far-fetched, if not disorienting. In fact, real democracy, in the classical sense of direct democracy, has nothing to do with civil liberties or the Internet, which refer to the liberal, or representative 'democracy'. It is this kind of 'democracy' and the related ideology of human rights that constitute the basis of the ideology of globalization. Furthermore, it is well known that it was exactly for the protection of such rights that the Transnational Elite has supposedly carried out a series of wars (Yugoslavia, Iraq, Libya) and encouraged several real massacres elsewhere, from Syria to Ukraine.

On the other hand, real democracy presupposes 'face-to-face' assemblies, where it is only through discussions between active citizens — and certainly not just between the 'experts' — that the collective political will can be really expressed. [267] In this sense, the Internet democracy, as I tried to show elsewhere, is a clear distortion of direct democracy:

> In this era of virtual reality which we live, it was inevitable that the dominant social-liberal ideology would demean even the fundamental concept of democracy. Thus, on top of the other kinds of illusory democracy (representative 'democracy', radical 'democracy' etc.) we now have discovered the virtual 'democracy' of the Internet, celebrated by well-known liberal writers and bloggers, in perfect harmony with supporters of the reformist Left. Such people extol blogs and the Internet in general as the "greatest democratic conquest in History," which brings about a real democratization of the media "from below," given that every person can now become a publisher of him/her self. It is worth noting that this mythology is fully compatible with the present social-liberal ideology of 'rights' which, of

---

[265] Takis Fotopoulos, *Subjugating the Middle East,* (vol 3 of the NWO in Action)
[266] Takis Fotopoulos, *Ukraine, The Attack on Russia and the Eurasian Union* (vol 2 of the NWO in Action)
[267] Takis Fotopoulos, *Towards An Inclusive Democracy,* (Cassell: London, 1997) chs 5-6

course, has nothing to do with social self-determination, individual and collective autonomy, and true democracy.[268]

It was therefore hardly surprising that *Time* magazine, a well-known mouthpiece of the American establishment, pronounced a few years ago the anonymous user of the Internet as "person of the year," while, in 2007, the Transnational Elite, which had gathered for its annual informal meeting in Davos, praised enthusiastically internet 'democracy'![269]

On top of all this, one cannot really assess the real significance of the Internet without taking into account its built-in deficiencies. First, it is well known that, even as late as 2013, only a minority of the world population (less than 40%) were considered internet users, most of them (77%) concentrated in the 'developed world', where the minority of the world population lives, and that even fewer of them (less than 10%) had a fixed broadband connection.[270] Needless to add that this is not a problem that will just disappear over time, despite the growth momentum in the number of users recently. It is a systemic problem directly related to poverty and economic and social inequality, which are phenomena inherent in a system of market economy and representative 'democracy'. Thus, economic inequality and poverty imply that billions of people on the planet cannot afford the hardware and software, as well as the connection expenses to the Internet. On top of this, there is the equally important social inequality, namely, the various social factors that deter large segments of the population from the Internet (cultural factors, education, old age etc.). The consequence is that one more social exclusion has been added to the present exclusions: "the digital divide"![271]

---

[268] See Takis Fotopoulos, 'The virtual "democracy" of the Internet', *The International Journal of INCLUSIVE DEMOCRACY*, vol.4, no.2, (April 2008), http://www.inclusivedemocracy.org/journal/vol4/vol4_no2_takis_virtual_democracy.htm

[269] Jackie Ashley, "Beware the powerful when they hail the new democracy", *The Guardian*, 29/1/2007

[270] *Key ICT Indicators for developed and developing countries and the world*, International Telecommunications Unions (ITU), Geneva, 27 February 2013

[271] Ken Loach's latest film *I, Daniel Blake* (2016), which received the Palme d'Or at the Cannes Film Festival, beautifully portrays this new social exclusion, as well as the plight of the victims of globalization. Yet, Loach, as a prominent member of the globalist 'Left', did not touch upon the issue of globalization as the cause of this plight and, in fact, he did not side with the workers and the victims of globalization

One frequently quoted myth about the supposed democratization of the media brought about by the Internet, is that the blogs have abolished the distinction between producers and consumers of information, so that today we can all be producers. However, this is another theoretical right and not a reality in the present system. Nowadays, there are tens of millions of blogs in the world, but in fact most of them are inactive, or not regularly renewed. Similarly, there are millions of websites, but in reality, few muster daily a considerable number of visitors, as it happens also with the blogs. The reason of course has less to do with the allegation that these few are the only really interesting blogs and Web pages — as the misleading social-liberal competitive ideology asserts — and more to do with the designing and especially the constant renewing of a blog or a website, which is an indispensable element of attracting many visitors. However, this calls for not just some significant expenditure but, above all, plenty of time, which of course in today's society is translated also into cash. A sophisticated and constantly renewable blog or website requires either teams of full-time administrators to run them, or bloggers who can spare the extra time (and/or the necessary hard cash) to do so. In other words, the producers of information are actually a very small minority, who, generally, as Glenn Reynolds, (author of *An Army of Davids*, which explored the explosion in web punditry), pointed out, "tend on average to be better off, better educated and, more importantly, employed."[272] Hence, as found in the same study, more than half of the Internet users on the continent are passive and do not contribute to the web at all, while a further 23% only respond when prompted.[273]

Still another myth is that the free access to the Internet secures the freedom of access to knowledge, while others see the medium as an anti-systemic means that could put pressure on power. However, both these functions are, also, illusory. The first is decisively undermined by the anonymity of the medium. The information provided anonymously is frequently unreliable, or even suspicious, as it has

in general on Brexit but, instead, he stated that he believes the solution is ultimately voting to stay and "make alliances with other European left movements" — presumably of the SYRIZA kind! (see Benjamin Lee, "Ken Loach: I'm pro-EU, but it's 'not doing us any favours at the moment'", *The Guardian*, 13/5/2016
[272] Quoted in Bobbie Johnson, "Ignore bloggers at your peril, say researchers," *The Guardian*, 18/4/2006.
[273] ibid.

frequently been demonstrated in the case of the free online encyclopedia Wikipedia. This website provides easy access to sometimes useful information, yet, interventions by state and secret services, politicians, TNCs and others have, repeatedly, been made on entries of political and socio-economic content, with the obvious aim of misrepresenting the facts.[274]

Also, concerning the operation of the Internet, as an anti-systemic means, (in the sense that it allows criticism of the rulers — something supposedly justifying anonymity) in reality, as it has repeatedly been shown, anonymity was frequently used by various mudslingers and slanderers (and probably by members of the state or secret services) to defame 'eponymous' analysts, (i.e. writers using their real names), even if they have a long service in the anti-systemic Left! However, if online anonymity is indeed necessary to protect those criticizing power — and in this sense it is a form of practicing freedom — then, like any real freedom, either it will be ***self-disciplined,*** or it will be ***no*** freedom. It is well known that the greatest danger that, historically, direct democracy had faced was precisely the lack of self-discipline, which demands a high level of civil consciousness. The non-publication, for instance, of defamatory or abusive comments as well as of unsubstantiated allegations and characterizations should be an obvious prerequisite for the use of anonymity. Even more so if similar mudslinging comments and characterizations are directed, not against the institutions of power, but against people who have shown absolute consistency over time in their struggle against power. Obviously, in this case anonymity is no longer used as a means of protection against power, but as a means to protect power itself and its institutions against their enemies! Thus character assassination is common in the internet and this has obviously nothing to do with freedom of speech, but rather with the freedom required by the professional slanderers to do their 'job' effortlessly. It was not therefore surprising to hear that even the EU authorities decided to spend almost 3m Euros out of taxpayers' money on trolling Eurosceptic critics in the internet, in a

---

[274] Robert Verkaik, "Wikipedia and the art of censorship", *Independent*, 18/08/2007; see, also, Billy Kenber & Murad Ahmed, "Wiki wipes of multinational companies exposed", *The Times*, 17/11/2012

vain attempt to control the anti-EU popular tsunami, during the run-up to the May 2014 Euro elections![275]

All this does not of course mean that the Internet has no significant positive aspects. Thus, the Internet plays an important role in mobilization for protests, occupations etc. On such occasions anonymity is, of course, a necessary precaution against power. Also, the work of *WikiLeaks* in revealing information inaccessible to the general public is well recognized — although there is of course another trap here related to the choice of the documents to be released, who does it and on what criteria. Particularly so as information on certain sensitive topics (e.g. related to Israel and its policies)[276] is missing, or it is sparse in the *WikiLeaks*. Furthermore, although it is true that usually it is only in the internet that anti-systemic opinions may be published, which would normally be excluded from the traditional media, there is still another trap here related to the fact that the internet itself is being ultimately controlled by the Transnational Elites, through multinationals (Google, Facebook, etc.), which have the final say on what goes in and how, online. In fact, there are several known examples of banning users, even websites, when their appeal starts becoming dangerous to the elites.[277]

In conclusion, the Internet in itself (as, generally, any technology) is neither 'neutral', by its nature, nor autonomous, and, therefore, by definition democratic either. It is not neutral, as it has been created within the context of a specific system (market economy and representative 'democracy'), expressing its logic and dynamic. And it is not autonomous, as it inevitably expresses specific power relations and the dominant social paradigm. In other words, the Internet is not just a means to an unspecified end that everyone may use the way s/he

---

[275] Bruno Waterfield, "EU to set up euro-election 'troll patrol' to tackle Eurosceptic surge", *Daily Telegraph*, 3/2/2013

[276] Dana Harman, "Bloggers Claim WikiLeaks Struck Deal With Israel Over Diplomatic Cables Leaks", HAARETZ, 17/12/2010
http://www.haaretz.com/bloggers-claim-wikileaks-struck-deal-with-israel-over-diplomatic-cables-leaks-1.331030

[277] See Tony Cartalucci on the role of facebook, "Don't Replace Facebook, Disrupt It", Localorg 11/11/2014 http://localorg.blogspot.co.uk/2014/11/dont-replace-facebook-disrupt-it.html; see, also, Glenn Greenwald. "How covert agents infiltrate the internet to manipulate, deceive, and destroy reputations", https://theintercept.com/staff/glenn-greenwald/; see for examples of blocking 'undesirable' blogs http://aegeanhawk.blogspot.co.uk/2014/08/facebook-blog.html

wants, since there are inherent limitations in it, expressing specific systemic values.

In general, the process that decides each time the actual technology-in-use (as opposed to available technology) is decisively determined by the power structures involved in the existing institutional framework and the corresponding dominant social paradigm. Similarly, the free flow of information that the Internet supposedly provides is another myth. These are issues that have been discussed for some time in the literature[278] and only uninformed users (and the mud-slingers themselves!) might ignore their conclusions.

On the basis of the above considerations, it is critical to define some generally accepted rules regarding the operation of the Internet (to the degree of course that this is possible within the existing institutional framework) in order to restrict phenomena that may have significant adverse social implications. But, in case this is not possible, the introduction of social controls for the self-protection of society from the Internet is imperative, as was also historically necessary the introduction of social controls for the self-protection of society from the market. This is because the Internet, as well as a perfectly competitive market (let alone a market controlled by oligopolies of various kinds), cannot secure by itself equality among all participants. As everyone knows, even under conditions of perfect competition, some are 'more equal' than others, as a result of the unequal distribution of income and wealth. Similarly, on the Internet, neither money nor time availability are equally distributed among users. Therefore, in the same way that the market, without some effective social controls for the self-protection of society, is bound to lead to a social jungle — as happens in the NWO with the phasing out of such controls — in a similar way the internet, without some effective social controls for the self-protection of society, is bound to lead into an online jungle. This is what is at stake today with the war pursued by the 'Internet neoliberals' (exactly like the war pursued by market neoliberals) against social controls for the self-protection of society from this jungle. The aim in both cases is the same: to enhance the power of the elites in controlling our "freedom"...

---

[278] See for a survey of relevant literature Takis Fotopoulos, "Towards a Democratic Conception of Science and Technology", *Democracy and Nature*, Vol. 4, No. 1, issue 10 (1997), pp.54-86

PART III

Towards a Democratic Community of Sovereign Nations

Chapter 7.

The pro-EU propaganda about "democratizing" Europe and the NWO

In this part of the book we may proceed to examine, first, a recent attempt to consolidate the NWO in the form of the EU — which has always been seen by the elites as a first step towards global governance — (Ch. 7) and, then, the significance of BREXIT as a move to the opposite direction (Ch. 8). Finally, I will examine the all important issue of the tasks that a movement for social liberation should undertake today towards the creation of a democratic community of sovereign nations. I will conclude with a proposal for a Democratic Community of Sovereign Nations, which, to my mind, represents a real option now, vs. the pseudo-options offered by this so-called 'manifesto' (DIEM25), which, has already been approved by the elites. (Chs 9-11).

DIEM25: A Manifesto for Perpetuating the EU Elites' Domination of the European Peoples

In the midst of a huge publicity, particularly by the mass media of the globalist 'Left' such as *The Guardian*, Y. Varoufakis — one of the protagonists of the present economic, political and social Greek catastrophe — presented himself as the 'savior of Europa,' as he was described by another well-known member of the same 'Left' in an article published (of all places!) in *RT*.[279] In this section, I will try, first, to examine the democratic credentials of this manifesto and, second, to explore its aims and strategy. Then, I will try to answer some crucial questions concerning the timing of this manifesto and who supports it.

Needless to add that the 'Manifesto's' options were also approved, albeit indirectly, by George Soros, one of Varoufakis's strongest supporters, who stressed (not accidentally at the same time) the need to save the EU–which is the main aim of the DIEM manifesto–so that Putin's aim to the opposite direction could be negated: "Putin's aim is to foster the EU's disintegration, and the best way to do so is to flood Europe with Syrian refugees."[280]

In fact, there is ample evidence that it was Soros who has helped (through his NGOs) to flood Europe and Greece in particular with dubious refugees–a fact indirectly confirmed by himself.[281] His aim was simply to impose a multicultural society everywhere and, effectively, break the European nations, so that freedom in the movement of labor, a basic component of the NWO, could be globalized (see Ch. 8). Victor Orban gave an eloquent description of Soros's role a year ago, as quoted in *Bloomberg*:

> His name is perhaps the strongest example of those who support anything that weakens nation states, they support everything that changes the traditional European lifestyle [...] These activists who support immigrants inadvertently become part of this international human-smuggling network.[282]

But it was Sam Gerrans, who in an excellent RT article, analyzed precisely the role of Soros (and the Soroses of this world), which he summarized as follows:

---

[279] Pepe Escobar, "It takes a Greek to save Europa", RT, 11/2/2016, https://www.rt.com/op- edge/332169-europe-diem25-yanis-varoufakis/

[280] G. Soros, "Putin is a bigger threat to Europe's existence than Isis", The *Guardian*, 11/2/2016, http://www.theguardian.com/commentisfree/2016/feb/11/putin-threat-europe-islamic-state

[281] AP, "Soros to Invest $500 Million to Help Refugees and Migrants", *ABC News*, 20/9/2016, http://abcnews.go.com/US/wireStory/soros-invest-500-million-refugees-migrants-42212000; see also "who protects the suspicious NGOs in the Greek isles who receive immigrants", *iThesis* (in Greek) 29/9/2016 http://www.ithesis.gr/politikh/pios-prostatevi-tis-ipoptes-mko-sta-nisia-pou-dechonte-metanastes/

[282] Andras Gergely, "Orban Accuses Soros of Stoking Refugee Wave to Weaken Europe", *Bloomberg*, 30/10/2015

This is cultural- and ethnic-cleansing in a business suit; it is the de facto usurpation of the nation state as a social construct for the peoples of Europe as part of a multi-purpose war – one designed to destroy oil-rich states and any state with no central bank, while simultaneously collapsing sovereign states.[283]

Varoufakis begins his 'manifesto' by stating that "for all their concerns with global competitiveness, migration and terrorism, only one prospect truly terrifies the Powers of Europe: Democracy…rule by Europe's peoples, government by the demos, is the shared nightmare of the European elites."[284]

Then he makes clear what he means by this when he presents the who's who of these elites:

- The Brussels bureaucracy and its lobbyists
- Its hit-squad inspectorates and the Troika
- The powerful Eurogroup that has no standing in law or treaty
- Bailed-out bankers, fund managers and resurgent oligarchies
- Political parties appealing to liberalism, democracy, freedom and solidarity
- Governments that fuel cruel inequality by implementing austerity
- Media moguls who have turned fear-mongering into an art form
- Corporations in cahoots with secretive public agencies investing in the same fear to promote secrecy and a culture of surveillance that bend public opinion to their will.

As is obvious from this list, the EU elites are defined in purely political terms and, particularly, in terms of their power to manipulate 'public opinion' through the lack of transparency and the framework of secrecy within which mostly unelected EU organs dominate their 'subjects', i.e. the European peoples. In other words, the defining characteristic of the members of these elites is their *political power*,

---

[283] Sam Gerrans, "Soros to make a killing with European 'forced migration'", RT, 2/10/2016 https://www.rt.com/op-edge/361376-george-soros-investing-forced-immigration/

[284] Y. Varoufakis, A MANIFESTO FOR DEMOCRATISING EUROPE, February 2016

through which they can manipulate the European peoples to serve their aims.

What is *not* mentioned at all is who the elites exercising *economic power* are and what their role is in manipulating the decision-making process of the EU. He only makes a meaningless reference to 'corporations in cahoots with secretive public agencies', which are only accused about their secretive practices! That is, there is not a single word about the Transnational Corporations (TNCs), particularly those of European origin, such as the European Round Table of Industrialists, which consists of the main Transnational Corporations (TNCs) running the EU.[285] Similarly, there is no mention of the various international economic institutions, which are controlled by the Transnational Elite and their role — behind the scenes — in determining the EU's decisions (economic and political as well as cultural).

The pseudo-democratic 'credentials' of DIEM25

In fact, the Manifesto does everything possible to stress the presumed purely political nature of 'democracy' (which it mostly identifies with human rights!), as when it points out that "the European Union was an exceptional achievement…proving that it was possible to create a shared framework of human rights across a continent that was, not long ago, home to murderous chauvinism, racism and barbarity".[286] Even when the Manifesto tries to allude to economic elites, again, it does not put the blame on the vastly unequal distribution of economic power on which the EU elites thrive, but, instead, on the unequal distribution of political power which, supposedly, makes it possible for the economic elites to exercise their power:

> A confederacy of myopic politicians, economically naïve officials and financially incompetent 'experts' submit slavishly to the edicts of financial and industrial conglomerates, alienating Europeans and stirring up a dangerous anti-European backlash… At the heart of our disintegrating EU there lies a

---

[285] See the official site of the European Round Table of Industrialists http://www.ert.eu See also the film by Friedrich Moser & Matthieu Lietaert, *The Brus$€ls Business : Who Runs the European Union?* (2012) https://www.youtube.com/watch?v=h4C5SgeVK-Q

[286] A MANIFESTO FOR DEMOCRATISING EUROPE

guilty deceit: A highly political, top-down, opaque decision-making process is presented as 'apolitical', 'technical', 'procedural' and 'neutral'. Its purpose is to prevent Europeans from exercising democratic control over their money, finance, working conditions and environment.[287]

It is therefore absolutely clear that, according to the Manifesto, it is the inequality in the distribution of political power that is the cause of all evil in the EU. This is a conclusion which, at best, betrays a complete ignorance of what democracy is really all about and, at worst, attempts to deceive the victims of globalization in Europe as to the real causes of their present ordeal. Needless to add that Varoufakis, as the ex-Finance Minister of the Greek government, knows a few things about political deception, since this is a government consisting not of the usual corrupt professional politicians but of pure con artists. This is anyway how they are referred to by most Greeks, currently in open revolt against the government, members of which (as well as cadres of SYRIZA) are currently finding it difficult even to go about on the streets without police protection, while Tsipras himself is protected in his office by hundreds of policemen, exactly as his predecessors social-liberal and right wing Prime Ministers did and were castigated by him accordingly!

Yet Varoufakis has no qualms about discussing political deception, as when he emphasizes that "the price of this deceit is not merely the end of democracy but also poor economic policies," by which he means — as he explains further on — the austerity policies implemented by the EU elites "resulting in permanent recession in the weaker countries and low investment in the core countries" and "unprecedented inequality." So, Varoufakis' lesson is that the present unprecedented inequality is not the inevitable result of the opening and liberalization of markets implied by globalization, but, instead, the outcome of the 'guilty deceit', which, as he asserts, is supposedly due to the 'non- democratic' character of the EU apparatus.

However, as I have tried to show elsewhere,[288] if we define political democracy as the authority of the people (*demos*) in the political sphere — a fact that implies political equality — then

---

[287] Y. Varoufakis, A MANIFESTO FOR DEMOCRATISING EUROPE, op.cit.
[288] Takis Fotopoulos,*Towards An Inclusive Democracy*, London: Cassell,1997), chs 5-6

economic democracy could be correspondingly defined as the authority of the *demos* in the economic sphere — a fact that implies economic equality. Economic democracy therefore relates to every social system that institutionalizes the integration of society with the economy. This means that, ultimately, it is the *demos* that controls the economic process, within an institutional framework of *demotic* ownership of the means of production. In a narrower sense, economic democracy also relates to every social system that institutionalizes the minimization of socio-economic differences, particularly those arising from the unequal distribution of private property and the consequent unequal distribution of income and wealth (as the old social-democratic parties used to preach). It should also be noted that economic democracy refers both to the mode of production and to the distribution of the social product and wealth.

In this sense, the EU apparatus is not, and could never be, a democracy within an institutional framework that secures, in fact, the unequal distribution of economic power, as the NWO of neoliberal globalization does. To put it simply, as long as a minority of people own and control the means of production and distribution, it is this minority (or elite) that will take all the important economic decisions, and not the political elite, which, crucially, depends on the former for the funding of their expensive election campaigns, or for their promotion through the mass media, which the economic elites also control and so on. Yet, James K Galbraith, a well-known member of the globalist 'Left' (and one of Varoufakis's political advisers when in government — presumably at the expense of the Greek people), did not hesitate to draw the following unflattering to the EU apparatus conclusion comparing it to the US congressional one:

> What struck me in particular from the standpoint of a veteran of the congressional staff was the near-complete absence of procedural safeguards, of accountability, of record-keeping, of transparency, and also the practical absence of an independent and sceptical press. These are the elementary functional components of a working democracy, and their absence is an enormous obstacle to the progress of democracy in Europe, and are therefore, an excellent place to begin.[289]

---

[289] see unofficial transcript of DIEM25 speeches at
https://pad.riseup.net/p/DiEM25_Transcript

So, according to this criterion of democracy (transparency etc.), which is also the Manifesto's main criterion, the model for EU democracy should be the US model. That is, a model which, in fact, represents the absolute degradation of any concept of democracy, as it is well known that Congressmen and the President himself are elected according to how much support they can muster from the economic elites (funding, mass media support etc.)! The Hillary Clinton example is particularly illuminating on this!

The aims of "authentic democracy" and the strategy of DIEM25

Having described this parody (or rather complete distortion) of democracy as 'authentic' democracy, the Manifesto then proceeds to define, in chronological order, the aims of the DIEM25 movement.

A. IMMEDIATELY

The immediate aim is "full transparency in decision-making," i.e. the publication of the minutes of EU institutions, the online uploading of important documents, the monitoring of lobbyists etc. Any comments here would obviously be superfluous, as it is clear that the reason such a petty aim is associated with 'authentic' democracy is clearly to distract people from the real conditions which must be met for political power to be distributed equally among all citizens.

B. WITHIN TWELVE MONTHS

The aim here is to address the ongoing economic crisis "utilizing existing institutions and within existing EU Treaties". The proposed policies, according to the Manifesto, "will be aimed at re-deploying existing institutions (through a creative re-interpretation of existing treaties and charters) in order to stabilize the crises of public debt, banking, inadequate investment, and rising poverty".

However, it was the EU institutions themselves that have created these crises, which therefore can never be 'stabilized' within the existing institutions and treaties. It was the proliferation of multinationals (or Transnational Corporations-TNCs), from the mid-1970s onwards, which has led to the phenomenon of neoliberal globalization — no relation to the failed attempt at globalization in the early 20th century [290] — through the opening and liberalization of markets for goods, services, capital and labor that was necessary

---

[290] See Takis Fotopoulos, *Towards An Inclusive Democracy,* (Cassell/Taylor & Francis, 1997), ch 1

within the globalization process. Thus, the opening and liberalization of markets brought about a structural change in the capitalist economic model, which most Marxists — with some notable exceptions like Leslie Sklair — have failed to understand. Hence, they could not see the direct link between neoliberalism and the opening/liberalization of markets and tried instead to explain neoliberalism, at best, as simply a kind of ideology and, at worst, as a capitalist 'project' or conspiracy. Yet, as I tried to show in this book, it was the famous 'four freedoms', i.e. the opening and liberalization of markets for capital, goods, services and labor, that were institutionalized first by the EU Maastricht Treaty and those following it, which were the ultimate cause of all the present EU crises (debt crises, rising inequality and unemployment, as well as the refugee crisis).

In other words, the aforementioned Marxists could not see that throughout the pre-globalization part of the post-war period from 1945-1975, the capitalist development model was based essentially on the internal market. This meant that the control of aggregate demand policies and especially fiscal policies (regarding taxation but also, more importantly, public spending — including public investment, social spending and the welfare state), played a critical role in determining national income and employment levels and, therefore, economic growth itself.

On the other hand, in the globalization era that followed with the opening and liberalization of markets, the basis of growth shifted from the internal to the external market. This meant that competitiveness became the key criterion for the success of a capitalist market economy. Consequently, the multinationals now play a key role in the growth process through the investments they finance, as well as through the expansion of exports they can bring about through the installation of affiliates in a country. The EU is, of course, the main expression of neoliberal globalization in the European area.

In this context, it is not the austerity policies imposed by some 'baddies' in the political and economic elites that are the cause of the present low growth economy, just because these elites do not wish to adopt Keynesian policies to expand incomes and demand. As I tried to show, the austerity policies are simply the symptom of globalization, as frequently it is the only means to improve competitiveness, which is the sole criterion of economic success in the NWO.

C. WITHIN TWO YEARS

A Constitutional Assembly should be convened consisting of 'representatives' from national assemblies (Parliaments), regional assemblies and municipal councils. The resulting Constitutional Assembly, according to the 'Manifesto', would be empowered to decide on a future democratic constitution that would replace all existing European Treaties within a decade. Here it is obvious that the author of the 'Manifesto' has no idea whatsoever about the meaning of classical democracy or the concept of *demos* which he so extensively (mis)uses, and yet he has no qualms about identifying representative 'democracy' with classical democracy!

In fact, however, it was only during the sixteenth century that the idea of representation entered the political lexicon, although the sovereignty of Parliament was not established until the seventeenth century. In the same way that the king had once 'represented' society as a whole, it was now the turn of Parliament to play this role, although sovereignty itself was still supposed to belong to the people as a whole. The doctrine that prevailed in Europe after the French revolution was not just that the French people were sovereign and that their views were represented in the National Assembly, but that the French nation was sovereign and the National Assembly embodied the will of the nation. As Anthony Birch stressed:

> [T]his was a turning point in continental European ideas since, before this, the political representative had been viewed in the continent as a delegate. According to the new theory promulgated by the French revolutionaries... the elected representative is viewed as an independent maker of national laws and policies, not as an agent for his constituents or for sectional interests.[291]

One may therefore conclude that the form of liberal 'democracy' that has dominated the West in the last two centuries is not even a representative 'democracy' but, instead, a representative *government*, that is, a government of the people *by* their representatives, as Bhikhu Parekh pointed out:

> Representatives were to be elected by the people, but once elected they were to remain free to manage public affairs as

---

[291] Anthony H. Birch, *The Concepts and Theories of Modern Democracy*, (London: Routledge, 1993) p.58.

they saw fit. This highly effective way of insulating the government against the full impact of universal franchise lies at the heart of liberal democracy. Strictly speaking, liberal democracy is not representative *democracy* but representative *government.*[292]

This European conception of sovereignty was completely alien to the Athenian conception, where the separation of sovereignty from its exercise was unknown. All powers were exercised directly by the citizens themselves, or by delegates who were appointed by lot and for a short period of time. In fact, as Aristotle points out, the election by voting was considered oligarchic and was not allowed but in exceptional circumstances (usually in cases where special knowledge was required), and only appointment by lot was considered democratic. [293] Therefore, the type of 'democracy' that has been established since the sixteenth century in Europe has had very little in common with the classical (Athenian) democracy. The former presupposes the separation of the state from society and the exercise of sovereignty by a separate body of representatives, whereas the latter is based on the principle that sovereignty is exercised directly by the free citizens themselves. Athens, therefore, may hardly be characterized as a state in the normal sense of the word.

D. BY 2025: ENACTMENT OF THE DECISIONS OF THE CONSTITUTIONAL ASSEMBLY

The ultimate aim of the process envisaged by DIEM25 is pure deception and Y. Varoufakis has shown in his career as a Finance Minister that he is a master of this. He claims that the Constitutional Assembly (or 'We, the peoples of Europe' as he calls it, copying the American Constitution) will bring about the 'radical' change envisaged by the Manifesto. Yet the American case is hardly a model for democracy, as A. Birch pointed out:

> The American Founding Fathers Madison and Jefferson were sceptical of democracy, precisely because of its Greek

---

[292] Bhikhu Parekh, "The Cultural Particularity of Liberal Democracy", *Political*, Volume 40, Issue Supplement s1, pages 160–175, August 1992

[293] According to Aristotle, "... I say that the appointment by lot is commonly held to be characteristic of democracy, whereas the process of election for that purpose is looked upon as oligarchic"; Aristotle, *Politics,* Book IV, 1294b, John Warrington, ed. (London: Heron Books)

connotation of direct rule. This is why they preferred to call the American system republican, because "the term was thought to be more appropriate to the balanced constitution that had been adopted in 1787 than the term democratic, with its connotations of lower-class dominance."[294]

Also, as John Dunn aptly stressed while describing the aim of representative government:

> It is important to recognize that the modern state was constructed, painstakingly and purposefully, above all by Jean Bodin and Thomas Hobbes, for the express purpose of denying that any given population, any people, had either the capacity or the right to act together for themselves, either independently of, or against their sovereign. The central point of the concept was to deny the very possibility that any demos (let alone one on the demographic scale of a European territorial monarchy) could be a genuine political agent, could act at all, let alone act with sufficiently continuous identity and practical coherence for it to be able to rule itself... . the idea of the modern state was invented precisely to repudiate the possible coherence of democratic claims to rule, or even take genuinely political action... representative democracy is democracy made safe for the modern state.[295]

Clearly therefore what Varoufakis had in mind with his 'Manifesto' was simply to repeat the American Founding Fathers' deception and create another 'democratic' monster, like his beloved American one, in Europe! Unsurprisingly, he tried to hide the fact that what he talked about had nothing to do with classical democracy, despite the misleading terminology he uses (*demos* etc.). Thus, as he stressed, "we consider the model of national parties which form flimsy alliances at the level of the European Parliament to be obsolete". He then goes on to effectively negate this statement by stressing that:

> While the fight for democracy-from-below (at the local, regional or national levels) is necessary, it is nevertheless insufficient if it is conducted without an internationalist

[294] Anthony Birch, *The Concepts and Theories of Modern Democracy, o.p.* p. 50.
[295] John Dunn, "Conclusion" in. *Democracy, the Unfinished Journey, 508 BC to AD 1993,* pp. 247-48.

strategy toward a Pan-European coalition for democratizing Europe. European democrats must come together first, forge a common agenda, and then find ways of connecting it with local communities and at the regional and national level.[296]

It is therefore obvious that his aim is purely to save the EU, rather than democracy, as he knows very well that the process he suggests could never lead to a democracy from below. Such a democracy could of course only start from the local level, and then local demoi could federalize into democratic regions, nations and finally a democratic Europe. Not the other way around, as he deceptively suggests, particularly so when we are talking about a continent which, unlike the USA, consists of a multiplicity of peoples with different languages, cultures and history. Yet Varoufakis goes on in the same wavelength, revealing in the process his real intentions:

> Our overarching aim to democratize the European Union is intertwined with an ambition to promote self-government (economic, political and social) at the local, municipal, regional and national levels; to throw open the corridors of power to the public; to embrace social and civic movements; and to emancipate all levels of government from bureaucratic and corporate power.[297]

However, what he obviously had in mind here was to deceive people into thinking that they are fighting for a conversion of the EU into a democracy through some sort of decentralization of power to the local, municipal, regional and national levels — while, of course, the economic and political elites would continue to monopolize economic and political power, exactly as at present. The deception becomes clearer when one remembers that the EU is also, in fact, supposed to encourage such decentralization through its principle of subsidiarity!

The timing of the manifesto and the rise of the neo-nationalist movement

One reasonable question arising with respect to the timing of the 'Manifesto' is why such a manifesto for the 'democratization' of the EU should be necessary at this particular moment. Given that this is not really a manifesto for the democratization of Europe but, rather, an

---

[296] Varoufakis, A MANIFESTO FOR DEMOCRATISING EUROPE, op.cit.
[297] ibid.

attempt to promote the EU, as we saw above, the motives behind this pseudo-manifesto are now clear. Particularly so if we consider that this is in fact the moment of truth for the EU, not just because of the refugee problem, but also because of the Eurozone crisis, the Brexit revolution and, generally, the rise of the neo-nationalist movement. Yet all these crises are not 'external' to the EU crises, but have actually been created by the EU itself and its institutions.

The opening of the labor market within the EU and the removal of border controls through the Schengen agreement was one of the main causes of the refugee problem. However, a decisive role was also played by the EU elites, which, as part of the Transnational Elite, destroyed the stable Ba'athist regimes in both Iraq and Syria, as well as the Libyan national liberation regime. The Transnational Elite's sole aim was "regime change", with the aim to integrate all these peoples, who were resisting the NWO and fighting to maintain their national sovereignty.

Then, it was the institutions of the Eurozone itself that created the Eurozone crisis, the debt crisis and the massive rise in unemployment and poverty. As I have shown elsewhere,[298] these institutions were tailor-made to create a mechanism for the transfer of economic surplus from the less developed members of the Eurozone (e.g. Greece, Portugal, Ireland and Spain) to the more advanced ones, particularly Germany.

Similarly, it was the resentment of the British people at the loss of their national sovereignty within the EU (despite the fact that the British elites are a constituent part of the Transnational Elite) that has led to a growing anti-EU movement within the country, which has already led to a Brexit vote — an event which could have catalytic implications for the EU itself and beyond. This is particularly so because, as the British elites themselves recognized, the anti-EU movement in Britain is actually a movement against globalization (a fact that the Globalist 'Left' ignores) — something that could also explain the rise of the neo-nationalist UKIP party.

However, it is mainly Le Pen's National Front party, as we saw in Part I, more than any other neo-nationalist party in the West, that has

---

[298] Takis Fotopoulos, "The real causes of the catastrophic crisis in Greece and the "Left", The International Journal of INCLUSIVE DEMOCRACY, Vol. 9, Nos. 1/2 (Winter-Summer 2013) — see, also, vol. 2 of the *NWO in Action*

realized that globalization and membership of the NWO's institutions are incompatible with national sovereignty. One could therefore assume that it was mainly the meteoric rise of neonationalist movements in Europe, which determined the timing of Varoufakis' Manifesto.

The Globalist 'Left' and the 'Manifesto'

It goes without saying that the neo-nationalist movement I considered in Ch3, which, in Europe, is usually an explicitly anti-EU movement as well, is presently engulfing almost every EU country: from Britain to France and from Hungary to Austria and Poland. The unifying element among the neo-nationalists is their struggle for national and economic sovereignty, which they rightly see as disappearing in the era of globalization. Although sometimes the main immediate motive of the victims of globalization is their opposition to uncontrolled immigration, it is clear that they are misguided on this (sometimes by the leaders of the neonationalist movements themselves), and do not realize that it is the opening up of all markets, including the labor markets, particularly within economic unions like the EU, which is the ultimate cause of their own unemployment or low-wage employment. In other words, the neo-nationalist movement is not a racist movement as such but a purely anti-globalization movement, although the Transnational and Zionist elites, with the help of the globalist 'Left', are trying hard to convert it into an Islamophobic movement — as the *Charlie Hebdo* case clearly showed — – so that they can use it order to terrorize the victims of globalization and recruit them in their developing war (supposedly against terrorism) in Syria.

It was of course hardly surprising that the neo-nationalist movement, in its struggle to recover economic and national sovereignty, would turn against not only economic globalization, but also political and cultural globalization . However, this does not mean that it is a movement against a specific foreign culture. It is in fact a movement for the defense of each people's culture, which is at present under threat by cultural as well as ideological globalization. Yet, the elites try hard to convert this neo-nationalist movement to an Islamophobic (if not racist) one, with the help of mass propaganda about the ISIS atrocities etc. This, despite the fact that it was the Transnational Elite itself that encouraged, directly, as well as indirectly (through its own atrocities in Iraq, Libya and Syria) the creation and expansion of ISIS![299] Unsurprisingly, extreme right wing parties like the Geert Wilders' Dutch Party For Freedom (PVV) exploited the opportunity given to them by the wave of Islamophobia created by several suspicious ISIS attacks in France and Germany to begin a "de-Islamization" campaign calling for the closure of all mosques and Islamic schools, a ban on the Koran, while declaring *"no more immigrants from Islamic countries."*[300] As we shall see below, this is one more reason why Popular Fronts for National and Social Liberation must be built in every country to fight not only the NWO — which is of course the main enemy — but also any racist trends developing within this new anti-globalization movement. This would also prevent the elites from using the historically well-tested practice of 'divide and rule' to create discord between the victims of globalization.

The neo-nationalist movement is embraced today by most of the victims of globalization all over Europe, particularly the working class that used to support the Left.[301] On the other hand the latter has effectively embraced not just economic globalization but also political, ideological and cultural globalization and has therefore been fully integrated into the New World Order — a defining moment in its present intellectual and political bankruptcy. The process of the Left's bankruptcy has been further enhanced by the fact that, faced with political collapse in the May 2014 Euro-parliamentary elections, it allied itself with the elites in condemning the neo-nationalist parties as fascist and neo-Nazi, while in extreme cases it has even consented to the use of blatantly fascist methods in order to suppress some of them (e.g. the Golden Dawn party in Greece).

However, following the successful emasculation of the anti-systemic movement against globalization (mainly through the World Social Forum, thanks to the activities of the globalist 'Left'),[302] it was up to the neo-nationalist movement to fight globalization in general

---

[299] see *Subjugate the Middle East,* (vol 3 of *the NWO in Action*)

[300] "Close all mosques & ban the Koran: Poll-topping Geert Wilders launches 'de-Islamization' manifesto", RT, 26/8/2016 https://www.rt.com/news/357340-geert-wilders-manifesto-islam/

[301] Francis Elliott et al. 'Working class prefers Ukip to Labour", *The Times,* 25/11/2014

[302] Takis Fotopoulos, "Globalisation, the reformist Left and the Anti-Globalisation 'Movement'", DEMOCRACY & NATURE, vol.7, no.2 (July 2001) http://www.democracynature.org/vol7/takis_globalisation.htm

and the EU in particular. It is therefore clear that the neo-nationalist parties which are, in fact, all under attack by the Transnational Elite, constitute cases of movements that have simply filled the huge gap created by the globalist 'Left'. It was this 'Left' which, instead of placing itself in the front line among all those peoples fighting globalization and the phasing out of their economic and national sovereignty, has indirectly promoted globalization, using arguments based on an anachronistic internationalism, supposedly founded on Marxism.

As one might expect, most members of the Globalist 'Left' have joined the new 'movement' by Varoufakis to democratize Europe, 'forgetting' in the process that 'Democracy' was also the West's propaganda excuse for destroying Iraq, Libya and now Syria. Today, it seems that the Soros circus is aiming to use exactly the same excuse to destroy Europe, in the sense of securing the perpetuation of the EU elites' domination over the European peoples and therefore the continuation of the consequent economic violence involved.

The most prominent members of the globalist 'Left' who have already joined this new DIEM 'movement' range from Noam Chomsky and Julian Assange to Suzan George and Toni Negri, and from Hillary Wainwright of *Red Pepper* to *CounterPunch* and other globalist 'Left' newspapers and journals all over the world. In this context, it is particularly interesting to refer to Slavoj Žižek's commentary on the 'Manifesto' that was presented at the inaugural meeting of Varoufakis's new movement in Berlin on February 2016. No need to add that Zizek's commentary was greeted enthusiastically by Varoufakis's globalist 'Left' supporters.

Zizek began by blatantly attempting to deceive the audience with respect to SYRIZA's rise to power. He talked about a 'defeat' but then he immediately added, "I don't blame them; their situation was hopeless from the beginning."[303] Of course, he 'forgot' to mention that the situation was hopeless only because SYRIZA took for granted what actually needed to be changed, if they were really keen to implement their promises. That is, to reverse the austerity policies imposed by the Troika, to 'tear up' the Memoranda along with them, to stop privatizations and so on. In other words, SYRIZA took for

---

[303] see unofficial transcript of DIEM25 speeches at https://pad.riseup.net/p/DiEM25_Transcript. See also the video itself at https://www.youtube.com/watch?v=fFNJYpwv39s

granted the very causes of the Greek crisis and in particular Greece's membership of the EU and the Eurozone.

No wonder Varoufakis, as a Finance Minister, never took any measures to implement a 'Plan B' so that, as soon as the European Central Bank began cutting off liquidity, (which led to capital controls that still continue to this day), the Greek government could have been in a position to re-introduce a national currency as a first step towards national sovereignty. Varoufakis simply said that he "had in mind" a Plan B and that he discussed it with close associates (like his friend Galbraith!), but of course he never thought of taking a single measure to facilitate the implementation of such a plan. Clearly, putting such a plan into action necessitated a huge preparatory process to mobilize Greek civil servants for this purpose. He did not even have the elementary political decency to resign when he discovered that such action was out of bounds for the SYRIZA leadership. Instead, he resigned (or, more accurately, was effectively forced to resign) only after the 'defeat' — as his friend Zizek euphemistically called it — had become inevitable. The very fact that Varoufakis connived in the catastrophe of the Greek people, as he did in his capacity as Greek Finance Minister for over six critical months, is of course a crime to which he took an active part together with the rest of the criminal SYRIZA leadership. This catastrophe was inevitable once the elites became certain that the government would surrender and accept whatever conditions they imposed on a defenseless people.

Zizek then launched a vitriolic attack on the rising neo-nationalist movements, following on the example of the entire globalist 'Left', which is of course 'inspired' by Soros and other members of the Transnational Elite:

> Sometimes even if you rationally know the situation is hopeless you have to experience it. The lesson was a very important one of the defeat of SYRIZA, the lesson was the crucial step forward, the way to undermine global capitalism cannot be done at the level of nation states. There is a great temptation now all around Europe, a kind of neo-Keynesian social democratic nationalist temptation. The idea is since we live in a global market, and this means international relations are dominated by the logic of capital, the only hope is to return to a stronger nation state, with all this implies a certain level of nationalism/populism and we establish again strong nation-

states which impose their own laws, regulate their own
financial policy and so on and so on. That illusion has to be
abandoned I claim. And this is why I think what DIEM is
doing is strictly linked to the failure of SYRIZA... [304]

In fact, along the same lines, the Manifesto itself stresses that,
"two dreadful options dominate: retreat into the cocoon of our nation-
states, or surrender to the Brussels democracy-free zone." Yet, this is a
pseudo-dilemma or, more to the point, a highly deceptive description
of the actual choices involved, as we shall see in the last chapter in
which we will present a real third option — unlike the Manifesto's
false options. But before we do this, let us see first the highly deceitful
way in which Zizek attempted to justify the globalist 'Left's' approach
which is, in fact, a celebration of the NWO. Thus, in his commentary
at the DIEM25 meeting, Zizek pointed out that:

> Our only hope is to engage in very concrete very specific acts,
> we have to choose very well our concrete act, our concrete
> demand... that is the art to demand something relatively
> modest, but if you follow to the end this demand, everything
> will fall apart. You open up the path to general rearrangement
> of social relations. [305]

Of course, for anybody with an elementary knowledge of what is
going on at present in Greece this can only be taken, at best, as a joke
and, at worst, as a deliberate attempt to justify SYRIZA's criminal
policies. These policies, in fact, aim to execute every single order that
comes from the Troika (although strictly speaking is not a Troika
anymore because of the addition of another EU institution in the
negotiations) perhaps with some minor modifications to create the
pretense of real negotiations. The aims currently pursued by the elites,
according to the new Memorandum (surely the worst ever) signed by
SYRIZA in July 2015, include:

- the effective smashing of farmers' incomes with heavy taxation
  and the destruction of their pension system. Farmers responded
  a few months later by blocking all the main roads, while the
  'Leftist' government did not have any qualms about using the
  special riot units to 'control' them!

---

[304] ibid.
[305] ibid.

- the actual pauperization of pensioners of all kinds — demonstrations over this issue had been occurring almost daily in Athens for several months afterwards, which culminated in early October 2016 when the world saw a supposedly radical 'Left' government using the special riot units to tear gas old age pensioners;[306]
- the sale off all social wealth, starting with seaports, airports and trains, with electricity, water etc. to follow.

It is clear now to everybody that SYRIZA's only aim is power for power's sake. No wonder that Greece, a country with a historical very strong Left tradition, may soon see the destruction of its Left movement altogether, given in particular the fact that KKE — the Greek Communist Party — engages in strong rhetoric not matched by its actions. As a result, most people turn to political apathy and the abstention rate in the last election, following the signing of the new Memorandum by SYRIZA, was at an all-time high! Others turn to the Golden Dawn Party, which, given the old sympathies of its leaders to Nazi collaborators and to the extreme Right, prevents the creation of a genuine neo-nationalist movement, as in the rest of Europe. Particularly so when KKE, instead of adopting the demand for national sovereignty and fighting for national as well as social liberation, (as it successfully did during the Nazi Occupation, when it became a mass popular movement) it simply joined the campaign of the Euro-elites against nationalism and the supposed rise of racism and fascism in Greece. Something which is in itself an insult against the Greek people, given its heroic fight against such phenomena in the past!

Of course, Zizek's stand on SYRIZA and the 'Manifesto' in general is far from unexpected. Not accidentally, he also supported (albeit indirectly) the campaigns for regime change in Libya and Syria, as when he advocated the need for a 'big' socio-economic revolution within Arab countries. He also did this directly when he adopted the propaganda of the Transnational Elite that Libya and Syria were governed by 'dictators' — not bothering (despite his high qualifications) to examine the history of these regimes, which were backed by strong national liberation movements and had achieved really significant social changes. Then, he celebrated the Ukrainian

---

[306] "Greek police use tear gas on pensioners at anti-austerity protest", *BBC News*, 3/102016 http://www.bbc.co.uk/news/world-europe-37544416; see also Anthee Carassava, Ban on tear gas after pensioners blinded", *The Times*, 5/10/2016

'revolution' in Kiev,[307] together with the likes of Victoria Nuland and John McCain, fully revealing to which camp he really belongs. No wonder that he never proposed any concrete alternatives to the present system, as a system, but instead just promoted changes guaranteeing the protection of human rights — as every good supporter of the ideology of globalization does. Alternatively, he talked about communism as an abstract ideal, without ever attempting to specify the preconditions for it, let alone any transitional strategy to achieve it.

---

[307] See the "Open letter on the future of Ukraine", signed by scores of Zizek-type globalization intellectuals, politicians et al, which declares their admiration for the Ukrainian 'revolutionaries': "They defended their democracy and their future 10 years ago, during the Orange Revolution, and they are standing up for those values again today ", *euobserver,* 27/1/2014 http://euobserver.com/opinion/122880

Chapter 8.

Brexit Revolution and Counter-revolution

Introduction

The aim of this long and important chapter is threefold. First, to show why the UK referendum result in favor of BREXIT from the EU was very much a popular revolution as almost the entire movement — apart from a small section consisting of a conservative nationalist minority and that tiny part of the economic elite not controlled by the multinationals — was a movement 'from below', i.e. from the victims of globalization themselves. In other words, Brexit was in fact a class issue, reflecting the popular reaction to the class nature of globalization.

The second aim is to show the extent and the aims of the counter-revolution launched by the Transnational Elite immediately after the initial shock of the referendum result. The ultimate aim of the counter-revolution is shown to be the effective annulment of the referendum result, given that a formal annulment of it is — at present at least — politically prohibitive. This would involve a Britain, formally outside the EU, but essentially implementing all the constraints on social and economic policies imposed by the full integration of the country into the New World Order of neoliberal globalization, apart perhaps from some controls on immigration.

The third aim, with which I will start the chapter, is to examine the fundamental change in the parameters determining the UK-EU relationship since 1975, when the first referendum on whether Britain will stay in the Common Market (the precursor of the EU) was held.

Furthermore, I will try to explain the apparent paradox that the British 'Left' (and the EU 'Left' in general) has now become much more pro-EU than ever before, despite the fact that the EU, during the globalization era, has become much more reactionary than ever before, given the unprecedented use of economic as well as military violence by its elites to achieve their aims.

The historical background of Brexit

June 23rd 2016 is a day that could, potentially, change history. Not only in Britain itself but also in Europe (which is presently fully controlled by the European branch of the Transnational Elite) and beyond. The British referendum was a terrific slap in the faces, not only of the Euro-elites, but also of the whole Transnational Elite and the neoliberal globalization run by it. That is, a globalization that has already pushed millions of people around the world, including many in Britain, to economic and social degradation, or, alternatively, to physical extermination and dislocation through the wars unleashed during its rule (from Yugoslavia to Iraq and Afghanistan, and from Libya and Syria to Ukraine).

It was a terrific slap to the elites because the British people did not buckle, despite the brutal campaign by the Transnational Elite to force them to vote against Brexit, using all means at its disposal, including the mass media which it controls. The `Project Fear' dismally failed because, as the flagship of the globalist 'Left' pointed out, its "fundamental mistake was that it did not understand that far too many Britons, already living insecure and uncertain lives, felt they had little to lose… the typical pay packet is the same now as at the time of the 2008 crash."[308] Even the war criminal, Nobel Peace laureate Obama, was mobilized to go to London to declare that Britain will suffer disaster if it leaves the EU, clearly worried by the possible serious ramifications of Brexit with respect to the forthcoming US elections. Meanwhile, the equally criminal Donald Tusk (who, after having organized the murderous coup in Ukraine as prime minister of Poland, was rewarded with the Presidency of the European Council!) spoke about a possible destruction of Western civilization following a

---

[308] Editorial, "Britain after Brexit: our economy, our union and our place in the world are all at stake", *The Guardian*, 25/6/2016

Brexit,[309] unashamedly identifying the latter with the criminal NWO of which he is a minor apparatchik.

However, the best way to understand the revolutionary character of the decision of the British people for Brexit might be to go back first to the historical background of the EU and Britain's relationship with it, the elites' Project Fear to terrorize the electorate against any decision for Brexit and the disorienting stand of the globalist 'Left' on Brexit.

In fact, the June referendum on whether Britain will remain a member of the EU or not was the second referendum on the issue. The British people was asked again to vote on the same issue some 40 years ago, in 1975, when they had to decide on whether to stay in the 'Common Market' (the precursor of the present EU) or not. At that time, the Left was not yet integrated into the New World Order (NWO) of neoliberal globalization that expresses the interests of multinational corporations — which were then emerging en masse. As a result, not only the anti-systemic Left but also most of the Labor party under the leadership of Tony Benn was fighting at the time for a British exit. Nowadays, Tony Benn's son is one of the most reactionary British politicians, a thorough globalist and one of the strongest opponents of Brexit and supporter of all the wars by the Transnational Elite. In fact, the entire Labor party, and the Trade Unions it controls, took a stand against Brexit, apart from a handful of its members in Parliament. So, what has changed since 1975? To answer this question we have to go back to the very origin and historical evolution of the EU.

a. The origin of the EU as the economic complement to NATO

As it is well known, the process of creating a single European market began in the 1950s with the Rome treaty. However, the EU project, far from reflecting the dream of the European peoples to unite and avoid another catastrophic world war, as the naïve western ideology had it, was in fact, from the beginning, a western capitalist project to fight communism which had been flourishing since the end of the Second World War. It can be shown that the 'European project' was very much, in effect, a product of the US capitalist elite that emerged as the hegemonic power of world capitalism at the end of the

---

[309] Kai Dieckmann, BILD, 13/6/2016 http://www.businessinsider.com/donald-tusk-bild-interview-brexit-2016-6

war. As Ambrose Evans-Pritchard, a distinguished *Telegraph* journalist and researcher recently put it, following long research on the matter:

> It was Washington that drove European integration in the late 1940s, and funded it covertly under the Truman, Eisenhower, Kennedy, Johnson, and Nixon administrations... The Schuman Declaration that set the tone of Franco-German reconciliation - and would lead by stages to the European Community - was cooked up by the US Secretary of State Dean Acheson at a meeting in Foggy Bottom. "It all began in Washington," said Robert Schuman's chief of staff. It was the Truman administration that browbeat the French to reach a modus vivendi with Germany in the early post-War years, even threatening to cut off US Marshall aid at a furious meeting with recalcitrant French leaders they resisted in September 1950... Truman's motive was obvious. The Yalta settlement with the Soviet Union was breaking down. He wanted a united front to deter the Kremlin from further aggrandizement after Stalin gobbled up Czechoslovakia, doubly so after Communist North Korea crossed the 38th Parallel and invaded the South.[310]

It was the same journalist and researcher who, sixteen years ago, revealed that the origins of the European federalist movement could also be traced back to the same source. Furthermore, declassified documents showed that, contrary to common 'European' myths, the US elite were always in favor of Britain playing a leading role in a federalized Europe:

> DECLASSIFIED American government documents show that the US intelligence community ran a campaign in the Fifties and Sixties to build momentum for a united Europe. It funded and directed the European federalist movement. The documents confirm suspicions voiced at the time that America was working aggressively behind the scenes to push Britain into a European state. One memorandum, dated July 26, 1950, gives instructions for a campaign to promote a fully-fledged

---

[310] Ambrose Evans-Pritchard, "The European Union always was a CIA project, as Brexiteers discover", *The Telegraph*, 27/4/2016
http://www.telegraph.co.uk/business/2016/04/27/the-european-union-always-was-a-cia-project-as-brexiteers-discov/

European parliament. It is signed by Gen William J Donovan, head of the American wartime Office of Strategic Services, precursor of the CIA...Washington's main tool for shaping the European agenda was the American Committee for a United Europe (ACUE), created in 1948. The chairman was Donovan, ostensibly a private lawyer by then. The vice-chairman was Allen Dulles, the CIA director in the Fifties... The documents show that ACUE financed the European Movement, the most important federalist organization in the post-war years. In 1958, for example, it provided 53.5 per cent of the movement's funds. The European Youth Campaign, an arm of the European Movement, was wholly funded and controlled by Washington.[311]

Of course, this is not just a conspiracy theory, as the Transnational Elite's mouthpieces usually characterize any similar kind of research, even if backed by official documents — following Dr. Goebbels's teachings to sow as much confusion as possible. However, the European project was not only a political aim of the Western elites, and particularly of the (hegemonic at the time) US elite, to create a politico-economic complement to NATO, its main military organ. It could be argued that the EU was also an important part of a US major project to restructure Europe and the world along the lines of the most predatory kind of capitalism the world has ever known: US capitalism, which, for most of its history, was based on the maximum possible market 'freedom'. In other words, it was a capitalism based on the minimization of any social controls on the markets for capital and commodities.

It was not therefore accidental that the main post-war economic institutions in the West created by the hegemonic US elite were the 'Holy Triad' — i.e. the International Monetary Fund (IMF), the World Bank (WB) and the World Trade Organization (WTO) — all of which aimed at the maximization of the freedom of markets. It was within this context that multinationals flourished and the era of neoliberal globalization began, which has led to the development of a new kind

---

[311] Ambrose Evans-Pritchard, "Euro-federalists financed by US spy chiefs", *Telegraph*, 19/9/2000
http://www.telegraph.co.uk/news/worldnews/europe/1356047/Euro-federalists-financed-by-US-spy-chiefs.html

of economic and political union of European nations, as a first step to global governance.

b. The EU evolution from an economic union of nation-states to a branch of the NWO of neoliberal globalization

The process of European integration accelerated in the late 1980s and the early 1990s with the 1992 Maastricht treaty (which replaced the 1957 Treaty of Rome that established the European Economic Community) and the Single Market Act that was put into effect in 1993. These Treaties implied a very significant acceleration of the integration process, which was made imperative for the elites because of the growing internationalization of the market economy — as expressed by the rapid expansion of multinationals — and the intensifying competition with the other two parts of the Triad (North America and Far East).

The supporters of the acceleration process maintained that, in the ultra-competitive internationalized market economy of the twenty-first century, only a market of continental dimensions could provide the security and the economies of scale needed for the survival of European capital — i.e. of the Europe-based multinationals. And indeed, during the last two decades of the 20th century, the economic gap between the European countries and the rest of the Triad has widened considerably. A characteristic indication of the widening gap was the fact that the European Union's world export share decreased by about 7 percent between 1980 and 1994, whereas at the same time the US share fell by only 2 percent and the Japanese share increased by a massive 31 percent. The main cause of Europe's failure was the fact that its competitiveness had, for long, been lagging behind the competitiveness of the other regions. Thus, European competitiveness has fallen by 3.7 percent since 1980, while US competitiveness has risen by 2.2 percent and Japanese competitiveness (which for many years has been on top of the competitiveness league) increased by 0.5 percent.[312]

The form that the integration had taken reflected, in various ways, the neoliberal trend, which had already become dominant by then, as required by the exigencies of globalization for open and 'liberalized'

---

[312] See for the sources of the data and an analysis of the historical background Takis Fotopoulos, *Towards An Inclusive Democracy* (London/NY, Cassel/Continuum, 1997/98), ch 2

markets. Thus, had, for instance, the acceleration of the integration process started about 10 years earlier a very different picture of European integration might have emerged. In fact, the 1979 European Commission's report was still foreseeing a European Union built on 'indicative planning' at the continental level. As such, it was accurately reflecting the essence of the social-democratic consensus still prevailing at the time — although the cracks in it had already become visible, e.g. in Britain, where Thatcherism was rising. In other words, thd EC proposal amounted to a kind of 'European Keynesianism' that should have replaced national Keynesianism, which had already become obsolete under conditions of increasingly free movement of capital.

However, the collapse of the social-democratic consensus, as a result of the rise of multinationals and the consequent flourishing of neoliberalism in the 1980's (Thatcherism, Reaganomics, about turn of Mitterrand etc.), brushed aside the proposals for a European Keynesian strategy. Thus, the tendency that was encouraged by the economic and political elites and eventually prevailed in the European Union was one that identified economic unification with the radical shrinking of national control on economic activity. Consequently, the European Union's executive power has been confined to creating a homogeneous institutional framework that allowed for unimpeded entrepreneurial activity, while, simultaneously, providing for some minimal guarantees (those compatible with the neoliberal consensus requirements) regarding the protection of the environment and labor.

The agreement for the single market rested on the main neoliberal assumption that the European Union's economies were suffering from a lack of 'structural adjustment', that is, from structural deficiencies due to inflexibilities of the market mechanism and barriers to free competition. Such barriers that were mentioned in the Cecchini Report,[313] on which the official ideology of the single market rested, were the various physical, technical and fiscal barriers that were assumed to obstruct the flow of commodities, capital and labor. As regards to the capital market in particular, freeing this market from any controls, that is, the creation of conditions for the easy and unrestricted flow of capital between countries, was considered to be a basic requirement in this process. This is why the abolition of all foreign

---

[313] P. Ceccini, *The European Challenge* (London, Wildwood House, 1988)

exchange controls has always been considered an essential condition for the 'Single European Market' of 1993.

However, the most important barriers were not the ones explicitly mentioned in the Report, but those implied by it and, in particular, the emphasis it placed on competition. These implied barriers were the 'institutional' barriers to free competition, which had been introduced by the social-democratic consensus and which the agreement for the Single Market undertook to eliminate — a task brought to completion by the Maastricht treaty. Such institutional barriers were the Keynesian type of state interventionism to secure full employment and the large welfare state that created fiscal and therefore competitiveness problems, the labor unions' restrictive practices' and the public corporations, which did not always act on the basis of micro-economic criteria to raise economic efficiency.

However, as long as the degree of internationalization of the European economies was still relatively low, these barriers did not have a substantial negative effect on economic growth. But, once the growing internationalization of the economy and, in particular, the enlarged mobility of capital, ceased to be compatible with the implementation of national macro-economic policies on Keynesian lines, their negative effect on growth became evident, as manifested by the stagflation crisis of the 1970s, which hit the European economies particularly hard.

The Maastricht treaty, therefore, simply confirmed the overtly neoliberal character that the Community had begun to acquire with the Single Market Act. The primary goal was the improvement of competitiveness and to this goal belong also the mechanisms that were established by the Economic and Monetary Union (1999-2002) and the Eurozone. Thus, this Union, as indeed the single market itself, signified neither the integration of peoples nor the integration of States, but just the integration of free markets. However, free markets mean not just the unimpeded movement of commodities, capital and labor, but also 'flexibility', that is, the elimination of barriers to the free formation of prices and wages, as well as overall curtailing of the state's control on economic activity. And this is, in fact, the essence of the neoliberal consensus that characterized the EU's new institutional framework, i.e. the continuation and expansion of the EU marketization. Therefore, the aim of the new institutions was obvious: to maximize the freedom of organized capital, the concentration of which was facilitated in every way possible (as it was witnessed, for instance, by the mass take-overs and mergers that took place in the late 1980s in view of the single market) and to minimize the freedom of organized labor, through any means available and, particularly, through the threat of unemployment.

So, in the interest of enhancing competitiveness, the 'European ideal' had degenerated into a kind of 'Americanized Europe', where luxury and extreme poverty stood side by side and the comfortable life of a minority was a mirror image of the marginalization of the rest. Britain, which was the first European country to embark on neoliberal policies that were then enshrined in the Maastricht Treaty, was showing at the time the future image of Europe. Therefore, the institutional framework that was established in Europe consisted of a model in which the continuation of growth depended on a process of further internationalizing its economy, through the destruction of local economic self-reliance and the continual expansion of exports to cope with a growing volume of imports.

c. The NWO of neoliberal globalization and the socialdemocratic dreams to improve it

All this implies that the rise of the NWO of neoliberal globalization was not just the result of a betrayal by social democrats that consented to the neoliberal content of the new Europe then emerging. Similarly, the present criminal policies implemented by a 'left' government in Greece are not just the result of a 'capitulation', as today's globalist 'Left,' asserts.[314] Nor simply is the present recession to be blamed on the austerity policies adopted by EU member-states etc. If we accept interpretations (or rather myths) such as these, then the replacement of the neoliberal institutional framework is simply a matter for the 'true' socialists and Leftists to gain power, who, in the context of economic recovery, would reinstate the institutional framework of the social-democratic consensus.

However, if a government takes for granted the institutional framework of the internationalized market economy and its institutions such as the EU and the WTO, then, it will simply *have to* implement the same neoliberal policies irrespective of whether it calls itself a

---

[314] see e.g. James Petras, "Global Economic, Political and Military Configurations", *Global Research*, 8/3/2016 http://www.globalresearch.ca/global-economic-political-and-military-configurations/5512722

government of the Left, including the communist Left. This is exactly what the globalist 'Left' does today, as we shall see next, when, in the name of an outdated internationalism, does not raise the issue of a new world order based on sovereign nations. This is why the issue is not simply one of Left betrayal and, also, this is why the radical change of the institutional framework 'from within' is not possible. This was proved both in the past (Mitterrand, Lafontaine and so on), as well as at present (SYRIZA) and will, undoubtedly, prove once more so in the future if Podemos take over in Spain, or the Labor party, under Jeremy Corbyn, in Britain.

In fact, Corbyn made a memorable about turn on the issue of Britain staying in the EU, presumably in order to meet the demands of the economic and political elites. Even worse was the justification he gave for his decision in a show of remarkable political amoralism:

> They (the Tories) would dump rights on equal pay, working time, annual leave, for agency workers, and on maternity pay as fast as they could get away with it…It would be a bonfire of rights that Labour governments secured within the EU…only by working across the continent could European countries protect social and human rights, tackle climate change and clamp down on tax dodgers.[315]

The obvious implication of this statement is that the working rights were not won because of the struggle of British workers but simply because of the 'struggle' of the Labor Party within the EU! In other words, the British people are not capable anymore of fighting for social and human rights but only their 'representatives' within the EU can do so. This, despite the fact, of which he was of course fully aware when he made the above politically dishonest statements, that the EU has excelled since the Maastricht Treaty in curtailing these rights in every way possible, so that more flexibility in the labor markets (for the sake of better competitiveness) could be achieved! Even worse, he made these appalling statements about better protection of worker's rights within the EU at the very moment when street battles in Paris, Toulouse, Rennes and all over France were still going on against the EU demands for restrictions of worker's rights.

---

[315] Jim Pickard and George Parker, "Jeremy Corbyn 'overwhelmingly' backs Britain staying in EU", *Financial Times*, 15/4/2016

Clearly, therefore, within the framework of capitalist globalization, the minimization of the state's social role and of national sovereignty in general does not constitute a choice but a pre-condition for TNCs based in Europe to effectively compete with those based in the USA or the Far East. Particularly so if we take into account the fact that the elites in the USA and the Far East face much weaker institutional barriers than in Europe due to the lack of a strong social-democratic tradition in their own countries. Within the NWO, social democracy and the globalist 'Left' in general, have, no meaning either at the national level or at the continental level, given the freedom of capital to move from one nation/continent to the other for profit maximization. Therefore, any attempt by European social democrats or globalist 'Leftists' to change the present institutional framework, in order to radically enhance the state's social role, or generally to expand national (or even European) sovereignty allowing states to impose more social controls on markets than those in the Far East or the USA, would simply make European multinationals less competitive than those based in the rest of the world and would result in a mass exodus of capital from Europe. On the other hand, a Popular Front government, like the one described in ch.10, would not even have to face such a problem when it comes to power, given that growth will be based mainly on the internal market within the context of a self-reliance strategy rather than on the external market and multinational investment.

By the same token, a new, Europe-wide kind of Keynesianism is not feasible, unless it is going to be combined with a self-reliant growth led by a highly protected European market economy. But, such a solution is in direct contradiction to the NWO's logic and dynamics. It is exactly for this reason that the proposals to re-negotiate the EU treaties, in order to introduce social-democratic aims in the European Union, are equally utopian in the negative sense of the word, if not totally disorienting, as is the case with Varoufakis' DIEM25.

In fact, the argument in favor of creating a European 'social market', which today's globalist 'Left' proposes within the framework of a supposedly 'new' movement like the aforementioned, is simply a repetition of the same arguments proposed by the previous generation of social democrats about 20 years ago. What differs is the packaging, as today's proposals are presented in the form of a pseudo-direct democracy proposal — which is particularly fashionable nowadays, following the various 'indignados' and 'occupy' movements of the last few years. Thus, Will Hutton, a major social democrat thinker, was arguing for a 'social market' Europe as follows, more than 20 years ago:

> The countries of EU together have the power to regulate the financial markets and control capital flows, and to play a part in compelling the US and Japan to regulate their relationship better, as part of a world deal ...Europe can insist on common social rights across the continent so that multinational corporations cannot play one state off against another in an effort to bid down wages and working conditions. Europe can set common environmental standards and common rules of corporate governance, establishing the concept of the stakeholder company. Indeed social market Europe can formalize its rules and codes so that ... a co-operative, more committed form of capitalism could be defended.[316]

However, our experience of the last two decades had amply shown that exactly the opposite was the case, following the higher integration achieved within the EU in the 1990s. The clear trend is for more liberalization of markets, rather than less. As I stressed in connection with the 2008 financial crisis, "much more is involved in the financial crisis than the deregulation of the financial markets. In fact, what is involved is the opening and deregulation of all markets, i.e., the very essence of neoliberal globalization."[317] No wonder that despite the catastrophic consequences of this crisis, the liberalization of markets, including the financial ones, continued unabated and many analysts already predict a repetition of a similar crisis (only worse as far as its effects are concerned) in the near future. Yet, even today, members of the globalist 'Left' repeat the same mantra, as if nothing had happened in the last quarter of a century. Thus, as Monbiot put it, in a supposedly 'objective' article on Brexit:

---

[316] Will Hutton, *The State We're In* (London, Jonathan Cape,1995) pp.315-16
[317] Takis Fotopoulos, "The myths about the economic crisis, the reformist Left and economic democracy" , *The International Journal of INCLUSIVE DEMOCRACY*, Vol. 4, No. 4 (October 2008)
http://www.inclusivedemocracy.org/journal/vol4/vol4_no4_takis_economic_crisis.ht
m

by instinct, like many on the left, I am a European. I recognize that many issues — perhaps most — can no longer be resolved only within our borders. Among them are grave threats to our welfare and our lives: climate change and the collapse of the living world; the spread of epidemics whose vectors are corporations; the global wealth-grab by the very rich; antibiotic resistance; terrorism and conflict.[318]

Therefore, a 'European social market paradise' is impossible, given the competition between the TNCs, unless of course EU imposes strict controls not only to the movement of labor but also to the free movement of capital and commodities from outside it. But this would mean the end of globalization as we know it, the essence of which is the free movement of capital, labor and commodities across the world. Furthermore, a European social market could only be based on a European self-reliance, something that would imply a very serious restriction of the TNCs' activities.

A determined globalist could at this point counter-argue that transnational agreements between economic unions in Asia, the Americas and the EU could do the trick, i.e. impose social controls on the markets (capital, labor and commodities) for the protection of society and the environment from them. But, in fact, the trend (which was created by the TNCs themselves!) is for less social controls, not more, as shown by the TTIP and TPP deals, which in effect attempt to bypass even the WTO. This becomes obvious by the fact that both Russia and China have been excluded from these trade deal negotiations. No wonder the Russian Duma chief Sergey Naryshkin and Xi Jinping, the Chinese leader, "described the Trans-Pacific Partnership treaty as an attempt to create a closed and secretive structure that would replace the World Trade Organization, adding that Russia and China are strongly opposed to it."[319] On the same theme, Xi Jinping, commenting on Barack Obama's recent remarks on global commerce — in which he said that the rules of international trade must be imposed by the United States and its allies, (i.e. the Transnational Elite) and not China — stressed that in his view, such rules must be

---

[318] George Monbiot, "I'm starting to hate the EU. But I will vote to stay in", *The Guardian*, 10/2/2016

[319] "Duma chief, China leader condemn 'US attempt to control international trade'", RT, 5/5/2016 https://www.rt.com/politics/341960-duma-chief-china-leader-condemn/

agreed jointly by all the nations of the world, not any particular one. Also, Putin, in his address to the Russian parliament in December 2015, had stressed that his proposal is for Russia "and other Eurasian Economic Union countries (to) kick-off consultations with members of the Shanghai Cooperation Organization [SCO] and the Association of Southeast Asian Nations [ASEAN] on a possible economic partnership."[320]

These developments are far from surprising. It is well known that the entire Transnational Elite is in favor of these transnational agreements (TTIP and TPP): from Obama to Hillary (despite her pre-election noises questioning it) and from Merkel to Cameron and May. What is not so widely known is that Zbiggie Brzezinski, who served as a counselor to Lyndon Johnson and National Security Advisor to Jimmy Carter, was also Obama's tutor on foreign policy, following his election in 2008. As Rappoport reports, Brzezinski, as early as in 1969, wrote that:

> The nation state as a fundamental unit of man's organized life has ceased to be the principal creative force: International banks and multinational corporations are acting and planning in terms that are far in advance of the political concepts of the nation-state. [321]

The inevitable conclusion drawn by Rappoport was that "these Globalist trade deals are, indeed, exercises in eliminating nations and turning over the economy of the world to mega-corporations."[322] But, this is exactly what the New World Order and the move towards global governance is all about. For the elites, therefore, Brexit is just an incident, or better a relatively small hurdle, that the Transnational Elite has to overcome in the process.

d. The NWO and the globalist 'Left'

In this section, I will refer briefly to the kind of 'Left' in general at the time of Brexit, while the specific role of it with respect to Brexit

---

[320] ibid.
[321] Jon Rappoport, "TPP, TTIP: Eliminating Nations, Turning over the World Economy To Mega-corporations. Obama's Secret Trade Deals vs. Trump and Bernie", *Global Research*, 2/5/2016 http://www.globalresearch.ca/tpp-ttip-eliminating-nations-turning-over-the-world-economy-to-mega-corporations-obamas-secret-trade-deals-vs-trump-and-bernie/5522947
[322] ibid.

will be examined below. As we saw in Ch 6, the globalist 'Left' that developed in the globalization era ceased questioning globalization itself, as well as its main institutions, such as the EU, the IMF and, WTO. At most, it would protest against new treaties to extend further the scope of globalization, such as TTIP and TPP, but never against globalization itself, which was taken for granted. This development was of course far from surprising, following the systematic destruction of the antisystemic movement against globalization by the reformist Left, mainly through the World Social Forum that emerged at Port Alegre (see ch.6).

For the reformist part of the globalist 'Left', neoliberalism is seen as just an ideology or a dogma, if not a 'doctrine' imposed by unscrupulous capitalists and 'bad' free-market economists, as well as politicians associated with them! This is, par excellence, what SYRIZA in Greece and Podemos in Spain represent, which, as we saw above, have not merely betrayed their Left voters, as some parts of the anti-systemic globalist 'Left' simplistically suggest. In fact, given the institutional constraints they took for granted, they had no other option. In other words, it is the institutions themselves that are taken for granted which are the real causes of the crisis in both countries. However, as the Greek and Spanish Left are the only surviving strong remnants of the historically hegemonic European Left, this is bound to have a pan-European , if not a global , negative effect on the Left as a whole.

On the other hand, for the antisystemic part of the globalist 'Left', there is nothing new in globalization, but simply the continuation of the trends for the internationalization of capital which emerged at the beginning of the 20th century. Therefore, for them, the problem is not globalization but, instead, capitalism itself, which, once overthrown, will lead, also, to the reversal of globalization. In other words, this part of the globalist 'Left' attempts to analyze a new systemic phenomenon — i.e. the NWO of neoliberal globalization that aims at the phasing out of national sovereignty — using theoretical tools developed in the 19th and early 20th centuries, despite the fact that imperialism, in the old Marxist sense of the world that they invoke, has disappeared long ago, together with the disappearance of the economic sovereignty of the nation-state, with which capital was intrinsically linked in the past. Consequently, this anti-systemic version of the globalist 'Left' fights against 'imperialism' in general and waits for the overthrow of capitalism in the next millennium or so to abolish the NWO institutions, which of course could perfectly be abolished even within capitalism, as long as nations restore their economic and national sovereignty.

Yet, although the ultimate aim of the fight of the victims of globalization should of course be the replacement of the capitalist system itself with a new socio-economic system of self-determination, such as the Inclusive Democracy one, the crucial precondition for this fight to become feasible is national self-determination. That is, the break from the NWO of neoliberal globalization which has created conditions of effective occupation in every country of the world that is integrated into the NWO. This is why, as we shall see next, Brexit is only the necessary condition for social liberation, but by no means a sufficient one.

What was really at stake with Brexit was national sovereignty and the lives of the victims of globalization

In view of the above, the answer to the question I raised at the beginning of this chapter on what has changed since 1975, when the first British referendum on EU membership took place, should be obvious. EU member-states, following the economic integration achieved since the 1990s, have lost most of their economic sovereignty — if not all of it in case they are also members of the Eurozone when they do not even control their own currency. Yet, it is clear that if a country does not control its own currency and therefore monetary policy it can hardly be called economically sovereign, as it would be at the mercy of the bureaucrats controlling the European Central Bank, who in turn work at the behest of transnational corporations. As the examples of Greece and Cyprus clearly had shown, the Eurozone elites can, at any moment, financially strangle any members that do not obey their instructions by simply turning off the liquidity tap. Even more so when these countries, in fact, do not control also their fiscal policies and have to obey the catastrophic austerity policies imposed on them 'from above' — supposedly through various stability 'pacts' etc. That is, the policies Eurozone members have to follow in case they cannot improve their competitiveness through alternative means (e.g. investment on research and development and high technology industries) while, at the same time, they are also pushed, directly or indirectly, to privatize their social wealth and therefore lose any remaining national control over their resources.

However, a country with no economic sovereignty does not enjoy also any national sovereignty. Yet, some of the EU apologists launched a disorienting campaign, through the elite controlled mass media, with the obvious aim to mystify what was really at stake with Brexit, by reference to the confusing distinction they make between sovereignty and power. I do not mean overt apologists like Varoufakis,[323] who threw this distinction around like a slogan, but serious commentators like Martin Wolf, the associate editor and chief economics commentator at the *Financial Times,* who argued that:

> The very fact that the UK is holding this vote proves that it remains sovereign. The referendum is not about sovereignty. It is about how best to exercise the country's power... Is the EU different from other treaties? The answers are: 'no' and 'yes'. The answer is no, because the UK can clearly withdraw... Thus the UK's membership of the EU does not limit its sovereignty... The political question in the referendum is not about sovereignty but about the delegation of powers within a treaty-governed system of particularly far-reaching obligations...The question then is whether membership of the EU is an appropriate exercise of UK sovereignty... UK sovereignty is not at stake in this referendum. It is, instead, proved by it. The referendum is rather about whether the UK has delegated excessive powers to the EU.[324]

The trick Wolf used to reach this untenable conclusion was that the EU membership is a Treaty like any other Treaty and therefore the UK can freely withdraw from it. If this is so, the EU treaty does not undermine sovereignty, and the referendum proves it. However, EU membership is not like any other treaty neither at present, nor is expected to be in the future, when the increase in the degree of integration within the EU seems to be a one-way street — if the EU is going to continue at all.

It is true that, as the UK is not a member of the Eurozone, it still has some degree of sovereignty left, at least as far as its currency and monetary policy is concerned, although even on this it had to follow policies similar to those adopted by the EU, which is its main market.

---

[323] Yanis Varoufakis, "Why we must save the EU", *The Guardian,* 5/4/2016
[324] Martin Wolf, "Brexit: sovereignty is not the same as power", *Financial Times,*3/5/2016

Thus, even as a member of the EU, it had to 'harmonize' its legislation with that of the EU. A clear indication of this is the fact that, according to several studies on the matter, at least 65% of domestic legislation of EU member states has its origin in Brussels. Thus, as a recent 'definitive study' on the British case study showed, "64.7 per cent of the laws introduced in the UK since 1993 either originated from the European Union (EU) or are deemed to be EU influenced by the House of Commons Library."[325] Also, according to Boris Johnson, the ex-Mayor of London, who was promoted by Theresa May to Foreign Secretary, the EU now generates 60 per cent of all the laws that pass through Westminster If you include both primary and secondary legislation. [326] All this, in a country which is, in fact, much less dependent on the EU than most other member countries.

Furthermore, withdrawing membership from the EU is far more difficult than withdrawing from any other Treaty, as the present UK experience clearly shows and last year's Greek experience also highlighted. Thus, before the referendum, the EU, given the huge means available at its disposal (money, control over mass media and over academic research through various research programs and subsidies), as well as its power to blackmail any member having strong trade links with its market, clearly had an incomparable power to influence any anti-EU referendum. This is exactly what the EU did during the Brexit referendum campaign, threatening that, following Brexit, the UK will have to renegotiate all its rights of access to the huge EU market and so on — a process that might take several years. Then, following a successful exit referendum, like Brexit, the EU still has vast powers to blackmail any "black sheep", as we shall see below in the context of the raging counter revolution against Brexit.

Even worse is the case of a Eurozone member that is tempted to withdraw only from the Euro but not the EU as well. As the Greek case clearly showed, any such attempt can be punished even more severely by the Euro-elites, which control the very liquidity of such a member and can easily force it to introduce a distorted form of capital

---

[325] "Definitive study reveals EU rules account for 65% of UK law", Business for Britain, 2/3/2015 http://businessforbritain.org/2015/03/02/definitive-study-reveals-eu-rules-account-for-65-of-uk-law/
[326] Boris Johnson, "UK and America can be better friends than ever Mr Obama... if we LEAVE the EU", *The Sun,* 22/4/2016

controls. That is, not social controls on the movement of capital, as we would also suggest, but, instead, a distorted form of control of the cash that citizens can withdraw from their own accounts! Furthermore, in case a member state has managed to print an alternative to Euro currency before the exit from it is announced, such an attempt could easily be crashed by the Euro-elites through the implementation of a myriad of EU regulations suitable for this purpose. As a result, a Eurozone exit becomes almost impossible, bar a revolutionary change through a Popular Front for National and Social Liberation, as proposed in this book.

It is therefore clear that nation-states have only a formal existence today, given that their national sovereignty has withered away within the EU. This loss of sovereignty of EU members within the framework of neoliberal globalization is aptly described by a British analyst as follows:

> This is the crux of the matter, namely the sovereign right of European nations to form their own policies for their own people and expect other states to do the same within sovereign borders...The Euro-project is also a study in the implementation of a Neo-Liberal Regime which benefits the corporations and which has seen small businesses vaporize from the streets. Gone is the butcher, gone is the baker, gone is the greengrocer selling local produce and in come the Big Spaces which offer fabulous GM goods smothered and charged with chemicals, deep-frozen meat products made in Vietnam, and Japan and Peru and Nigeria, washed with ammonia, compressed into blocks and frozen for years before being marketed as 100% Prime British Beef! [327]

It was therefore the resentment of the British people at the loss of their national sovereignty within the EU (despite the fact that the British elites are a constituent part of the Transnational Elite), which has led to a growing anti-EU popular movement in Britain. This movement in turn, which was also reflected among several Tory MPs facing the loss of their parliamentary seats because of the rise of the neo-nationalist UKIP party, managed to force the Cameron

---

[327] Timothy Bancroft-Hinchey, UK-EU: IN or OUT? There is no "no", English Pravda.Ru, 19/2/2016 http://www.pravdareport.com/opinion/columnists/19-02-2016/133529-eu_uk-0/

government to have a referendum on Brexit, which the people won against all the odds. In fact, the outcome of the referendum could well have catalytic implications for the EU itself. This is particularly so because, as the British elites themselves recognize, the anti-EU movement in Britain is actually a movement against globalization (a fact that the Globalist 'Left' ignores!) — another reason that helps explain the rise of UKIP.

A further confirmation of the lack of economic and national sovereignty, even with regards to a country which is a member of the Transnational Elite such as Britain, was provided a couple of months before the referendum with the threatened steel industry closure by its Indian owner Tata, with the loss of up to 40,000 jobs. Clearly, if Britain was a truly sovereign nation, as in the past, it could have imposed, long ago, tariffs to protect its own industry from imported steel at an impossibly low price because of the miserable wages and the gross violation of the environment in countries such as China. As it was reported recently, the Chinese steel producing company is "based in Hebei province, China's steel-producing heartland where cities are shrouded in toxic smog and factories churn out millions of tons of cheap steel to undercut western rivals, such as Tata Steel UK."[328]

Yet, in fact, steel production is impossible within the EU, even if the Tories were prepared to nationalize it — which is of course anathema not only to them but even to 'left'-wingers like Corbyn and the rest of the Labor party, who did not even dare to raise the issue! As a British systemic paper put it:

> Even if Whitehall was prepared to take control of Tata's UK steel business, Europe's strict rules on state aid could preclude it. Member states are not allowed to prop up or subsidize uncompetitive businesses.[329]

Therefore, as a result of globalization and the consequent freeing and liberalizing of markets, as well as the privatizations and general de-industrialization following the migration of Transnational Corporations (TNCs) to low-cost 'paradises', the jobs of tens of thousands of people are being condemned to oblivion, as has happened

---

[328] Danny Fortson, "Chinese steel profits recycled into London luxury homes", *The Sunday Times*, 24/4/2016
[329] John Collingridge, "Sunset on steel: is there any hope for Tata's workers?", *The Sunday Times*, 3/4/2016

repeatedly in the recent past. No wonder Britain today is a service economy with three quarters of its national output produced in the services sector. The result is that present growth is based mainly on consumption, often on borrowed money, with official figures showing Britain having now the highest current account deficit since modern records began in 1948.[330]

This does not necessarily mean a capitalist crisis, as globalist Marxists believe. Profits of TNCs thrive from transferring their production cost, including taxes, to cheap labor and/or low-tax paradises. What it means is that neoliberal globalization destroys the productive structure of countries like Britain, as the steel industry case showed. As a very recent investigation by a think tank reported, since 2000, the share of GDP accounted for by foundation industries (i.e. industries supplying basic goods — such as metal and chemicals — used by other industries) has fallen by 43% in Britain vs. a fall by 21% across the rich nations. This could well explain the fact that whereas at the end of the 1990s, imports accounted for 40% of UK demand for basic metals, today they account for 90% of it![331] Of course, this is nothing new within the EU marvelous world. A similar process has destroyed the Greek economic structure since the country entered the Common Market in 1981, leading to a consumer society funded by borrowing, i.e. to a debt trap, which, as I predicted a quarter of a century ago,[332] inevitably had led to the present informal bankruptcy and the consequent Greek economic and social catastrophe.[333]

Brexit as a precondition for sovereignty

However, it is not only the Britons but also millions of other Europeans who increasingly realize that true independence and self-reliance, the preconditions of national and economic sovereignty, are impossible within the NWO in general and the EU in particular, which

---

[330] Larry Elliott, "Britain's low grade free-market model is bust", *The Guardian*, 4/4/2016

[331] ibid.

[332] Takis Fotopoulos, "Economic restructuring and the debt problem: the Greek case", *The International Review of Applied Economics,* Volume 6, Issue 1 (1992), pp. 38-64

[333] Takis Fotopoulos, "The real causes of the catastrophic crisis in Greece and the "Left"", *Global Research,* 16/1/2014 http://www.globalresearch.ca/the-real-causes-of-the-catastrophic-crisis-in-greece-and-the-left/5365013 & The International Journal of INCLUSIVE DEMOCRACY, Vol. 9, Nos. 1/2 (Winter-Summer 2013)

has systematically dismantled sovereignty in the last two decades or so. But is an exit from the EU by itself a sufficient condition to restore sovereignty? Here is how a reader of the *Guardian,* the flagship of the globalist 'Left', aptly put it:

> The 'Brexit buccaneers' would suggest that an out vote would enable us to regain our sovereignty. That is a fantasy. As a nation, with the encouragement of successive governments, we have ceded sovereignty to a variety of external powers, including the EU, over many years. Major, foreign-owned multinationals determine levels of investment and jobs in this country as a consequence of decades of British national institutions and businesses being privatized or sold to the highest bidder. It is an illusion to believe that leaving Europe will somehow restore national sovereignty when our energy security is largely dependent on the French and Chinese governments deciding whether or not Hinkley C is built; Canadian multinationals decide how many aerospace jobs there will be in Northern Ireland; and Indian entrepreneurs preside over the survival of our steel industry. These same Indian entrepreneurs, and their German and Japanese counterparts, will decide the long-term health of our automotive manufacturing. Similarly, decades of privatization of the public sector has seen outsourcing contracts (particularly in the NHS) let to US corporations, among others. Brexit will not diminish the power and influence of these institutions over our economic future and our elected representatives. Nor will the government suddenly be in a stronger position to persuade them to pay a fairer contribution towards our civil society through taxation.[334]

No wonder this is an argument which would be supported also by apologists of globalization and the EU, like Varoufakis, who stated the obvious when he said that "it's impossible to stay in the single market and keep your sovereignty".[335] However, for systemic writers, pretending to be radicals like him, the implication of this fact was not the need to fight for national sovereignty but, instead, exactly the

---

[334] Mark Dodd, *The Guardian*, 24/2/2016 (comment under the general heading, "Sovereignty, autonomy and Britain's relationship with Europe")
[335] Yanis Varoufakis, "Why Britain should STAY in the EU", *LSE blogs,* 8/3/2016 https://yanisvaroufakis.eu/2016/03/08/why-britain-should-stay-in-the-eu-lse-blogs/

opposite: to persuade people about the necessity of the NWO on the basis of the famous Thatcherite principle TINA "There Is No Alternative." Thus, using the cheap trick of creating a pseudo-dilemma in order to draw the 'right' answer, the same author stressed that:

> Neither withdrawing into the safe cocoon of the nation state, nor giving in to the disintegrating and anti-democratic EU, represent good options for Britain. So, instead of seeing the referendum as a vote between these two options, and these two options alone, the UK needs a third option: to vote to stay in the European Union so that it can fight tooth and nail against the EU's anti-democratic institutions. [336]

Yet, both the first option as well as his own third option are, in fact, false options. The first one because fighting for national sovereignty does not of course mean withdrawing into the safe cocoon of the nation state, as he and some calamity 'Marxists' suggest. It could well mean, instead, laying the foundations for a new democratic world order of sovereign nations (ch.11).

In fact, sovereignty is a necessary condition (though not a sufficient one) for any radical social change, given that such a change is impossible within the NWO of open and liberalized markets for commodities, capital and labor. Therefore, those like Varoufakis, Zizek and the self-declared 'anarchist' [337] Chomsky (who promptly joined Varoufakis' movement!), as well as the rest in the globalist 'Left' (including 'anarchists') who talk today about open borders, are in fact deceiving the victims of globalization. That is, they exploit the old libertarian ideal for 'no borders' in order to indirectly promote the NWO. No borders is of course an important ideal, provided however that the peoples themselves control the economy — not 'the markets' (i.e. Goldman Sachs [338] people and the likes, recently joined by

---

[336] Yanis Varoufakis, "The UK should Stay in the EU to Fight Tooth and Nail against the EU's Anti-democratic Institutions", *Global Research*, 22/2/2016 http://www.globalresearch.ca/the-uk-should-stay-in-the-eu-to-fight-tooth-and-nail-against-the-eus-anti-democratic-institutions-yanis-varoufakis/5509652

[337] Chomsky, according to Murray Bookchin, the doyen of post-war anarchism, has very little, if any, relation to anarchism; see Murray Bookchin's interview in Janet Biehl's *The Politics of Social Ecology* (Black Rose Books, 1998) pp.148-149

[338] Matt Taibbi, "Goldman Sachs – in the center of World Power", *Defend Democracy Press*, 25/7/2016 http://www.defenddemocracy.press/goldman-sachs-center-world-power/

Emmanuel Barroso the ex-President of the European Commission!) or, alternatively, some central planners.

Open borders in an internationalized capitalist market economy simply mean that multinational corporations will be absolutely free to exploit the productive resources of any country in the world — and particularly labor — in order to maximize their economic power at the expense of societies. In other words, societies, in a state of open borders, will be unable to impose any effective social controls to protect themselves from markets, as Polanyi aptly pointed out long ago.[339] Furthermore, as regards the free movement of people in general — rather than just of labor — it was the policy of open borders that was secured by the Schengen Treaty, which contributed significantly to the present huge migration problem. This is the problem that the EU has temporarily 'solved' at the expense of the Greek people, through the conversion of their country (with the connivance of SYRIZA) into a huge depository of migrants. However, the migration of a huge number of people from Asia and Africa is bound to create cultural problems among peoples with very different cultures, unless it is the peoples themselves in each country who decide the number of migrants they wish to host, rather than the economic elites (as at present) according to their own economic interests.

It is for these reasons that a huge resentment has been created among European peoples at the moment against uncontrolled migration, which is of course another indication of the effective undermining of national sovereignty. Thus, according to a recent poll carried out by France's Institute for Opinion Research (IFOP), Europeans overwhelmingly would like to see Schengen halted and the re-establishment of border controls between neighboring countries: 72 percent of French want their borders sealed, while 66 percent of Germans and 60 percent of Italians want the same for their own countries.[340]

On the other hand, Varoufakis' supposed third option, i.e. to "fight tooth and nail against the EU's anti-democratic institutions" in order to democratize the EU, is another pure deception, as we saw in Ch. 7. Therefore, a Brexit, by itself, is not enough to restore

---

[339] Karl Polanyi, *The Great Transformation,* (Beacon Press, 1944), chs 5-6
[340] "French, Germans & Italians overwhelmingly in favor of abandoning border-free Europe – poll" , RT, 7/4/2016 https://www.rt.com/news/338837-europeans-want-border-control/

sovereignty as long as a country is integrated into the NWO and is subject to the regulations stipulated by the Transnational Elite and implemented through the transnational institutions controlled by it. That is, the institutions, which the latter set up in order to impose the free movement of capital, commodities and labor (e.g. WTO, IMF, World Bank) and the corresponding military institutions such as NATO.

So, the discussion in Britain today on whether Brexit should be followed by the establishment of the Canadian model, or the Norwegian model and similar models, is completely disorienting. The Norwegian case is particularly illuminating since, unlike Canada, which has always been a fortress of Anglo-American liberalism (despite the introduction of some significant social democratic programs during the post-war statist phase of capitalism), Norway has always been a stronghold of social democracy. Norway is not of course a member of the EU, as two referendums on joining it failed, even if it was by narrow margins, in 1972 and 1994. However, the Norwegian elite decided to harmonize the country's policies with those of the EU anyway, while at the same time the country has always been a member of the WTO, IMF, as well as NATO. The consequence was that despite Norway's rich energy resources, Norwegians saw a massive retreat from social democracy in their country during the NWO era!

Thus, despite the fact that social services are still supported in Norway, social democrats participated enthusiastically not only in the brutal NATO bombing of Libya, but also, in a continuous process of intensifying and worsening working conditions. In other words, as the Norwegian social democrats, adopting their elite's options, did not break with the NWO of neoliberal globalization, they had to follow the policies imposed on them both directly, that is, through the country's participation in the transnational institutions of globalization (i.e. WTO, IMF etc.) and, indirectly, through the harmonization of Norway's policies with those of the EU. No wonder, as Norwegian social democrats such as Andreas Bieler rightly pointed out, "Norway is sliding gradually toward more and more mainstream and soft neoliberal positions." [341]

---

[341] Andreas Bieler, "Norway: What Future for Social Democracy?", *Global Research*, 11/10/2013 http://www.globalresearch.ca/norway-what-future-for-social-democracy/5353922

Yet, although Brexit by itself is by no means a sufficient condition for sovereignty, it definitely is a necessary condition for it. Not only because sovereignty is a precondition for any radical social change today but also because Brexit, potentially, could have catalytic effects on the NWO. The Italian Finance Minister Pier Carlo Padoan, in an interview with *The Guardian*, rightly pointed out the possible domino effect of a Brexit, which terrorizes the elites:

> Brexit would be the demonstration that if you have an anti-European program you can implement that programme... It would be a message sent to many anti-European parties and to some anti-European governments. It would have, especially in the medium term, quite dramatic implications. We are already seeing a domino effect with anti-European parties gaining a lot of support, starting in France.[342]

In fact, the likelihood of a domino effect is the main possible negative (for the elites) consequence of a Brexit. Particularly so, at a moment when the repeated terrorist attacks in Europe lately and the parallel massive influx of migrants are bound to boost the neo-nationalist and Eurosceptic parties in general and those supporting Brexit itself in particular. This has already happened in Hungary, where, in the recent referendum, Hungarians overwhelmingly rejected mandatory EU migrant quotas, asserting, once more after Brexit, national sovereignty.[343] No wonder the Transnational Elite and its media launched, immediately after the result of the referendum was announced, a huge campaign to declare the referendum legally invalid because the required by Hungarian law minimum participation rate of 50 per cent was not achieved. This, despite the fact that almost 98 per cent of the voters approved it and 'forgetting' in the process that many US Presidents and western PMs have been elected by a much smaller proportion of their electorates!

---

[342] Patrick Wintour Rajeev Syal, "British EU exit 'could spark domino effect'", *The Guardian*, 7/3/2016

[343] James Rothwell, Peter Foster and Balasz Cseko, "Hungary referendum: 98 per cent of voters say 'no' to EU migrant quotas", *The Telegraph*, 3/10/2016
http://www.telegraph.co.uk/news/2016/10/02/hungary-votes-no-to-migrant-quotas-polls-suggest---but-what-does/

The elites' Project Fear on Brexit

As soon as the June referendum was announced at the beginning of 2016 a formidable campaign against Brexit was launched by the entire Transnational Elite, as well as by the largest part of the British elite, in a huge effort to exorcise any idea of a Brexit. Even the titular head of the Transnational Elite, Obama, was sent to London to speak against Brexit and threaten the British people that in the crucial talks between the main constituents of the Transnational Elite (i.e. US and EU) for the future of globalization within the TTIP framework, "the UK is going to be in the back of the queue" if it chooses Brexit.[344] At the same time, Lord Bramall, former chief of UK's general staff, had no qualms about stating that "a broken and demoralized Europe just across the Channel … would constitute a far greater threat to our future, indeed to the whole balance of power and equilibrium of the western world."[345]

Even the communist Chinese President Xi Jinping felt the need to make the following memorable (for a 'communist') statement:

> China hopes to see a prosperous Europe and a united EU, and hopes Britain, as an important member of the EU, can play an even more positive and constructive role in promoting the deepening development of China-EU ties.[346]

This statement clearly shows the degradation of present day so called "socialism with Chinese characteristics" (something that Mao had accurately predicted knowing the kind of party cadres that were going to succeed him) which, however, as we shall see next, is reflected in almost the entire 'Left' today. In fact, the explanation for this stand, given by 'Chinese diplomats,' is revealing of the opportunism of Chinese communists. According to these diplomats, "Britain's potential exit from the EU worries Beijing that believes free-market supporting Britain strengthens the EU, which China sees as important ballast to American market dominance." [347]

---

[344] 'Back of free trade queue': Brits slam Obama for 'threats' over Brexit', RT, 23/4/2016 https://www.rt.com/uk/340682-brits-obama-trade-queue-brexit/

[345] George Parker, "Brexit could destabilise Europe amid populist upsurge and damage UK's biggest export market", *Financial Times*,18/2/2016

[346] " Xi Jinping urges Britain to stay in EU as ballast to US market dominance", RT, 23/10/2015, https://www.rt.com/uk/319488-china-eu-brexit-referendum/

[347] ibid

Thus, not only these 'communists' showed complete ignorance of the present neoliberal globalization, as a new phase in the development of the capitalist market economy, but they also imagined important differences between the two blocs, i.e. the North American and the European capitalist blocs, presumably seeing them as inter-imperialist conflicts for the division of markets! Clearly, such calamity Marxists in the East, like the corresponding globalist 'Leftists' in the West, do not see that Lenin's theory of imperialism is irrelevant in the globalization era, as it was of course based on nation-states, which were indeed in conflict between them for the division of markets — a fact that led to two world wars. Therefore, either the Chinese leaders have not yet assimilated the fact that nation-states are phased out in the globalization era or, at worst, they wish to hide in this way their own integration into neoliberal globalization.

In other words, today's blocs are by no means empires in the above sense of the word, as they consist of elites based on transnational corporations with overlapping specific economic interests and a common general interest: the reproduction of the NWO of neoliberal globalization. It is the protection of this general interest that is the main function of the Transnational Elite. This is why any military conflict between the states on which the Transnational Elite is based (mainly the G7 states and its associates in Scandinavia, Australia etc.) is inconceivable today and any differences between them, like those that arose in connection to the Iraq war or Syria, are purely tactical and do not reflect conflicting antagonisms. Similarly, the famous 'deepening capitalist rivalries' between USA and EU regarding TTIP or the taxing of US multinationals like Apple[348] represent, as we saw in Ch. 6, more of a storm in a teacup than an inter-imperialist conflict! Therefore, if we follow these calamity 'Marxists' and 'Leftists', the only 'imperialisms' around, among whom an intra-imperialist conflict could arise, are the US and the Russian imperialisms! And a USA-Russia conflict is indeed in the cards at the moment. But is it an inter-imperialist conflict?

However, even if we accept this kind of Paleolithic Marxism and call USA an imperialist power today, Russia can hardly be characterized as an imperialist power. Although its economic elite, which consists mainly of the oligarchs created by Yeltsin and the

---

[348] See Prof. James Petras, "Inter-Capitalist Rivalries and Political Rebellion against the US Multinational Corporate Elite", Global Research, 8/9/2016, c.f.

Transnational Elite following the collapse of USSR, would like to play the role of a subordinate member of the Transnational Elite (so that their privileges could be secured by it), the political elite under Putin is divided between two factions, as we saw in past chapters: the globalists, who follow the same line as the oligarchs, and the patriots/neo-nationalists who support a sovereign Eurasia in a new economic and political union of sovereign states. Furthermore, Russia can hardly be characterized as an 'imperialist' power, as it never attacked another country and even its present involvement in Syria was a result of a request by the Syrian government to protect Syrian people from having the fate of the Libyan people at the hands of the mercenaries of the Transnational Elite and the Gulf states.

Needless to add that the rest of the European economic elites came also out in force against Brexit. Thus, the directors-general of the business federations of Germany, France, Spain, the Netherlands, and *BusinessEurope* — representing organizations in 34 European countries — joined the UK's CBI to argue that EU membership is an important factor in maintaining and attracting investment into the UK. The meeting was also attended by the heads of companies including Siemens, L'Oréal, Banco Sabadell and Scottish Power, which is owned by Spain's Iberdrola. [349] Unsurprisingly, the Transnational Elite's think tanks, often masquerading as 'independent' research organizations but in fact funded directly or indirectly by the political and economic elites, such as the OECD, presented an almost cataclysmic view of the effects of Brexit. Thus, according to the OECD's central estimate, Britain's gross domestic product (GDP), within four years, would be 5 per cent lower than if Britain remained in the EU, this being "equivalent to Britons losing a month's income." That was of course a ridiculous prediction based on 'heroic assumptions', which induced even the *Financial Times* to point out that "these figures put the organization very close to the Treasury's estimate" and concluding with the catty remark "the OECD has been a consistent supporter of the economic policies of George Osborne, the UK chancellor." [350]

---

[349] "European business warns against Brexit", *Financial Times*, 13/4/2016
[350] Chris Giles, "Brexit sparks outbreak of agreement among economists-The FT considers the latest view from the OECD and asks what it is worth", *Financial Times*, 27/4/2016

No need to stress that the reason for this general mobilization of the elites to torpedo Brexit was solely motivated by the knowledge that a Brexit could well lead to a breakup of the EU, therefore thwarting for many years to come the completion of the Transnational Elite's plan for global governance. A plan that, in the first stage, seems to assume the creation of economic unions like the EU, NAFTA etc., which, in a second stage, are going to be united through agreements similar to the TTIP agreement, towards a final stage of global governance. In fact, Obama's enthusiasm about the EU and his rage against Brexit was purely motivated by the need to protect at all cost the TTIP, as a step towards the completion of the plan for global governance.[351]

The domestic front of the elites against Brexit was equally formidable. The entire political elite — apart from a few exceptions, mainly in the Tory party, and of course the UKIP party — was against Brexit. Particularly pro-EU was the entire 'progressive' part of this elite i.e. the Labor party, the Green Party, Social Liberals and the rest. Thus, whereas the Tory party was more or less split with about 45% of its Members of Parliament (MPs) being in favor of BREXIT and 55% against (although Cameron had taken care to select a Cabinet which was overwhelmingly pro-EU), in the Labor Party only 7 of its 222 MPs were in favor of Brexit! Similarly, the Liberal Democrats and all the autonomist parties (Scots, Welsh and Irish in Northern Ireland) were 100 percent against Brexit![352] Given therefore the strong influence that the Labor party still exerts on trade unionists, we can assume that a significant part of the Bremain vote was due, mainly, to the fact that the British 'Left' (as well of course as the globalist 'Left' world-wide) is completely integrated into the NWO — the surest proof of its political bankruptcy.

As regards the economic elite, it almost unanimously came out against Brexit, if we exclude from it the medium or small businesses, with some 250 of them coming out publicly in favor of Brexit.[353] Thus,

---

[351] "Why Obama really wants Britain to stay in the EU… to impose TTIP on Europe – NGO", RT, 22/4/2016 https://www.rt.com/uk/340605-ttip-obama-uk-visit/; see also "'Time for US-German leadership'? Obama, Merkel pushing EU into unpopular TTIP free trade deal", RT, 25/4/2016 https://www.rt.com/news/340796-obama-merkel-pushing-ttip-deal/

[352] BBC, "EU vote: Where the cabinet and other MPs stand", *BBC News*, 24/3/2016 http://www.bbc.co.uk/news/uk-politics-eu-referendum-35616946

[353] EU referendum: 250 business leaders sign up as backers of Vote Leave, *The Guardian*, 26/3/2016

the economic elites and the financial elites in particular, headed by the financiers controlling central banks, hedge funds etc., have played a leading role in the 'Project Fear'. The Canadian governor of the BoE and former Goldman Sachs employee, i.e. a man with impeccable links to the financial constituent of the Transnational Elite — which plays a crucial role in the exercise of economic violence against the victims of globalization all over the world — came out first to declare that the prospect of leaving "is the biggest domestic risk to financial stability because, in part, of the issues around uncertainty," adding that some city companies would leave the UK in the event of Brexit.[354] This forced even Lord Lawson, the former chancellor, to say to the BBC that it was "quite wrong for a governor of the Bank of England to enter the political fray in this way. I believe he is talking nonsense and if I may say so he was doing it for political reasons," he said, pointedly adding, "I think it would please the Chancellor of the Exchequer who appointed him."[355] In fact, the governor of the Bank of England was more interested in pleasing his former employer, Goldman Sachs, rather than his political appointer (who is also controlled by the same economic elites!). Naturally, Carney could defend himself that he simply expressed the views of the Bank. This is of course true but hardly surprising as several key senior positions within the Bank of England are also held by former Goldman officials![356]

No wonder that, following Carney, HSBC also said publicly that it might move thousands of jobs from London in the event of Brexit, while Morgan Stanley warned that leaving the EU would have a devastating effect on financial markets within six months[357] and Goldman Sachs itself (rightly described by Boris Johnson as "the people who engineered the biggest financial disaster of the last century") warned as far back as 2013 that if Britain left the EU "every European firm [of investment banks] would be gone in very short

[354] Chris Giles and Emily Cadman, "Carney supports Cameron's deal with Brussels", *Financial Times*, 9/3/2016
[355] ibid.
[356] Prof Michel Chossudovsky "Who Controls the Central Banks? Mark Carney, Governor of the … "Bank of Goldman Sachs", *Global Research*, 9/3/2016 http://www.globalresearch.ca/mark-carney-governor-of-the-bank-of-goldman-sachs/5512969
[357] Lianna Brinded, "MORGAN STANLEY: Brexit would devastate the markets in just 6 months", *Business Insider*, 14/6/2016 http://uk.businessinsider.com/morgan-stanley-eu-referendum-and-brexit-impact-on-financial-markets-2016-6?r=US&IR=T

order."[358] Similarly, the rating agency Moody's took immediately part in the Project Fear by declaring that "Britain's biggest companies could face a credit downgrade – potentially forcing up their borrowing costs — should the UK vote to leave the EU in June'.[359] Needless to add that the City (i.e. the British financial center in London) came out in full support of the EU. Thus, *TheCityUK*, the financial services lobby group, declared on February 20th: "Membership of a reformed EU and continued access to the single market is vital ... It is also the preferred outcome for the majority of our members."[360]

Of course, the campaign of the economic elites against Brexit was not only rhetorical. They also used their economic power in order to blackmail their working force. This method was particularly used by major TNCs like BMW. As it was reported at the time, the chief executive of Rolls-Royce Motor Cars, which is owned by BMW, had written to all its workers in Britain, warning that exit from the European Union would drive up costs and prices and could affect the company's "employment base."[361] The letter was one of six sent by bosses of each of BMW's British companies, including Mini, to their staff warning of the dangers of UK withdrawal. Both Rolls-Royce and BMW admitted that emails and letters had been sent out to 8,000 employees, including workers at car plants in Goodwood, West Sussex, and Oxford. BMW was, also, among the signatories of a business letter, organized by the government, backing EU membership. Paul Stephenson, a Vote Leave spokesman gave an insightful explanation about this industrial blackmail:

> Big foreign multinational companies like the EU because they spend millions lobbying it in order to stitch up the rules in their favor – forcing smaller players out of business.[362]

---

[358] Jim Pickard and Laura Noonan, "Boris Johnson hits out at pro-EU stance of City", *Financial Times,* 6/3/2016
[359] Phillip Inman, "Brexit 'could trigger credit threat' for UK firms", *The Guardian,* 22/3/2016
[360] Patrick Jenkins, "Brexit is the last thing City banks need", *Financial Times,* 22/2/2016
[361] see the report by Anushka Asthana and Heather Stewart on this interference by a German multinational, "Rolls-Royce warns its staff of Brexit risks", *The Guardian,* 3/3/2016
[362] ibid.

Needless to add that the campaign against Brexit had been fully using the state mechanism to promote its stand. That is, taxpayer's money, which included the money of the majority that proved to be pro-Brexit, was unashamedly used to finance the propaganda of the elites! In fact, this created a minor political scandal when it was announced that £9m of taxpayers' money (on top of the general allocations given to the 'Yes' and 'No' campaigns) would be spend on leaflets to send to every UK home in order to promote the EU case. Cameron had of course no qualms about doing this, as he knew very well that a victory for Brexit will cost him his premiership (as indeed it did!), despite the fact that this made a mockery of the referendum. As if it was not enough that the elite-controlled media (particularly the TV channels, with BBC playing, as always, its role of the systemic medium par excellence) clearly discriminated against Brexit, Cameron and the elites behind him decided also, that every home in the country should get an official leaflet. That is, a leaflet bearing the official HM government stamp, which supposedly was telling 'the facts' (i.e. the 'truth') about the EU, but which, in fact, was just repeating the EU black propaganda. Here is how the BBC described its contents:

> The leaflet claims that a vote to leave the EU would cause an economic shock that "would risk higher prices of some household goods and damage living standards". It further claims that the only way to "protect jobs, provide security, and strengthen the UK's economy" is by staying in the EU, arguing that leaving would create risk and uncertainty. [363].

As regards the BBC's role in particular with respect to Brexit, recent research by a media-monitoring group, News-watch, showed the shamelessly biased practice of this supposedly objective medium on the referendum. As the report mentioned:

> One of the BBC's flagship news programs has shown a 'strong' bias towards Britain staying in the European Union (EU). From the 13th of January to the 11th of March 2016, News-watch analysed 40 editions of the popular current affairs program Newsnight. News-watch noted that 25 of the guests who appeared on the program were in favor of Britain staying

---

[363] BBC News, "EU referendum: PM 'makes no apology' for £9m EU leaflets", BBC, 7/4/2016 http://www.bbc.co.uk/news/uk-politics-eu-referendum-35984991

in the EU, compared to only 14 who advocated the UK leaving the union. [364]

It should be added however that the supporters of Brexit were, inevitably, much more divided than their opponents, as they ranged from conservatives and neo-nationalists up to genuine antiglobalists, from the Left or the Right. The main demand of the former (conservatives and neo-nationalists) was the strict control of borders, but only as far as it concerned the movement of people and not necessarily also the much more important movement of capital and commodities through the activities of TNCs. On the other hand, the real anti-globalists were fighting for genuine national sovereignty, which is incompatible with globalization and the integration of the country into the NWO and its institutions — such as the EU, the WTO, the IMF and the World Bank. In other words, all those institutions that preclude any policy of self-reliance, which is of course the sufficient condition for national sovereignty.

The disorienting stand of the globalist 'Left' on Brexit

As regards the stand of the British 'Left' on Brexit, particularly damaging to the campaign — although far from surprising — was the stand of the Labor Party. Whereas in the 1975 referendum the Party was split on the Common Market issue — despite the fact that at that time the issue of sovereignty was far less significant — the Party was now almost unanimous in supporting the EU. Thus, apart from a few exceptions, all sections of the Labor party were united against Brexit, including its 'progressive' leadership under Corbyn, who in the past was himself against the EU! The very fact that he appointed as one of the Party's economic advisers the highly connected with the Euro-elites (and the Transnational Elite in general) Varoufakis, well-known for his enthusiastic globalism and his role on the Greek catastrophe, was highly significant. However, the Labor Party's stand was far from surprising since it had abandoned long ago its close links to workers — I do not mean of course the trade union bureaucrats who are fully integrated into the NWO — and the victims of globalization. That is, since the time Tony Blair, another con artist and war criminal, took the party over, which was then converted into a middle-class party

---

[364] Steven MacMillan, "BBC Bias, Brexit, the EU, Bilderberg and Global Government", *Global Research*, 6/4/2016 http://www.globalresearch.ca/bbc-bias-brexit-the-eu-bilderberg-and-global-government/5518878

expressing mainly the interests of that part of the middle class, which did not suffer from globalization. Naturally, trade unionists linked to Labor also stood against Brexit, supposedly to protect jobs. This, at the very moment when the French people had, for several weeks in the Spring of 2016, been protesting against the present attempt by the EU and the French elites (under the 'socialist' Hollande!) to pass legislation eroding further the workers' rights, while in Greece, Spain, and Portugal unemployment has taken mass proportions, mainly because of the labor market liberalization reforms imposed by the EU.[365] In fact, the French 'socialists' who govern France, in pure contempt of this mass movement from below, decided to force the reforms by means of bypassing Parliament in an extraordinary cabinet meeting, which invoked a controversial article of the French constitution.[366]

No wonder the blue-collar workers, the unemployed and those paying the consequences of globalization have moved towards neo-nationalist parties in Europe in general and, in Britain, towards UKIP. This is, of course, another indication of the total political bankruptcy of today's 'Left'. However, what many people in the Green Left found difficult to understand was the stand of the British Green Party, which was also opposed to Brexit. Thus, its co-leader and single MP, Caroline Lucas, (who, needless to add is, also, a supporter of Varoufakis' DIEM25 'movement'!) had no qualms about supporting the myth of a peaceful EU. But, although this stand may be surprising to some Greens, it was in fact far from unexpected, following the full integration of the European Greens into the NWO. This became inevitable, once the German Green Party (the most influential Green Party) was taken over by the 'realos,',[367] while the despicable Kohn-Bendit was leading the European Greens to enthusiastically support

---

[365] Adam Sage, "Hollande buckles as students in a haze of cannabis occupy Paris", *The Times*, 23/4/2016; see also Simon Schama New revolutionaries generate much heat but little action, *Financial Times*, 22/4/2016

[366] "French labour reforms: Government to force plan through", *BBC News*, 10/5/2016 http://www.bbc.co.uk/news/world-europe-36259120

[367] see the section "The end of the Greens as an antisystemic movement" in the article "The End of Traditional Antisystemic Movements", DEMOCRACY & NATURE: The International Journal of INCLUSIVE DEMOCRACY, vol. 7, no.3, (November 2001), pp. 415-455
http://www.democracynature.org/vol7/takis_movements.htm

every single war of the Transnational Elite in the last quarter of a century or so.

Moving further to the Left, a number of communists, Trotskyites, trade unionists and others signed a common declaration published in the flagship of globalist 'Left' under the title "EU is now a profoundly anti-democratic institution" and concluding with the following statement:

> We stand for a positive vision of a future Europe based on democracy, social justice and ecological sustainability, not the profit-making interests of a tiny elite. For these reasons we are committed to pressing for a vote to leave the EU in the forthcoming referendum on UK membership. [368]

Unsurprisingly, the issue of globalization and of economic and national sovereignty was not even mentioned, despite a passing reference to the Transatlantic Trade and Investment Partnership, which was mentioned as just a bad Treaty that had to be abandoned. Instead, the non-democratic character of the EU was emphasized, (exactly as Varoufakis and the rest of the globalist 'Left' did), the only difference being that this declaration asked also for a Brexit, presumably in the hope that this could precipitate the overthrow of capitalism.

Further to the 'Left', the Socialist Workers party (which supported the Libyan and Syrian 'revolutionaries', and up to a point even the Ukrainian ones!) took a stand, which can be well summarized by the following extract of an article in their theoretical organ:

> [socialists] shouldn't feel compelled to back the austerity-driven, racist EU project simply because the leave camp is led by such hateful figures as Nigel Farage, Michael Gove and Boris. In fact, it is important to note the racism and pro-business arguments dominating both camps. Socialists have a responsibility to put a principled internationalist, anti-racist, anti-austerity case for a left exit. Neither should we be afraid that if Britain left the EU it would automatically benefit only the right. …Crucially, a vote to leave would destroy David Cameron, tear apart the Tory party, weaken the EU project and throw all kinds of questions up for debate. We vote to leave in

---

[368] Mick Cash et al, "EU is now a profoundly anti-democratic institution", *The Guardian*, 17/2/2016

solidarity with our brothers and sisters in Greece suffering under the EU institutions — as well as those risking death in the Med to reach Fortress Europe's shores.[369]

The purely tactical stand adopted on such a crucial issue (to "destroy Cameron, tear apart the Tory party" etc.) is fully explained by the fact that this 'Trotskyite' party, far from understanding the significance of globalization and national sovereignty, in fact, fully adopts the ideology of globalization on open borders (promoted by Soros and the likes). It is very difficult indeed to believe that it is just out of ignorance (or idiocy) that this kind of 'Trotskyites' cannot understand the real significance of open borders in an internationalized capitalist market economy on unemployment, wages, the (remnants of) the welfare state etc. Needless to add that far from the Brexit victory "tearing the Tory party apart", as they predicted, in fact it strengthened the party, which adopted the line that it is the only party that unites Brexiteers (some of them in the new government) and Bremainers!

Similarly, the point implicitly raised by the stand of the British 'left' in general on the issue of Brexit cannot just be discussed in terms of the free trade vs. protectionism debate, as the liberal (or globalist) 'Left' attempted to do (see for instance Jean Bricmont[370] and Larry Elliott[371] of the *Guardian*). This is because such a discussion ignores the main point of the debate, i.e. whether it is globalization itself, which has led to the present mass economic violence against the vast majority of the world population and the accompanying it military violence.

In other words, what all the aforementioned 'Left' trends effectively were trying to hide was the fact that globalization is a class issue. But, *this is the essence of the bankruptcy of the "Left", which is reflected in the fact that, today, it is the neo-nationalist Right which has replaced the Left in its role of representing the victims of the system in its present globalized form,* while the Left mainly represents those in the middle class or the petty bourgeoisie who benefit (or hope

---

[369] Sally Campbell, "The bosses Europe is not for us", *Socialist Review*, March 2016, http://socialistreview.org.uk/411/bosses-europe-not-us

[370] Jean Bricmont, "Trump and the Liberal Intelligentsia : a view from Europe" , *Counterpunch*, 30/3/2016 http://www.counterpunch.org/2016/03/30/trump-and-the-liberal-intelligentsia-a-view-from-europe/

[371] see for instance Larry Elliott, "How free trade became the hot topic vexing voters and politicians in Europe and the US" , *The Guardian*, 28/3/2016

to benefit) from globalization. Needless to add that today's bankrupt 'Left' promptly characterized the rising neo-nationalist parties as racist, if not fascist and neo-Nazis, fully siding with the EU's black propaganda against the rising movement for national sovereignty. This is obviously another nail in the coffin of this kind of 'Left', as the millions of European voters who turn their back on this degraded 'Left' are far from racists or fascists but simply want to control their way of life, rather than letting it to be determined by the free movement of capital, labor and commodities, as the various Soroses and Varoufakises of this world wish!

In Britain itself, very recent research by the Joseph Rowntree Foundation found that 668,000 households (containing 1,252,000 people, including 312,000 children) are unable to afford essentials such as food, heating and clothes: "More than a million people in the UK are so poor they cannot afford to eat properly, keep clean or stay warm and dry, according to a groundbreaking attempt to measure the scale of destitution in Britain."[372] The study stressed that this was an underestimate because the data did not capture poor households who eschewed charity handouts or used only state-funded welfare services with high destitution rates found, in particular, in former industrial areas in the north-west and north-east of England, Scotland, south Wales and Northern Ireland, as well as inner London.[373] These are of course the areas particularly hit by unemployment, as a result of neoliberal globalization policies consistently applied by Conservatives and Labor governments alike since the 1980s. It is therefore clear that the question of Brexit is indeed a class issue, although we have to re-define 'class' to give it a broader meaning than the traditional Marxist sense, more appropriate to the globalization era, as I tried to do elsewhere.[374]

In other words, globalization is the class issue par excellence in the era of globalization. However, as in every class struggle in history, there are two main camps opposing each other: those directly or indirectly benefiting from the status quo (today globalization) and

---

[372] Patrick Butler, "More than a million people in UK living in destitution, study shows", *The Guardian,* 27/4/2016
[373] ibid.
[374] Takis Fotopoulos, Class Divisions Today — The Inclusive Democracy approach, *DEMOCRACY & NATURE*, vol.6, no.2, (July 2000)
http://www.democracynature.org/vol6/takis_class.htm

those who are its victims. Therefore, as we shall see below, academics who function like the lackeys of the Transnational Elite in order to enjoy the economic and social benefits of their profession are, in fact, class enemies when they try, for instance, to diminish the significance of the Brexit vote on pseudo-scientific grounds and in full knowledge that Brexit functions today as a symbol of revolt of the vast majority of the world population against the minority benefiting from globalization.

Why the Brexit vote was a revolution?

Perhaps one of the best descriptions of the revolutionary nature of Brexit was given by the *Observer,* which together with its sister paper the *Guardian* play a leading role in the globalist 'Left', although the following statement was intended more as a warning to the British people if it persists with Brexit rather than as a recognition of its revolutionary character:

> Anyone who has witnessed the aftermath of a super typhoon in countries such as the Philippines or seen the devastation caused by the hurricanes that occasionally ravage the Caribbean and southern US would readily recognize the dramatically altered political, economic and social landscape of the United Kingdom following last week's thunderous vote to leave the European Union. The damage caused by this constitutional mega-storm is ubiquitous, unquantifiable and, in some key instances, irreparable. The political establishment, including the leaders of the two main parties, David Cameron and Jeremy Corbyn, and the Brussels hierarchy, was squashed flat. The hitherto dominant influence of the City, big business, financial institutions, the US government, international watchdogs such as the IMF and myriad economic experts was contemptuously blown aside.[375]

Even more significant was the direct connection the paper made with neoliberal globalization, although the conclusion it drew was the usual one expected from this kind of 'Left', i.e. — to exonerate the NWO and the EU itself, as "possibly the greatest democratic achievement of the postwar era" and to directly blame the 'bad' Tory

---

[375] Editorial, "We ignored the 'left-behind'", *The Observer*, 26/6/2016

governments (but not necessarily also the equally 'bad' Blairite governments!):

> So what about globalization? How have free markets benefited the steel worker put out of work by the EU-sanctioned dumping of cheap Chinese products? Seen from Wearside or the Welsh valleys, booming London and the southeast, with its Monopoly money property prices and £70 a head restaurants, resembles Gold rush City, a foreign and hostile land. Does anybody in Westminster understand or even care? No, not really, so these alienated voters seemed to believe…For 30 years, the 'leftbehind' (the working poor, the 'strivers', the zero hours contract workers) have waited for a new economic reality based on fairness and equality to rebalance the effects of late capitalism as it advantaged a smaller and smaller number of people with grotesque income inequalities. [376]

Then, it was the turn of *Guardian*, the flagship of the globalist 'Left' par excellence, to expand on the significance of globalization and put the blame directly on it (in order to draw, of course, the wrong conclusions!) Thus, beginning with a brief history of globalization, which started in the late 1970s and accelerated throughout 1980s and reached a climax with the collapse of 'actually existing socialism in Eastern Europe at the end of the decade and the beginning of the 1990s, it described the essence of globalization as "the free movement of capital, people and goods; trickle-down economics; a much diminished role for nation states; and a belief that market forces, now unleashed, were inexorable." [377] However, further on, the aim of the paper to simply exonerate the EU itself (as a NWO institution) and put instead the blame on its bad practices and policies becomes obvious:

> In the age of globalization, the idea was that a more integrated Europe would collectively serve as the bulwark that nation states could no longer provide. Britain, France, Germany or Italy could not individually resist the power of transnational capital, but the EU potentially could. The way forward was clear. Move on from a single market to a single currency, a single banking system, a single budget and eventually a single

---

[376] ibid.
[377] Editorial, "The age of globalisation showed how weak the EU is. Now for the age of disintegration", *The Guardian*, 27/6/2016

political entity. That dream is now over. As Charles Grant, director of the Centre for European Reform think-tank, put it: "Brexit is a momentous event in the history of Europe and from now on the narrative will be one of disintegration not integration…The reason is obvious. Europe has failed to fulfill the historic role allocated to it.[378]

So, although the *Guardian* admits that Britain's rejection of the EU was, in fact, a protest against the economic model that has been in place for the past three decades, it is clear that its real aim was simply to criticize the EU as not being 'progressive enough' — following the well-trodden path of Varoufakis![379] All that the globalist 'Left' had to do, according to this completely disorienting view, was to introduce some reforms to cover its democratic 'deficit', without of course touching the EU's cherished '4 freedoms' in the movement of capital, labor, goods and services. In other words, without making the life of multinational corporations, which control the world economy, more difficult in any sense of the word.

In fact, the entire globalist 'Left' has engaged in a huge attempt of gross deception of the victims of globalization when it argued that globalization is not by necessity neoliberal but that it is instead the result of 'bad' policy of some 'bad' political parties and economists! Yet, it can be shown that no other 'good' globalization is possible within a system of open and liberalized markets for capital, commodities and labor. All this is therefore a resurgence of the old deceptive Porto Alegre slogan of the World Social Forum that 'another world is possible' even within the present globalization, as long as the good Left politicians replace the present bad ones. This was in essence, also, the argument repeated by the criminal Tony Blair's anointed heir Gordon Brown, who, following the Brexit decision, stressed that Historians will see it as "the largest popular revolt against political, business and financial elites, the nearest Britain has come in centuries to a revolution."[380]

---

[378] ibid.
[379] see, ch.7 and, also, Takis Fotopoulos, "The DIEM25 Manifesto: 'Democratizing Europe' or Perpetuating the Domination of the EU Elites? *Global Research*, 19/2/2016 http://www.globalresearch.ca/the-diem25-manifesto-democratizing-europe-or-perpetuating-the-domination-of-the-eu-elites/5508950
[380] Gordon Brown, "Leaders must make the case for globalisation", *Financial Times*, 18/7/2016

However, the growing anger at the EU is not simply a British phenomenon. In fact, the victims of globalization all over Europe have begun rising even before Brexit, as early as 2011 in Greece and then Spain but, unfortunately, due to the recent past of these countries with a military junta in the former case and fascism in the latter, the globalist 'Left' (Syriza and Podemos) managed to control the rising popular indignation, deceiving the peoples that it was just the austerity policies that the 'bad' Germans imposed which was the cause of their misery. All that was needed therefore was to elect con artists like Tsipras (who at present is busy imposing arguably the worst kind of neoliberal policies ever imposed on any country in the world — all for the sake of the people of course!) so that good days come back again.

Fortunately, in the rest of Europe this kind of 'Left' is politically bankrupt and people in France, Belgium and elsewhere have been frequently on the streets protesting against the measures to 'liberalize' the labor market which another con artist, the 'socialist' Hollande, has been trying to impose. Even in the USA, Donald Trump successfully appealed to the victims of globalization there with slogans against it, so that — following the (far from unexpected!) selling out of Bernie Sanders to save the favorite of the Transnational Elite Hillary Clinton — another popular revolution from below in the USA could not be ruled out (although Trump's limitations and inconsistencies are well known).

Furthermore, as I mentioned in other parts of this book, the revolts against globalization in Hungary, Poland and elsewhere in Europe are in full progress at the moment. Here, we may mention just one more incident of the growing revolt which, for obvious reasons, received very little publicity in the Transnational Elite's media. Thus, the result of the referendum in the Netherlands was highly indicative of the explicitly anti-EU and implicitly anti-globalization wind blowing all over Europe and beyond at the moment. The way in which a conservative newspaper like the London *Times* described it in an editorial was highly significant. It began with reference to an earlier referendum:

> In 2005 the Dutch voted against an EU constitution and were
> dismayed when the Lisbon treaty, in effect, introduced one by
> the back door. Many other EU countries share this suspicion

that the integration process has become automatic and unquestioning.[381]

In other words, the Dutch simply expressed their indignation for the loss of any national sovereignty that became particularly evident in the last ten years or so. When, therefore, they recently found out that their elite (as also the elites of all other EU countries), had decided without of course consulting them, to have an EU association Treaty with the Ukraine — a protectorate created by the Transnational Elite following the coup of 2014 — they presumably concluded 'enough is enough'. A clear movement 'from below' was set in motion — which the European 'Left' ignored — when an Internet petition demanding a referendum on the issue (using a new Dutch law designed to promote democracy) attracted more than 400,000 signatures, significantly more than the 300,000 required by the law. As even the fully pro-EU BBC had to admit at the time, "from the start activists said this was a chance for Dutch voters to express frustration at the EU, in particular what they see as its desire to expand despite democratic shortcomings." By doing so, the Dutch voters completely ignored the stern warning by EU Commission President Jean-Claude Juncker, who had described the stakes in the run-up to the vote as being high, warning that a 'No' vote could trigger a wider crisis in the 28-member bloc.[382] Yet, the "No" campaign won with 61.1 per cent, against 38.2 per cent for the "Yes" group, despite the latter being backed by all mainstream Dutch political parties. As the *Times,* again, reported about the low turnout (which, however, was well over the minimum required 30%), this was a miraculous expression of popular will against all the odds:

> The result is a major blow for the EU at a time when Euroscepticism is growing across the continent…Campaigners for No accused the government of trying to keep the turnout low by providing only half the normal number of polling stations used in a national election. "It is outrageous," Harry Van Bommel, an MP for the Eurosceptic Socialist party, said.[383]

---

[381] Editorial, "Dutch Torpor", *The Times,* 7/4/2016
[382] Alex Forsyth Analysis on "Netherlands rejects EU-Ukraine partnership deal", BBC News, 7/4/2016 http://www.bbc.co.uk/news/world-europe-35976086
[383] Bruno Waterfield, "Boost for Brexit campaign as Dutch voters reject EU deal", *The Times,* 7/4/2016

This, despite the fact that "during a lackluster but ill-tempered campaign, Dutch ministers and Yes campaigners warned that a No vote would signal support for President Putin, Russia's aggression and annexation of Ukrainian territory."[384] As part of the same campaign, the infamous 'Panama papers' were published at the same time with the obvious aim to target Putin and Russia, (as WikiLeaks revealed), given that the 'Putin attack' was funded by the US Agency for International Development (USAID) and American hedge fund billionaire (sponsor of many NGOs) George Soros.[385] Not accidentally, again at the same time, Western papers reported a new flare-up in Ukraine![386] Needless to add that the EU elites showed once more their contempt towards expressions of popular will, particularly if they are not compatible with their own will. Thus, as Luxembourg's Foreign Minister Jean Asselborn told *Hannoversche Allgemeine* newspaper, following the elites' defeat in it, in a memorable statement of the elites' despise of popular will:

> Referendum is not an appropriate instrument to solve complex issues in a parliamentary democracy. If you want to make Europe collapse, you only need to hold more referendums." (sic!)[387]

Last, but not least there is an indirect link between the Brexit 'revolution' and the events following the unsuccessful coup in Turkey — an event which is particularly significant given Turkey's importance with respect to the Middle East campaign of the Transnational Elite to integrate the area fully into the NWO. Particularly so, when it is now known that the coup was backed by the CIA with direct involvement by Victoria Nuland, who seems she specializes in organizing coups in the NWO, directly or indirectly aimed at Russia — from Ukraine up to Turkey.[388] The British peoples'

[384] ibid.
[385] "US government, Soros funded Panama Papers to attack Putin – WikiLeaks", RT, 6/4/2016, https://www.rt.com/news/338683-wikileaks-usaid-putin-attack/
[386] Jack Losh, "Ukraine clashes shatter ceasefire", *The Times*, 6/4/2016
[387] "Referendums not part of parliamentary democracy, Luxembourg FM says after Dutch vote on EU/Kiev deal", RT, 11/4/2016 https://www.rt.com/news/339250-referendum-eu-democracy-ukraine/
[388] F. William Engdahl, "Top USA National Security Officials Admit Turkey Coup", New Eastern Outlook, 31/8/2016 http://journal-neo.org/2016/08/31/top-usa-national-security-officials-admit-turkey-coup/

slap to the elites had surely influenced the Turkish people, who turned in their millions onto the streets to demand the right to govern themselves, as the British had done just a month before. Furthermore, in case the failed coup eventually leads to a radical change in the geopolitical strategy of Turkey[389] — as it seems possible, following also revelations by members of Erdogan's government on the role of the USA in it — then the unsuccessful coup could well lead to a radical change in the geopolitical map of this crucial area for the NWO. This was obviously Putin's intention when he invited Erdogan, soon after the failed coup, for a discussion on a potential cooperation via the Eurasian Economic Union.[390]

In fact, following this meeting, a much closer economic co-operation was announced, particularly as regards to energy.[391] This co-operation effectively frustrates the Transnational Elite's plan to abort any substantial energy cooperation between Russia and Turkey/Greece, although the plan of the Transnational Elite was — unsurprisingly — successful as regards to Greece, thanks to its 'Leftist' protectorate there. Furthermore, the announcement after the Putin-Erdogan meeting that the two leaders agreed to discuss further a new Syria policy is significant. Particularly so, as it seems that Erdogan and the US elite try hard lately to restore their ties, possibly in view of a possible attack by the Transnational Elite against Syria's army in the near future, with the aim of "regime change".

At the moment of writing, there is much uncertainty about the future relations of Turkey with the West, as well as with Russia.[392] Thus, a small scale Turkish invasion in Northern Syria, which was followed by the breakdown of the ceasefire in Syria agreed in early

---

[389] See e.g. Andrew Korybco, "Post coup Turkey will be distinctly Eurasian", *Global Research,17/7/2016 http://www.globalresearch.ca/post-coup-turkey-will-be-distinctly-eurasian/5536229*
[390] Andrew Korybco, "Why The Failed Turkish Coup Attempt Wasn't A "False Flag" Power Grab By Erdogan", *Global Research,* 18/7/2016 http://www.globalresearch.ca/why-the-failed-turkish-coup-attempt-wasnt-a-false-flag-power-grab-by-erdogan/5536341
[391] "Turkey to transit Russian natural gas to Europe via Turkish Stream pipeline – Erdogan", RT, 9/8/2016 https://www.rt.com/business/355245-turkey-restart-tukish-stream/
[392] Mike Whitney, "Washington Slapdown: Turkey Turns to Moscow for Help, *Global Research,* 9/8/2016 http://www.globalresearch.ca/washington-slapdown-turkey-turns-to-moscow-for-help/5540384

September between USA and Russia, led to a sharp worsening of US-Russia relations. The pretext for the truce breakdown was a double provocation by the Transnational Elite and its proxies on the ground, both presumably aiming at setting the wheels in motion to the final stage of their original plan for 'regime change' in Syria. Thus, first, there was the serious incident with the US bombardment of Syrian positions 'by error' that led to many army casualties.[393] This was followed by the bombing of a UN humanitarian convoy, which was blamed, with no evidence, as usually, on Syria and Russia.

The aim of the Turkish invasion was obviously to ensure that no Kurdish state will emerge out of the present Kurdish action in the area — supposedly aimed against ISIS. On the other hand, the Transnational Elite's plan seems to be exactly the opposite: to achieve the integration of at least part of Syria into the NWO, through its dismemberment, with the creation of another protectorate in the area: a fully integrated into the NWO Kurdistan, extending from Northern Iraq and Northern Syria to Southern Turkey. This is indirectly confirmed also by a very recent report in the *New York Times*, according to which the Turkish intervention disrupted the US timetable for taking Raqqa, prompting the plan to arm the Kurds directly — a plan which "both the officials who leaked the plan's existence to the paper and experts at Washington think-tanks agree that would complicate US relations with Turkey."[394] However, the very recent attack on Mosul by an alliance of the Transnational Elite and its allies on the ground (Iraq and Kurds — excluding the Turks) highlighted yet again the significance of the creation of a Kurdish state on Turkey's southern borders, which is clearly the Transnational Elite's aim, as part of the 'regime change' plan in Syria I mentioned. This plan is, at present, perfectly feasible for the Transnational Elite, given that all Kurdish movements, (including the ex anti-imperialist PKK!)[395] are now US allies in the fight — supposedly aimed against ISIS.

---

[393] Federico Pieraccini, "US Attack in Syria Opens Disturbing and Unpredictable Scenarios. The Danger of "Direct Military Confrontation" between US-NATO and Russia", *Global Research*, 21/9/2016 http://www.globalresearch.ca/us-attack-in-syria-opens-disturbing-and-unpredictable-scenarios-the-danger-of-direct-military-confrontation-between-us-nato-and-russia/5546975
[394] Samira Ghaderi, "Obama mulls arming Syrian Kurds against ISIS", *RT*, 21/9/2016 https://www.rt.com/usa/360194-obama-arming-kurds-syria/
[395] see *Subjugating the Middle East* (vol 3 of the NWO in Action)

Whether the Erdogan leadership will reach some compromise on this crucial issue with the Transnational Elite, on the condition that no Kurdistan in Turkey's borders will be created, or whether instead a new state will be created in the Middle East, at the expense, partly, of Turkey — a development which will surely push Turkey towards the Eurasian Union — remains to be seen. The very fact that the EU has for all intents and purposes effectively ruled out any EU entry for the country[396] (as the globalist part of the Turkish elite always wanted) is highly indicative of the geopolitical changes in the area. Similarly, the recent raising of territorial demands by the Erdogan leadership against Greece is not irrelevant to the geopolitical game played by the Turkish elite at the moment in its attempt to frustrate at all cost the creation of a Kurdish state in its borders.

Brexit as a class issue

It is, therefore, clear that the Brexit revolution, far from being an isolated incident, related — as some globalists argued in order to defame it — to the ideological paraphernalia of old British imperialism, reflects, in fact, a world revolutionary phenomenon. In fact, it was the IMF itself that lately came out in recognizing the revolutionary character of Brexit, — of course, in order to express the Transnational Elite's panic about it and draw the appropriate conclusions. Thus, as *The Times* described the statement by Maurice Obstfeld, the IMF's chief economist on recent world economic developments:

> Brexit may be the start of a growing revolt against globalisation and technological advance in the developed world that threatens to depress living standards, the International Monetary Fund has warned. Persistently weak growth is unleashing "negative economic and political forces" that are fuelling protectionism in Britain, the rest of Europe and the US, according to the IMF, and governments need to respond before the problem gets worse.[397]

---

[396] Turkey says Germany's remarks on EU accession amount to 'cultural racism', RT, 31-08-2016 https://www.rt.com/news/357724-turkey-germany-cultural-racism/
[397] Philip Aldrick, "Brexit was just the start of a global revolt, IMF warns", *The Times*, 5/10/2016

This is hardly surprising, in view of the analysis in this book which tried to show that Brexit is, in fact, a class issue — although we have to re-define 'class', so that it could reflect the new realities of the globalization era, as I tried to do elsewhere.[398] Briefly, 'class' has to be redefined to include not just the old working class (which has diminished in Europe in general and Britain in particular as a result of de-industrialization — a by-product of globalization itself) but also:

- all those who became unemployed;
- those who became partially employed at subsistence wages;
- those working at zero hours contracts;
- those trying to survive in some sort of self-employment and, finally;
- all those who cannot adequately cover even basic human needs like health, education and social care because of the systematic destruction of the welfare state in the NWO of neoliberal globalization.

The fact that Brexit is, in effect, a class issue, expressing the popular reaction to the class nature of globalization, has even prompted some of the world's most powerful investment houses to turn their focus to inequality, with both Bank of America and the international investment firm Pimco warning their clients about the growing risks resulting from the fact that the gulf between rich and poor has been continually rising in the globalization era. Thus, Joachim Fels, global economic adviser at Pimco, wrote in a research note: "The vote in the UK is part of a wider, more global, backlash against the establishment, rising inequality and globalization." [399] Similarly, in a research note entitled "Brexit and the war on inequality", Bank of America strategists stressed, "Brexit is thus far the biggest electoral riposte to our age of inequality."[400]

All this points once more to the bankruptcy of the 'Left', which still talks about imperialism, ignoring globalization, as if we are still

---

[398] Takis Fotopoulos, Class Divisions Today — The Inclusive Democracy approach, *DEMOCRACY & NATURE*, vol.6, no.2, (July 2000) http://www.democracynature.org/vol6/takis_class.htm
[399] Katie Allen, "UK vote is part of global backlash, investors told", *The Guardian*, 28/6/2016
[400] ibid.

living somewhere at the beginning of the 20th century when nation-states were dominant.[401]

Furthermore, as I will try to show here, Brexit was very much a popular 'revolution' as the entire movement was a movement 'from below', i.e. from the victims of globalization themselves. The main factor which created a movement 'from below' for Brexit was the growing realization by the British people that its national and economic sovereignty has been decisively eroded within the EU, forcing the elites, albeit reluctantly, to accept the demand for a referendum. This realization was inevitable if one takes into account that Britons, who used to live in one of the strongest nation-states in the world, have now been forced to watch, powerless, the effective destruction of their industrial base, in the very place where industrialization was born.

Needless to add that the globalist 'Left' academic/politicians supporters of the EU, such as Piketty and Varoufakis (the two 'left-wing gurus who try to save Europe', according to another EU acolyte)[402] have nothing to say about all this and the loss of national sovereignty. Instead, they talk about a mythical and disorienting European 'sovereignty', which just suffers from the present lack of internal democracy. This, while at the same time, both Varoufakis and Piketty, following Soros, are in full favor of open borders, without bothering to explain how exactly open borders are compatible with any conception of sovereignty in an internationalized capitalist market economy![403]

No wonder most members of the old working class have abandoned their 'natural' leaders, i.e. the Left parties (Labor party, Green party etc.) and even their own Trade Union leaders, who, (apart from a very few honorable exceptions) declared themselves against Brexit on the basis of a variety of excuses, as we shall see next, usually centered around the issue of immigration. Furthermore, as we have

---

[401] A typical example of this is an archaic 'Marxist' Left supporter who, completely ignorant of my analysis on imperialism, has discovered that "what's missing from Fotopoulos's argument is any reference to Imperialism". See William Bowles, 'The Tory Chickens Come Home to Roost. Brexit, What Next?', *Global Research*, 24/6/2016 http://www.globalresearch.ca/the-tory-chickens-come-home-to-roost-brexit-what-next/5532608?print=1

[402] Paul Mayson, "Can two leftwing gurus save Europe?", *The Guardian*, 1/4/2016

[403] Piketty: "EU should welcome one million immigrants a year", *BBC News*, 7/4/2016 http://www.bbc.co.uk/news/business-35982528

already seen, even when the parties of the supposedly anti-systemic Left, reluctantly — usually for tactical reasons — supported Brexit (e.g. the Trotskyite SWP) they never uttered a single word against globalization itself, the Transnational Elite and its institutions! Yet, the Transnational Elite has a much better picture than the 'Left' of the real significance of Brexit, as George Soros, a significant member of the Transnational Elite, made clear in his first article after Brexit, adding a menacing threat in case the referendum result is not effectively annulled somehow:

> Now the catastrophic scenario that many feared has materialized, making the disintegration of the EU practically irreversible... I am convinced that as the consequences of Brexit unfold in the weeks and months ahead, more and more people will join us.[404]

In fact, this was a referendum in which an unprecedented number of voters took part, and in which well over a million more people voted for change than for the status quo on UK's membership of the EU. Two important characteristics of the referendum were usually minimized by the Transnational Elite's media: first, the geographical pattern of the vote, which is particularly revealing as regards the class nature of Brexit and, second, the age pattern of the vote, which is very much related to the ideological and cultural aspects of globalization.

As regards first, the geographical pattern of the vote, the way in which people voted was a clear indication of the fact that this was a 'revolution from below' of the victims of globalization. Thus, the only region in England to vote for Remain was London, which voted for this option by 60 to 40 percent. Every other region voted Leave, by 58 percent in Yorkshire and Humberside, 54 percent in the North West, 59 percent in the West Midlands, and more than 50 percent in both the South East and South West.

The London result is far from surprising as it is well known that, as the major urban center of the country dominated by the City of London, (effectively the financial center of Europe), it attracts not only the economic elites and the upper-middle class, but also the victims of globalization from Britain, the EU and beyond. Therefore, the Bremain victory in London is due to the fact that the majority of the population

---

[404] Soros warns of EU disintegration, *BBC News,* 25/6/2016
http://www.bbc.com/news/business-36630468]]

there consists of either those benefiting from globalization, who are concentrated in the capital that attracts the relevant lines of activity (finance, management and services in general), or of those immigrants or descendants of them, who may or may not belong to the beneficiaries of globalization but aspire to become ones or, alternatively, have been persuaded by the EU propaganda that a Brexit could somehow lead to their expulsion from UK. No wonder a second generation Pakistani yuppie and fanatic supporter of Bremain, who was elected Mayor of London a few months ago, was campaigning after Brexit for an 'independent' London within the EU! In fact, he is a reactionary Blairite, of the kind that dominates the Labor Party at present and see even Jeremy Corbyn, the globalist 'Left' leader of the party, as a kind of radical threat, fighting for his replacement by another Blairite!

On the other hand, the Brexit victory was overwhelming in the deprived areas of England, where the victims of globalization live, i.e. the victims of the criminal de-industrialization imposed by the multinational corporations, which they moved en masse to the Chinese and Indian labor 'paradises'. That is, to the places offering multinationals not only a very disciplined work force that is paid survival wages, but also all the tax concessions possible, in order to induce them to invest and create a pseudo kind of development. This was the kind of development that led to the emergence of a few hundred billionaires in those countries, while the mass of the population has suffered the effects of economic as well environmental strangulation. Therefore, the victory of Brexit in these deprived areas has nothing to do with the low concentration of immigrants in them and has everything to do with the 'structural factors' in these areas (high unemployment due to de-industrialization as a result of globalization, a decaying system of social services etc.).

This implies that the statistical correlations that some academics tried to establish between the high proportions of Brexit voters with areas characterized by low levels of immigration are simply spurious resulting in nonsensical (or better, utterly biased) conclusions. Obviously, it does not require a high level of sophistication, or some sort of high-powered statistical analysis, to substantiate these facts. Yet, two British academics with admitted connections to EU funding (although — as they stated in advance — not for this particular work!) attempted to do exactly this: to use high powered statistical analysis to draw conclusions consistent with the Bremain propaganda. That is, the black propaganda that those who voted Brexit did so mainly because of their anti-immigrant or racist feelings rather than because they were angry with the phasing out of their country's economic and national sovereignty within the EU and the fact that their economic position had significantly deteriorated since the opening and liberalization of markets for capital, commodities and labor imposed by Thatcherism first and then by the Maastricht Treaty and the other EU treaties that followed.

Thus, according to a supposedly 'objective' scientific research, those who voted for Brexit did so simply because they were ignorant anti-immigrant (the implicitly insinuation is that they were racists) who in fact live in areas where immigration is low and therefore were hardly in a position to judge whether immigration is good or bad! The two academics, starting with the clearly biased premise that "the EU referendum was, for many people, a referendum on immigration", made a major 'discovery' based on supposedly "hard evidence". Their premise was substantiated by such an 'objective' source as a survey conducted on behalf of Lord Ashcroft, the well-known businessman and politician who is the 74th richest person in the UK, as ranked by the *Sunday Times* Rich List 2015. And their 'discovery' was that "in most cases, high proportions of Leave voters were not concentrated in areas of high immigration. Apart from a few outliers, the districts with the highest vote for Leave were those with the lowest levels of immigration."[405]

Of course, you do not need any sort of statistical analysis but just common sense to realize that immigrants do not have any economic or other incentive to move to deprived areas populated mostly by the victims of globalization and, instead, they tend to concentrate in areas where the beneficiaries of globalization also live, such as London. Inevitably, some of the victims of globalization also live in such big urban areas and inner London areas are full of victims of globalization. But, at this point, the 'objective' analysis of the *Conversation* makes another heroic jump to 'justify' the biased premise it started with. Relying on the conclusions of the well-known systemic think-tank

---

[405] Chris Lawton and Robert Ackrill, "Hard Evidence: how areas with low immigration voted mainly for Brexit", Conversation, 8/7/2016
https://theconversation.com/hard-evidence-how-areas-with-low-immigration-voted-mainly-for-brexit-62138

Demos (presumably based on a similar kind of 'research') according to which "contact with migrants and members of ethnic minority communities 'takes the edge off negative perceptions', something reinforced by assimilation," [406] they drew, hey presto, the pre-conceived conclusion they wanted to 'prove':

> So, where migrants were not present, it appears they were held partly to blame for the all-too-real, but much deeper-seated, economic difficulties experienced by locals.

Clearly, this is just another distortion of the voting behavior of the victims of globalization. The "economic difficulties experienced by locals" that the research implies, mainly, refer to the squeezing of wages as a result of immigration. The obvious inference is that the absence of such a serious squeeze in a area should be taken to mean that, if Brexit was victorious in it, the locals should have been motivated by anti-immigration feelings. However, as I am going to show in the next section, the victims of globalization voted for Brexit not just because they suffered a squeezing in their wages during the globalization era but, even more important, because of the general deprivation in their areas, as a result of the closing down of entire industries following the move of the TNCs to the 'labor paradises' of the Far East. Furthermore, they voted for Brexit because of the decaying of the social welfare system, which of course has been directly due to the drastic cut in social spending in the globalization era that we examined in previous parts. Obviously, the mass influx of immigrants (see data below), on top of the cuts in social spending, had surely made the situation worse.

At this point, bad faith supporters of the globalist 'Left' resort to playing their last card: the supposed 'lack of evidence' (e.g. surveys etc.) showing why people voted the way they did. However, the victims of globalization usually do not have the necessary background to analyze the precise causes of their discontent and therefore surveys of this sort are bound to be lacking, given in particular the various forms that the effects of globalization take. In fact, even if such surveys did exist, they would have been mostly irrelevant or misinformed, as they could have easily been manipulated by those setting the questions to be asked, while the answers would crucially

---

[406] ibid.

depend on the willingness and/or ability of those asked to give meaningful/frank replies and so on.

Yet, for bad faith 'Left' globalists, the above study simply confirms their belief in the racist and anti-immigrant motives of those who voted for Brexit. Clearly, it has not dawned on them that, even if some of the victims of globalization share anti-immigrant feelings, this is directly related to globalization and how its victims internalize its effects and not to any sort of racism as these globalists viciously imply!

In other words, the real motives of those who voted for Brexit cannot, be found on the basis of empirical research, as they idiotically imply, but only on the basis of historical analysis. Thus, the fact that before globalization there were no serious anti-immigrant or Islamophobic trends in Europe is far from accidental. Common sense makes crystal clear that the effects of globalization I mentioned above, as well as those of the mass Islamophobic campaign — supposedly aimed against terrorism but, in fact, aimed to cover up the crimes of the Transnational and Zionist elites in the Middle East during the globalization era — are highly related to the present outburst of anti-immigrant and Islamophobic trends.

At the same time, even Blairite politicians with a 'progressive' profile, like Gordon Brown, Tony Blair's heir in the throne of the Labor Party, felt the need to make the following statement in the aftermath of the referendum, perceiving much more than the 'objective' academics and their acolytes in globalist 'Left', that the real causes of the Brexit vote had to be traced back to globalization and not to anti-immigration, which is only the symptom of it:

> The elephant in the room is globalization. And the most obvious manifestation of the world we have lost is the hollowing out of our industrial towns as a result of the collapse of manufacturing in the face of Asian competition. These towns are home to a disproportionate share of the semi-skilled workers who have, not surprisingly, become recruits to an anti-globalization movement whose lightning rod is migration.[407]

---

[407] Gordon Brown, "It's now clear, globalisation must work for all of Britain", *The Guardian*, 29/6/2016

Not surprisingly, the 'solution' proposed by Gordon Brown was another Commission of Inquiry, this time on migration, not omitting to express the Transnational Elite's line that "we have to decide that we cannot simply be an antiglobalization party that exploits grievances but offers no answers!"[408]

Finally, as far as the age distribution of the Brexit vote is concerned, the most significant exception to the voting pattern described above was among those under the age of 24, where the Remain vote was 75 percent in favor.[409] In fact, Bremain was supported by an apolitical youth — the perfect subject for manipulation by the elites and its media (including social media) — who are brainwashed by ideological and cultural globalization. Thus, it has been estimated that while there was a turnout of 82% among those aged 55 and over, barely a third of the 18-24 age group managed to cast their vote. But those youngsters who did bother to vote were fanatical opponents of Brexit, who as soon as the referendum result was announced, began demonstrating against it with the direct or indirect support of the local elites, as well as of the Transnational Elite (George Soros, the well-known 'master of ceremonies' of pink revolutions of every kind, played a leading role on this).[410] Yet, when these youngsters were asked to explain their fanatical support for the EU, they were usually at a loss to justify their stand! The following description in Dominic Lawson's *Sunday Times* column is characteristic:

> The journalist Melissa Kite described in the Catholic Herald being accosted by neighbors who, when they discovered she was voting 'leave', began to rant at her that she was on the side of the killer of the Labor MP Jo Cox. And one of them told Kite: "I don't understand any of the detail of the EU, but I know whose side I'm on.... A similar sort of rage has been directed at 'the old', for voting in such vast numbers to leave.

[408] ibid.
[409] Chris Marsden & Julie Hyland, ""Seismic Shock": UK Vote to Leave the EU Triggers Economic and Political Crisis, *Global Research*, 24/6/2016
http://www.globalresearch.ca/seismic-shock-uk-vote-to-leave-the-eu-triggers-economic-and-political-crisis/5532656?print=1
[410] G. Soros, "The promise of Regrexit", *Project Syndicate*, 8/7/2016
https://www.project-syndicate.org/commentary/the-promise-of-regrexit-by-george-soros-2016-07

Speaking of voters dragging themselves to the ballot box, a friend of mine saw an elderly woman moving inch by agonizing inch to the voting booth. If she had voted for "remain", it might easily have been described as 'heroic' in a BBC report, but if the old lady voted for "leave", it is categorized as 'selfish'.[411]

No wonder therefore that the EU elites fully support further lowering the age of qualifying for voting (Tsipras has already pioneered a new electoral law to this effect). This is hardly surprising given that SYRIZA — as well as Podemos in Spain — owe much of their electoral appeal to an a-political (or pseudo-political) youth, which essentially is supporting the status quo (including even the EU!) and demanding its reform. This, in contrast, to the really radicalized and mostly anti-systemic youth of the pre-globalization era, culminating in May 68, as well as the anti-globalization youth in Seattle and Genova, before it was suppressed by the pseudo 'Left' of the World Social Forum.[412]

The smearing of the Brexit revolution as a prelude to the counter-revolution

In the aftermath of the Brexit revolution a new smear campaign began by all those at the service of the NWO of neoliberal globalization aiming, directly or indirectly, to justify the parallel counter-revolution that was launched immediately after it. The obvious aim was to effectively reverse the results of the referendum.

Some talked about the return of nationalism and therefore of nationalist wars, which plagued Europe, particularly in the 20th century. Others talked about the victory of German 'imperialism', which allegedly attempts to reverse the results of its defeats in the last two world wars, while still others talked about the nostalgia for British imperialism among many of the voters for Brexit. Most, however, of the 'serious' commentators stressed either the supposed re-emergence of nationalism, or, alternatively, the assumed increase of anti-

---

[411] Dominic Lawson, "OK, you're angry. But ignore the vote and tanks could be on the streets", *Sunday Times*, 3/7/2016
[412] See "Globalization, the reformist Left and the Anti-Globalization 'Movement'", *Democracy & Nature*, vol.7, no.2 (July 2001)
http://www.democracynature.org/vol7/takis_globalisation.htm

immigration feelings and the related rise of Islamophobia and xenophobia in general.

In fact, as I will try to show briefly, these are all parts of a huge propaganda campaign orchestrated by the Transnational Elite and its media, NGOs etc. to divert attention from the real revolutionary nature of Brexit that I described above. That is, from the fact that Brexit is a victory of the victims of globalization against the NWO and as such it is a class victory, in the sense I defined 'class' above.

But, let us consider in more detail the two basic charges raised against supporters of Brexit and by implication against supporters of neo-nationalist movements, (including supporters of Trump in the USA) by the NWO and its media, as well as by the globalist 'Left'. That is, the charges of nationalism and racism used as an effective means of smearing these movements.

a. The nationalist smear

As regards, first, the relationship of Brexit to nationalism, those who talk about the revival of nationalism and possible national conflicts have no clue (or pretend they don't) that nationalism effectively ended with the phasing out of economic and national sovereignty for all those states that were integrated into the NWO, i.e. most of the world. Furthermore, as I showed elsewhere,[413] the nationalist movements of the 19th and 20th century have very little, if anything, to do with the neo-nationalist movements rising today, such as UKIP in Britain and FN (Le Pen's movement) in France. The former movements aimed to create nation-states, usually following a national liberation struggle, whereas the latter aim to restore the economic and national sovereignty lost in the globalization process. Therefore, by their nature, neo-nationalist movements are not aggressive movements against other peoples living beyond their borders but essentially defensive movements fighting for the fundamental right of any nation for self-determination, which is under severe attack by the elites controlling political-economic unions, such as the EU. That is, a union that is 'justified' under the pretext of creating a supranational super-state, which will protect the peoples'

---

[413] Takis Fotopoulos, "Globalization, Rise of Neo-Nationalism and the Bankruptcy of the Left", *Global Research*, 26/5/2016
http://www.globalresearch.ca/globalization-the-massive-rise-of-neo-nationalism-and-the-bankruptcy-of-the-left/5527157

rights better against globalization than any single nation-state could do acting alone.

However, this has already been proven to be a pure fantasy to deceive the European peoples, given that the EU, far from protecting working people's rights is, in fact, the main organ of the NWO in the European area, as its 'constitution' (i.e. the Maastricht Treaty, and the subsequent Treaties that established the basic '4 freedoms' of globalization), clearly showed. In other words, all significant legislation to impose the opening and 'liberalization' of all markets (labor, capital and commodities) has gone through the EU. Also, as I showed in the past, it was through the integration into the EU that the productive structure of countries like Greece had been destroyed and, as a result, the Greek people has been transformed — thanks to the criminal policies presently implemented by the pseudo-'Left' of Syriza — into a beggar of financial capital in order to secure its very survival.[414] A similar story could be told about countries such as Portugal and Spain, which have also lost their economic sovereignty, following their entry into the EU.

Last, but not least, neo-nationalist movements are not purely 'nationalist' movements, which ignore class issues and fight only for the 'nation', as used to be the case with the old nationalist movements. Thus, unlike old nationalists, neo-nationalists raise also demands that in the past were an essential part of the Left agenda, such as the demand for greater equality (within the nation-state and between nation-states) and the demand to minimize the power of the elites. In fact, neo-nationalist movements raise even anti-war demands, as when they side against the NWO's wars in the Middle East,[415] taking effectively sides in favor of informal patriotic movements such as the Russian one (which also fights against its own globalist 'Left' that is supported by Russian oligarchs, the media and so on). In other words, neo-nationalist movements become themselves, even by default, class movements, as when they fight, directly or indirectly, against globalization, which as we saw above is a class issue.

---

[414] See "The Real Causes of the Catastrophic Crisis in Greece and the "Left"", *Global Research,* 17/10/2015 http://www.globalresearch.ca/the-real-causes-of-the-catastrophic-crisis-in-greece-and-the-left/5365013
[415] See e.g. Anne-Sylvaine Chassany and Roula Khalaf, "Marine Le Pen lays out radical vision to govern France", *Financial Times* (5/3/2015).

So, on the one side, are the pro-globalization movements and parties appealing to all those benefiting from globalization (the elites, the upper middle class and part of the petty bourgeoisie which aspires to join them) and, on the other, are the anti-globalization movements and parties appealing to the victims of globalization. No wonder therefore that the old working class (or the remnants of it, following globalization) moved en masse towards these movements in countries such as Britain,[416] France and Austria, abandoning the old Left parties, which now survive mainly through the support they receive from that part of the middle class which benefits from globalization. In a nutshell, the 'Left' today mostly expresses those benefiting from globalization (or those believing the 'Left' mythology about the benefits of globalization in general and the EU in particular). At the same time, those pro-globalization Left parties (which I called the globalist 'Left') do not have any qualms about characterizing the popular strata which have moved to the neo-nationalist parties as nationalist, racist, anti-immigrant and so on.

Therefore, the present political bankruptcy of the Left everywhere is simply the inevitable consequence of the abandonment of its traditional role in supporting the victims of the social system rather than the elites, as it does at present. Even worse, those 'Left' parties such as SYRIZA, which still pretend that they fight for the victims of globalization, while in effect they implement without any objection the most criminal policies imposed by the Transnational Elite, are, in fact, con artists and as such are already seen by the majority of the Greek people. In fact, the argument used by political crooks of this kind (and their supporters in the globalist 'Left') that they had to submit, having to face a superior force, is another expression of their dishonesty. Obviously, if a honest Left political fighter sees that there is no chance to implement his/her program, s/he resigns, rather than staying in power under the pretext that the occupation under a Left government would be better than under a Right one — a well trodden argument used in the past by every collaborator with occupying forces!

Needless to add that the international 'Left' which supported and still supports SYRIZA (such as Chomsky, Zizek and the likes) are also seen in the same light. Unsurprisingly, the political bankruptcy of the Left follows its theoretical bankruptcy, given that, apart from a few

---

[416] Francis Elliott et al. 'Working class prefers Ukip to Labor", *The Times* (25/11/2014).

honorable exceptions, the Marxist Left never grasped the significance of globalization as a structural change in the capitalist system, following the emergence and mass expansion of multinational corporations, which have very little, if anything, to do with the monopolies and cartels of the classical theory of imperialism.

Naturally, given the origin of many neo-nationalist parties and their supporters, adherents of the old nationalist ideology have penetrated them, in the form of Islamophobic and anti-immigration trends within them, providing therefore the excuse for the elites to dismiss all these movements as 'far right'. However, such trends, which have always existed, are by no means the main reasons why such movements have expanded rapidly in the last few years.

On the other hand, today's autonomist movements, like those in Scotland, Northern Ireland and Catalonia, are purely nationalist movements of the old type, which are effectively controlled by the middle class nationalists who mostly benefit from globalization. Unsurprisingly they ignore class issues or pretend that the social problems affecting their regions are simply caused by the reactionary policies of British (or Spanish) governing conservative parties. They thereby conveniently 'forget' "that the corresponding 'progressive' parties (i.e. the old social democratic parties), when in government, have followed exactly the same policies.

No wonder that these autonomist parties have played a purely reactionary role with respect to the Brexit revolution, and instead of joining the struggle forged by the British victims of globalization, they raised the flag of 'Independence' from Britain in order to remain in the EU, fully siding with the Transnational Elite and the EU elites! At the same time in Wales, where the class issue in the above broader sense has always been dominant, as Welsh people had known at first hand the consequences of globalization (following the massive de-industrialization of their region within the globalization process) the popular strata fully supported Brexit, showing a level of maturity completely lacking by the other autonomist movements today. In other words, Welsh autonomists, by voting for Brexit, managed to merge successfully their own demand for national and cultural autonomy with the general demand for national self-determination and economic sovereignty. On the other hand, the Scots, Irish and Spanish autonomists, as well as — lately — the Kurdish autonomists (including the ex-anti-imperialist PKK, which now co-operates with

US 'imperialism' against ISIS)[417] function today, objectively, as the vassals of the Transnational Elite.

b. The anti-immigrant and racist smear

Finally, with regards to the smearing of the Brexit revolution as 'racist', the flagship of the globalist 'Left' and its principal 'radical' columnists set the line of attack based firmly on the ideology of globalization in general and the supposedly anti-immigration nature of the Brexit vote in particular. Thus, a *Guardian* editorial following the Brexit victory, declared:

> The country has embarked on a perilous journey... The immediate outlook for progressive and even humanitarian values in the UK is not encouraging. There is no denying that, even if only on the Faragiste fringes, xenophobia had its part to play in the leave campaign... Most, but not all, of the Conservatives' Brexit wing opposed, for example, gay marriage, the one solid progressive achievement on the home front.[418]

Then, never stepping out of line, Owen Jones and George Monbiot, its two main 'radical' columnists, predicted a doomsday scenario as a result of Brexit. Thus, Owen Jones first, saw in Brexit a disaster:

> The referendum fallout looks terrifying: economic chaos, a resurgence in racism, the break-up of the UK. We need to fight these multiple threats... Just thinking about the coming years is as exhausting as it is terrifying. From economic chaos to the legitimization of xenophobia and racism; from the coming dismantling of the UK to the stress placed on the Northern Ireland peace process; from the ascent of the Tory hard right to the coming attacks on everything from workers' rights to the NHS; from the inevitable anger that will follow the leave campaign's abandonment of their unachievable premises to the inevitable retribution from a European Union that fears for its existence and that suffers from the Brexit aftershocks. Any one

---

[417] See *Subjugate the Middle East* (vol. 3 of *the NWO in Action*)
[418] Editorial, "Britain after Brexit: our economy, our union and our place in the world are all at stake", *The Guardian*, 25/6/2016

of these in isolation would be difficult to deal with. They are all coming together, and they are coming fast.[419]

Next, it was the turn of its second 'radical' columnist, George Monbiot to describe his own version of doomsday that will follow Brexit:

> Yes, the Brexit vote has empowered the most gruesome collection of schemers, misfits, liars, extremists and puppets that British politics has produced in the modern era. It threatens to invoke a new age of demagoguery, a threat sharpened by the thought that if this can happen, so can Donald Trump. It has provoked a resurgence of racism and an economic crisis whose dimensions remain unknown. It jeopardizes the living world, the NHS, peace in Ireland and the rest of the European Union.[420]

Leaving aside the doomsday scenarios presented by these two 'radical' Left thinkers of the globalist 'Left', one has to remember that they are supposed to support the victims of the elites (in this case of neoliberal globalization) but it seems in this case they 'forgot' this mission and, instead, they supported the elites themselves, i.e. those running the NWO in general and the EU in particular, in their struggle against the victims of globalization!

Yet, the working class has voted overwhelmingly for Brexit and this was far from a big surprise. Thus, other *Guardian* columnists, just a week before the referendum, predicted this result. Nonetheless, the flagship of the globalist 'Left' did publish their conclusions, clearly for the sake of the image of "objectivity" that it tries to convey — an image that of course does not extend to any really heretical views challenging its line on the NWO and its institutions. John Harris, a liberal left columnist, drew the following conclusion following a local research in England and Wales, (after correctly excluding Scotland from his research, rightly perhaps perceiving that most of the Scottish people are a 'lost cause' to the anti-globalization struggle):

---

[419] Owen Jones, We cannot succumb to inevitable disaster. It's time to campaign to save our future, *The Guardian*, 28/6/2016

[420] George Monbiot, Brexit is a disaster, but we can build on the ruins, *The Guardian*, 29/6/2016

To quote the opinion pollsters Populus: "Both socioeconomic groups C2 and DE disproportionately back the UK leaving the EU." To be a little more dramatic about it, now that Scotland has been through its political reformation, England and Wales are in the midst of a working-class revolt... make no mistake: in an almost comical reflection of the sacred lefty belief that any worthwhile political movement will necessarily be built around the workers, the foundation of the Brexit coalition is what used to be called the proletariat, large swaths of which are as united as in any lefty fantasy, even if some of their loudest complaints are triggering no end of anxiety among bien-pensant types, and causing Labor a great deal of apprehension.[421]

Then, referring directly to the supposed racist nature of Brexit, he implicitly assumed (rightly) that the 'refugee problem' is in fact, part and parcel of globalization and of the '4 freedoms' that the globalization ideology preaches:

Yes, some people — from bigots in the stockbroker belt to raging gobshites in south Wales shopping precincts — are simply racist. But in a society and economy as precarious as ours, the arrival of large numbers of people prepared to do jobs with increasingly awful terms and conditions was always going to trigger loud resentment. For many places, the pace of change and the pressures on public services have arguably proved to be too much to cope with. Before anyone with a more right on view of all this explodes with ire, they might also consider the numbers. Between 1991 and 2003, on average about 60,000 migrants from the EU came to the UK each year. Between 2004 and 2012, that figure rose to 170,000. The 2011 census put the number of UK residents from Poland alone at 654,000.[422]

In fact, figures released in May this year by the Office for National Statistics showed 2.15 million EU migrants working in the UK — up 224,000 on a year earlier. A further 1.19 million people from non-EU countries are also working in UK, which means foreign

---

[421] John Harris. "We are in the midst of a working-class revolt, *The Guardian*, 17/6/2016
[422] ibid.

nationals account for 10.6% of the British workforce. As a result, many industries say they depend on migrant labor and that restricting freedom of movement will cause big problems.[423] In fact, even Gideon Rachman, who may be considered as the ideological father of Global Governance, had stressed that the benefits of globalization inevitably are unevenly distributed:

> Those at the top of the British social scale have generally done pretty well out of the globalization they occasionally decry: their salaries are higher, their houses are worth more, their horizons and those of their children are broadened by living in one of the most internationally connected countries in the world. The impact of globalization on the poorer parts of the country is much more ambiguous. It is the working-class whose wages are most likely to be held down by competition with immigrants, and whose areas are most likely to be transformed by mass migration.

This development, far from unexpected, represents in effect the essence of globalization. It is well known that because of demographic trends, several countries in Europe, particularly in the North, came out in favor of facilitating the influx of cheap labor from the European South to the North, as well as from Asia and Africa. This applies in particular to Germany, which has faced a rising demand for labor during the globalization era — especially since the emergence of the Eurozone, which is effectively controlled by this country. Furthermore, the criminal wars of the Transnational Elite in Yugoslavia, Iraq, Afghanistan, Libya and Syria, as well as the equally criminal economic violence against the Greek people, have also created a massive exodus from the corresponding countries in the South to the North and particularly to Germany.

But it was particularly in the last few years that the ideology of open borders was massively promoted by the media of the Transnational Elite, accompanied by a mass, supposedly humanist, campaign to save the refugees. That is, the mass of dislocated people who were of course created in the first place by the Transnational Elite itself, through its wars in the Middle East! Needless to add that 'open borders' — the policy promoted by Soros, the Transnational Elite,

---

[423] Sarah Butler, "Employers dependent on foreign workers seek reassurances from Whitehall", *The Observer*, 3/7/2016

Varoufakis and the likes — in fact exploits an old libertarian ideal, completely distorting its essence in the process, as I explained in a previous section. I will further add here that open borders is meaningful only in a democratic world order where the peoples of the world are really self-determined, controlling themselves the productive resources at their disposal, including human resources. That is, a world with no exploitation and no inequality, where it is peoples themselves that determine how best to meet the needs they decide to satisfy, through social control of some sort (e.g. through an economic democracy as I described it elsewhere)[424] rather than through the anarchy of the markets. Clearly, the world we live in today is exactly the opposite of this kind of ideal world and those fighting for open borders are in fact the elites and their associates aiming to maximize their profits through the free movement between countries not only of capital and commodities but of cheap labor as well. The inevitable effect is the equalization 'to the bottom' of the real value of wages and salaries (their 'cost of production') all over the world.

This is therefore the essence of the economic side of immigration and not the pseudo-humanist black propaganda about helping the masses of refugees and the victims of globalization. Particularly so, when both the former and the latter are simply the byproducts of political and economic globalization respectively. Clearly, it was the unprecedented economic violence of the NWO (initiated by the opening and liberalization of markets) and military violence (unleashed by the wars of the Transnational Elite in the globalization era) that created the billions of the victims of globalization and the millions of refugees respectively. In other words, the successful attempt by the Transnational Elite to convert an economic consequence of globalization, and the economic and military violence it implies, into a (supposedly) humanitarian refugee problem and an issue of satisfying the libertarian principle of 'open borders', is perhaps its greatest deception of humanity today and one of the great deceptions of all times. What is even worse is the general acceptability of this deception by almost every country in the world (including Russia, let alone China) which has been integrated into the NWO.

---

[424] See *Towards An Inclusive Democracy*, op.cit. ch. 6

In the light of these facts, the case of the academics I mentioned above[425] who attempted to defame the Brexit vote as a pure expression of anti-immigration (if not racist) feelings is a perfect example of the interconnection between the transnational economic and political elites with the transnational academic elites. That is, the prominent systemic academics in various transnational organizations (foundations, institutes, think tanks and the likes), which are in charge of creating/improving the ideology of the NWO and globalization, 'scientifically' justifying the need for globalization, as well as disorienting people on the real causes of the present multi-dimensional crisis (see ch 1). The fact, therefore, that most so-called 'experts' (mainly academic economists) are strongly against Brexit is far from surprising. Particularly so, if one takes into account not only their general class position, which classifies them beyond the victims of globalization, but also their vested specific interests in the EU I mentioned also in Ch.4 (e.g. the various EU programs financing their research and their trips all over the globe — well appreciated by them — to participate in conferences, seminars etc. funded by the EU).

However, immigration is not only an economic consequence of globalization. As I discussed in Part 1, there is another equally important side of globalization: the cultural globalization, i.e. the present homogenization of culture, as expressed for instance by the fact that almost everybody in today's 'global village' watches more or less the same TV serials and videos, consumes — or aspires to consume — the same products-, 'learns' the news from the same sources (TV channels and websites), all of them — apart from a few exceptions allowed to exist so that an image of 'fair play' is created — repeating the same view of the world and so on.

A national culture is of course in clear contradiction with the globalist culture, like the one imposed now 'from above' by the Transnational and local elites. Thus, a national culture includes all major aspects of culture created by a nation during its history (language, ideas, beliefs, customs, taboos, codes, institutions, tools, techniques, works of art, rituals, ceremonies and so on). A nation in this sense can be defined as a community of people which has been formed historically on the basis of a common culture (language etc.), but also of a common territory and economic life .

---

[425] Chris Lawton and Robert Ackrill, "Hard Evidence: how areas with low immigration voted mainly for Brexit", Conversation, 8/7/2016, op.cit.

Therefore, the globalist culture is effectively the negation of national culture, as it is based on the globalization ideology of multiculturalism etc., which in fact is the globalist version of classical liberal ideology. It is also well known that the criminal wars launched by the Transnational Elite during the globalization era aimed mainly to "protect" human rights (Yugoslavia, Iraq, Afghanistan, Libya and indirectly Syria).

In fact, however, cultural globalization is not only some sort of 'automatic' effect of globalization. It can be shown that it is also a deliberate policy of the Transnational Elite with the aim of creating the mass immigrant flow to the EU — something which euphemistically is called the 'refugee problem'. Thus, Peter Sutherland, the UN migration chief, has authoritatively expressed the Transnational Elite line on immigration and cultural homogeneity. In fact, Sutherland is a prominent member of the Transnational Elite himself, as he was the first director-general of the World Trade Organization — one of the main institutions of neoliberal globalization. He has also served for twenty years as Chairman of Goldman Sachs International and is a former chairman of oil giant BP. Given his high NWO 'qualifications' he naturally played a leading role in the campaign against Brexit. Yet, what is even more important is to examine his views with respect to 'the migration crisis' and the 'refugee problem', as revealed by the BBC itself, a leading organ of the Transnational Elite propaganda.

Thus, Sutherland, quizzed by the UK House of Lords committee four years ago on migration, inadvertently revealed who and why created the mass exodus of migrants into Europe in the last few years, as well as the motives behind the so-called 'refugee problem'. That is, he revealed that, in fact, it was the Transnational Elite which, in order to meet the needs of neoliberal globalization for cheap labor, used the ideology of globalization in terms of multiculturalism and open borders, effectively, in order to achieve its aims of both economic and cultural globalization. The means to achieve this major aim was through the undermining of cultural homogeneity of EU nations, i.e. of the national cultures of member-states!

This is how the BBC reported the crucial House of Lords committee meeting with Sutherland:

> An ageing or declining native population in countries like Germany or southern EU states was the "key argument and — I hesitate to the use the word because people have attacked it

— for the development of multicultural states", he added. "It's impossible to consider that the degree of homogeneity that is implied by the other argument can survive because states have to become more open states, in terms of the people who inhabit them. Just as the United Kingdom has demonstrated." At the most basic level, individuals should have a freedom of choice. The UN special representative on migration was also quizzed about what the EU should do about evidence from the Organization for Economic Cooperation and Development (OECD) that employment rates among migrants were higher in the US and Australia than EU countries. He told the committee: "The United States, or Australia and New Zealand, are migrant societies and therefore they accommodate more readily those from other backgrounds than we do ourselves, who still nurse a sense of our homogeneity and difference from others." And that's precisely what the European Union, in my view, should be doing its best to undermine" (My emphasis).[426]

So, for this frequent attendant of the meetings of the Bilderberg Group,[427] the EU, through its migration and refugee policies, should be doing its best to undermine cultural homogeneity at the national level, on the pretext of supporting the 'sacred' right of freedom of choice and the humanist 'European values' on refugees respectively. It is on the basis of this disorienting argument, expressing the liberal values of individual autonomy (in contrast to the libertarian and socialist values of collective or social autonomy), that the huge Transnational Elite propaganda to 'save the refugees' was built, which had multiple aims:

a) To assist economic globalization, by providing plenty of cheap labor to cover the growth needs of the European North and, at the same time, by equalizing to the bottom wages and salaries;

b) To promote effectively cultural globalization by undermining cultural homogeneity within each nation, as the precondition for creating an integrated political and economic EU, which will also be the first step in the process of global governance

---

[426] Brian Wheeler, "EU should 'undermine national homogeneity' says UN migration chief", *BBC News*, 21/6/2012 http://www.bbc.com/news/uk-politics-1851
[427] This the well known top level international networking organization, which has been often criticized for its alleged secrecy and clearly constitutes another informal institution of the Transnational Elite.

(the next step will be the effective merging of EU and NAFTA through TTIP);

c) To destroy any remnants of economic and national sovereignty within a borderless EU. It was in reaction to this trend and the consequent rise of neo-nationalist movements all over Europe that several European countries were forced in the last few months to close their borders, apart from those which have already lost any trace of sovereignty, such as Greece.

This was therefore another important reason why the decision of the British people for Brexit was a revolutionary one, as it was torpedoing this carefully planned long-term process for global governance. This was also the reason for the huge counter-revolution we shall consider next, which was set in motion by the Transnational Elite immediately after the referendum result was announced. The aim was to 'punish' in every way possible the British people who had the temerity to resist neoliberal globalization, so that nobody else would even think of trying to imitate them.

However, the NWO of neoliberal globalization has brought about not just a huge economic divide among the British population but also an equally huge cultural divide, as described above. As regards the economic divide, a recent Social Market Foundation (SMF) study has shown that the rich had become 64% richer than before the recession, while the poor became 57% poorer. [428] Also, as regards the cultural divide, Paul Mayson, a well-known ex-Trotskyite and presently EU acolyte broadcaster and globalist 'Left' admirer of Varoufakis and the likes, gave a good description of this divide and of the a-political youth which voted overwhelmingly against Brexit:

> The other half (who voted for Remain) is symbolized by the bearded hipster — his trips to Berlin for art, Ibiza for dancing, now in question, and the assumed cultural dominance of his social liberalism and anti-racism under threat. [429]

The raging counter-revolution against Brexit

Immediately after the Brexit result, Craig Roberts rightly described what was to follow in the aftermath of the dismal failure of the elites to terrorize the victims of globalization:

---

[428] Nigel Morris, "Britain's divided decade: the rich are 64% richer than before the recession, while the poor are 57% poorer", *The Independent*, 10/3/2015
[429] Paul Mason, "UK: lost, divided and alone", *Le Monde Diplomatique*, July, 2016

The propagandists who comprise the Western political and media establishments succeeded in keeping the real issues out of public discussion and presenting the leave vote as racism. However, enough of the British people resisted the brainwashing and controlled debate to grasp the real issues: sovereignty, accountable government, financial independence, freedom from involvement in Washington's wars and conflict with Russia. The British people should not be so naive as to think that their vote settles the matter. The fight has only begun.[430]

He then went on to describe how the Fed, ECB, BOJ, and NY hedge funds would 'pound the pound' and short British stocks in order to convince the British voters that their vote is sinking the economy. Also, how they would try to 'soften' the leaders of the Brexit campaign. In fact, it seems they already succeeded, through various ways, in getting rid of all of them including Boris Johnson and Nigel Farage!

In effect, the counter-revolution, despite the obvious shock of the elites for a result they did not expect, began immediately after the announcement of the referendum result and it took not only a media form but also a political and an economic form.

1. The political dimension of counter-revolution

At the political level, PM Cameron, instead of announcing his immediate resignation from both the leadership of his clearly divided party and the government — as any defeated leader of a similar campaign would have done, setting in motion a process whereby the new popular mandate for Brexit will be implemented — he adopted delaying tactics. His obvious aim was to create the conditions for the effective reversal of the popular will. Thus, first, he announced that his resignation would take effect in September, following a new party leadership election and, second, that he will set in motion the EU procedure for Brexit at the same time.

Yet, it seems the Transnational and local elites had different plans and could not forgive his serious mistake to put such a crucial issue, as Britain's position in the EU, at the mercy of the plebs. Particularly so

---

[430] Dr. Paul Graig-Roberts, "Despite the Brexit Vote, the Odds Are Against Britain Leaving the EU, *Global Research*, 25/6/2016 http://www.globalresearch.ca/despite-the-vote-the-odds-are-against-britain-leaving-the-eu/5532728

as the EU elites have never won in the past any referendum on the first attempt (even on the constitution itself) and had to force the electorates to vote again and again — under constant pressure from the elites — until they got the desired result! So, the elites effectively cancelled the new party leadership election by forcing out of the race both Boris Johnson and the pro-Brexit candidate Andrea Leadsom. This is how the honest liberal journalist Neil Clark graphically described the process:

> In the Conservative Party leadership election, we've witnessed a master-class in how the Establishment engineers the result it desires. Theresa May was obviously the anointed one, but in order for her to be crowned a few things had to happen first. The maverick Boris Johnson, who was decidedly dodgy on foreign policy had to be knocked out of the race. And then, after she had beaten Murdoch's favourite, Michael Gove, onto the final short-list it was time for the Establishment's attack-dogs to be unleashed on Mrs. Andrea Leadsom... It was no surprise that after a tearful weekend Leadsom pulled out of the Tory leadership race. With Leadsom successfully tripped up, the Tory party's 150,000 members (were) deprived of having their democratic say in their party's leadership election.[431]

Following the coronation of the pro-Remain Theresa May as PM, the road was open for the effective reversal of the referendum result, as planned by Cameron before he was thrown out, so that the aim of the counter-revolution could be achieved. For Neil Clark this aim is "to make sure there is no major deviation from elite-friendly, neo-liberal, crony capitalist pro-war policies,"[432] or, as I would put it, to make sure that people realize that any country's exit from the New World Order of neoliberal globalization, even if it constitutes a prominent member of the Transnational Elite, is punishable, so that other peoples do not even think of repeating the same mistake.

Theresa May, immediately after her coronation, announced that she would adopt the very time-consuming procedure of her predecessor for Brexit, i.e. the one envisaged by article 50 of the EU Lisbon Treaty. Of course, instead she could have pursued a unilateral

---

[431] Neil Clark:"British politics: The Establishment versus Democracy", RT, 13/7/2016 https://www.rt.com/op-edge/350895-british-politics-establishment-elite/
[432] ibid.

withdrawal of the UK from the EU, through a Parliament Act, as the British Parliament had the power to do. However, given that the majority in Parliament consists of ardent supporters of the EU, such an Act would have easily been blocked. This procedure therefore, although it might have ended up with an easy victory for the elites, could have turned into a Pyrrhic victory, as the elite contempt for the popular will would have been made all too clear for everybody to see. In other words, the risk was that, at the end of this process, the sort of 'democracy' prevailing in Britain, the 'mother of parliamentary democracy' would have been revealed. This is also the reason why the alternative road suggested by many in the elites, i.e. to have the result of the referendum annulled, was not pursued.

Therefore, the path chosen by the elites to achieve the main aim of the counter-revolution — i.e. to keep Britain fully integrated within the NWO even if outside the EU — was to follow the Byzantine exit process envisaged by the EU Treaty, which has been designed with the clear aim to make the exit of any member state almost impossible and anyway, absolutely controlled by the Euro-elite. This process could take up to two years of negotiations, (unless the two parties (EU and UK) took a joint decision to prolong them further), i.e. a process long enough to soften people up for eventual surrender of their most radical demands, i.e. those that were incompatible with the position of Britain as a fully integrated member of the NWO. In fact, it seems at the time of writing that the UK government will not set in motion article 50 of the Treaty before March 2017, possibly delaying actual Brexit further, well into 2019![433]

Clearly, given the crucial nature of the decision, not only strong political forces could be set in motion within such a long period of time to effectively reverse the popular will, but, even more so, world economic forces with an obvious interest to achieve a similar aim would also be able to do the same. Particularly so as the entire Transnational Elite, i.e. the transnational political, economic, media and cultural elites, had already taken a strong line to avert a meaningful British exit at all cost.

The outcome therefore of the negotiations with the EU is predetermined: a new Treaty with the EU, which for all intents and

---

[433] Aimee Donnellan & James Lyons, "Brexit 'will be delayed until end of 2019', *The Sunday Times,* 14/8/2016

purposes will secure the continuation of Britain's full integration of into the NWO, the difference being that the country will, formally, not be an EU member anymore, although it could still remain a member of the European Economic Area (EEA). So, one way or another, UK will still have to implement fully the '4 freedoms' of the Maastricht Treaty (open and liberalized markets for capital, labor, goods and services), which it will have to implement anyway as a member of the World Trade Organization. Perhaps, as a 'concession' to the popular will, some modifications concerning the number of refugees allowed into Britain and also the number of new immigrants from the EU may also be allowed.. What would seem to be the object of hard negotiations is the degree of British access to the single EU market and vice versa as regards the degree of immigration control. It seems the EU elites want to 'punish' Britain for Brexit, as a lesson to any other EU elite thinking to hold a similar referendum and may not allow any access to the single market unless the British elite is prepared to water down significantly any immigration controls, particularly against EU citizens — something which is of course against the spirit of the result of the referendum.

Thus, more than three months after Brexit, it seems that Britain is being forced to a 'hard' Brexit, (widely interpreted as meaning leaving the single market and moving to WTO deals), which some analysts estimated that it could cause a "black hole" in tax revenue of £10bn in lost taxes.[434] In other words, the Euro elites blackmail the British elites either to completely water down Brexit, in which case they would face the anger of the British people, or, alternatively, to proceed to a hard Brexit that may have dire economic (and electoral) consequences. Some even threaten Britain to have Greece's fate![435]

Clearly, any significant postponement of Brexit works in favor of the forces working for the effective 'neutralization' of the referendum result, given that a formal annulment of it is politically prohibitive, at least in the short run. Obviously, the longer the process takes, the longer the Transnational Elite can inflict punishment on the victims of globalization in Britain, who not only dared to express their discontent with their lot in life but also to question the very fabric of British

---

[434] Sam Coates & Oliver Wright, "Hard Brexit could cost £10bn in lost taxes", *The Times*, 27/9/2016
[435] Bruno Waterfield, "'Brussels will gang up on UK like it did to Greece'", *The Times*, 5/10/2016

society: neoliberal globalization itself! What therefore the elites obviously have in mind is that, by the end of negotiations, the people will be so beaten down by economic punishment and propaganda that it will be easy to force them to accept essentially the same social fabric as before but in a different 'package deal'. This could perhaps better be achieved through a new general election at the end of the long negotiating process.

Yet, for this aim to be achieved, the necessary condition is the existence of strong parties, such as those introduced all over the West in the post-war period, following the bipartisan US system that was highly successful over time in deceiving the masses that they enjoy full democracy. However, the rise of neo-nationalist parties all over Europe has effectively broken this system, since such parties are presently kept out of power in most countries only thanks to electoral systems, which, in a scandalous way, discriminate in favor of the two leading parties. But the electoral decay of mainstream pro-EU parties, both in the conservative space but also in the liberal and socialdemocratic ones is such, so that the only way to restore the authority of the economic elites and the associated political elites is by facilitating the creation of an institutionalized multi-party governing system (i.e. coalition governments) like the one in Israel. Proportional representation is the way to facilitate this radical political change and the Syriza government, which has converted Greece into a full protectorate of the Transnational Elite (as well as of the Zionist Israeli elite), is already taking constitutional steps in this direction. Here is how an FT columnist described how Britain could imitate Greece:

Of course, it is possible that an election would not solve anything. The fragmentation of politics leaves the two big parties struggling to win a majority in the best of times. These are the worst. Pre-election paralysis might be followed by post-election, well, paralysis. This would be the moment for otherwise cautious politicians to think radically. The referendum disenfranchised the centrist, internationalist majority in parliament. To borrow a phrase from the leavers, these moderates should be planning to take back control. Many centrist Tories have more in common with their counterparts on the Labor side than with English nationalist Brexiters; and, likewise, middle-of-the-road Labourites are closer to pro-European Tories than to Mr. Corbyn's brand of 1970s state socialism. Political realignments do not happen often in British politics, mostly because the first-past-the-post electoral system has been merciless towards third parties. But the space may be opening up for a new, pro-European, economically liberal and socially compassionate alternative to pinched nationalism and hard-left socialism. The wait, of course, would be infuriating for Britain's erstwhile partners. But at least they have had the experience of dealing with Greece.[436]

In other words, the adoption of such an electoral system would make much easier the coalitions of pro-EU (or pro-NWO) governments, consisting of the pro-EU parts of the two main parties (e.g. of the Tory and Labor parties in Britain) to crush the rise of neo-nationalist parties, which, although they will be able to secure a bigger representation in Parliament (for the sake of 'democracy'!) they will be permanently ostracized from power through these coalitions. A similar option might be adopted by the French elites to keep Le Pen's FN permanently out of power, following the forthcoming Presidential elections of 2017, which the elites may still win within the existing system — for the very last time!

2. The economic dimension of the counter-revolution

As far as the economic dimension of the counter-revolution is concerned, George Soros, the well-known member of the Transnational Elite, immediately after the result became known declared in his *Project Syndicate* website: "Britain eventually may or may not be relatively better off than other countries by leaving the EU, but its economy and people stand to suffer significantly in the short-to medium term."[437] Then, he came back even bolder to make the following statement, revealing in the process his leading role in the counter-revolution against Brexit, (as well as on Ukraine):

> The post-referendum turmoil has highlighted for people in Britain just what they stand to lose by leaving the EU. If this sentiment spreads to the rest of Europe, what seemed like the inevitable disintegration of the EU could be instead creating positive momentum for a stronger and better Europe. The

---

[436] Phillip Stevens, "Britain is starting to imitate Greece", *Financial Times*, 30/6/2016
[437] "Soros warns of EU disintegration", *BBC News*, 25/6/2016
http://www.bbc.com/news/business-36630468

process could start in Britain. The popular vote can't be reversed but a signature collecting campaign could transform the political landscape by revealing a newfound enthusiasm for EU membership. This approach could then be replicated in the rest of the European Union, creating a movement to save the EU by profoundly restructuring it. I am convinced that as the consequences of Brexit unfold in the months ahead, more and more people will be eager to join this movement...the EU must strengthen its defences to protect itself from its external enemies, who are liable to take advantage of its current weakness. The EU's greatest asset is Ukraine, whose citizens are willing to die in defence of their country. By defending themselves, they are also defending the EU – rare in Europe nowadays.[438]

Then, it was the turn of multinationals themselves warning of risks to jobs and profitability as a result of Brexit. Major US banks said they might move staff abroad while some of the world's largest companies warned they could relocate their British-based operations following the referendum result. Thus, Investment bank JP Morgan, plane maker Airbus and car manufacturers Toyota and Ford all said they will review their investments in the UK after the country voted to leave the European Union.[439]

The 'big guns' followed, such as the 'socialist' French President Hollande, who excelled in braking old-established working rights in France in order to make labor more 'flexible' (i.e. more competitive and profitable for multinationals), leading to a long struggle with street fighting this Spring and early summer. Speaking at the end of a Brussels summit, Hollande warned that it would be unacceptable for clearing — a crucial stage in trading of derivatives and equities — to take place in the UK:

> The City, which thanks to the EU was able to handle clearing operations for the Eurozone, will not be able to do them," he

[438] G. Soros, "The promise of Regrexit", *Project Syndicate,* 8/7/2016
https://www.project-syndicate.org/commentary/the-promise-of-regrexit-by-george-soros-2016-07
[439] Graham Ruddick, "Multinationals warn of risk to jobs and falling profits", *The Guardian,* 25/6/2016

said. "It can serve as an example for those who seek the end of Europe... it can serve as a lesson."[440]

Yet, this was an old point of dispute between EU's main financial centers. The City's right to clear in Euros is a long cherished goal of the European Central Bank in Frankfurt, which was previously thwarted by the UK in the EU courts. The ECB had argued that it was unfair for it to be expected to provide emergency support to clearing houses that operated outside its jurisdiction, while the UK had argued that a 'location policy' would discriminate against Britain and challenge its role in the single market. George Osborne, UK chancellor, described the UK's court victory in 2015 as a "major win for Britain."[441]

The counter revolution signified what Graham VanBergen aptly put it, when he stressed that "what you are witnessing is anarchy by the rich and powerful and now the gloves are off. Get ready to be bludgeoned like never before until you are on your knees begging for their neoliberal mercy." This was particularly so if one takes into account, as he went on to point out, that "Britain's rich are 64% richer than before the recession, while the poor are 57% poorer – all that in just 8 years. Overall, about 20 per cent of the population is doing much better and 80 per cent are doing much worse. This was the real reason for 'Brexit'."[442]

However, the initial effect of this counter-revolution on the British economy has been much smaller than expected by the prophets of gloom. Even a survey by the BBC (which excelled in its bias against Brexit!), completed almost a week after Brexit, concluded that, the actual effect was far from the catastrophe predicted by various 'experts' — mainly economists and institutions supported by the elites and particularly the EU elites.[443]

Of course, the highly expected downgrading of the UK's credit rating has already materialized by such 'objective' institutions as the

---

[440] Jim Brunsden and Anne-Sylvaine Chassany, "Hollande heightens City Brexit fallout fears", *Financial Times*, 29/6/2016
[441] ibid.
[442] Graham VanBergen, "Brexit – Why Things will get Worse and What's coming Next", *Global Research*, 26/6/2016 http://www.globalresearch.ca/brexit-why-things-will-get-worse-and-whats-coming-next/5532899
[443] BBC News, "What has Brexit done to the economy?" 29/6/2016 http://www.bbc.com/news/uk-politics-eu-referendum-36661918

rating agencies Fitch and S&P, which express the Transnational Elite's assessment about the safety of lending the UK government. This implied that lending money to the British government is less safe now and therefore less attractive. In fact, however, exactly the opposite has happened as the yield, or return, on government bonds (which is a good indicator of the interest rate the government would have to pay to borrow money) has fallen, indicating that UK government bonds are more attractive now than before!

As regards stock markets, although there were big falls in stock markets immediately after the referendum, the stock index hovered near a one-year high in the summer.[444] Lately, the shares index has reached almost record levels and in fact the surge in share prices since the Brexit vote was dubbed "the most hated bull market of modern times."[445]

Similarly, the bogey of recession following a Brexit and a decline in exports was also part of the same black propaganda of the elites. Particularly so as the European elites are as keen not to lose a big market like the British one, as the British elites are keen not to lose an even bigger European market. Thus, the first indications of the economic effects of Brexit were far from catastrophic, as even the flagship of the globalized 'Left' agreed.[446]

In fact, the post-Brexit news at the time of writing are the opposite than those expected by the prophets of gloom, as described by Katherine Griffiths, the Banking Editor of the London *Times*:

> Another blow for Project Fear. A dramatic rebound in the manufacturing sector has boosted the prospects of the UK economy continuing to grow, despite widespread fears that Britain could slip back into recession.[447]

This development was further confirmed a few days later by another report according to which "the UK construction sector recovered from the seven-year low it hit in the wake of Britain's vote

---

[444] Sudip Kar-Gupta, "FTSE 100 rises, hovers near one-year high", Reuters, 8/7/2016 http://uk.reuters.com/article/uk-britain-stocks-idUKKCN0ZO0M3
[445] Patrick Hosking, "FTSE soars near record high as the pound slides", *The Times*, 5/10/2016
[446] Larry Elliott, "Benign beginning for Brexit", *The Guardian*, 21/7/2016
[447] Katherine Griffiths, "Manufacturers ride the weak pound", *The Times*, Business News, 1/9/2016

to leave the European Union" and concluding that "economists said the improvement within the construction industry will again fuel hopes that the short-term repercussions of the referendum result could "prove less severe than feared.""[448] In fact, the latest news is that there was "an unexpected upbeat news from the construction sector" at the beginning of October, which helped to push the shares index even higher.[449]No wonder the very latest news (good news again!) came from UK's Office for National Statistics, according to which "Britain's economy has held up well since the Brexit vote in spite of warnings that it would collapse".[450] Even the full pro-NWO Organisation for Economic Co-operation and Development (OECD), which, as we saw above, before the referendum adopted an almost cataclysmic view of the effects of Brexit, has also announced that it was upping its forecast for growth![451]

In fact, it seems, that the post-Brexit statistical data are so good up to now that they made even the deputy governor of the Back of England (and sworn enemy of Brexit, like the Governor) to start worrying about the effectiveness of the counter revolution. No wonder that he was forced to warn not to rely on short run statistical data, as "the Brexit effect is coming!"[452] Yet, the very latest news before going to the printers also give a very different economic picture than the doomsday predicted by the prophets of doom. Thus, data from the Office for National Statistics for the third quarter, the first full quarter since the referendum in June, showed that the Treasury was wrong to suggest that the economy would collapse into recession after a vote to leave. Instead, Britain's economy has defied expectations of an immediate post-Brexit crash by growing 0.5 per cent in the three months to September, a stronger rate than the start of the year.[453] Not surprisingly, even the BBC had to admit that "Brexit supporters will

---

[448] Callum Jones, "Construction industry shrinks less than expected", Business News, *The Times*, 2/9/2016

[449] Patrick Hosking, "FTSE soars near record high as the pound slides", *The Times*, 5/10/2016

[450] Patrick Hosking, "Strong economy confounds predictions of Brexit doom", *The Times*, 22/9/2016

[451] ibid.

[452] Phillip Aldrick, "We can't rely on data — the Brexit effect is coming, says Bank deputy", *The Times*, 5/10/2016

[453] Philip Aldrick, "Economy defies Brexit slowdown fears", *The Times*, 27/0/2016

take these figures as a sign that warnings about the economic costs of voting to leave the EU were nothing more than scaremongering."[454]

Therefore, the biggest perhaps negative impact so far on the economy is the fall in the value of the pound, which has dropped considerably both against the US dollar and the Euro. This was of course highly expected, as currency speculation is the specialty of such world benefactors as George Soros, who will do everything in their power to make Brexit fail and particularly to frighten the middle class to press even more against Brexit, after seeing that their highly valued holidays in the Mediterranean and the US have suddenly become much more expensive than before. Even more important is the expectation that the victims of globalization will also pay a high price later on, when the price of imported commodities will start rising significantly, as a result of the pound depreciation. Thus, the pressures of the transnational economic elites on the British pound have already sank it to its dismal 1980s levels and as financial analysts stressed:

> Renewed weakness for the currency follows Prime Minister Theresa May's speech to the Conservative party conference on Sunday, which investors seized on as pointing to a so-called "hard Brexit" that prioritizes Britain's control of immigration over full access to Europe's single market.[455]

As exchange strategists at Commerzbank made clear, "until an amicable agreement can be reached in this matter, sterling will therefore remain under pressure."[456] Needless to add that all this is a pseudo dilemma caused by the fact that the British elites have no intention to take the next radical step following Brexit, i.e. to break completely with the NWO and its institutions, as we shall see at the end of this chapter.

Yet, despite the mild effects of this attack by the elites so far, the counter revolution is still raging at the moment with the Governor of the Bank of England unnecessarily lowering the interest rates to record levels in the Bank's 322-year history. This move is bound to hit hard, mainly, small savers and pensioners, who, as we saw voted

---

[454] "UK economy grows 0.5% in three months after Brexit vote", *BBC News*, 27/10/201, http://www.bbc.co.uk/news/business-37786467
[455] Michael Hunter and Joel Lewin, "Pound sinks to post-Brexit vote low as FTSE 100 nears record", *Financial Times*, 4/102016
[456] Ibid.

overwhelmingly for Brexit. They will be affected on two fronts, first as a result of the interest fall, which will influence negatively their pensions and savings and, second, as a result of the rising inflation, following the fall in the value of the pound — something that will further squeeze their purchasing power. However, even orthodox economists stressed that the dramatic fall in interest rates was completely unnecessary and will have the opposite effect of the supposedly desired boost of the economy. As Oliver Kamm, *The Times* economics editor pointed out:

> Paradoxically, a measure to ease credit conditions further might actually cause a decline in lending... The bigger risk now is of a totally unnecessary recession brought on by the demand shock of a vote for Brexit. Looser fiscal policy is a prudent way of trying to contain the damage.[457]

No wonder the former Goldman Sacks employee and presently Bank of England Governor was summoned by the Treasury Select Committee to explain his precipitous action, as his 'impartiality' was seriously questioned by British MPs. [458] Naturally, the neoliberal executives of the Transnational and local Elites do not want to hear anything about fiscal policies and their Keynesian connotations, which could imply more social spending on the decaying British welfare state — something that is obviously anathema to the elites administering the NWO.

So, the aims of the counter-revolution are now becoming clear: the punishment of the victims of globalization is supposed to involve further squeezing of their income through a combination of the above induced measures (pushing the pound and interest rates down) and a parallel stagflation of the economy. That is, a decline in real income and employment accompanied with inflation. The clear plan of the elites is to continue this 'medicine' to the 'English patient' until he softens up and, through a new general election, is -prepared to accept not only more concessions regarding in particular the movement of labor but also the kind of agreements, such as TTIP and TPP, that the Transnational Elite tries hard to push at the moment.

---

[457] Oliver Kamm, "Cutting rates would do more harm than good", *The Times,* 4/8/2016
[458] Phillip Aldrick, "Carney faces Brexit showdown with MPs", *The Times*, 7/9/2016

The options for the victims of globalization following the Brexit vote

However, irrespective of the elites' actions following the Brexit referendum, the crucial issue for the victims of globalization concerns the major options available to them. To my mind, there are two major options between which they have to choose. The first option involves the adoption of some version of the present model, while the second option involves a complete break not only with the EU but also with the NWO of neoliberal globalization itself.

a. Adopting a variation of the present model

Clearly, in case Brexit is followed by the introduction of a variation of the present model, as is more likely at the moment, this would imply the continuation of the present dependence on TNCs, which of course aim to determine economic growth and the economic process in general according to their own objectives of profit maximization. However, a simple variation of the present model is highly unlikely to involve any significantly different economic effects compared to the present situation. Particularly so if a Brexit is accompanied by a new agreement with the EU as regards to trade (which anyway even after Brexit will still be ruled by the WTO regulations) and the re-confirmation of the other treaties on the movement of capital and labor, which most likely will remain unchanged — apart perhaps from the present British obligations as regards the movement of labor.

However, quite apart from the possible economic effects of adopting a variation of the present model following Brexit, one has to consider also the political implications involved and particularly the propaganda about peace, supposedly secured by the EU, as this argument has been frequently used in favor of adopting a variation of the present model. Thus, Gideon Rachman, the well-known Zionist chief foreign affairs commentator of the *Financial Times*, aptly put, before the referendum, the following political case against Brexit:

> But, perhaps paradoxically, the fact Europe is in crisis actually strengthens my own resolve to vote for Britain to stay inside the EU. For all its faults, the EU champions ideas that are crucial to peace and freedom in Europe. These include co-operation between nations, the rule of law, the protection of human rights and the promotion of free trade. Nationalist political forces that challenge all of these ideas are growing in

strength across Europe, from France to Poland, and they are united by their hostility to the supranational EU. Outside the EU, a hostile and freshly aggressive Russia is cheering on the possible collapse of the European project — and is probably funding some of its most ardent internal opponents. Given Europe's bloody past and troubled present, helping to destroy the major vehicle for European co-operation cannot be a good idea. It is true that the crisis within the EU may soon require a fundamental rethink of the organization's aims and methods, well beyond the minor changes that Mr. Cameron is able to negotiate... It would be a serious mistake for the UK to undermine an organization that, whether we realize it or not, is crucial to Britain's own security. [459]

I reproduced at length this view as, to my mind, it is in fact a monument of misinformation and distortion of truth, endemic among the practitioners of the Project Fear. Of course, the EU is as much a champion of peace and freedom as the US and the other members of the Transnational Elite are also champions of world peace. That is, as much as the very countries, which instigated or carried out all the bloody wars of the last quarter of a century or so, not just on Iraq, Afghanistan, Libya and Syria but even in Europe itself (Yugoslavia).[460].

In fact, however, the only reason that wars among major capitalist countries are inconceivable today is the high degree of economic interdependence between the TNCs based in these countries. It is this reason alone that precludes any wars between members of the Transnational Elite and not the economic unions such as EU and NAFTA etc., which have simply been created to complete the opening and liberalization of markets that globalization requires — in the process leading to global governance, as envisaged by Rachman himself.

Yet, Caroline Lucas, the single Green Party MP and present co-leader of it, had no qualms in a pre-Brexit lecture at the London School of Economics to use the 'peace argument' against Brexit,

[459] Gideon Rachman, "Brexit is no way out of a Europe in crisis", *Financial Times*, 1/2/2016
[460] Takis Fotopoulos, "New World Order and NATO's war against Yugoslavia", *New Political Science*, vol. 24, no.1, (March 2002), pp. 73-104

warning that EU membership is Britain's best defense against the risk of Europe descending into war, repeating essentially Gideon Rachman's argument:

> Europe is not, historically, a very peaceful place. It would be sheer folly to think that armed conflict cannot return. We cannot know what dangers lie ahead. But we can be sure that a strong and stable European Union, with Britain as an active and positive participant, provides the surest guarantee of our national security. [461]

However, the values mentioned by Rachman and repeated by Lucas (co-operation between nations etc.) refer only to the Transnational Elite and its associate states and not to any states questioning its hegemony in any way, such as Russia, China as well as the Arab states based on national liberation movements (e.g. Ba'athist regimes in Iraq and Syria). Peace and co-operation between the Transnational Elite and all these states is impossible unless they submit to the Transnational Elite's authority. These are not of course inter-imperialist conflicts — as globalist 'Marxists' describe them, confusing and disorienting the victims of globalization — but simply conflicts between those controlling the NWO and those refusing to be controlled by the Transnational Elite. This applies also to the case when a state (e.g. Russia, or better, the globalist part of the elite within it), aspires to join the Transnational Elite as an equal member, not realizing that the only position offered to them in the NWO is one of a subordinate member. Finally, it is hardly surprising that Rachman (as well as Lucas) adopted the misleading and completely disorienting ideology of the globalist 'Left' (Varoufakis and his mentor Soros, Piketty and the rest) that the way out of the present crisis is not a break with the globalization institutions like EU but, instead, an attempt to 'democratize' it 'from inside'!

b. Breaking with the NWO of neoliberal globalization

But let us now move to the second radical option following Brexit which involves a complete break with the NWO. To my mind, the maximization of the positive effects of Brexit for the vast majority of

---

[461] Cf. Bruno Waterfield, "Boost for Brexit campaign as Dutch voters reject EU deal"

the population, who are the victims of globalization, are intrinsically linked to a complete break with the NWO of neoliberal globalization, which would lead to real economic, as well as national sovereignty. Only this way the peoples themselves, instead of the economic and political elites, as at present, will be able to take the fundamental economic decisions concerning what, how and for whom to produce.

But, under the present conditions, i.e. the formidable campaign of the elites against Brexit and the despicable stand of the globalist 'Left', in Britain and beyond, only the full mobilization of a social movement fully conscious of its aims and the strategies needed to achieve them would be able to succeed. This is also another reason for them to press for a real Brexit, involving a self-reliant economy, which is a precondition for economic and national sovereignty. However, given that neither the governing Tory Party, nor of course the Labor Party would ever move in such direction, a Front for National and Social Liberation, which would function as a catalyst for fundamental political and economic change, is the only kind of change that could get the victims of globalization out of the current mire, while also creating the basis for a new true internationalism based on the self-determination of each nation.

The social subject in this movement would be the victims of neoliberal globalization and of the consequent de-industrialization. Such a full mobilization of the victims of globalization never took place in the past, even on the occasion of the Scottish independence referendum, as we have seen in Ch.4. Instead, there was a full mobilization of those who benefit from globalization and the Transnational Elite's aggressive policies. This is why the independence movement was defeated, as the victims of globalization were not fully mobilized — and could never be — by a movement, which was overtly a nationalist one of the old type and had no relation to the present neo-nationalist movements against globalization. No wonder that, not only the Scottish nationalists, but also the Irish nationalists (Sinn Fein) were against Brexit, playing exactly the game of the establishment (i.e. the English elites as part of the Transnational Elite) on this crucial referendum. In other words, unless the victims of globalization in Scotland, Ireland and Catalonia realize that no real political independence (i.e. political sovereignty) will ever materialize without economic independence and sovereignty, they will continue to be the victims of globalization, either under the British flag, or under their own national flags within the EU.

At the same time in England, not only a very significant part of the working class but also part of the middle class as well, which is also squeezed at present as a result of globalization, have realized that, without economic self-reliance and national sovereignty, self-determination is impossible in the era of neoliberal globalization. It was because of this real danger that the elites and those benefiting from globalization had mobilized all their supporters in the country (the Labor Party, most of the Conservative Party, the Liberals, the Greens, the Scots and the Welsh nationalist parties) to avert any possibility of British exit from the EU. But exit from the EU is, as I already stressed, only a necessary condition for any political and economic independence. In fact, the reason why Nigel Farage's (UKIP) social policies did not significantly differ from those of the Tories was exactly because he, like Salmond (the leader of the Scottish nationalist party during the Scottish referendum), mostly represented the nationalist part of the bourgeoisie rather than the victims of globalization as a whole. This, unlike the economic program for instance of the National Front in France, which is much more to the Left than SYRIZA's or Podemos' 'Left'! Yet, due to the very fact that significant parts of the working class in Britain have moved to UKIP lately, mainly because they bore the brunt of globalization (unemployment, austerity policies, degradation of the welfare state and so on), one could hope that this party will be forced "from below" to introduce more radical social policies in the future and, following the Brexit victory, will be more socially radicalized.

As far as the political subject of this movement is concerned, it is obvious that only if the present informal front, which fought for a Brexit, is formalized after Brexit into a Front for National and Social Liberation (FNSL), it could achieve the required huge mobilization, so that the aim of national sovereignty could lead to self-reliance. Such a front can be achieved 'from below' or 'from above', as I will try to show in Ch. 10, where I will examine in more detail the functions of a FNSL and the process leading to a new Democratic Community of Sovereign Nations.

Therefore, as regards to the economic (as well as the social, cultural and ecological) effects of a Brexit, they would be radically different from the present situation only in case Britain adopts a real anti-globalization policy. This implies a break not only with the EU but also with the other transnational institutions of the NWO (WTO, IMF, NATO and so on). In other words, as we shall see in more detail in the last section, Brexit makes sense only if it signals a complete break with the NWO of neoliberal globalization.

This is particularly the case today, when the capitalist system as such is taken for granted by almost everybody, even by the working class (particularly in countries like China and India where capitalist industry has moved in the era of globalization), as today's workers feel more like consumers rather than like workers with the corresponding proletarian consciousness. No wonder that there has been not a single pan-European strike against the systematic demolition of workers' rights in the era of globalization. As a result, following the collapse of the soviet bloc, there is no conceivable threat against capitalism as a system, in any foreseeable future. The only 'threat' to the NWO comes from Russia and the Eurasian Union but, mainly. on geopolitical rather than on economic reasons. This is why the only real threat that the elites face today is the one arising from the struggle of the victims of globalization against them, which increasingly takes the form of a mass struggle all over Europe and beyond. Even in the USA, a rudimentary (and sometimes distorted) form of an anti-globalization front has been developing around Donald Trump, the Republican candidate against whom (not accidentally!) the entire US establishment has turned. In fact, the very fate of the Transnational Elite plan for global governance may be determined by the crucial US elections in November.

Finally, the argument that a Brexit followed by a break with the NWO will lead Britain to political isolation, particularly if it is accompanied with an exit from NATO as well, is baseless and promoted by the elites themselves for well understood reasons. It was NATO participation which led Britain to a series of wars in the last quarter of a century or so (Yugoslavia, Iraq, Afghanistan, Libya) for the sake of the transnational elite's interests and those of its members based in Britain. If we take into account that during the same period, as a direct result of the opening and liberalization of markets imposed by the NWO through the EU, the welfare state has been systematically dismantled, while the 'flexibility' of the labor market introduced meant the effective abolition of full time jobs and their replacement by part-time jobs, zero hours contracts and so on, then, it becomes obvious that membership of the EU and of the NWO in general has hardly helped the victims of globalization in Britain, or anywhere else. No wonder that on average, according to the latest Eurostat data, well over 20 percent of EU citizens are at risk of poverty or social exclusion (in Portugal this percentage is close to 30%, while in Greece it is close to 40%!)[462]

In conclusion, leaving the EU and the NWO could indeed lead to 'isolation' but only if by this we mean isolation from the elites who rule the world today. But, Brexit could mean anything but isolation as far as the vast majority of the world population, who are the victims of globalization, is concerned. Therefore, Brexit could indeed be harmful to the transnational elites and the British elites but it could also be very beneficial to the victims of globalization all over the world. In fact, a radical change in Britain could well function as the catalyst for the creation of a new democratic world order of sovereign nations. This is also the aim pursued by an informal patriotic front that has emerged in Russia — a country which, exactly for this reason, is subject to an unprecedented attack by the Transnational Elite. The latter's aim is clear: yet another 'regime change', this time the definitive regime change, which will determine the future of the present NWO.

However, in both the British and the Russian cases, unless the victims of globalization unite and fight the economic elites and the associated political and media elites, the Transnational Elite will come out of this Titanic conflict victorious again and the present criminal World Order will be strengthened further, particularly if the formalization of the Transnational Elite at the global level is completed. And it is a criminal world order, since the dominant characteristic of it is the economic and military violence exercised by elites over the vast majority of the world population.

---

[462] Valentina Romei, "Over 71 per cent of non-EU citizens in Belgium are at risk of poverty", *Financial Times*, 23/3/2016

Chapter 9.

The Brexit revolution in the USA

From Brexit to Trump

a. A very different Presidential election

As soon as the first edition of this book went to the printers, a major and dramatic development took place in the USA: a new Brexit-style revolution, this time in the metropolis of globalization itself, the USA. The tremendous implications of this event, which was the result of the victory against all the odds of Donald Trump, a neo-nationalist candidate explicitly attacking globalization, hardly need to be stressed. Of course, neither Trump, nor his likes in Europe (Farage, Le Pen, Grillo and so on) can be credited for the creation of the mass popular anti-globalization movement itself, which is flourishing today all over Europe and beyond. All these politicians simply tried to exploit, for electoral reasons, the rising world-wide movement against globalization, given that the globalist 'Left', which is fully integrated into the NWO of neoliberal globalization, cannot even think of questioning globalization and its institutions — the EU, WTO, IMF, WB, NATO etc. — as well as the multinationals and the elites running it. Instead, it simply criticizes their 'excesses' and sides fully with the middle classes (i.e. that part of them which has not been pauperized during globalization) in expressing the interests of the beneficiaries of globalization against its victims, who in the past formed the Left's political clientele. It is therefore only to the extent that these politicians express the real demands of the new anti-globalization movement that the victims of globalization can support them, until they find their own natural leaders from within the Popular Fronts proposed in ch.10.

Therefore, the Trump victory in the USA simply confirmed the fact, recognized also even by systemic writers, that the movement for Brexit in Britain, as well as the movement for Trump in the United States and similar movements all over Europe, are in fact all parts of a rising new anti-globalization movement which began in Europe and has spread all over the world. This new movement has nothing to do with the old anti-globalization movement that began in Seattle and Genova in the beginning of the new millennium, and which was then systematically undermined and eventually destroyed at the hands of the globalist 'Left' and the Soroses of this world in Porto Alegre etc. As we saw in previous chapters, this new movement is a global movement of the victims of globalization — who constitute the vast majority of the world population — for economic and national sovereignty, as the necessary condition for any radical social change.

As regards the 2016 US Presidential election itself, there is little doubt that it was one of the most controversial in US history. This had nothing of course to do with the various personal 'scandals' supposedly marring the two candidates, i.e. the emails scandal vs. the sexual utterances that were incompatible with the political correctness imposed by the ideology of globalization. These were obvious diversions created by the systemic media in order to disorient the American victims of globalization from the real issues of these elections. In fact, if we talk about real politics rather than politicking, the personalities of the two candidates mattered little anyway, as both were 'products of the system,' and in this sense one could argue that there was no real difference between them. Yet, there were some crucial differences not only between these two candidates but also between them and previous post-war candidates, who were also 'products of the system'.

Thus, previous candidates in the post-war period were distinguished only by their (usually minor) differences as regards aspects of their economic policies, mostly referring to the extent of social controls over markets. However, none of these candidates ever questioned the very fundamentals of a system, which eventually — helped by post-war US hegemony — led to the emergence of Transnational Corporations and the present NWO of neoliberal globalization. In other words, the fundamental principle guiding all post-war US Presidents was the principle of maximizing market freedom — i.e. not just 'free trade' but, also free movement of capital, services and labor in general. On the other hand, the historical differences between protectionists (usually belonging to the Republican Party) and free traders referred mainly to commodity trade, which constitutes only one of the (in)famous "four freedoms" (free movement of goods and services, as well as of capital and labor), which no post-war US President would question. Therefore, to simply characterize Trump as a protectionist, as the globalist 'Left' does ("Trump followed the legacy of protectionism in US policies established by George Washington and Alexander Hamilton and carried into the administrations of Franklin Roosevelt and others"[463]) betrays, at best, an ignorance of the fundamental differences between protectionism (which was a phenomenon of the nation-states era) and neo-nationalism (which is a phenomenon of the globalization era).

These "freedoms" constituted the post-war systemic fundamentals in the US, which were later institutionalized by the EU and NAFTA, and adopted by every country integrated into the NWO, including "communist" China. In fact, the entire world economic, political and military structure created by US hegemony in the 'free' World (i.e. the non-communist world) was based on three main institutions — the IMF, its sister organization, the WB, and the WTO — which, backed by the huge military power of NATO, functioned as the main pillars of 'market freedom' in general, which created the foundations of the present globalization era. At the same time, in the so-called 'communist' world, which covered more than half the world in the early post-war period, the basic principle of economic organization was central Planning. This was a socially controlled way of allocating economic resources that secured full employment and meeting the basic needs of all citizens (although at a generally low level), in contrast to the 'anarchy of the market' in the West, which was characterized by endemic catastrophic economic crises, high

---

[463] Prof. James Petras, "Trump and the "Collapse of Capitalism" (COC): Foibles, Fables and Failures, The Financial Press and its Keepers", *Global Research*, 23/11/2016 http://www.globalresearch.ca/trump-and-the-collapse-of-capitalism-coc-foibles-fables-and-failures-the-financial-press-and-its-keepers/5558610

unemployment and the failure to meet even the basic needs of many millions of people.[464]

It was the institutional economic framework created in the immediate post-war period which, in combination with the grow-or-die dynamic of the capitalist system, have led to the rise of multinationals that today, through the Transnational Elite, run the NWO. The victory of Brexit in the UK and the election of Trump in the USA drastically affected the NWO by explicitly questioning globalization. Both phenomena also constitute major social revolutions from below, against the concerted attack of the transnational elites (political, economic, cultural, academic and media) to complete the globalization process and lead to the creation of a system of global governance.

b. The real differences between Clinton and Trump

The real differences between the two Presidential candidates in the 2016 election were not the ones propagated by the systemic media, including most of the social media, but, first, those referring to their stand with respect to the systemic fundamentals I mentioned above and, second, the degree to which the two candidates are controlled by the system.

As regards the former, the very fact that Trump questioned the Trans-Pacific Partnership deal (TPP), NAFTA, and the role of the multinationals and free trade in destroying US industry and jobs, was a clear indication that this was a candidate moving well 'beyond the boundaries' set by the system. Particularly so, as this happened at the very moment the NWO was being widely questioned all over Europe and beyond, with Brexit marking a crucial landmark in this development. As Trump, almost immediately after his election, repeated his intention to quit TPP as soon as he took office, it is clear that the future of both TPP and TTIP (and therefore of globalization itself) is being seriously questioned, for the first time in the globalization era. Clearly, what the upshot of this Brexit-style revolution in the USA will be, as also of Brexit in Britain, will depend on the outcome of the class struggle. That is the struggle going on the

---

[464] See for an analysis of the capitalist and the socialist growth economies, Takis Fotopoulos, *Towards an Inclusive Democracy*, (London & N.Y: Cassell, 1997), chs. 1-2.

moment, which takes the form of a conflict between the revolution of the victims of globalization and the counter-revolution launched against it by the systemic forces supporting the NWO.

As regards the latter, i.e. the degree of elite control over the candidates, it is well known that Donald Trump, the candidate who dared to question the systemic fundamentals, is a product of the same system himself, yet he is a self-made product of it, who managed to become a candidate for the highest post of the Transnational Elite, without any direct or indirect support by it and its institutions (mass media, economic, political, academic, and cultural institutions). In fact, he was the target of an unprecedented attack by all these elites and institutions, not of course because he is a revolutionary of some kind, but simply because he is not as controllable by the elites, as all previous post-war US presidents — not to mention the Clintons (husband and wife) who have been executive assistants of the elites, par excellence. Hillary, as the first woman candidate and a perfectly controllable ambitious politician, was therefore the perfect candidate to carry out their criminal plans, exactly as Obama was before her a similar perfect candidate of the elites, being the first black candidate — one of the relatively few privileged blacks of course — and a perfectly controllable ambitious politician. No wonder, Hillary Clinton, a typical 'product of the system', was systematically promoted by it, in order to carry out faithfully the demands of the elites in the implementation of the above market fundamentals and what these demands imply, both at the domestic and at the foreign and geopolitical levels. She is well known anyway for her criminal role in the massacre of the Libyan people at the hands of the barbaric terrorists, who were funded by the Transnational Elite and supported by the State Department, which she headed at the time. It is the same kind of 'revolutionaries' who today are employed in Syria (some of them moved from Libya to Syria immediately they finished the 'job' there), with the same aim for regime change.

Therefore, the twin problem the elites had with Trump was that he not only was an 'unknown quantity' — the biggest crime for the elites — but he also professed policies that firmly put him within the rising world movement against globalization. That is, a movement which had already given the elites Brexit, a genuine revolution of the victims of globalization in the UK. No wonder that in the USA, because also of the much higher stakes involved, the counter-revolution began immediately it became clear that one candidate was adopting many of the demands of the victims of globalization. Particularly so as the elites were well aware of the fact that Trump had drawn mass support and won elections and public opinion not just because he was a 'populist demagogue' (as the elites were claiming in public) but because, as even a prominent member of the globalist 'Left' admitted,[465] he rejected the free trade agreements which allowed multinationals to exploit labor all over the world. Similarly, as even a columnist for the flagship of the globalist 'Left' recently stressed — after dutifully expressing first his dislike for Trump and Farage — the assumptions that globalists (he calls them 'free traders') make about the beneficial effects of free trade are wrong and as the latest transatlantic deal (CETA, the deal between Canada and the EU) showed, globalization is all about protecting big business — from the public. Thus, according to Aditya Chakrabortty, who (as expected for a *Guardian* writer), is also a globalist 'Left' supporter:

> For decades, presidents and prime ministers, policymakers and pundits have told voters there is only one direction of travel: free trade. Now comes Brexit and Donald Trump — and the horrible suspicion that the public won't buy it any more. And the elites don't know what to do, apart from keep insisting the public listen.[466]

Of course, as I pointed out above, the differences between Hillary and Trump are much deeper than just free trade. In fact, as it was rightly pointed out, the hard difference between Hillary who "has done nothing but advocate or agree to endless US-led war crimes without any life gain but only mass murder, social ruin and terror which she ignores" and Trump — which is also the difference between him and his Republican predecessors — is "Trump's denunciation of NAFTA and willingness to have peace with other nations not bowing to Uncle Sam".[467] This difference, plus — I would add — Trump's

---

[465] See James Petras, "Obama versus Trump, Putin and Erdogan: Can Coups Defeat Elected Governments?", Global Research,10/8/2016
http://www.globalresearch.ca/obama-versus-trump-putin-and-erdogan-can-coups-defeat-elected-governments/5540500*p
[466] Aditya Chakrabortty, "I hate Trump, but on the issue of free trade he has a point", The Guardian, 19/10/2016
[467] Prof. John McMurtry, "President Trump: Big Liar Going to Washington or Tribune of the People?", Global Research, 10/11/2016

determination to neutralize, if not abolish, TPP and TTIP, are defining the main aim of the counter-revolution against Trump. Needless to add that the crooked globalist 'Left' simply ignores these crucial differences and sides with his haters who "cannot say this [as] they stick to the politically correct repudiations, and call him 'racist', 'sexist', 'bigot' and so on, even if the conclusion does follow from what he says or does. Selected instances are the ruling fallacy here."[468]

The class nature of the Trump vote

As I tried to show in this book with respect to Brexit, globalization is a class issue, reflecting the popular reaction to the class nature of globalization. Furthermore, it was exactly the abysmal failure of the 'Left' in the UK and US to grasp this fact (either for dogmatic reasons or because it has already been fully integrated in the NWO) which has led to its theoretical and consequently political bankruptcy. As we saw in previous chapters, the entire US 'Left' (from Chomsky and Znet up to the Greens) had no qualms about siding with the criminal candidate of the elites, with the latter even demanding a recount of the vote, aiming to reverse the election result in favor of Clinton! Thus, all those 'Leftists', instead of supporting the victims of globalization in their struggle against the elites, they preferred to adopt the cause of those in the middle class or in the petty bourgeoisie, who benefit (or hope to benefit) from globalization! Their excuse was the liberal excuse (firmly based on the ideology of globalization) that human rights and identity politics should be the Left's mission, in place of its traditional mission for social liberation and class politics! No wonder the neo-nationalist Right has replaced the Left in its role of representing the victims of the system in its present globalized form.

However, one note of caution has to be added here about the meaning of class, as liberal apologists of the system, such as Fukuyama, blatantly distort the term. Thus, as he writes, referring to both Brexit and Trumpism:

> Social class, defined today by one's level of education, appears to have become the single most important social fracture in countless industrialised and emerging-market countries. This,

http://www.globalresearch.ca/president-trump-big-liar-going-to-washington-or-tribune-of-the-people/5556141
[468] ibid.

in turn, is driven directly by globalisation and the march of technology, which has been facilitated in turn by the liberal world order created largely by the US since 1945.[469]

Of course, education does not define class, but only in the narrow liberal view that he adopts, pretending he is unaware of the fact that education is, particularly today, a commodity, which can be bought by those controlling economic power. Class is therefore defined by one's economic power, as expressed by control of the means of production, income and wealth, as I defined it elsewhere.[470]

a. The geographical and age distribution of the vote

As in the case of Brexit, the class nature of Trump's electoral base can be shown by both the geographical and the age distribution of pro-Trump voters, with striking similarities characterizing the vote pattern in the two countries. A post-election editorial in the *Financial Times*, which together with the *Wall Street Journal* are the flagships of the Transnational Elite, summarized well their views on the election result, as the following extract show:

> Mr Trump's campaign appealed to nativism, isolationism and protectionism… In the US, as told by Mr. Trump, globalization and free trade have rewarded only a privileged few. There is a kernel of truth in Mr Trump's generalizations… Inequality has risen and median incomes have stagnated or fallen in recent years, especially among those without a college degree. There is an alternative narrative that highlights the resilience of the US economy, its capacity to innovate and produce world-class winners, especially in technology… Similarly, the free movement of capital, goods, and labor is one of the great achievements of the postwar era. Globalization has lifted millions out of poverty, especially in Asia.[471]

It is clear that the TE's campaign, following the Brexit and US election results, was based on two blatant lies: first, that both results

[469] Francis Fukuyama, "US against the world? "Trump's America and the new global order", *Financial Times,* 11/11/2016
[470] Takis Fotopoulos, "Class divisions today*", Democracy & Nature,* vol 2 no 6 (July, 2000), pp. 211-251 http://www.democracynature.org/vol6/takis_class.htm
[471] FT View, "Donald Trump's victory challenges the global liberal order", *Financial Times,* 9/11/2016

express feelings of 'nativism', which is as untrue a slander with respect to the US case as it is with respect to British 'racism' in the UK and, second, that globalization has lifted millions out of poverty. The latter is an allegation which, as we have seen above (ch. 5), is mainly based on a statistical trick used by the post-Mao 'communist' Chinese leadership, which removed from the list of the world poor more than 400 million Chinese in the period 1981-2001, simply by re-classifying them as proud earners of US$ 1 dollar a day![472]

Within the context of the vicious mass campaign of lies and disinformation launched by the systemic media, supported by supposedly 'objective' statistical (or generally 'scientific') analyses of the results by systemic academics and analysts (whose career depends on supporting the 'right side' on this crucial issue), it is impossible to draw any sort of objective or 'neutral' conclusions, even on as simple a question as who voted for Trump and why. This is hardly surprising, as I tried to show twenty years ago:

> Any attempt to objectivize the interpretation of social reality either takes the existing socio-economic order for granted, implicitly aiming at the justification of its reproduction, or discards it explicitly aiming at drastic social transformation.[473]

In this case, media and social analysts, taking for granted the NWO of neoliberal globalization, are bound to draw very different conclusions on the US vote results from those who questioned it. Thus, the former ('globalists') on the basis of dubious exit polls, usually asking the wrong questions (e.g. the income level of voters and their education but not their class position, or even their profession so that their class position can be indirectly derived), conclude that white wealthy voters gave victory to Donald Trump:

> Far from being purely a revolt by poorer whites left behind by globalization, who did indeed turn out in greater numbers for the Republican candidate than in 2012, Trump's victory also

---

[472] World Bank, *World development indicators* 2005, Table 2.5a. See Takis Fotopoulos, The "elimination of poverty", The International Journal of INCLUSIVE DEMOCRACY, vol.4, no.1, (January 2008)
http://www.inclusivedemocracy.org/journal/vol4/vol4_no1_takis_poverty.htm
[473] Takis Fotopoulos, *Towards an Inclusive Democracy*, op. cit. p.307

relied on the support of the middle-class, the better-educated and the well-off.[474]

In the same vein, a more sophisticated academic analysis in the flagship of globalist 'Left', compares Brexit with 'Trumpism' to draw essentially the same conclusions:

> Both majored on concerns about immigration. Both questioned whether the existing global financial order necessarily benefitted the ordinary man in the street. And both portrayed themselves as the underdogs campaigning against an allegedly complacent and out of touch political establishment. In the UK these stances have been shown to appeal in particular to the so-called "left behind", that is, voters who feel they have lost out economically in recent years and who are uncomfortable with some of the social changes that have been going on around them.[475]

The obvious intention of this kind of analysis is to discard any idea that the Trump vote in the USA (or, similarly the Brexit vote in the UK) had anything to do with class and globalization, and everything to do with racism and anti-immigration! Yet, the academic analysis mentioned could not escape some indirect hints to the class nature of the vote, as when it mentioned the fact that "Donald Trump was remarkably successful in such mid-West Rust Belt states as Michigan, Ohio and Wisconsin, where the decline of manufacturing industry has seemingly created a part of America that can also be said to have been 'left behind.'"[476] It is not accidental of course that the main Brexit voters were also concentrated in the areas which have been de-industrialized by globalization, or euphemistically as this academic described it, "those who are uncomfortable with some of the social changes that have been going on around them"!

The same analysis rightly pointed out that the age pattern of Brexiteers was similar to those who voted for Trump: "There are certainly some striking similarities between the UK and US voting

---

[474] Jon Henley, "White and wealthy voters gave victory to Donald Trump, exit polls show", (based on a CNN national election poll), *The Guardian* 9/11/2016
[475] John Curtice, Professor of politics at Strathclyde University, "The Trump-Brexit voter revolt", BBC News, 11/9/2016 http://www.bbc.co.uk/news/election-us-2016-37943072
[476] ibid.

trends. To begin with, older voters in the UK were inclined to vote to leave the EU, whereas a majority of younger voters were in favor of remaining, according to exit poll data. Similarly, in the US, Mrs Clinton was ahead among younger voters, while Mr. Trump was more likely to be preferred by older citizens".[477] Clearly, therefore, when the analysis concentrates on the geographical and age distributions of voting, the class nature of Brexit and 'Trumpism' becomes obvious.

However, not surprisingly, the same writer rushed to undermine any conclusion about globalization being the ultimate cause behind both Brexit and the Trump vote when he noted further on (presumably using the same CNN exit polls) that "in other respects the claim that it was the "left behind" who took Mr Trump to victory does not match the evidence. But Mr Trump was not particularly successful among low-income voters. In fact, just over half of those with incomes of less than $30,000 (£24,000) voted for Mrs Clinton. Conversely, those on more than $100,000 (£80,000) a year only preferred Mr. Trump by the narrowest margins".[478] Yet, such figures could mainly reflect the population in urban conglomerations such as N.Y. or California, which, because of their sheer size, affect disproportionately the averages, as we shall see next with reference to the liberal myth of the 'undemocratic' character of the result. Inevitably, the disorienting globalist 'Left' adopted a similar line concluding, without any evidence mentioned (unless it referred implicitly to the same unsupportable CNN exit poll on the basis of income levels) that it was not blue-collar workers in areas de-industrialized by globalization who gave victory to Trump but, instead, disappointed middle class professionals! It is obvious that the globalist 'Left' attempts in this pathetic way to dismiss the valid accusation against it that it ceased to express the interests of its traditional supporters, the working class voters, who as a result, have moved *en masse* to the neo-nationalist parties, of which Trumpism is an expression.

"[Trump voters] were not overwhelmingly unemployed, bitter former industrial workers or minimum wage, uneducated racists from the gutted 'heartland'. 'Angry white male workers' constituted only a fraction of the Trump electorate. Trump received the vote of large sections of suburban middle class

---

[477] ibid.
[478] ibid.

professionals, managers and local businesspeople; joined by
downwardly mobile Main Street shopkeepers, garage owners
and construction contractors. A majority of white women voted
for Trump. City household residents, still trying to recover
from the Obama-Clinton era mortgage foreclosures, formed an
important segment of the Trump majority, as did underpaid
university and community college graduates — despairing of
ever finding long-term stable employment. In short, low-paid,
exploited and precarious business owners and service sector
employees formed a larger section of the Trump majority than
the stereotyped 'deplorable angry white racists' embedded in
the media and Clinton-Sanders propaganda.[479]

b. The myth of the 'undemocratic' character of Trump's victory

Another myth, particularly exploited by George Soros, the master
of ceremonies for pink revolutions par excellence, in order to initiate
demonstrations against the election result, was the apparent
'undemocratic' character of Trump's victory, given the small gap
between popular votes and electoral college votes. Yet, although this
was not of course the first time that the popular vote for the
presidential candidate who lost was higher than the vote for the winner,
one cannot remember as many demonstrations of protest and for so
long after the election, as today. Clearly, Soros' absence in the past
was decisive for this unfortunate lack of support for past losers!

However, it is a distortion of democracy to call the result of the
Presidential election as 'undemocratic', simply because the popular
vote was in favor of the criminal Hillary (by a margin of something
between 1.5% and 2% of the total vote). This is not simply because the
Presidential electors' result, as prescribed by the US constitution, went
clearly for Trump but, also, because such an argument could have any
validity only in the case of a small *demos*, such as the demos of
classical Athens, where the population was small enough (some tens of
thousands) that citizens could take all important decisions through
face-to face assemblies. Furthermore, the citizenry was more or less
homogeneous, given the lack of any significant class divisions, a fact
recognized even by Karl Marx, as a result of the mode of production
prevailing at the time. This, despite the fact that some degree of

---

[479] Prof. James Petras, "Trump and the "Collapse of Capitalism", op.cit.

economic inequality was present even at the time of classical democracy — a fact which, to my mind, was the main reason of its eventual collapse.[480] Needless to add that there were also significant divisions beyond the citizen body, as both women and slaves were excluded from it, something which, however, was hardly surprising 2,500 years ago (despite some idiotic liberal arguments to the opposite), when the abolition of slavery and the granting of voting rights to women had to wait for another 22 centuries or so to be established in the West!

On the other hand, modern states have populations reaching into hundreds of millions (as in the USA), which are sharply divided socially, according to social class, area they live, education levels and so on. Therefore, the requirement for an absolute majority of all US voters, as far as Presidential elections is concerned, far from being more democratic, would in fact be an absolute distortion of democracy. This is because, as we have seen above, urban centers, such as New York and California (or London in the UK), concentrate disproportionate numbers of the total population in the globalization era. Given that the vast majority of the beneficiaries of globalization (or those aspiring to benefit from it) live also in such centers (for the reasons I explained in ch. 8), such mega-population centers possess a built-in mechanism in favor of globalization in any election where counter-balancing mechanisms to take regional or class differences into account are missing.

In this sense, the electoral system in the US presidential elections, or the one-constituency system in British parliamentary elections respectively, do function as counter-balancing mechanisms to the above built-in mechanism for globalization. Therefore, the argument of liberals and the 'Left' about the size of the popular vote being ignored by the electoral system of US Presidential elections is not only phony but devious as well. Clearly, in a representative 'democracy', such huge population centers could determine, just by their size, the final result on such crucial issues as globalization, making the vote of everybody living outside these centers redundant. On top of this, the inevitable concentration of the service sector (which is a major globalization sector particularly in countries such as US and UK), functions as another factor attracting higher proportions of the beneficiaries of globalization in them.

---

[480] Takis Fotopoulos, *Towards an Inclusive Democracy*, op.cit. pp.192-194

294   The New World Order in Action

Finally, it should not be forgotten that the above arguments refer to different cases of representative democracy. Clearly in a genuine democracy, that is a direct democracy where citizens take all important decisions in face-to-face assemblies, the problem will not even arise at all in the first instance. This is because a basic component of such a democracy is economic democracy (i.e. the equal distribution of economic power that complements the equal distribution of political power), which is completely incompatible with globalization and its institutions.

Revolution and counter-revolution in the USA

a. Why the polls on globalization are usually wrong?

Roger Altman, Bill Clinton's deputy Treasury secretary, wrote the following in the *Financial Times*, more than 2 months before the US election, on the basis of opinion polls and various, supposedly 'informed', academic and media analyses:

> The biggest American political question today is not the outcome of the November presidential election. For all practical purposes, that is over and Hillary Clinton will be the next president. No Democratic or Republican nominee since 1948 has overcome, at this late stage, the 7-10 point deficit that Donald Trump currently suffers in respected national polls. In particular, his deficits among non-white and college educated voters, especially women, are so huge as to make it virtually impossible for him to win the necessary 270 electoral votes. Yes, there are still just over two months left before November 8; and, yes, an asteroid could collide with Earth before then, but the fact is that this is decided.[481]

In fact, Hillary's defeat proved much more likely than an asteroid's collision with Earth! Yet, the question remains: how can we explain this phenomenon, which happened yesterday with Brexit and was repeated today in Italy, while the possibility of 'Frexit' tomorrow (i.e. France's exit from the EU), which will mark the definite end of the European Union, seems growing all the time. This, in turn, will constitute a major step towards economic and national sovereignty and the beginning of the end of the NWO of neoliberal globalization, that

---

[481] Roger Altman. "Trump will lose. Can the Republicans recover,?" *Financial Times,* 6/9/2016

is, a very significant step in the fight against globalization and for social liberation. Of course for the elites and the beneficiaries of globalization this will be 'a tragic development', as the self-declared 'anarchist' Noam Chomsky, (who like Soros, is an enthusiastic supporter, of Varoufakis' DIEM25 Movement) characterized the dismantling of the EU !

The question however still remains whether this blatant failure of the NWO's pollsters, which has already discredited them, is just due to the fact that most of these polls are funded to produce the results liked by their funders, or whether instead this is due to their real ignorance about voters' intentions faced with crucial plebiscites or elections. To my mind, both these factors are at work. Thus, it is highly likely that the ferocity of the huge propaganda campaigns launched by the transnational and local elites, with the clear aim to avert at all cost crucial popular decisions affecting their own vital interest in reproducing the present enormous concentration of income and wealth in their hands, deters people from revealing their true intentions. Particularly so, when they are fully aware of the fact that, given the total control of all forms of power by the elites, they may well pay a price if they come out publicly against their plans. Clearly, therefore, if this assumption is right, the present polls which predict an overwhelming defeat of Le Pen in the forthcoming Presidential elections in France, may prove to be as accurate as the polls in the UK and US...

Indicative of these trends is the extract below of a report from Youngstown, Ohio, a traditionally blue-collar Democratic bastion, that voted for Trump, accurately describing the feelings of the victims of globalization in blue collar working class America:

> All the media and all the pollsters just didn't understand that the little people like us all over the country were quietly supporting Donald Trump, said John Vass, a 66-year-old engineer and former Democrat. And today we made our voices heard.[482]

Clearly, the victims of globalization in the USA had their own important reasons for "quietly" supporting Trump...

---

[482] Jon Swaine, "White, working-class and angry: Ohio's left-behind help Trump to stunning win", *The Guardian*, 9/11/2016

b. The Brexit revolution in the UK and USA and the 'Left'

There is no doubt that the election of Trump, as well as the vote for Brexit, represented a kind of popular revolution, as each signaled the peoples' revolt against globalization and the elites' plans for global governance. Below is a first-hand description of how working class people (who, effectively, have given up voting long ago, both in Britain and the USA, having concluded that elections cannot change anything), decided to try the election process and they won against all the odds! That is, against the combined forces of all parties (even the Republican Party turned against its own candidate!), against all media, against most academics (including 'Left' Nobel prize winners), against Hollywood and the entire culture industry and, of course, against the middle classes, apart from that part which became a victim of globalization:

> The Trump effect is more than, as the man himself put it, "Brexit plus plus plus". It is nothing less than a revolution, not just in American and global politics, but in the way we see politics and in the way we do politics. I saw first-hand in Mississippi how Donald Trump had rallied thousands and thousands of people to his banner; a forgotten generation of voters who had given up on elections long ago after being trodden down by the inexorable march of globalisation, but bursting with patriotism and enthusiasm now that they had found a candidate who would speak for them. Mr Trump reached these people by breaking the mould. The legacy media wanted no part of him, and American broadcasting rules allowed them to be even more obviously biased against his campaign than they were against Brexit in the UK.[483]

In fact, this is far from an isolated incident and every honest journalist who attended similar gatherings in both the UK and US reported exactly the same picture of a revolutionary atmosphere prevailing among the victims of globalization. John Harris, for instance, who visited the Brexit areas as well as the areas who voted for Trump had drawn the same conclusion in an article subtitled

---

[483] Arron Banks, "We're on the cusp of a new era", *The Times,* 10/11/2016

"Workers I met in Indiana were as much victims of globalisation as those in Stoke or Merthyr Tydfil".[484]

Of course, this was not a revolution of the kind we saw in the last three centuries or so, as part of the revolutionary era that began in the 17th century and probably ended in the last century.[485] It is clear that, following the collapse of 'actually existing socialism,' this kind of revolution is not possible any more, at least in any country fully integrated into the NWO of neoliberal globalization with a relatively strong middle class. Yet, this does not rule out insurrections, or even electoral 'revolutions', such as Brexit or 'Trumpism', where the electorates turn against the entire establishment, rejecting any kind of elites (political, economic, cultural, media etc.) The fact that both Brexit and Trumpism signal a new era, as every revolution has done in the past, was well summarized by another analyst who is also the founder of Leave.UK:

> No more NATO massing troops on Russia's borders to stir up the tensions which justify its existence. No more casual acceptance of mass immigration, persistent low-level terrorism and the erosion of national identity as "the normal" in the West. We're on the cusp of a new era, and we'll know soon if the crest of the Trump wave is about to break on Paris and Berlin, too.[486]

No wonder that the so-called 'Left' attempted to diminish the significance of these events and academics such as Noam Chomsky mentioned above and James Petras played a leading role in the disorientation of peoples in their struggle against globalization and the NWO, turning in the process even against the traditional supporters of the Left — under a supposedly 'Left' cover.

---

[484] John Harris, "The reasons for Trump are also the reasons for Brexit", *The Guardian*, 11/11/2016

[485] For Bookchin, "the era of the great revolutionary movements, from that of the English Revolution of the 1640s to that of the Spanish Revolution of 1936-39, is waning today", *The Third Revolution*, vol 1, (London & NY) Cassell, 1996, p. vii

[486] Arron Banks, "We're on the cusp of a new era", op.cit.

Thus, Petras, apparently demystifying the result of the last Presidential election,[487] referred to the "myth" of the Trump revolution, while not mentioning once the words "globalization" and "sovereignty"! Yet, sovereignty and globalization are what the entire world movement now developing is all about, which these 'radical Left' academics presumably have not heard of. Instead, he talks about the "Trump revolution", following the familiar devious approach of constructing a straw man argument in order to avoid the real arguments about the revolutionary character of Brexit and the presidential election results.

There is no doubt — and all serious analysts accept the fact — that what happened in the US, as in Britain, was a revolution, but not of course in the ridiculous sense discussed by these 'radical' academics who should know that revolutions are not made anyway by individuals (the Farages and Trumps of this world). Surely, a real Marxist, or anarchist, intellectual for that matter, would be the last one to suggest such a monstrosity. Revolutions are made by people and the very fact that the victims of globalization, in both Britain and the US, were mobilized 'from below' to rise against globalization is in itself a revolution, given that the essence of the entire NWO is globalization and the running of all economies integrated into this Order by multinationals.

Clearly, therefore, this process has nothing to do with what the British government, or the new US Administration, for that matter, will do, or will not do, in the future. Neither Farage nor Trump nor Le Pen are leaders of this global movement. This is obviously a leaderless global movement expressing concrete demands for national and economic sovereignty, which is exactly the form that the struggle for self-determination takes in the globalization era. Political parties therefore such as UKIP in Britain, the Republicans in the USA and FN in France simply attempt to exploit this movement for electoral reasons and do not in any sense lead it. This is why politicians such as Farage, Trump or Le Pen come in conflict with the elites when they support the demands of this movement. This is also why it is highly

---

[487] Prof. James Petras, 'Presidential Elections: Myths and Deceits', *Global Research*, 18/11/2016, http://www.globalresearch.ca/presidential-elections-myths-and-deceits/5557621

likely that the counter-revolution going on at present both in Europe and in the US against this popular movement for economic and national sovereignty and against globalization will manage, eventually, (with all the power still held by the elites controlled by multinationals) to water down both Brexit and 'Trumpism'. Yet, this will not stop this huge movement of global dimensions, which will simply abandon parties and 'leaders' that break their promises in power.

Below is a perceiving analysis of the contradictions involved in this process, which are ignored by the myopic analyses of the globalist 'Left':

> [Trump] identified a split between the party's donors, who tended to benefit from globalization, and its rank and file, who felt victimised by it. And he took the side of the latter. He attacked free trade, mass immigration and military intervention... Mr Trump appealed to working class whites,[488] taking about 70 per cent of their votes, according to preliminary exit polling... Mr Trump outpolled Mitt Romney, the 2012 candidate, among both blacks and Hispanics, and lost white university-educated women only narrowly... Here is the Republican party's problem. Thanks to Mr Trump it has received a mandate to speak on behalf of globalisation's losers. But its personnel consists of the global-economy winners who ran the party before he arrived on the scene... The Republican party has become something it has never been since it was founded a century-and-a-half ago: the party of outsiders. Mr Trump's toughest job may be bringing his colleagues to terms with that.[489]

The conclusion is that to scorn the really revolutionary character of these phenomena (Brexit, election of Trump, possible election of Le Pen) on the grounds that their leaders when in power will simply 'forget' their promises, as Petras and the likes do, far from being a radical analysis of any sort in this crucial moment in History, is at least disorienting, unless it is aiming to defuse the entire movement,

---

[488] Demetri Sevastopulo, "US election: the rise of the Trump Democrats", *Financial Times*, 4/10/2014
[489] Christopher Caldwell, "The Republicans are now the party of outsiders", *Financial Times*, 9/11/2016

supposedly because it is not revolutionary enough! The obvious implication of such a distorted logic is the millenarian 'strategy' of waiting for the overthrow of capitalism, while in the meantime supporting the Hillarys of this world, as, supposedly, the 'least evil' — exactly as Chomsky, Sanders, the Greens and similar 'radicals' have done…

c. Immigration, cultural globalization and the racist card against Trump

As mentioned in ch. 2, globalization does not involve only an economic and political dimension but an equally important cultural dimension as well, of which the immigration problem is a significant aspect. In other words, immigration is not only an economic consequence of globalization.

As we saw in ch 8, the dominant globalist culture in the NWO effectively constitutes the negation of national culture, as it is based on the globalization ideology of multiculturalism etc., which in fact is the globalist version of classical liberal ideology. Furthermore, as I showed in Part I, cultural globalization is not only some sort of 'automatic' effect of globalization, but it is also a deliberate policy of the Transnational Elite. The aim of this policy is helping the expansion of immigration, given that a plentiful supply of cheap immigrant labor is necessary for the expansion of multinationals 'at home', that is in the US and Germany. This means that a plentiful supply of cheap Mexican labor in the former case and of Asian and African labor in the latter is necessary, so that the multinationals face more or less the same wages and working conditions, whether they operate 'at home', i.e. in their home bases, or abroad, e.g. in China, India and the other countries integrated into the NWO.

It is hardly surprising therefore that Lionel Barber, the FT editor, aptly identified cultural and identity politics as the common thread of instability running through the world right now:

> From Donald Trump's triumph to Brexit and the rise of a new caliphate in the Middle East, the tension is likely to get worse before it gets better. In the US, Trump played on middle class and working class fears about immigration and cultural nostalgia for a bygone era in America. He brilliantly exploited anger about political correctness, especially among elites, including the mainstream media. Ultimately, as in Brexit

Britain, identity politics may have "trumped" pocketbook politics.[490]

Yet both the globalists in the US (i.e. the Democrats as well as the globalist 'Left') and those in the UK did not have any qualms about playing the racist card, in their desperate effort to rule out 'Trumpism' and Brexit respectively. The pretext in the US was Trump's senseless promise to build a wall around America and particularly on the border with Mexico to stop mass illegal immigration from that country. On this, he was conveniently 'forgetting' in the process that it was the US elites in the first instance, which, in collaboration with the Mexican elites, created the present dependent development of Mexico, whose growth depends on foreign (i.e. US) investment and trade, as these elites destroyed any possibility of economic self-reliance in that country. Of course Mexico's dependent development goes back to the history of its relation to the USA in the last century but NAFTA, the agreement between the local and US elites that institutionalized this dependence relationship (exactly as the EU agreement institutionalized Greek dependence on Northern Europe[491]) and opened and liberalized markets, played a crucial role in destroying any degree of self-reliance in Mexico and in creating a mass of unemployed and underemployed people, who were pushed beyond the border to the US to find cheap employment in that country.[492] Ironically, in the globalization era, metropolitan countries like the US and UK, suffer a similar fate in reverse, when their own multinationals have either to import cheap labor from abroad or move themselves abroad in order to win the war of competition with other multinationals. However, what angered the elites was not of course that Trump blamed Mexicans, whereas in fact

---

[490] Lionel Barber, "Seven takeaways from the victory of Donald Trump", *Financial Times,* 11/11/2016

[491] Mexico is of course a typical case of dependent development in North America, as Greece is similarly a typical case of dependent development in Europe; see Takis Fotopoulos, *Dependent Development: the case of Greece* (Athens: Exantas, 1985 & 1987 — shortly in a new 2017 edition, published by Koukkida Press, Athens)

[492] see for data and research on the catastrophic effects of NAFTA on Mexico, Timothy Alexander Guzman, "Is it Fact or Fiction? US Media Says that New World Order is in Jeopardy with a Trump Presidency", Global Research, 11/11/2016 Is it Fact or Fiction? US Media Says that New World Order is in Jeopardy with a Trump Presidency http://www.globalresearch.ca/is-it-fact-or-fiction-us-media-says-that-new-world-order-is-in-jeopardy-with-a-trump-presidency/5556295

302 The New World Order in Action

it was corporations to be blamed. What angered them, as McMurtry pointed out was that:

> The Mexican wall does not fit the borderless neo-liberal program either. But all of it is welcome to citizens' ears. That is why the establishment hates Trump for exposing all these issues long kept in the closet and covered over by politically correct identity politics.[493]

In view of the above it is not therefore surprising that Trump campaigned against the effects of America's free trade deals with Canada and Mexico, and (what he alleged to be) China's unfair trading tactics. Yet, can we characterize Trump's attitude antidemocratic or even racist? As a British supporter of Brexit pointed out (from a conservative point of view), "while Trump's remarks about Mexican illegal aliens were incendiary and deliberately so, there is nothing anti-democratic about the idea of protecting a country's borders and nothing inherently racist in voting for such a proposal".[494] Clearly, a people which has lost the ability to control its borders has lost one of the defining characteristics of what it is to be a nation. Yet, as the same author rightly pointed out, the prevailing electoral strategy of the Democrats in the United States and then Labour in the UK was based on the idea of balkanizing the electorate into "communities", and aggregating their votes. Thus, for the Democrats, it was a matter of identifying "the African-American community" and the "Hispanic community" as political client groups; for Labour — and this was a particular skill of the former London mayor Ken Livingstone — the task was to do the same with "the Muslim community" or "the black community". It purported to create a less segregated country, but, if anything, it was a recipe for the opposite.

In fact, Trevor Phillips, a prominent member of the London ethnic community in his capacity as former head of the Commission for Racial Equality, aptly explained why he broke with this: "The idea was to corral certain groups of people, to make people like me — someone from an ethnic background — a political category, which they could move around. It was treating me as just a pawn and that the only thing

---

[493] Prof. John McMurtry, "President Trump: Big Liar Going to Washington or Tribune of the People?," op.cit.
[494] Dominic Lawson, "Until the left gets beyond wooing 'communities', it will remain in the cold", *Sunday Times,* 13/11/2016

that mattered about me was my color."[495] In other words, Trevor Phillips implicitly raised the issue of the all-important class element in the identity of a person, irrespective of skin color, sexual identity etc. From this point of view, identity politics, a basic element of liberal ideology, can be seen as a way to obscure class divisions, or, alternatively, as the present-day tactics of the ruling elites to 'divide and rule' in the pseudo-democracies of the Western world. So, what about the 'racist' vote for Trump? As the same writer stressed:

> it is clear that a substantial number of the votes Trump won in the Rust Belt — thus seizing the formerly solid Democrat territories of Pennsylvania and Wisconsin — were from those who had voted for Obama in the two previous presidential elections. They could hardly be defined as racists. This has been described as a "whitelash". But if the Democrats insisted on defining other ethnic groups as specific political entities to be "corralled" (as Phillips might put it) then they could hardly complain if Trump targeted something that could be categorized as "the white working class". What is clear is that the Democrats took their support for granted (Clinton never once visited Wisconsin).[496]

The conclusion is that, in a capitalist society, communities will have to be class-based communities in order to be meaningful (e.g. miners' communities and so on). Even neighborhood communities are, in effect, class-based communities, as obviously it is the level of income and wealth that ultimately determines who lives in a particular neighborhood. In other words, real communities existed only in pre-capitalist societies, although even within such communities, as we saw in relation to the Athenian demos, one could distinguish between various implicit 'class based' communities. At the same time, ethnic communities simply play the role described above by Trevor Phillips, i.e. the role of political pawns, while class barriers develop within these communities as well. Obama's color did not make any difference as regards the domestic or foreign policies he implemented, as he simply protected the interests of his class and he used his skin color to climb the social and political ladder. Similarly, the sex of Thatcher or

---

[495] ibid.
[496] ibid.

Hillary did not make the slightest difference as regards their policies in office.

All this is absolutely relevant to a sort of 'debate' going on at present within the 'Left' on whether class politics take priority over identity politics or not. The usual answer given by the globalist 'Left' is one attempting to reconcile the two kinds of politics under the umbrella of working class politics as follows:

> There are those who argue the left has abandoned class in favour of identity politics. There is certainly a type of liberal who has done this: who argues for solutions such as more women in corporate boardrooms rather than addressing systemic inequality. But socialists argue that class is absolutely central to understanding society's ills, but cannot be understood without gender, race and sexual orientation. [497]

However, as it is obvious from the above answer, this crucial question cannot be answered in terms of (liberal in effect) platitudes, as too often nowadays, deliberately or not, identity politics come into conflict with class politics. The clearest example was the Brexit revolution in both the UK and USA. Is it accidental that supporters of identity politics were fully supporting the enemies of a Brexit kind of revolution in both cases ? Or is it perhaps that the fanatic supporters of Bremain and Clinton were motivated mainly by their class position (i.e. the fact that they mainly belonged to the beneficiaries of globalization) rather than from other criteria in voting? Or, to put it in another way, is perhaps the main reason why beneficiaries of globalization voted against Brexit and Trump the fact that, as they had already sorted out their own survival problems within the NWO of neoliberal globalization, they could then afford to vote the way they did, whereas the victims of globalization could not afford to ignore their own survival for the sake of identity politics and political correctness?

As John Wight aptly put it:

> Trump represents a backlash against a liberal establishment that had become so fixated with identity politics it refused to tackle a growing ocean of alienation and poverty across large swathes of the country... It is an economic system that acts as a

---

[497] Owen Jones, "Don't be divided – minorities are part of the working class", *The Guardian*, 17/11/2016

tyrant over the lives of the mass of people rather than one that serves their needs, producing a race to the bottom involving workers around the world competing for the crumbs from the table of a multinational corporate dictatorship that in its ability to destroy or raise living standards arrogated to itself more power than most governments. The result in the US was manufacturing jobs that once provided a decent income and a sense of dignity and worth in working class communities being exported abroad to China, Mexico, Vietnam, and elsewhere in the Global South. They were replaced by low paid jobs in the new service economy, forcing people to take two, even three jobs just in order to survive.[498]

d. The mass counter-revolution to suppress the Brexit revolution in the USA

A similar counter-revolution to the one developing in the UK is raging in the USA at the moment. In the UK, the elites have launched a huge campaign financed by millions of pounds and headed (unofficially at the moment) by the war criminal Tony Blair in order to impose a 'soft Brexit,' implying a Britain only formally out of the EU. Similarly, the campaign in the USA aims to 'soften' Trump's policies, so that the NWO will remain essentially the same as before, perhaps with some cosmetic modifications. Soros, who has played a leading role in the counter-revolution in the UK, does the same in the USA, always on behalf of the Transnational Elite.

Thus, immediately the election result was announced, scores of anti-Trump demonstrations took place all over America. These demonstrations were as impromptu as the corresponding demonstrations during the Arab Spring, or the Ukraine coup![499] As Paul Craig Roberts stressed:

> I think I know who they are. They are thugs for hire and are paid by the Oligarchy to delegitimize Trump's presidency in the way that Washington and the German Marshall Fund paid

---

[498] John Wight, "Trump's election - a scream from the swamp of alienation created by liberal America", RT, 14/11/2016, https://www.rt.com/op-edge/366883-trump-liberal-us-split/

[499] see Takis Fotopoulos, *The New World Order in Action,* vol. 2 on Ukraine demonstrations, and vol. 3 on the Arab Spring events.

students in Kiev to protest the democratically elected Ukrainian government in order to prepare the way for a coup.[500]

In fact, George Soros, the master of ceremonies behind every 'pink revolution' in the world, played a role in all of them and is now in action again, both in the UK and USA. Thus, it has been shown that some at least of the anti-Trump protests in the US have been organized by groups that were sponsored by Clinton sympathizer Soros through MoveOn.org. As is well known, "among Wikileaks' Podesta emails was a strategy document involving the Soros-supported MoveOn.org and grassroots organizing and funding."[501]

Furthermore neither Hillary, nor Obama, not even Bernie Sanders had uttered a single word to stop these demonstrations, and when the full pro-systemic leader of the US Greens set in motion the recounting process, again, nobody attempted to stop her. As an activist blog noted:

> Is it just me or have you also noticed that Hillary Clinton, Bernie Sanders, and President Obama have been silent about the protests? The very people who have the power to stop these protests and riots with just a few well-spoken words have been completely silent on the issue... Bernie Sanders, the one from whom the Democratic primary was fraudulently stolen, the one who backed up Hillary Clinton anyway, has also been uncharacteristically silent, especially for an aging peace-and-love hippie kind of guy... Then there's the President, who met cordially with Trump. His Twitter account is likewise mute on

[500] Paul Craig Roberts, The Anti-Trump Protesters Are Tools of the Oligarchy. Their Objective: Delegitimize Donald, Install "Madam President", *Global Research*, 11/11/2016 http://www.globalresearch.ca/the-anti-trump-protesters-are-tools-of-the-oligarchy-their-objective-delegitimize-donald-install-madam-president/5556434
[501] See "Soros-fronted orgs among groups calling for anti-Trump protests (VIDEO)", RT, 12/11/2016 https://www.rt.com/usa/366579-soros-orgs-driving-trump-protests/; See, also, Wayne Madsen, "The Clintons and Soros Launch America's Purple Revolution", *Strategic Culture*, 11/11/2016 http://www.strategic-culture.org/news/2016/11/11/clintons-and-soros-launch-america-purple-revolution.html

the subject of vandalism, arson, and violence in reaction to the election.[502]

The fact that a discussion had already begun on whether the electoral college could deny Trump's victory shows the extent of pressures on the forthcoming Administration to deter it from making any significant changes on foreign policy, in particular, but, also, on economic policies with respect to 'market freedom', (the euphemism for multinationals' freedom to move capital and labor in and out of the country as they like it). In fact, the US Green leader (Jill Stein) plays exactly the same dirty role on this that European Greens have played under Danny Cohn-Bendit — the ex-May '68 'revolutionary' who turned to an enthusiastic supporter of all the Transnational Elite's criminal wars, from Yugoslavia up to Libya![503] Alternatively, one could take the general apathy of Greens everywhere about globalization and its social effects as another proof that the ecological movement, during the globalization era, has been converted into a fully middle-class movement, whose sole reason of existence is the ecological damage going on, while the original aim of the antisystemic Green movement for social liberation has quietly been abandoned, at least since the defeat of the "fundos" at the hands of the "realos".[504]

In fact, the elites had not any qualms even about using the secret services to doubt Trump's victory, on the basis perhaps of their familiar false flag operations concerning a supposed Russian hackers meddling in the elections, prompting even the BBC to point out that the present situation "set the incoming commander-in-chief against intelligence services that he will preside over".[505] It is therefore clear that the real aim of the elites is to crush the underlying "revolution in

[502] Obama, "Clinton, And Sanders Could Stop The Riots But They Just Watch", Activist Post, 13/11/2016 http://www.activistpost.com/2016/11/obama-clinton-sanders-stop-riots-just-watch.html
[503] Robert Bridge, "Is The Donald trumped? Clinton scheming to seize White House through backdoor", RT, 3/12/2016, https://www.rt.com/op-edge/369019-donald-trumped-hillary-clinton-us-presidency/
[504] Takis Fotopoulos, "The End of Traditional Antisystemic Movements and the Need for A New Type of Antisystemic Movement Today", *DEMOCRACY & NATURE*,, vol.7, no.3, (November 2001) pp. 415-455 http://www.democracynature.org/vol7/takis_movements.htm
[505] "Trump mocks Russian hacking 'conspiracy theory'", *BBC News*, 12/12/2016 http://www.bbc.co.uk/news/world-us-canada-38292392

thinking" that marked the Presidential election. As Prof. John McMurtry aptly put it:

> An underlying revolution in thinking has occurred. Trump has tapped the deep chords of worker rage at dispossession by forced corporate globalization, criminally disastrous Middle East wars, and trillions of dollars of bailouts to Wall Street. He never connects the dots on stage. But by Clinton's advocacy of all of them, she has made them her own and will go down because of it... But this is not a Republican-Democrat division. It is as deep as all the lost jobs and lives since 2001, and it is ultimately grounded in the tens of millions of dispossessed people which the life-blind global market system and its wars have imposed on America too.[506]

So, as in the case of Brexit, what is important today is not whether Brexiteers or Trump 'will deliver' or not. This is an utterly disorienting question raised by a crooked globalist 'Left', which insults this popular movement as racist, nationalist etc. The real issue is whether this revolution in thinking going on at the moment, from Britain and USA yesterday, to Italy today, and France tomorrow, will mature into a global anti-globalization movement for economic and national sovereignty and self-reliance, as well as a new internationalism based on the principles of solidarity and mutual aid rather than competitiveness and profit.

---

[506] Prof. John McMurtry, "President Trump: Big Liar Going to Washington or Tribune of the People?," op.cit.

Chapter 10.

The imperative need for a shift of strategy in the struggle for self-determination

Breaking with the NWO, the fundamental aim of the social struggle today

Fifteen years ago, in an article examining the theoretical aspects of globalization and the related approaches, I had drawn the following conclusion in describing the dilemma faced by humanity at the dawn of the new millennium.

> I think that humanity faces a crucial choice in the new millennium. Either we continue our present patterns of life, within the present institutions that secure today's huge and growing concentration of power at all levels and the consequent continuous deepening of the present multidimensional crisis, or, alternatively… we embark on a process which would create the preconditions for the establishment, for the first time in History, of a new and truly Democratic World Order.[507]

However, at that time, globalization had not taken on its present dimensions in terms of concentration of power at all levels. More important, globalization did not mean yet the complete loss of economic and therefore national sovereignty for most countries integrated into the New World Order of neoliberal globalization. Yet,

---

[507] Takis Fotopoulos, *"Globalisation, the reformist Left and the Anti-Globalisation "Movement" Democracy & Nature*, Vol. 7, No. 2 (July 2001), pp. 233-80

the Eurozone that was created at the same time signaled, in fact, the abolition of economic and therefore national sovereignty of all 19 European states in the Eurozone, in various degrees, of course, depending on the economic power of each country involved.

Since then, as we saw in Part I, national sovereignty has increasingly been replaced by various degrees of transnational sovereignty, which, however is enjoyed only by some countries, i.e. those where the major TNCs are based (mainly the G7 countries). So, today, the economic and national sovereignty of every country integrated into the NWO has been effectively eroded (again in various degrees depending on the economic power of each country).

A main instrument of the economic elites in this process was the World Trade Organization (WTO) and, as far as Europe in particular is concerned, the EU. These transnational institutions had imposed various rules for the opening and liberalization of markets on most countries of the world that joined them, apart from a few recalcitrant countries like Iran, Algeria and Syria. On the other hand, Russia and China, which were not members of WTO at the beginning of the millennium, have since joined it. In fact, Russia joined the WTO relatively late (2012) and its relationship to it has always been precarious, given the political will of the Russian elite under Putin to maintain the country's sovereignty and consequently a significant degree of self-reliance — a will that was particularly enhanced after the launching of the Transnational Elite's economic warfare against Russia.

Today, therefore, it is clear that the fundamental aim of the social struggle should be a complete break with the present NWO and its institutions and the building of a new democratic world community that would be founded on sovereign nations. Particularly so, as peoples who are fully integrated into the NWO increasingly realize (as the rise of neo-nationalism shows) that they are in a state of occupation, in relation to the Transnational Elite that controls it. This is, an 'occupation', however, which is not simply military as in the past, but multidimensional, in tandem with the dimensions of globalization as economic, political, ideological and cultural. We may therefore describe the following forms of 'occupation' today:

- *Economic occupation*, in the sense that, all countries integrated into the NWO had to implement policies dictated by the economic elites which are mainly based in the G7 countries — from where the main Transnational Corporations (TNCs) originate. It is these economic elites that imposed the '4 freedoms' (freedom of movement for goods and services, capital and labor) on which the entire NWO of neoliberal globalization is founded. Furthermore, it is the same elites that design global economic policy through the international institutions they control (WTO, IMF, European Commission, etc.);

- *Political occupation*, in the sense that local parliamentary juntas, elected through pseudo-democratic processes, have as their basic mission the faithful implementation of each directive coming from the Transnational Elites, deceiving the citizens of each country that these decisions are their own. However, it is a bad joke to assume that e.g. Tsipras' vote in the European Commission, or in the Eurogroup decision-taking process, is of equal weight to Merkel's or Hollande's vote, unless we believe the similar myths of representative 'democracy' that the vote of a worker or a small farmer is of equal weight to that of a media tycoon, or of a shipping-magnate! Clearly, for each vote to represent equal political weight there should be an equal distribution of economic power among all voters. Or, to put it in another way, as a genuine political democracy presupposes an equal distribution of political power, in the same way economic democracy is inconceivable without an equal distribution of economic power,[508] and, of course, political democracy is meaningless if not accompanied by economic democracy;

- *Ideological occupation*, in the sense that the values and ideas that define the kind of ideological hegemony prevailing in each country fully integrated into the NWO, are those associated with the ideology of globalization (ideology of individual human rights, identity politics, multicultural society etc.). This ideology is systematically used by the Transnational Elite in order to strengthen non-class social divisions (e.g. religious, cultural, ethnic, etc.)

---

[508] Takis Fotopoulos, *Towards An Inclusive Democracy*, (London/NY: Cassell/Continuum,1997/1998), chs 5- 6

with the clear aim to perpetuate its dominance ('divide and rule');

- *Cultural occupation*, in the sense that the same multinationals that control the economic, political and ideological processes, also control the cultural process, through the direct or indirect control they have on international media and the production and distribution of cultural products — which in the NWO are just commodities.

Therefore, it is exactly the state of occupation under which the vast majority of the global population lives in the era of globalization, which creates the need for new tools in the struggle for liberation and self-determination. Particularly so as, historically, peoples fighting for their liberation against occupation (colonialist or military) have always faced a serious dilemma: should they fight first for their national liberation and then for social liberation, or, alternatively, for a simultaneous national as well as social liberation? The former implies that national liberation is a precondition for social liberation whereas the latter implies the opposite.

A social struggle for national and social liberation to fight the NWO occupation

Resistance movements against military occupation during the Second World War faced the same crucial dilemma of whether to fight first for national liberation and then for social liberation. The answer given by every important such movement in Europe was that national liberation is a precondition for social liberation. This was dictated by the crucial need to unite everybody opposing the occupation (apart, of course, from the social groups collaborating with the occupiers) against an all-powerful enemy. Therefore, the Popular Front for National Liberation was the usual political subject, which was playing the role of the avant-garde in this struggle. It was clearly understood at the time by most in the Marxist Left that the issue of the desired systemic change would divide not only bourgeois from proletarians but also the working class itself, given its highly uneven levels of consciousness, the significance of nationalism etc. In sum, the necessary, though not the sufficient, condition for social liberation was considered to be national liberation, whereas a socialist revolution was considered to be utterly utopian under conditions of occupation , when, inevitably, the social struggle was much more difficult both subjectively and objectively.

Citizens who wanted to fight the military occupation at the time were joining en masse popular resistance fronts all over Europe, with the aim to get rid, first, of the occupying powers, in the form of the Nazi and fascist armies. Then, once liberated from occupation, they dealt with the broader aim to achieve social liberation in terms of the desired systemic change. No wonder that it was only some extreme Trotskyite currents, and similar pseudo-libertarian ones, which, completely alienated from popular feelings, were urging the proletarians of the opposing armies to unite in a class war and fight together the capitalist elites, which were supposedly behind both the opposing armies — something which in effect implied that people should not resist the occupation until a socialist revolution occurred! No wonder some shrewd occupiers in the past and some 'left' Zionists today in Palestine have implicitly promoted similar 'progressive' ideas, which of course are very useful in perpetuating their domination over the occupied peoples.

Yet, under military occupation, it was much easier than today for peoples to decide what the answer to the above mentioned dilemma should be. The enemy, in the form of a foreign occupying military power, was obvious to everybody, irrespective of one's aspirations for a future ideal society. But, this is exactly the missing element today. People do not find it easy today to understand who their real enemy is. In fact, many find it difficult even to grasp the very idea that they live under occupation in the first place! In other words, today, national and social liberation are much more interconnected than in the past, as globalization implicitly interlocks the issue of social liberation to the issue of national liberation.

However, the very fact that social liberation is much more interconnected today to national liberation than in the past makes the struggle for social liberation not easier but, in fact, even more difficult than in the past. This is because, in the past, military occupation was visible and therefore it was much easier for everybody who was not collaborating with the occupiers (usually a very small minority) to realize that the issue of social liberation had to wait for national liberation. Today, not only is the occupation an invisible one, as only those with a high level of consciousness can grasp this crucial fact, but also significant parts of the population are in favor of the occupation, as they benefit from globalization.

It is therefore clear that the social struggle today cannot just take the form of national liberation, given that the two kinds of liberation are closely interlinked. But, by the same token, the social struggle cannot just take the form of social liberation either, i.e. the form of a popular front for social liberation, which explicitly raises the issue of the desired socio-economic system. Clearly, following the collapse of actually existing socialism (which, as I mentioned above, has been one of the two main factors leading to the rise of the NWO), any popular front aiming simply to revive the socialist project, or any anti-capitalist project for that matter, is doomed today. Not of course because the 'objective' conditions are not ripe today for an anti-capitalist revolution. In fact, the opposite is true, given the unprecedented degree of inequality characterizing all countries integrated into the NWO. However, the 'subjective' conditions are perhaps worse than ever, for a variety of reasons beyond the scope of this book. If therefore, in the past, anti-capitalist activists were the avant-garde of revolution, today, it is the usual activists of the various 'anti-capitalist' occupation movements that are supposed to play this role. However, such activists, without any concrete program for a new world and no transitional strategy are, at best, irrelevant naïve leftists.

The shift of strategy required for the building of a democratic world order

The need for a social struggle aiming at national as well as social liberation, with national liberation being the precondition for social liberation, requires a basic shift of strategy, particularly as regards anti-systemic movements aiming at social change "from below". In other words, the old radical approaches, such as the "limits to growth" and the corresponding ecological approaches, including the social ecology and the de-growth approaches, (even Inclusive Democracy (ID) itself), have become irrelevant today. Not of course in terms of the ideal society each envisages but in terms of their transitional strategies which have become irrelevant, if not disorienting, in the NWO.

In fact, their transitional strategies, which are based at the local level, have become incompatible with present reality. Therefore, to continue fighting along these lines today, instead of joining an anti-globalization Front for National and Social Liberation is, in effect, taking the wrong side on the developing class struggle today. As in any class struggle in history, there are two main camps in this struggle: those benefiting directly or indirectly from the status quo (today, the NWO of neoliberal globalization) and those who are its victims., who are the vast majority of the population. But, while the beneficiaries of globalization are united to fight for their interests, the victims of globalization are at the moment completely disunited and many of them, inadvertently, support the parties of globalists in the Left' or the Right. Those therefore in the Left (including the Greens etc.) who, instead of fighting against globalization, devote all their energies on irrelevant struggles at the local level (with the indirect support of the Transnational Elite, as this sort of struggle creates the perfect diversion from the real class struggle), objectively — and sometime even deliberately — function as the organs of the Transnational Elites. It is exactly this huge political gap that the Popular Fronts are called to fill today, if humanity can ever hope to overthrow the present criminal NWO, which speedily moves towards a global governance. That is, the most authoritarian kind of regime, disguised as 'democracy', that the world has ever known.

The Inclusive Democracy (ID) strategy, for instance, was based on the aim of building an Inclusive Democracy from the bottom up, not only because of ecological considerations but, also, because of fundamental democratic exigencies. Direct democracy presupposes small scale *demoi*, so that face-to-face assemblies (the cornerstone of direct democracy) are feasible, although, of course, these demoi could be confederated, so that national identities and cultures are supported. But, radical decentralization within the institutional framework of the internationalized market economy — whether such decentralization is realized through local IDs in action, eco-villages, or urban villages, the 'Simpler Way' and so on — is impossible today. Thus, even if a truly democratic World Order based on Inclusive Democracies (IDs), (i.e. societies characterized by the equal distribution of political and economic power among their citizens), was perhaps still feasible at the beginning of the millennium, this is certainly no longer the case. This is so because no significant degree of self-reliance is still possible today for any country or nation-state integrated into the NWO.

But there is an additional important reason why the strategy I was suggesting in the 90s in order to move to a new world democratic order is not possible anymore. This strategy involved the building of a massive programmatic political movement, with an unashamedly universalist goal to change society along genuine democratic lines, i.e. a movement that should explicitly aim at an institutional change as well as a change in our value systems, i.e. a systemic change. In other words, this strategy implied the gradual involvement of increasing numbers of people in a new kind of politics and the parallel shifting of economic resources (labor, capital, land) away from the market economy. As I wrote then:

> the aim of such a strategy should be to create changes in the institutional framework, as well as to value systems, which, after a period of tension between the new institutions and the state, would, at some stage, replace the market economy, representative 'democracy', and the social paradigm 'justifying' them, with an inclusive democracy and a new democratic paradigm respectively.[509]

Furthermore, as I also stressed at the time, the rationale behind this strategy was that, as systemic change required a rupture with the past which extended to both the institutional and the cultural levels, such a rupture was only possible through the development of a new political organization and a new comprehensive political program for systemic change, which would create a clear anti-systemic consciousness on a massive scale — rather than at the level of *avant-garde*, (as in the case of state socialists), or at the commune level as in the case of libertarian greens etc.

That implied, in turn, that the creation of a new culture — which had to become hegemonic before an Inclusive Democracy could be launched — was only possible through the parallel building of new political and economic institutions at a significant social scale. As I proposed elsewhere, *"it is only through action to build the new institutions that a mass political movement with a democratic consciousness can be built."*[510] This was the reason why I proposed that the objective of an ID strategy should be the creation, from below,

---

[509] Takis Fotopoulos, "*Globalisation, the reformist Left and the Anti-Globalisation "Movement"* op.cit.

[510] Takis Fotopoulos, "The transition to an Inclusive Democracy" (The Barcelona Talks), *The International Journal of INCLUSIVE DEMOCRACY*, Vol. 6, No. 2/3 (Spring/Summer 2010)

of 'popular bases of political and economic power', that is, the establishment of local Inclusive Democracies, which, at a later stage, would confederate in order to create the conditions for the establishment of a new confederal Inclusive Democracy. Yet, this condition, i.e. the establishment of local IDs, is also non-feasible in the NWO, with the huge concentration of political and economic power it implies.

In fact, a crucial element of the ID strategy was that the political and economic institutions of Inclusive Democracy should begin to be established immediately after a significant number of people in a particular area have formed a base for 'democracy in action' — preferably, but not exclusively — at the massive social scale that is secured by winning in local elections under an ID program. Such a strategy, as Murray Bookchin also stressed with regards to his social ecology approach,[511] had nothing to do with a 'power-seeking approach', as some 'libertarians' accused it, for reasons I will explain next.

But, first, I would like to clarify an important point concerning the relationship of social ecology to the Inclusive Democracy (ID) approach, as some confusion has (deliberately) been created about it lately. It is of course well known that there are certain similarities between the social ecology and ID approaches, as there are also similarities between most, if not all, Left projects aiming at radical social change: from the Marxist 'communist stage' to left libertarianism and from the latter to green anarchism and so on. Such similarities were therefore bound to be evident in a liberatory project such as Inclusive Democracy, which explicitly aimed to achieve a synthesis of radical libertarian traditions. However, there are also fundamental, (in fact, defining) differences between social ecology and Inclusive Democracy, at both the philosophical and economic levels, which have been established long ago.[512] Bookchin himself rightly perceived that his "basic theoretical disagreements" with me were irreconcilable and consequently felt the need to dissociate himself

---

[511] Murray Bookchin, *Remaking society* (Black Rose, 1990), pp.179-85
[512] see e.g. Takis Fotopoulos, "Addendum: The ID project and Social Ecology", *The International Journal of INCLUSIVE DEMOCRACY*, Vol. 1, No. 3 (May 2005) http://www.inclusivedemocracy.org/journal/vol1/vol1_no3_addendum.htm

from the journal, of which I was the editor at the time,[513] but it seems his companion Janet Biehl (who also signed his resignation letter!) never managed to grasp these differences![514]

However, after this brief, but necessary, digression let us return to the reasons why neither a social ecology approach nor the ID approach have anything to do with a "power-seeking approach". Clearly, for a power-seeking approach to have any meaning at all, it should aim at taking over central power. However, taking over a local authority is far from a serious way of taking over central power, even if we talk about the local authority of a capital city! Particularly so today, in the NWO, when local authorities have been deprived of any important functions, either because they have been taken over by the market (through subcontracting of public services etc.), or by the state itself. In fact, one of the first jobs of Thatcher, for instance, as soon as her neoliberal government took over, was to re-centralize some of the functions of local authorities, so that subcontracting to private businesses could become easier. Therefore, as I stressed in the past, contesting local elections simply provides the most effective means to massively publicize a program for an inclusive democracy, *as well as the*

---

[513] See «Advisory Board Resignation Letter» by M. Bookchin & Janet Biehl', *Democracy & Nature* Vol. 3, No. 3 (Issue 9), 1997 pp. 198-202 http://www.democracynature.org/vol3/vol3_no3_1997.htm and "Editorial Response"pp. 203-211 http://www.democracynature.org/vol3/editorial_response.htm

[514] This is the only rational explanation one can give to her recent dishonest and unprovoked personal attack against me (see Janet Biehl, *The ecology of catastrophe: the life of Murray Bookchin*, Oxford University Press, 2015, p.291) in which she accused me that I had 'borrowed' some of his ideas! In fact, Biehl's behavior is not surprising after all, as, following the death of Bookchin (who never attacked me personally), she revealed that "[she] reverted to her pre-1987 political identity, which was what leftists call a social democrat"! (see "Janet Biehl breaks with Social Ecology Institute for Social Ecology", 14/4/2011) http://social-ecology.org/wp/2011/04/biehl-breaks-with-social-ecology/. Given that social democracy is anathema to any libertarian and Bookchin had (rightly) attacked even the self-declared "anarchist" Chomsky for his deviation towards social democracy, one would safely assume that he would surely turn in his grave on hearing this news about his ex-companion (although she tried to ameliorate the impact of her statement by alleging that she told Bookchin about her reversion before his death — without producing, however, a shred of evidence to support her allegation!) Yet, although Biehl seemingly never believed Bookchin's libertarian project, she nevertheless used it extensively in the past, presumably for social recognition, as she was of course completely unknown before she met him.

opportunity to initiate its immediate implementation on a significant social scale.

However, it is now more than obvious that the radical changes, which characterize the political and economic structures of a country integrated into the NWO, make such a strategy non-feasible. In other words, 'economic localism', i.e. the change in production relations, through the creation of self-reliant communities, is non-feasible in an integrated country where the transnational corporations and their subsidiaries are spread into every community. But, if economic self-reliance is impossible today even at the national level, unless national and economic sovereignty has been restored first, one could imagine how feasible such self-reliance is at the local level (unless one talks about a Robinson Crusoe kind of self-reliance!)

The Mondragon case perfectly illustrates the above argument. Before globalization flourished in Spain in the mid-1980s, the Mondragon co-ops were an example of political and economic democracy, as well as of self-management 'from below'. However, the Mondragon co-op group was based on a sovereign nation-state (Spain) and on the strong support of its local base (Basque area), as the co-op group itself was founded on self-reliance principles caring mainly for the production and consumption needs, principally, of the Basques and, also, of the people of Spain at large. Yet, once Spain joined the EU in 1986 and the Eurozone, at the end of the 1990s, and therefore became fully integrated into the NWO, none of the fundamental preconditions for local democracy were valid anymore (i.e. national/ economic sovereignty and self-reliance). So, although the Mondragon co-op group survived, it did so only by transforming itself into a Mondragon Corporation, that is a mini-transnational corporation working strictly within the rules imposed by the NWO in general and the EU in particular, so that it could survive competition. In other words, the organization and functioning of today's Mondragon Corporation is as close to political/economic democracy and self-management as are the parliamentary juntas of the NWO to parliamentary democracy!

The inescapable conclusion is that the aforementioned structural changes of countries integrated into the NWO, signal the need for a fundamental shift in the strategies aiming to radical social change. This is because, today, even the minimal degree of national and economic self-determination needed for the creation of 'popular bases of political and economic power' is missing, either at the local, or the national level. It is therefore obvious that the social struggle in the globalization era, as I will try to show next, has to be primarily about the re-creation of this minimal degree of national and economic self-determination, (i.e. conquering national and economic sovereignty) as a precondition for any radical social change (a systemic one).

In conclusion, in the era of globalization, it does not make sense anymore to talk about a radical social change that will come about from the local or the community level. The present complete and unprecedented control of economic, political, and cultural life by the Transnational Elite makes the building of such institutions completely non-feasible today and has decisively shifted the social struggle terrain from the local to the national level, and from it to the international one, with economic and national sovereignty becoming a precondition for any kind of systemic change, in the form of an ID, an ecological society, a socialist society, etc.

In fact, the Transnational Elite and the local elites today, exploit the need that people at the local level have to self-organize in order to help the most destitute victims of globalization. The elites' aim is to turn such people away from fighting the real cause of destitution.. Thus, they encourage — even through legislation — various kinds of 'social economy' projects, while propagating at the same time the ideology of globalization. Such projects flourish, particularly in the EU area, as it is its institutionalized policy to fund and help such projects in every way possible, so that people do not turn against the EU itself and its policies aiming at the gradual demolition of the welfare state and the squeezing of wages and pensions, as a result of austerity policies. This way, entire armies of NGOs volunteers find also employment for themselves (sometimes paid employment), or at least a meaning to their lives — exactly as the Salvation Army and similar religious organizations (not in fashion anymore in the globalization era) used to do in the past.

Chapter 11.

National and Social Liberation Fronts Everywhere

Why a front for national and social liberation? (FNSL)

In the era of neoliberal globalization the social struggle can no longer be just a struggle for social liberation, as obsolete Marxists still believe today and some Trotskyites have always believed. This becomes obvious when one considers the fact that, as soon as a state (which is not belonging to the Transnational Elite — mainly the 'G7') is fully integrated into the NWO of neoliberal globalization, it loses most, if not all, traces of economic and, consequently, national sovereignty, either because it has to obey the EU rules (in Europe), or because it has to follow the corresponding WTO and IMF rules (in the rest of the world), as well as the orders given by capitalist lenders, bankers, the TNC's executives and the likes. On the other hand, in case a state has no objection to be integrated into the economic institutions of the NWO but wishes, at the same time, to keep some degree of economic and national sovereignty, it will be treated as a pariah (e.g. Russia and China). Finally, states which try to keep their national and economic sovereignty outside the NWO (such as North Korea and Syria) are declared rogue states by the Transnational Elite and could well have the fate of similar countries which were declared rogue states in the past, such as Iraq and Libya.

Clearly, therefore, any real struggle for social liberation today is impossible unless it has already gone through national liberation. The occupying troops that are now destroying and 'plundering' countries such as Greece, Portugal, Spain, Argentina etc., as well as the weakest social strata in all countries, (with the full cooperation of local privileged elites, which control the media, the political parties, the 'Left' intelligentsia etc.), are not a regular army in uniform with lethal weapons of physical violence at their disposal. The occupying army today is an economic army in suits, possessing equally lethal instruments of economic violence, as well as the means to justify it (mass media and social media, NGOs etc.)

So, at this crucial historical juncture that will determine whether we shall all become subservient to the NWO of neoliberal globalization and the transnational elite that runs it, or not, it is imperative that Popular Fronts are created in every country integrated into the NWO. Such Fronts should include all the victims of globalization among the popular strata, regardless of their current political affiliations. In other words, under conditions of effective occupation, as many describe the present situation, the creation of Popular Fronts of National and Social Liberation (FNSL) in every country is the only way to regain a minimum level of self-determination, through recovering our economic and national sovereignty, on the way to complete social liberation.

In Europe, in particular, where the popular strata which constitute the victims of globalization are facing economic disaster, what is urgently needed is not an 'antifascist' Front within the EU, as proposed by the 'parliamentary juntas' in power and the Euro-elites. This is a policy, which is also supported by the globalist 'Left', that is, by such movements as Diem25, Plan B and Die Linke in Europe, the Socialist Workers' Party in the UK, SYRIZA in Greece, or, correspondingly, the movement around Znet in US, and so on. Such 'antifascist' movements would, in effect, unite the victims of globalization with its beneficiaries and simply disorient the masses and make them incapable of facing the real fascism being imposed on them by the political and economic elites that constitute the transnational and the local elites.

Instead, what is needed today is a Popular Front that could attract the vast majority of the people that would fight for immediate unilateral withdrawal from the EU, or, generally, from the NWO institutions, as well as for economic self-reliance, thus breaking with globalization.

In other words, it is only the creation of broad Popular Fronts that could lead the struggle for each country's exit from economic unions such as the EU, NAFTA etc., and fight for achieving economic self-reliance. Re-development based on self-reliance is the only way in which peoples, breaking away from globalization and its institutions, could rebuild their productive structures, which have been dismantled by globalization. This could also, objectively, lay the ground for future systemic change, decided upon democratically by the peoples themselves. To expect that the globalization process will itself create the objective and subjective conditions for a socialist transformation — as some 'Paleolithic Marxists' believe — or alternatively, that the creation of self-managed factories, local communes etc., within the present globalized system of the NWO will lead to a self-managed economy, as a variety of life-style 'anarchists', 'greens' and others suggest, is, in effect, to acquiesce in the completion of the globalization process, as planned by the elites. Even worse, to adopt the globalist 'Left' propaganda, according to which, even within the NWO, an institution like the EU could be converted into a 'good' EU and that, consequently, a 'good' capitalist globalization will emerge at the end (as DIEM25, SYRIZA, Podemos and the likes suggest), amounts to a pure disorientation of the peoples. This, at the end, is of course helpful in the implementation of the Transnational Elite's plan for global governance.

Therefore, the conditions of occupation we live under today mean that people resisting it have to make broad political alliances with everybody concerned who accepts the aims of a Popular Front for National and Social Liberation, and particularly the basic aim to break with the NWO. Under conditions of effective occupation, as many describe the present situation, the creation of a Popular Front for National and Social Liberation (FNSL) in each country, allowing peoples to achieve their economic and national sovereignty, is a precondition for social liberation. Then and only then, the crucial issues of the form that a future society should take, and the strategy needed to achieve it, could be raised.

The political-economic framework, within which the required measures for national liberation will be taken, should be determined democratically by the people themselves, within the framework of a strong democratic state. The general aim at this stage would be to impose adequate social controls on markets, so that society and particularly labor, as well as the environment, are protected from them.

This is only feasible (as has always been the case in the past) at the national level, at which the real sovereignty of a people is only possible. Of course, the nation could consist of a confederation of communities bound together by a common culture.

The Front could initially demand an immediate general election, in which it could participate with a program for the realization of the above general aim and the specific tasks to be described below. These aims would become feasible if the Popular Front Government, following a victory in the elections, convened a Constitutional Assembly, which would cancel all the extortionate and colonialist agreements with the EU, NATO, NAFTA etc., (loans and the various 'Memoranda' and implementation 'Laws'). Then, a real struggle for economic self-reliance could begin in earnest, through the radical restructuring of the productive base, with the aim of meeting the basic needs of all citizens, rather than meeting market demands, as prescribed by the Transnational Elite. Furthermore, citizens could then enjoy the benefits of Social Health, and Education, as well as Social Insurance (through new public organizations that they themselves would control directly) and recover the public assets and social goods, which are currently being sold out to multinational corporations and loan sharks.

Furthermore, a Popular Front Government could also create the preconditions for a democratic solution to the problem related to which socio-economic system the people would adopt for the future society, i.e. whether it would be an Inclusive Democracy, State Socialism, a libertarian society, or a radical form of Social Democracy etc. Thus, a FNSL government could create all the necessary conditions for the people to get direct experience of the various alternative forms of social organization to the present disastrous system of society, so that they could become able to take an informed decision on the form of future society they prefer. This is why it is vital that the FNSL should include members expressing all political trends, from the extreme Left up to the extreme Right, as long as they accept its main aim for national and social liberation through the recovery economic and national sovereignty first. Such a wide ranging membership will be the best guarantee that, in the struggle for social liberation that will follow national liberation, no proposals for alternative forms of society will be excluded from the rational debate on forms of social organization. This would be in place of present 'democratic dialogue' which is conditioned by the fact that present societies are founded on the concentration of all forms of power to a very small minority of the world population and 'justified' either through pure deception or brute force.

Then, at a later stage, the people could decide, through a definitive referendum, the form that a future society would take, following a thorough discussion, which, to be meaningful, presupposes a democratic control of the media (e.g. by committees representing the main options under discussion), instead of the present system of media control by the political and economic elites. The main possible options to be discussed at this stage could include the Inclusive Democracy project, as I described it elsewhere, [515] which implies *demotic* ownership and control of productive resources, so that an allocation of resources that transcends the limitations of both the market mechanism and central planning could develop. An alternative option might be a kind of a socialist planning based on social ownership of resources, or even a social democratic model — as it was originally designed rather than as it developed in the hands of social-liberal con artists pretending to be social democrats (e.g. Blair and his followers in the British Labor party).

Needless to add that the mere existence of a mass FNSL could play a very significant role in the struggle itself to bring about a liberatory society. For example, if such a Front existed in Greece at the time the economic catastrophe began in 2010, when the savage austerity measures were adopted on top of various 'structural reforms' to liberate the markets according to the prescriptions of neoliberal globalization, the fight against economic violence would have been much more effective. This is because the main weapon used by the parliamentary juntas today against any sort of resistance is to turn one section of the population against another: "consumers" against "producers" (e.g. transport users against striking transport workers, pupils against striking teachers etc.), or even one section of workers against another and so on. This way, people become unable to unite, as citizens, in a political action against the parliamentary junta itself (and indirectly against the Transnational Elite), which is ultimately responsible for the economic violence against all citizens who are the victims of globalization. Yet, there is no greater crime than to

---

[515] *Towards An Inclusive Democracy*, (London/NY, Cassell/Continuum, 1997), Chs. 5-6

condemn someone to slow death through economic violence, on the basis of 'laws' passed by a bunch of privileged professional politicians at the service of the elites, with the support of those benefiting from globalization.

In other words, a FNSL should function as a catalyst for fundamental political and economic change, which is the only kind of change that could get us out of the current mire, while also revealing the systematic deception by the globalist 'Left'. That is, the 'Left', according to which we could somehow emerge from this catastrophe, even without breaking with the NWO and its institutions, as e.g. Varoufakis et.al. preach in Europe[516] and as its latest counterpart, under the pompous title OUR REVOLUTION (sic!) similarly does in America (M. Albert, N. Chomsky et. al.).[517]

The social and political subject of the Front

a. The social subject

The social subject of a mass popular front pursuing the aims described above would consist of all the victims of neoliberal globalization. That is:

- the unemployed and the partially employed;
- wage-earners on the very edge of survival (zero-hour contracts, occasional workers etc.);
- those seeking various kinds of self-employment which, as a rule, are bound to end in failure in an environment of open and 'liberalized' markets;
- children without education who are 'punished' for being 'unlucky' enough to be born to non-'privileged' parents;
- those at the subsistence level (pensioners, the sick who lack medical insurance et. al. — amounting to one third of the population today — and others.

But it is not only the victims of economic violence exercised by the NWO — through the opening and liberalization of markets (particularly the labor markets) and of the opening of the borders — who are the victims of globalization. It is also the victims of the Transnational Elite's military violence in other countries, such as

---

[516] see DIEM 25, ch. 7
[517] see OUR REVOLUTION (Campaign created by Michael Albert)
https://diy.rootsaction.org/petitions/support-and-improve-our-revolution

Yugoslavia, Iraq, Afghanistan, Libya, Syria and possibly in the future even Russia. It is therefore this combination of military and economic violence, which has convinced the victims of globalization everywhere to turn against the NWO of neoliberal globalization.

b. The political subject: *'from below' or 'from above'?*

As far as the political subject is concerned, there are two possible options concerning the method to bring about a Front for National and Social Liberation (FNSL): a front 'from below' or a front 'from above'. The preferred, of course, option is the former, but in case this becomes unfeasible because the level of political consciousness of the victims of globalization and their will to fight is inadequate for this huge task, then the only other option is for existing political forces to take over the task of achieving sovereignty and self-reliance.

A FNSL 'from below' could be organized from among local assemblies, committees, groups and initiatives consisting of the victims of globalization (namely, the vast majority of the world's population) who ought to join as ordinary citizens, irrespective of party affiliations and ideologies or religious and other differences — as long as they share the ultimate aim of national and economic sovereignty. The intermediate target should be the exit from the international institutions of the NWO such as the EU, so that the victims of globalization could escape the present process of economic catastrophe.

However, in the event that the formation of a FNSL from below is impossible, then the only other way in which people could fight for their economic and national sovereignty is by supporting those political forces that are committed to a struggle for sovereignty, something that presupposes the exit from the international institutions set up by the NWO (EU, NAFTA and the likes). Fortunately, despite (or rather because of) the bankruptcy of the Left, which, as we saw above, has joined the globalization bandwagon — whether it belongs to the anti-systemic or the reformist parts of it — new political movements have emerged (like UKIP in Britain), or old ones have been transformed into anti-NWO movements (like the National Front in France), which could lead the way against neoliberal globalization and its institutions.

Yet, the problem with these movements is that usually they are just neo-nationalist or, at best, patriotic movements, rather than internationalist movements fighting for a new democratic community of sovereign and self-reliant nations. Although their nationalism is not of the pre-war aggressive kind and more of the new defensive neo-nationalist or patriotic kind, which developed in the globalization era aiming at national sovereignty, still, many of these parties do tend to exploit the immigration issue. Such parties sometimes cultivate even racist feelings (islamophobic instincts and the like), while at the same time they usually reject social controls on markets for the protection of labor and the environment.

Yet, as we saw in chapter 3, immigration is a byproduct of globalization and of the opening and liberalizing of markets, including the labor market. This, apart from the fact that a large part of the present mass expansion of immigration is due to the wars of the Transnational Elite against other countries in order to integrate their peoples into the NWO. Therefore, much of the problem could be sorted out just by imposing social controls on markets (including the market of labor) and allowing new immigrants in, only to the extent that the economic needs of each country require them and its people decide. Of course, immigrants who have established themselves for a minimum number of years (to be determined by each society) would be free to stay if they wished so, provided they would be paid the same wages and salaries as the indigenous population and share the same social burdens with them (taxes, social insurance etc.). Needless to add they should enjoy the same social benefits as locals, so that no pressure on local labor is created by the exploitation of cheap immigrant labor, as at present. It is well known, anyway, that the main function of immigration in the NWO is to homogenize downwards the real incomes of working people all over the world for the benefit of expanding the profits of the TNCs. It is therefore only the creation of a new democratic world community, like the one described in the next chapter, which could stop this form of modern slavery.

Even worse, some of these neo-nationalist parties, although they do understand the nature of the NWO and the aim of the struggle against it, they cannot get rid of some of the ideological paraphernalia of old nationalist parties. As a result, they are making life easy for the Transnational Elite and the globalist lackeys at its service (including the globalist 'Left'), so that they can pretend fighting a pseudo-antifascist war, in this way dividing the victims of globalization and pushing many of them to fight irrelevant a-historical struggles.

To my mind, the only way in which such harmful trends within the new anti-globalization movement can be checked is, first, by pressure 'from below' to push the anti-NWO political parties away from old nationalism and, second, by pushing them towards social objectives (free education, free health, free social care and so on). Fortunately, such moves from below have already influenced parties like the NF in France and even UKIP in Britain, which have adopted such traditional Left objectives as nationalizations that are presently taboos for 'Left' parties like SYRIZA, whose government is busy at the moment at de-nationalizing everything still not sold away to foreign 'investors'!

However, perhaps the only effective way to ensure that all those neo-nationalist/patriotic movements, when they come to power, will be forced to reject old nationalist paraphernalia and create, instead, a new democratic world community of sovereign and self-reliant nations (to replace the NWO), is the development of an economic union of sovereign and self-reliant nations, as we shall see in Ch. 11.

An intermediate socially-controlled market economy

As regards the form of economic model that an economy has to choose, once a PF government has been elected in power, there are three basic options available, depending on the method of allocation of economic resources chosen and the form of the economy selected:

a) Continuing the catastrophic process of fully integrating the economy into the NWO, within the present economic model;

b) Creating a non-market economy outside the NWO or, alternatively,

c) Transcending the present model and creating an intermediate socially-controlled market economy, which will open the way for people to decide, at a later stage, when economic and national sovereignty has been restored, the preferred sort of economic, political and social model to be adopted.

Given that the first option, as I have been trying to show in this book, has to be ruled out and that the second option, although ideal, is not feasible unless sovereignty has first been restored, it seems that the only feasible solution today is an intermediate one. Particularly so, as a struggle for a simultaneous national and social liberation is non-feasible under today's objective and subjective conditions and the lack of any mass revolutionary movements aiming at systemic change. Therefore, what is required today is an intermediate socially controlled economy, which will stop the present economic and social catastrophe of the vast majority of the world population by creating conditions of covering, at least, the basic needs at every citizen. This implies a socially controlled market economy that will provide successful welfare systems and create the conditions for all the country's resources (human and natural) to be fully utilized, mainly through domestic socially controlled enterprises.

The process to be followed in the transition from 'here', (i.e. the present catastrophic integration into the NWO), to 'there' (i.e. the stage where people can be in a position to decide the sort of economic system they would like to live in), could be described in terms of the following three stages, through which the liberation process may go, following the taking over of power by FNSL governments (either from below or from above), and the associated tasks.

Stage I: the short term tasks of a FNSL government

The immediate measures that should be taken in this process by a FNSL government should include the following:

a) The unilateral exit from the EU and the Eurozone (for a country-member of the EU/Eurozone) or from the WTO the IMF and similar institutions, as well as from NATO (for any other country), which will create the necessary conditions for economic and national sovereignty;

b) The unilateral cancellation of all Public Debt, given that as a rule, it consists of loans approved only by the elites for projects usually favoring only the beneficiaries of globalization.

c) The annulment of all treaties and laws aiming at further opening and liberalization of markets, privatizations and other 'structural reforms' imposed by the Transnational Elite;

d) The cancellation of sell-outs of social wealth by the parliamentary juntas, followed by expropriation without compensation of social wealth acquired by transnational corporations through privatizations;

e) Strict social controls on all markets for goods and services (including the markets for labor and capital), which will be allowed only under exceptional circumstances to cater for basic social needs;

f) The creation of a new 'social services sector' run by the social services workers themselves, under the guidance of society at large — through government and local authorities — and funded exclusively through a steeply progressive tax system based on national and local taxes. This sector will include Health, Education and other social services that will be provided free to all citizens;

g) The re-structuring of the wider public sector (civil service, banking, energy, transport, communication and so on) in such a way so as to secure national and economic sovereignty through the exclusion of TNCs activities in these sectors and the minimization of private business activity. The wider public sector could be run by the employees themselves under the guidance of the FNSL Government;

h) The re-structuring of trade relations either on a bilateral basis, or on a multilateral basis within a political and economic union of sovereign nations, such as the Eurasian Union, or any other similar union to be created. This will ensure trade is compatible with the self-reliance aim pursued by the FNSL Government, as well as with the aim of covering the consumer needs, as expressed individually and collectively;

i) The FNSL government will undertake to secure full employment for all, through a massive public investment program, aiming not only at infrastructure (the usual kind of public investment imposed by the Transnational Elite to facilitate imports!) but, mainly, at the socialized key sectors of the economy needed for the revival of the productive structure;

j) The FNSL government will have to secure a minimum income for all, covering at least the survival needs for food, clothing, housing etc. and a drastic redistribution of income and wealth effected by means of a highly 'progressive' system of income and wealth taxation;

k) Finally, the FNSL government will have to adopt a radical change of geopolitical relations, through the formation of an international alliance of all countries presently resisting the NWO — unless a Eurasian Union, as originally designed, (i.e. as an economic and political union of sovereign and relatively self-reliant countries, which means breaking its ties with the NWO) undertakes this task.

Stage II: Medium-term tasks

The second stage in this intermediate process involves the medium term measures that should be taken by a FNSL government aiming at re-building the production and consumption structures, given that the existing structures have effectively made impossible any self-reliance within the process of integration into the NWO. Steps in this direction could be:

- The establishment of a new mixed system of allocation of resources for this transitional stage, which will consist of a mix of planning, economic democracy and the market mechanism. In this intermediate stage the market will still be dominant, although production and distribution will be determined through the partnerships described below;

- The regeneration of the primary sector with the double aim of economic self-reliance as well as radical decentralization. Agricultural partnerships controlled by farmers, as well as by society at large through the FNSL government, could determine jointly the production targets and methods to be used for the development of a self-reliant agricultural sector;

- The creation of an industrial sector which, through direct production or trade creation, would be meeting at least the basic needs of all citizens. Workers' partnerships controlled by workers, as well as by society at large through the FNSL government, could determine jointly the production targets and methods to be used for the development of a self-reliant industrial sector;

- The new primary and secondary sectors will have as an overall aim the development of a new production structure that could lead to a new consumption pattern meeting the economic, cultural and ecological requirements of each country;

- The development of various forms of collective ownership (with respect to the means of production) and private ownership, (with respect to housing), covering the residential needs of each citizen, following the introduction of a tax system aiming at a fair system of distribution according to need, rather than according to inheritance and profit, as at present. Forms of collective ownership could range from socialized industries (e.g. in energy, communication, transport etc.) to 'demotic' enterprises in which the people running them will be the workers employed by them, under the guidance of the 'demotic' assemblies, i.e. the citizens' assemblies in the municipalities where the enterprises are based.[518]

• Media and the production/dissemination of culture should be socially controlled, i.e. by those employed in these industries in collaboration with the FNSL government.

Stage III: Long-term tasks

The second stage will prepare the ground for the transition to the third stage, at which the crucial decision on the form of the desired systemic change will be taken democratically by the citizen's assemblies. Such assemblies could federate into a Constitutional Assembly that would determine each country's constitution accordingly. In other words, it is at this stage that citizens will decide democratically the form of self-government they prefer for the future. It is hoped that by this stage, both the objective and subjective conditions for systemic change would have been created.

Thus, as far as the objective conditions are concerned, (particularly self-reliance), it is assumed that by this stage these conditions would have already been achieved, otherwise the new system would be under a constant risk of collapse.

As far as the subjective conditions are concerned, one could reasonably expect that these conditions would have fully been developed by the time a considered decision is taken on the matter, rather than one on the basis of the media's brain washing, as has been the practice in the past. In other words, the decision on the form of the future society would have to be taken by a fully informed citizenry on the form of society they want, which would be based on their own experience of the various forms of economic self-management.

---

[518] Takis Fotopoulos, *Towards An Inclusive Democracy*, (London/NY: Cassell /Continuum, 1997/1998), Ch. 6

Chapter 12.

From the NWO to a Democratic Community of Sovereign Nations

Why a Democratic Community of Sovereign Nations?

  The fundamental aim of the social struggle today, which, as we saw in the previous parts, in the globalization era, takes the form of a new class struggle,- should be a complete break with the present NWO and the building of a new global democratic community, in which economic and national sovereignty have been restored, so that peoples could then fight for the ideal society, as they see it. The conditions of occupation we live under today mean that people resisting it have to make broad political alliances with everyone concerned who accepts the aims of a Popular Front for National and Social Liberation, particularly the basic aim of breaking with the NWO. Similar broad political alliances should be formed between nations which have already achieved their economic and national sovereignty.

  Thus, in the same way in which people who wish to fight for their self-determination against the internal occupation imposed by the Transnational Elite in association with the local elites, should join a Popular Front within each country to fight them, the victims of globalization living in different parts of the world, which wish also to fight for their sovereignty and self determination, should join forces together in a democratic community in a new pole of sovereign nations to fight the unipolar NWO. This is the only way they can sort out between them, on a sovereign basis, the economic problems arising from trade and investment — instead of, as at present, on the basis of the rules imposed by the Transnational Elite through the controlled by its institutions (WTO, IMF, EU and so on). Furthermore, this is the only way these sovereign nations could create a democratic self-protection mechanism against the violence the Transnational Elite would certainly launch against them.

This is also the reply to the criticism of globalist 'Leftists' that the Popular Front strategy will likely fail, given that the TNCs, who control the world economy, could easily boycott such "rogue nations" and thus send their economies into a tail-spin. However, this non-argument, which is based on the usual 'Project Fear' about the unknown, ignores the possibility of sovereign peoples to organize on the lines suggested here to protect themselves not only against the economic violence of TNCs (which anyway would by definition be minimal against an economic union organized on the basis of self-reliance) but also against the military violence of the Transnational Elite. If this elite cannot even dare to touch a small country of determined people, such as North Korea, one could imagine what are the chances of success of attacking a political and military union of many millions, from Iran and Syria up to Latin America and Southern Europe and, highly likely, to the Eurasian Union and even China.

Clearly, therefore, the new democratic order will have to be based on very different values and principles of organization than the present order, otherwise it will not have any raison d'être and no sane person would fight for it! This will be a new international community of sovereign and self-reliant nations based on the principle of mutual aid rather than competitiveness — the guiding principle behind the present criminal NWO. Furthermore, as long as the member countries share complementary production structures, the possibility of an involuntary transfer of economic surplus from some countries (usually the weaker ones, as is the case in the EU) to other countries in the union could be ruled out. Therefore, a collective kind of self-reliance could be achieved within the economic area covered by such a union, which should be based on the sovereignty of each participating country.

So, the crucial issue today in the fight for the building of a new democratic world order is how we c a n create an alternative pole of sovereign self-reliant nations, in full knowledge that the Transnational Elite will use every kind of economic or physical violence at its disposal to abort any such effort, with all the huge means at its disposal. Then and only then, the crucial issues of the form that a future society should take, and of the strategy to achieve it, could be raised. In fact, such an alternative pole could function also as a magnet attracting the victims of globalization from all over the world. Particularly so as the peoples in the West (the so-called 'world community') never hear anything about the real significance of globalization and are spoon-fed information about it, which either distorts the truth, or is economical with the truth — let alone any information about the possibility of an alternative democratic world!

Even more so as, at the moment, there is no organized global system of alternative information against the NWO of neoliberal globalization. Thus, *Russia Today*, the only channel which could provide such information, criticizes only the geopolitical aspects of this Order and rarely — usually in a contradictory way — criticizes the even more important economic aspects of it. This simply reflects the internal contradictions within Russia, which constitutes of course the core of the Eurasian Union to which we now turn.

Can the Eurasian Union be the foundation for a real multipolar world?

The Eurasian Economic Union (EEU), which was founded by Russia in 2014 as an economic union of sovereign states, consists of the former Soviet republics Belarus, Kazakhstan, Armenia, Kyrgyzstan and Russia. The original idea, as was expressed by Putin himself, was for an economic and political union. Thus, as described by the flagship of the globalist 'Left', Putin's plan was for the EEU to grow into a "powerful, supra-national union" of sovereign states like the European Union, uniting economies, legal systems, customs services and military capabilities to form a bridge between Europe and Asia and rival the EU, the US and China."[519] Also, according to the *Financial Times*, the EEU, despite its name, is not just an economic union:

> For Russia's president Vladimir Putin, this is about much more than just the economy. While he has repeatedly rejected the idea that he wants to resurrect the Soviet Union, Mr Putin says its former member republics share a common infrastructure, regional specialisation and culture that they should use as a

---

[519] Jon Henley, "A brief primer on Vladimir Putin's Eurasian dream", *The Guardian*, 18/2/2014

resource for joint development. "We suggest a powerful supranational association capable of becoming one of the poles in the modern world and serving as an efficient bridge between Europe and the dynamic Asia-Pacific region," Mr Putin wrote in 2011.[520]

However, since then, important developments (induced, as can be shown by the Transnational Elite) reversed this process, at least for the time being. Thus, when Ukraine was ready to join the Eurasian Union — a crucial stage in the EEU development — a coup organized by the Transnational Elite led to the overthrow of the pro-Russia regime and its replacement by an EU protectorate, whose first job was to sign an association agreement with the EU! It is therefore clear that the Transnational Elite attack on Ukraine was clearly an attack against not just Russia, but principally the Eurasian Union as a whole. [521] Furthermore, it possibly implied a perfectly designed plan to subordinate Russia into the NWO, while converting the Eurasian Union into a kind of a geographical extension of the EU into the Eurasian area. This is a plan particularly favored by the German elite, which seems prepared to even accept the 'Finlandization' of Ukraine — i.e. its neutralization as far as NATO is concerned — as long as it is integrated, one way or another, into the EU.

In fact, it seems now that the Transnational Elite plan has already had a significant degree of success: the Transnational Elite's present economic war on Russia, rather than convincing the country's entire elite to back the informal Popular Front that seems united against all aspects of globalization, encompassing the broadest possible political spectrum ranging from patriots and neo-nationalists to communists and orthodox Christians, has led, instead, to the opposite! That is, the Russian leadership, instead of utilizing the golden opportunity given by the sanctions, to advance a plan to massively enhance the self-reliance of the Russian economy, within an expanded and also self-reliant Eurasian Union, it seems to have taken mainly defensive measures and always within the confines of WTO regulations. Thus, for instance, instead of expanding the controls on the markets for capital, commodities and labor, it simply took painless for the elites measures, such as import substitution.

---

[520] Kathrin Hille, "Russia: Dangers of isolation", *Financial Times,* 8/1/2015
[521] See *Ukraine: The Attack on Russia and the Eurasian Union (vol 2 of the NWO in Action)*

This had a direct effect on the Eurasian Union itself. The economic war against Russia that was launched at the same time by the Transnational Elite and involved strict sanctions and, even more important, the mass decline in the price of oil, led to a serious economic recession in Russia and frictions within the EEU itself, which was modeled at the end on the EU.

But, to understand these developments, one has to refer to the basic division within the Russian elite, with part of it (the 'nationalists/patriots') aiming at creating a Eurasian Union of sovereign nations, inevitably leading Russia outside the NWO, and another part (the 'globalists' or "liberals" as they are called in Russia) aiming at full integration into the NWO as an equal member of the TE — something the latter could never allow for economic, geopolitical and cultural reasons. The globalists include all those who do not question globalization and the economic significance of the NWO. At the moment, the globalists seem to be in control not only of the economic elite (in terms of its oligarchs, as one could well expect) but also of a significant part of the Russian political, academic and media elites. On the other hand, Putin seems to be attempting to accommodate both factions of the Russian elite under a 'united Russia' tent — as it is also the name of the governing party in Russia — although he was heavily involved later in the creation of the movement with the symbolic name "All-Russia People's Front (ONF)", of which he was elected as its leader in its inaugural congress in June 2013.[522]

So, at present, the chosen development path by the elites in Russia (or of China, for that matter) would never allow the country to develop a strong productive base geared to the needs of the Russian people. But, this is exactly why, historically, the present advanced capitalist countries in the Transnational Elite never opened their markets to competition until after they had fully developed their productive bases.

Others in the globalist Left at large, on the basis of the flawed argument of the existence of fundamental divisions between US and EU — particularly Germany — end up by fully supporting the idea of a "common European Space," which would include both EU and EEU (the Eurasian Union) as an alternative pole to the American empire. This approach, objectively, expresses the interests of the Transnational

---

[522] Steve Rosenberg, Putin inaugurates new movement amid fresh protests, *BBC News*, 12/6/2013 <http://www.bbc.co.uk/news/world-europe-22879644>

Elite, as well as of the globalist part of the Russian elite, in integrating the Eurasian Union in general and Russia in particular into the NWO. Needless to point out the tremendous opportunities that such a 'common space' (i.e. a free trade area) would offer to western TNCs in expanding their activities into the vast Eurasian space and at the same time in frustrating any hopes for the Eurasian Union to develop as a political and economic union of sovereign nations, that is as a real alternative pole to the NWO. Thus, Mahdi Darius Nazemroaya, assuming an imaginary conflict between the US 'empire', (which is assumed to be aiming to integrate, through the Transatlantic Pact, the rest of the world under its domination) and the EU, and completely ignoring the NWO of neoliberal globalization, in effect sides with the Transnational Elite, and the globalist part of the Russian elite in stressing that "Russia and the EEU want to ultimately establish a free trade zone encompassing the entire EU and EEU — a Common Economic Space."[523] Of course, such a development would inevitably imply the loss of Russia's economic and national sovereignty and the creation of a new level of transnational sovereignty, controlled, at the economic level, by the TNCs, which are more competitive and financially more powerful than the corresponding Russian companies.

But, even worse is the fact that this view, which expresses the globalist part of the Russian elite, seems now to be adopted also by the Russian Foreign Ministry, as well as by Russian media, such as RT, which seem also to be mostly controlled by the same elite. This became obvious recently when Vladimir Chizhov, Russia's EU ambassador, at the very moment when the EEU was being formally launched, described the Eurasian Union as a better partner for the EU than the US, stressing that the EEU "is designed to serve as an effective link between Europe and the Asia-Pacific region" and adding:

> Our idea is to start official contacts between the EU and the EEU as soon as possible. [German] chancellor Angela Merkel talked about this not long ago. The EU sanctions [on Russia] are not a hinder. I think that common sense advises us to explore the possibility of establishing a common economic space in the Eurasian region, including the focus countries of

---

[523] Mahdi Darius Nazemroaya, Berlin and Paris look East: How close are we to a Common Economic Space?, RT, 2/3/2015 http://rt.com/op-edge/236741-west-east-eurasian-union-cooperation/

the Eastern Partnership [an EU policy on closer ties with Armenia, Azerbaijan, Belarus, Georgia, Moldova, and Ukraine].We might think of a free trade zone encompassing all of the interested parties in Eurasia.[524]

Strangely enough a similar view was supported recently by Alexander Dugin, one of the principal proponents of the Eurasianist ideology. Clearly Dugin, on the basis of an exclusively geopolitical approach to the present world order, which is completely uninformed about the NWO of neoliberal globalization,[525] ends up with a supposed conflict between the 'baddies' (i.e. Anglosaxon hegemonism) and the 'goodies' ('Europe'). This way he indirectly endorses the elites of the EU, as something separate from the Transnational Elite, which supposedly functions as an alternative global pole. In other words, he effectively sides with the fifth column in the Russian elite, the globalist part of it:

> [A]fter Brexit, Europe got the chance to somewhat deviate from America's suffocating control and, as always, the two pillars of continental Europe, real Europe, remain France and Germany, who are least of all controlled by Anglo-Saxon domination... the only chance for salvation is to immediately abandon the US and NATO at breakneck speed.[526]

No need to stress that such a view significantly undermines the plan for an alternative bipolar world in which the second pole would be centered on the Eurasian Union, (i.e. a political and economic union of sovereign nations). This is because sovereignty, as we saw in Ch. 4, can only be based on self-reliance, which makes possible the imposition of social controls on markets particularly on capital and commodity markets — something that is by definition ruled out within a free trade area zone within the NWO.

However, the EEU, even in its present form of a purely economic union, has two fundamental differences clearly differentiating it from the EU. First, the EU, as we saw in previous parts, consists of pseudo-

---

[524] A. Rettman, "Russia calls for EU talks with newly born Eurasian Union", *EU Observer*, 2/1/2015

[525] see e.g. Alexander Dugin, "Europe vs. the West", Katehon/ *Dugin's Guideline*, 2/8/2016

[526] Alexander Dugin, "Europe: War Mechanism Launched", Katehon/ *Dugin's Guideline*, 1/8/2016 http://katehon.com/directives/europe-war-mechanism-launched*

sovereign states, as their economic policies, (even their currency as regards members of the Eurozone), are determined by the EU economic organs, i.e. the Euro-elites and the TNCs behind them. In fact, lately even their foreign policies are determined by the same elites, as the examples of sanctions against Russia on account of Ukraine and the EU policies on Syria showed.

Second, the EU consists of highly unequal states as regards the level of their economic development leading to the constant transfer of economic surplus from the European South to its North, as we saw with reference to Greece. On the other hand, the EEU consists of countries at equal level of development, which are therefore complementary in economic terms. As the Armenian Prime Minister put it, "Russia, Belarus and Kazakhstan are now at about the same level of development, and no country is going to live at the expense of another."[527]

Yet, for the Eurasian Union to develop and flourish in the future, breaking its links with the NWO is the necessary condition for the creation of a new democratic community of sovereign nations. In that case, countries such as Greece, as well as Latin America countries, Iran and other countries in the Arab world and Asia could join it, creating another pole and leading the struggle for the emergence of a real bipolar world, which is in fact the only way the present NWO could be challenged. That is, through an economic and political union in which countries maintain their national sovereignty and their economic sovereignty, as well as their political and cultural identity. This way, countries could also have different principles to base their co-operation, instead of being involved in a cutthroat competition, as is the fundamental principle imposed by the NWO. In this sense, the present EEU can be the foundation for a future political and economic union of sovereign nations, as originally planned. But, this presupposes a break with the NWO of neoliberal globalization and its institutions (WTO, IMF, NATO and so on). In that case, the Eurasian Union could perfectly function as an alternative pole to the present unipolar world, as is shown by the fact that all forms of transnational power today, as we saw above, are mainly controlled by the Transnational Elite. Alternatively, if the globalist part of the Russian

---

[527] Maria Snytkova, "USSR to rise from ashes through joint Eurasian currency", *Pravda.ru*, 19/11/2012 http://www.pravdareport.com/business/finance/19-11-2012/122851-joint_eurasian_currency-0/

elite prevails in its struggle with the anti-globalist patriotic front, then the Eurasian Union may well develop into another part of the NWO — as has always been the aim of the EU elite and particularly the German elite within it.

In other words, self-reliance is impossible within the World Trade Organization framework and the limited degree of import substitution allowed by its rules, whereas it could be feasible within an economic and political union. This, provided of course that the EEU does not evolve into something like a free trade zone, i.e. an extension of the NWO in the Eurasian area, (as Russian globalists, and the Transnational Elite itself wish), but, instead, evolves into a political and economic union of sovereign nations based on self-reliance (as Russian patriots and neo-nationalists demand).

It is therefore clear that unless Russia returns to the policies of economic self-reliance of the Soviet era and cuts all ties with neoliberal globalization and its institutions (e.g. WTO), proceeding full speed ahead with the Eurasian Union, as originally designed — i.e. as an economic and political union of sovereign states, at about the same level of development — it is doomed to become a subordinate member of the Transnational Elite. Therefore, the argument of Russian 'globalists' in favor of further expanding trade and investment relations with the West, within the framework of neoliberal globalization and free/'liberalized' markets, far from leading to a new multi-polar world, would simply further enhance the present concentration of economic and political power at the hands of the Transnational Elite and Russia's subordination to it.

In fact, it is this potential of the Eurasian Union to play a really alternative role to the present NWO that could also explain, at least partly, why Russia under Putin has been targeted by the entire Transnational Elite. It should also be added that another important side effect of creating an alternative pole of sovereign nations is that this may perhaps be the only effective way to ensure that all those neo-nationalist/patriotic movements in Europe, when they come to power, they would be forced to reject old nationalist paraphernalia and create, instead, a new democratic world community of sovereign and self-reliant nations (to replace the NWO). Joining such a political and economic union would commit members to a program of short, medium and long term measures, like the ones described in Ch.10, which directly or indirectly rule out old nationalism.

If, on the other hand, such a political and economic union does not finally materialize and the Eurasian Union, which is supposed to develop in this direction, eventually becomes simply an extension of the present NWO (as will be the case if Russia finally succumbs to the Transnational Elite and does not break with the NWO), then, the only way out will be an intensification of the pressure 'from below' to force governments to create/join such a union.

In this sense, the completion of a Eurasian Union, would be an event of a tremendous global significance for the development of a new democratic global community of sovereign nations to replace the present criminal NWO of neoliberal globalization, which has already destroyed the lives of billions of people all over the world. Particularly so if the Eurasian Union could expand to cover, in addition, all those peoples in the world who presently fight against the Transnational Elite for their sovereignty and self-determination, either in the Arab World (Syria and Iran, as well as those who were forcibly integrated into the NWO like Iraq and Libya), or in Latin America (Cuba, Venezuela, Bolivia, Brazil and others) and in the rest of the world.

To sum it up, for the EEU to develop, as originally conceived, into an economic union of sovereign nation-states in which nations could secure self-reliance within the Union as a whole and would have the ability to impose whatever social controls on markets they decided there is a basic condition that has to be met: the Eurasian Union should not just be an extension of the present NWO into the Eurasian space, as the Transnational Elite itself (particularly the German elite) wish, and, of course, as the 'liberal globalists' within the Russian elite — the 'fifth column', as Putin called it in his Crimea speech — also want. There is no doubt that the aim of all these elites is simply to expand the geographical area of activity of TNCs even further, into the vast Eurasian space, which is not yet fully integrated into the NWO. The way therefore in which the Eurasian Union will develop is of crucial significance with respect to the emergence of a new democratic world order.

At the moment of writing, it seems the issue of whether the Russian leadership will proceed along this road, or whether instead it will continue the present policy, is open. Thus, a significant ray of hope with respect to Russia's breaking with the NWO may be emerging with the possibility of the 'nationalization' of the ruble, which will be a very important step towards Russian self-reliance. As is well-known, since the time of Yeltsin's selling-out of Russia to the NWO in 1990, money creation in Russia was removed from state sovereignty and was tied to the US dollar. Now, the Stolypin club report effectively advises the nationalization of the ruble, so that the amount of printed rubles will not be determined anymore by how many dollar reserves the country has but by the actual needs of the economy.[528] Clearly, if Putin's acceptance of this advice is confirmed, this will be the first important step towards Russian self-reliance and break from the NWO — although his interview to Bloomberg a few days later, seemed to cast doubt on such hopes:

> Russia made the decision "for the long haul" to allow the ruble to trade freely, according to the president. The same applies to upholding the principle of allowing unrestricted flows of money across borders. Putin said he opted against reintroducing capital controls despite proposals made in 2015 and the year before that.[529]

It seems therefore that the policy aiming to materialize the impossible dream of the globalist part of the Russian elite, for Russia to become an equal member of the Transnational Elite, still is predominant. Thus, at the very moment the Russian attempt to sort out the Syrian 'problem' through negotiations with the Americans was obviously deadlocked by the Transnational Elite, which directly or indirectly threatened Russia with war if it does not accept their terms, Vladimir Chizhov, now in its capacity as the Russian envoy to the European Union, was welcoming the French proposal, recently voiced by French ambassador to Russia Jean-Maurice Ripert, to start work on a common economic bloc "from Lisbon to Vladivostok"! As Chizhov put it:

> [I]n the long term the project could encompass not only the EU and Russia, but the EU and the Eurasian Economic Union – the bloc that also includes Belarus, Armenia, Kazakhstan and Kyrgyzstan. It will be the binding of all integration processes

---

[528] The Daily Bell, "Dollar Disaster Looms? China and Russian Currencies Break Away", *Global Research*, 20/8/2016 http://www.globalresearch.ca/dollar-disaster-looms-china-and-russian-currencies-break-away/5541849

[529] Ksenia Galouchko, "Putin Says Russia's Self-Sufficiency Lets It Skip Bond Dash", Bloomberg, 2/9/2016 http://www.bloomberg.com/news/articles/2016-09-02/putin-says-russia-s-self-sufficiency-lets-it-sit-out-bond-dash

and structures that had been created lately that can give our European continent, or, we can also call it the Eurasian continent, the confidence in the changing multi-polar world.[530]

To my mind, as the Transnational Elite will never accept equality of Russia with the other members of the Transnational Elite and particularly the USA there is no way for a peaceful expansion of the NWO into the Eurasian space. This means an indefinite continuation of the present conflict situation with Russia, which gives hope that the Putin leadership will eventually take the decisive step to break with the NWO and build a real alternative pole to the present unipolar world.

The transition from the NWO to the democratic community of sovereign nations

It is clear therefore that the crucial issue today, in the fight for the building of a new democratic world order, is how we create this alternative pole of sovereign self-reliant nations, in full knowledge that the Transnational Elite and those benefiting from globalization will fight tooth and nail not to lose their privileges. But, assuming that such an alternative pole is finally created, preferably through the transformation of the present EEU into a full political and economic community of sovereign nations, the next question is what will follow such a dramatic development when the NWO will be challenged directly and its plan for global governance will be in ruins.

The pessimistic scenario is that the Transnational Elite will launch a war to overthrow the Russian regime, if efforts to overthrow it 'from inside' fail. However, such a war will not be possible even to be launched in case the victims of globalization at large have realized that this would be a war not against the 'dictator' Putin et al but against themselves. In that case the criminals of the Transnational Elite would know that a new popular Nuremberg will wait to judge them for their crimes against humanity. So, in case such a war is not launched, one can expect that once an alternative pole for a new democratic world order has been created, there will be a transitional period between the present uni-polar world order (which is disguised as a pseudo multi-polar world), and a future new Democratic World Order based on self-reliant and sovereign nations that is obviously incompatible with it. It

---

[530] "Europe & Russia will eventually have common economic space "– envoy, RT, 23/9/2016 https://www.rt.com/politics/360372-europe-and-russia-sanctions-envoy/

seems therefore that the most likely scenario for the transitional period involves a bi-polar world, in which the present NWO will co-exist in tension with the emerging real multi-polar world of self-reliant and sovereign nations.

The new Democratic World Community of Sovereign Nations should also take the opportunity to set the foundations to transcend the historical systems of control over the means of production and distribution. That is, the private vs. the state control of the means of production and distribution. In fact, the crucial historical issue today is how the conditions can be created for the control of the means of production to be exercised directly by society, through the citizens' assemblies, which will determine the economic and political processes.

This is particularly urgent today when it is fully realized that the collapse of the Cold war bipolar world, instead of leading to the creation of a mass movement in the same direction, had led to exactly the opposite: the creation of the present criminal uni-polar world and the parallel development of a globalist 'Left' that, directly or indirectly, (or, at least, 'objectively'), supports it.

Thus, part of the globalist Left adopts the usual mantra, according to which effective change from within the system is still possible. This, despite the fact that social democracy, historically, has proved to be a total failure in stopping the reversal of all major social conquests of the last century concerning the right to full employment, working conditions, the rights to strike and demonstrate, let alone the right to a 'social wage' in terms of the social welfare state that was condemned to death by the Transnational Elite.

Similarly, the anti-systemic part of the Left (including the anti-systemic Green part of it, which lives in a world of its own imagination, involving Green communes, radical changes in the way of living, through changes in radical imaginaries etc.) has, mostly, not a clue about globalization as a new systemic phase, nor of the present struggle of working class people and the victims of globalization everywhere for national and economic sovereignty, as a precondition for any radical change. Instead, it still talks about intra-imperialist struggles, and waits patiently for a global revolution, presumably sometime in the next millennium. This, despite the fact that, in the globalization era, there has not been, for instance, even a single Pan-European workers' strike against the dramatic reversal of historical working class social conquests!

However, it is clear that the alternative pole I described above for the transitional period, will not establish such direct democratic institutions for as long as the present uni-polar NWO still prevails. That is, for as long as the transitional period continues — involving the necessary co-existence between the NWO and the emerging new Democratic Community of Sovereign Nations in tension with each other — before the final establishment of a new democratic world of sovereign nations. Yet, just by challenging the present NWO and also by implicitly questioning the Soviet Bloc's way of allocating resources, the new pole, even objectively, will raise again the crucial issue of direct control of resources by society in the new democratic world community to emerge, following the overthrowing of the NWO of neoliberal globalization.

In other words, only an economic and political union of peoples resisting today's uni-polar NWO would be in a position to create the pre-conditions for transcending the present homogenization and put, instead, the foundations for a different, really self-managed society — something obviously impossible today when the vast majority of the world population, the victims of globalization, live under conditions of effective occupation fighting for their own survival.

The proposed, therefore, transition strategy hopes to create the conditions for the development of a democratic world community of sovereign and self-reliant nations to replace the present New World Order of neoliberal globalization. It is also hoped that such a strategy would allow a genuine, new form of internationalism to be built 'from below', which will be inspired by the principles of solidarity and mutual aid, rather than the catastrophic principles of competitiveness and profit-making, as at present.

La Lutte Continue

Index of Names

Progressive Press Books

In bookstores, online, or on sale from ProgressivePress.com

Six by Webster Griffin Tarpley

9/11 Synthetic Terror: Made in USA — by a network of moles, patsies, killers, corrupt politicians and media. The authoritative account of 9/11. "Strongest of the 770+ books I have reviewed" – R. Steele. 5th ed., 569 pp, $19.95. In Spanish: *11-S Falso Terrorismo*. 408 pp, $19.95.

George Bush: The Unauthorized Biography Vivid X-ray of the oligarchy dominating U.S. politics, with a full narrative of GWHB's long list of crimes. How Skull-and-Bonesmen Bush and Brown Bros Harriman made fortunes building up Hitler's war machine. Bush Sr is linked to Iran-Contra, Watergate, and genocide in Iraq after luring Saddam Hussein to attack Kuwait. 700 pp, $19.95.

Just Too Weird: Bishop Romney and the Mormon Putsch Against America: Polygamy, Theocracy and Subversion. Mormonism exposed as part of the British-neocon financier plot to take back the colonies. 284 pp, $16.95.

Barack H. Obama: the Unauthorized Biography The abject corruption of a Wall Street lackey, and a richly detailed profile of the finance oligarchy. 595 pp, $19.95.

Obama – The Postmodern Coup: Making of a Manchurian Candidate. The Obama puppet's advisors are radical reactionaries. This study distills decades of astute political insight and analysis. 320 pp, $15.95.

Surviving the Cataclysm, Your Guide through the Greatest Financial Crisis in Human History, by W.G. Tarpley. The unwinding of the hedge funds and derivatives bubble, and with them, life as we knew it in the USA. Richly detailed history of the financier oligarchy, how they plunder our nation. Plus, How to cope with the crisis. 668 pp, $25.

Five by F. Wm. Engdahl

A Century of War: Anglo-American Oil Politics and the New World Order. The classic exposé; the empire controls the oil to control the world. 352 pp, $25.

Full Spectrum Dominance: Totalitarian Democracy in the New World Order. They are out for total control: land, sea, air, space, cyberspace, media, money, movements. 258 pp, $23.95.

Gods of Money: Wall Street and the Death of the American Century. The banksters stop at nothing: setting world wars, plunging our world in chaos and corruption. 390 pp, $24.95.

Seeds of Destruction: The Hidden Agenda of Genetic Manipulation. A corporate gang is out for complete control of the world by patenting our food. Inside the corporate boardrooms and science labs, a world of greed, intrigue, corruption and coercion. 340 pp, $25.95.

Target China: How Washington and Wall Street Plan to Cage the Asian Dragon. The secret war on many fronts to thwart the Chinese challenge. 256 pp, $24.95.

Three by Michel Chossudovsky

Towards a World War III Scenario: The Dangers of Nuclear War. The Pentagon is preparing a first-strike nuclear attack on Iran. 103 pp, $15.95.

The Global Economic Crisis: The Great Depression of the XXI Century, by Prof. Chossudovsky, with a dozen other experts. 416 pp, $25.95.

The Globalization of Poverty and the New World Order. Brilliant analysis how corporatism feeds on poverty, destroying the environment, apartheid, racism, sexism, and ethnic strife. 401 pp, $27.95.

History

Two by George Seldes, the great muckraking journalist, whistleblower on the plutocrats who keep the media in lockstep, and finance fascism. *1,000 Americans Who Rule the USA* (1947, 324 pp, $18.95) Media concentration is nothing new!

Two by Stewart H. Ross. *Global Predator: US Wars for Empire.* A damning account of the atrocities committed by US armed forces over two centuries.

Propaganda for War: How the US was Conditioned to Fight the Great War Propaganda by Britain and her agents like Teddy Roosevelt sucked the USA into the war to smash the old world order. 350 pp and $18.95 each.

Afghanistan: A Window on the Tragedy. An eloquent photo essay on life amidst the ruins of war. 110 pp, $9.95.

Enemies by Design: Inventing the War on Terrorism. A century of imperialism in the Middle East. Biography of Osama bin Ladeen; Zionization of America; PNAC, Afghanistan, Palestine, Iraq. 416 pp, $17.95.

The Iraq Lie: How the White House Sold the War, by former Congressman Joseph M. Hoeffel. Bush Lied about WMD — and went ahead with war. $14.95

Inside the Gestapo: Hitler's Shadow over the World. Intimate, fascinating Nazi defector's tale of ruthlessness, intrigue, and geopolitics. 287 pp, $17.95.

Sunk: The Story of the Japanese Submarine Fleet, 1941-1945. The bravery of doomed men in a lost cause, against impossible odds. 300 pp, $15.95.

Troublesome Country. Throughout its history the US has failed to live up to our guiding democratic creed. 146 pp, $12.95.

Psychology: Brainwashing

The Rape of the Mind: The Psychology of Thought Control, Menticide and Brainwashing. Conditioning in open and closed societies; tools to defend against torture or social pressure. Classic by Dr Joost Meerloo, survivor of Nazism and McCarthyism. 320 pp, $16.95.

The Telescreen: An Empirical Study of the Destruction of Consciousness, by Prof. Jeffrey Grupp. How mass media brainwash us with consumerism and war propaganda. Fake history, news, issues, and reality steal our souls. 199 pp, $14.95. Also by Grupp: *Telementation: Cosmic Feeling and the Law of Attraction.* Deep feeling is our secret nature and key to self-realization. 124 pp, $12.95.

Conspiracy: False Flag Operations

9/11 on Trial: *The W T C Collapse.* 20 proofs the World Trade Center was destroyed by controlled demolition. 192 pp, $12.95.

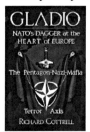

Gladio, NATO's Dagger at the Heart of Europe: *The Pentagon-Mafia-Nazi Terror Axis.* The blood-red thread of terror by NATO death squads in Europe, from WW2 to the present. 490 pp, $25.

Conspiracies, Conspiracy Theories and the Secrets of 9/11, German best-seller explores conspiracy in history, before tackling competing theories on 9/11. 274 pp, $14.95.

In Search of the Truth: *An Exposure of the Conspiracy,* by Azar Mirza-Beg.

ISIS IS US: The Shocking Truth Behind the Army of Terror. How and why the US and its allies created ISIS. 268 pp, $14.95

A portrait of our times, society and religion, and the threat we face. 208 pp, $17.

JFK-911: 50 Years of Deep State., by Laurent Guyénot. The Greater Israel strategy behind the JFK and 9/11 murders. 238 pp, $15.95.

Terror on the Tube: Behind the Veil of 7/7, an Investigation, by Nick Kollerstrom. The glaring evidence that all four Muslim scapegoats were completely innocent. 7/7 clinched the assault on our rights. 3rd ed, 322 pp, $17.77.

The War on Freedom. The seminal exposé of 9/11. "Far and away the best and most balanced analysis of September 11th." – Gore Vidal. 400 pp, $16.95.

Truth Jihad: *My Epic Struggle Against the 9/11 Big Lie.* Kevin Barrett's profound and humorous autobiographical testament. 224 pp, $9.95.

Unmasking ISIS: *The Shocking Truth.* 150 pp, $13.95.

Coming Soon

A Prisoner's Diary, by Hussain M. Al-Amily.

Numbers of the Gods, by Sylvain Tristan

E-Books

9/11 Synthetic Terror; Barack Obama Unauth. Biography; Fall of the Arab Spring; Gladio; In Search of the Truth; Iraq Lie; ISIS IS US; JFK-911; Just Too Weird; Killing Us Softly; Nazi Hydra; Obama: Postmodern Coup; Subverting Syria; Surviving the Cataclysm; Target: China; Unmasking ISIS.

THE "WAR ON TERROR" IS A HOAX
SUPPORT THE TRUTH about 9/11 & 'NWO.' Books & DVD's from
ProgressivePress.com
SEE HOW THE TOWERS FALL? THAT TELLS IT ALL!

Lightning Source UK Ltd.
Milton Keynes UK
UKOW03f2302090117
291695UK00001B/18/P